Lecture Notes in Computer Science 8697

Commenced Publication in 1973
Founding and Former Series Editors:
Gerhard Goos, Juris Hartmanis, and Jan van Leeuwen

Jeffrey Parsons   Dickson Chiu (Eds.)

Advances in Conceptual Modeling

ER 2013 Workshops, LSAWM, MoBiD, RIGiM,
SeCoGIS, WISM, DaSeM, SCME, and PhD Symposium
Hong Kong, China, November 11-13, 2013
Revised Selected Papers

 Springer

Volume Editors

Jeffrey Parsons
Memorial University of Newfoundland
Faculty of Business Administration
St. John's, NL, A1B 3X5, Canada
E-mail: jeffreyp@mun.ca

Dickson Chiu
The University of Hong Kong
Faculty of Education
Division of Information and Technology Studies
Hong Kong, China
E-mail: dicksonchiu@ieee.org

ISSN 0302-9743   e-ISSN 1611-3349
ISBN 978-3-319-14138-1   e-ISBN 978-3-319-14139-8
DOI 10.1007/978-3-319-14139-8
Springer Cham Heidelberg New York Dordrecht London

Library of Congress Control Number: 2014956976

LNCS Sublibrary: SL 3 – Information Systems and Application, incl. Internet/Web
and HCI

Typesetting: Camera-ready by author, data conversion by Scientific Publishing Services, Chennai, India

Printed on acid-free paper

Springer is part of Springer Science+Business Media (www.springer.com)

Preface

This volume contains the proceedings of the workshops associated with the 32nd International Conference on Conceptual Modeling (ER 2013) and the papers associated with the PhD Symposium of ER 2013. For the first time, the proceedings are published as a post-conference volume, enabling authors to submit revised versions of papers that take into account feedback from the workshops.

Continuing the ER tradition, the ER 2013 workshops provided researchers, students, and industry professionals with a forum to present and discuss emerging, cutting-edge topics related to conceptual modeling and its applications. After a call for workshop proposals, the following eight workshops and symposia were selected and organized from the submissions made:

- DaSeM, Data Mining and Semantic Computing for Object Modeling
- LSAWM, Legal and Social Aspects in Web Modeling
- MoBiD, Modeling and Management of Big Data
- RIGiM, 5th International Workshop on Requirements, Intentions and Goals in Conceptual Modeling
- SeCoGIS, 7th International Workshop on Semantic and Conceptual Issues in Geographic Information Systems
- WISM, 10th International Workshop on Web Information Systems Modeling
- SCME, Symposium on Conceptual Modeling Education
- PhD Symposium

The workshops cover different conceptual modeling topics, as indicated in the titles above. The workshops received a total of 57 submissions. Following the rule of the ER workshops, the respective workshop Program Committees carried out peer reviews and accepted a total of 25 papers with an acceptance rate of 44%. Several wporkshops also invited speakers who significantly enhanced the perspectives and quality of the workshop program.

Setting up workshops required a lot of effort and involved many people. We would like to thank the workshop organizers, for their invaluable collaboration and their significant effort to provide a successful workshop edition, and the workshops Program Committees and external reviewers for their professional contribution to the paper review that ensured such a high-quality program.

We also thank the conference co-chairs, Valeria De Antonellis and Stefano Rizzi, for their continuous support and the help in setting up the final program. A very special thanks to Jaison Kuriakose for his hard work in editing this volume.

Finally, we would like to express our sincere appreciation to the authors of all the submitted papers for the high-quality contributions. We rely on their continuous support to keep up the high quality of the ER conference.

August 2014

Dickson Chiu
Jeffrey Parsons

Organization

LSAWM 2013 Workshop Chair

Eleanna Kafeza   Athens University of Economics and Business, Greece

LSAWM 2013 Workshop Co-chair

Dickson Chiu   The University of Hong Kong, Hong Kong, SAR China

LSAWM 2013 Program Committee

Constantine Coutras	Pace University, USA
Ho-fung Leung	The Chinese University of Hong Kong, Hong Kong, SAR China
Patrick C.K. Hung	University of Ontario Institute of Technology, Canada
Irene Kafeza	Kafeza Law Office, Greece
Dickson K.W. Chiu	Dickson Computer Systems, Hong Kong, SAR China
Andrianos Tsekrekos,	Athens University of Economics and Business, Greece
Vasilis Vasalos	Athens University of Economics and Business, Greece
Giannis Tzimas	Technological Educational Institute of Messologhi, Greece
Christos Makrhs	University of Patras, Greece

MoBiD 2013 Workshop Chairs

Il-Yeol Song	Drexel University, USA
David Gil	University of Alicante, Spain
Carlos Blanco	University of Cantabria, Spain

MoBiD 2013 Program Committee

Yuan An	Drexel University, USA
Marie-Aude Aufaure	Ecole Centrale Paris, France
Michael Blaha	Yahoo Inc., USA

Rafael Berlanga   Universitat Jaume I, Spain
Gennaro Cordasco   Università di Salerno, Italy
Alfredo Cuzzocrea   University of Calabria, Italy
Gill Dobbie   University of Auckland, New Zealand
Eduardo Fernandez   University of Castilla-La Mancha, Spain
Matteo Golfarelli   University of Bologna, Italy
Inma Hernandez   University of Seville, Spain
Magnus Johnsson   University of Lund, Sweden
Nectarios Koziris   Technical University of Athens, Greece
Jiexun Li   Drexel University, USA
Alexander Loeser   Universität Berlin, Germany
Antoni Olive   Universitat Politècnica de Catalunya, Spain
Jeff Parsons   Memorial University of Newfoundland, Canada
Oscar Pastor   Universitat Politècnica de Val'encia, Spain
Mario Piattini   University of Castilla-La Mancha, Spain
Nicolas Prat   ESSEC Business School, France
Sudha Ram   University of Arizona, USA
Carlos Rivero   University of Seville, Spain
Colette Roland   University of Paris 1-Panthèon Sorbonne,
                                     France
Pablo Sanchez   University of Cantabria, Spain
Keng Siau   University of Nebraska-Lincoln, USA
Alkis Simitsis   Hewlett-Packard Co., USA
Julia Stovanovich   University of Pennsylvania, USA
Juan Trujillo   University of Alicante, Spain
Alejandro Vaisman   Université Libre de Bruxelles, Belgium
Panos Vassiliadis   University of Ioannina, Greece
Ambrosio Toval   University of Murcia, Spain
Marta Elena Zorrilla Pantaleon   University of Cantabria, Spain

RIGiM 2013 Workshop Organizers

Colette Rolland   Université Paris1 Panthéon Sorbonne, France
Lin Liu   Tsinghua University, China
Eric Yu   University of Toronto, Canada
Jennifer Horkoff   University of Trento, Italy

RIGiM 2013 Program Committee

Raian Ali   Bournemouth University, UK
Thomas Alspaugh   University of California, USA
Daniel Amyot   University of Ottawa, Canada
Mikio Aoyoma   Nanzan University, Japan
Ian Alexander   Scenario Plus, UK
Daniel Berry   University of Waterloo, Canada

Jaelson Castro	Universidade Federal de Pernambuco, Brazil
Luiz Cysneiros	York University, Canada
Fabiano Dalpiaz	Trento University, Italy
Vincenzo Gervasi	University of Pisa, Italy
Aditya K. Ghose	University of Wollongong, Australia
Paolo Giogini	University of Trento, Italy
Renata Guizzardi	Universidade Federal do Espírito Santo (UFES), Brazil
Patrick Heymans	University of Namur, Belgium
Zhi Jin	Chinese Academy of Sciences, China
Haruhiko Kaiya	Shinshu University, Japan
Aneesh Krishna	Curtin University, Australia
Régine Laleau	Université Paris XII, France
Axel van Lamsweerde	Université Catholique de Louvain, Belgium
Alexei Lapouchnian	University of Toronto, Canada
Sai Peck Lee	University of Malaya, Malaysia
Julio Leite	Pontificia Universidade Catolica, Brazil
Emmanuel Letier	University College of London, UK
Sotirios Liaskos	York University, Canada
Peri Loucopoulos	University of Manchester, UK
Andreas Opdahl	University of Bergen, Norway
Xin Pen	Fudan University, China
Anna Perini	Fondazione Bruno Kessler, Italy
Yves Pigneur	HEC, Lausanne, Switzerland
Naveen Prakash	MRCE, India
Jolita Ralyte	University of Geneva, Switzerland
Motoshi Saeki	Tokyo Institute of Technology, Japan
Camille Salinesi	Université Paris 1 Panthéon, Sorbonne, France
Pnina Soffer	University of Haifa, Israel
Sam Supakkul	Keane, USA
Angelo Susi	FBK - Fondazione Bruno Kessler, Italy
Juan Trujillo	University of Alicante, Spain
Roel Wieringa	University of Twente, The Netherlands
Carson Woo	University of British Columbia, Canada

SeCoGIS 2013 Workshop Committee

Mir Abolfazl Mostafavi	Université de Laval, Canada
Esteban Zimányi	Université Libre de Bruxelles, Belgium
Claudia Bauzer Medeiros	University of Campinas, Brazil
Michela Bertolotto	University College Dublin, Ireland
Roland Billen	Université de Liège, Belgium
Jean Brodeur	Natural Resources Canada
Christophe Claramunt	Naval Academy Research Institute, France
Eliseo Clementini	University of L'Aquila, Italy
Esteban Zimányi	Université Libre de Bruxelles, Belgium

SeCoGIS 2013 Program Committee

Alia I. Abdelmoty	Cardiff University, UK
Andrea Ballatore	University College Dublin, Ireland
Phil Bartie	University of Edinburgh, UK
Claudia Bauzer Medeiros	University of Campinas, Brazil
David Bennett	University of Iowa, USA
Michela Bertolotto	University College Dublin, Ireland
Roland Billen	Université de Liège, Belgium
Patrice Boursier	University of La Rochelle, France
Jean Brodeur	National Resources Canada, Canada
Bénédicte Bucher	Institut Géographique National, France
Adrijana Car	German University of Technology, Oman
Christophe Claramunt	Naval Academy Research Institute France
Maria Luisa Damiani	University of Milan, Italy
Clodoveu Davis	Federal University of Minas Gerais, Brazil
Gilles Falquet	University of Geneva, Switzerland
Fernando Ferri	Istituto di Ricerche sulla Popolazione e le Politiche Sociali, Italy
Paolo Fogliaroni	University of Bremen, Germany
Andrew Frank	Technical University of Vienna, Austria
Bo Huang	Chinese University of Hong Kong, SAR China
Marinos Kavouras	National Technical University of Athens, Greece
Ki-Joune Li	Pusan National University, South Korea
Thérèse Libourel	Université de Montpellier II, France
Jugurta Lisboa Filho	Universidade Federal de Viçosa, Brazil
Miguel R. Luaces	Universidade da Coruña, Spain
Jose Macedo	Federal University of Ceara, Brazil
Pedro Rafael Muro Medrano	University of Zaragoza, Spain
Peter van Oosterom	Delft University of Technology, The Netherlands
Dimitris Papadias	Hong Kong University of Science, and Technology, Hong Kong, SAR China
Dieter Pfoser	Institute for the Management of Information Systems, Greece
Ricardo Rodrigues Ciferri	Universidade Federal de São Carlos, Brazil
Andrea Rodriguez Tastets	University of the Concepción, Chile
Markus Schneider	University of Florida, USA
Sylvie Servigne-Martin	INSA de Lyon, France
Shashi Shekhar	University of Minnesota, USA
Spiros Skiadopoulos	University of the Peloponnese, Greece

Emmanuel Stefanakis	
Harokopio	University of Athens, Greece
Kathleen Stewart Hornsby	University of Iowa, USA
Kerry Taylor	CSIRO, Australia
Sabine Timpf	University of Augsburg, Germany
Antonio Miguel Vieira	Monteiro INPE, Brazil
Nancy Wiegand	University of Wisconsin, USA
Stephan Winter	University of Melbourne, Australia

WISM 2013 Workshop Committee

Flavius Frasincar	Erasmus University, The Netherlands
Geert-Jan Houben	Delft University of Technology, The Netherlands
Philippe Thiran	Namur University, Belgium

WISM 2013 Program Committee

Syed Sibte Raza Abidi	Dalhousie University, Canada
Mahmoud Barhamgi	University of Lyon, France
Djamal Benslimane	University of Lyon, France
Maria Bielikova	Slovak University of Technology in Bratislava, Slovakia
Marco Brambilla	Politecnico di Milano, Italy
Jose Alfonso Aguilar	Calderon University of Sinaloa, Mexico
Sven Casteleyn Vrije	Universiteit Brussel, Belgium
Richard Chbeir	Pau University, France
Jose Palazzo Moreira de Oliveira	UFRGS, Brazil
Olga De Troyer Vrije	Universiteit Brussel, Belgium
Roberto De Virgilio	Università di Roma Tre, Italy
Oscar Diaz	University of the Basque Country, Spain
Peter Dolog	Aalborg University, Denmark
Flavio Ferrarotti	Victoria University of Wellington, New Zealand
Flavius Frasincar	Erasmus University, The Netherlands
Martin Gaedke Chemnitz	University of Technology, Germany
Hyoil Han	Marshall University, USA
Geert-Jan Houben	Delft University of Technology, The Netherlands
Zakaria Maamar	Zayed University, UAE
Oscar Pastor	Valencia University of Technology, Spain
Dimitris Plexousakis	University of Crete, Greece

Hajo Reijers   Eindhoven University of Technology,
                                     The Netherlands
Davide Rossi   University of Bologna, Italy
Shazia Sadiq   University of Queensland, Australia
Philippe Thiran   Namur University, Belgium
Riccardo Torlone   Università di Roma Tre, Italy
Lorna Uden   Staffordshire University, UK
Guandong Xu   University of Technology Sydney, Australia

DaSeM 2013 Workshop Committee

Yi Cai   South China University of Technology
Dong Li   South China University of Technology

SCME 2103 Workshop Committee

James Cheng
Il-Yeol Song

Table of Contents

LSAWM 2013 – Legal and Social Aspects in Web Modeling

Glocal News: An Attempt to Visualize the Discovery of Localized Top Local News, Globally 1
  Dimitris Spathis, Theofilos Mouratidis, Spyros Sioutas, and Athanasios Tsakalidis

Identifying Personality-Based Communities in Social Networks 7
  Eleanna Kafeza, Andreas Kanavos, Christos Makris, and Dickson Chiu

Towards a Domain-Specific Conceptual Modeling Approach of Open Source CMS 14
  Vassiliki Gkantouna, Zafeiria-Marina Ioannou, Athanasios Tsakalidis, John Tsaknakis, and Giannis Tzimas

MoBiD 2013 – 1st International Workshop on Modeling and Management of Big Data

Preface to MoBiD 2013 21
  David Gil, Carlos Blanco, and Il-Yeol Song

Challenges and Opportunities in the Evolving Data Web 23
  George Papastefanatos

Improving Massive Open Online Courses Analysis by Applying Modeling and Text Mining: A Case Study 29
  Alejandro Maté, Elisa de Gregorio, José Cámara, and Juan Trujillo

Functionality for Business Indicators in Data Warehouse Requirements Engineering 39
  Naveen Prakash and Hanu Bhardwaj

RIGiM 2013 – 5th International Workshop on Requirements, Intentions and Goals in Conceptual Modeling

Preface to RIGiM 2013 49
  Collette Rolland, Lin Liu, Jennifer Horkoff, and Eric Yu

Requirements Engineering in Business Analytics for Innovation
and Product Lifecycle Management 51
  Clotilde Rohleder, Jing Lin, Indra Kusumah, and Gülru Özkan

Modeling the Impact of Non-functional Requirements
on Functional Requirements 59
  Christophe Gnaho, Farida Semmak, and Regine Laleau

A Framework for Business Rules 68
  *Naveen Prakash, Deepak Kumar Sharma, Deepika Prakash,
  and Dheerendra Singh*

SeCoGIS 2013 – 7th International Workshop on Semantic and Conceptual Issues in GIS

Preface to SeCoGIS 2013 75
  Mir Abolfazl Mostafavi, and Esteban Zimanyi

Integration of Heterogeneous Spatial Databases
for Disaster Management 77
  *Imen Bizid, Sami Faiz, Patrice Boursier,
  and Jawahir Che Mustapha Yusuf*

An Ontology for Submarine Feature Representation on Charts 87
  Jingya Yan, Eric Guilbert, and Eric Saux

A Human-Enhanced Framework for Assessing Open
Geo-spatial Data.. 97
  Roula Karam and Michele Melchiori

Supporting Disaster Management with Real-Time-CPAR Platform 107
  Mohamed Bakillah and Steve H.L. Liang

A Semantic Web Approach for Geodata Discovery 117
  Helbert Arenas, Benjamin Harbelot, and Christophe Cruz

Mob-Warehouse: A Semantic Approach for Mobility Analysis with a
Trajectory Data Warehouse 127
  *Ricardo Wagner, José Antonio Fernandes de Macedo,
  Alessandra Raffaetà, Chiara Renso, Alessandro Roncato,
  and Roberto Trasarti*

WISM 2013- 10th International Workshop on Web Information Systems Modeling

Preface to WISM 2013.. 137
  Flavius Frasincar, Geert-Jan Houben, and Philippe Thiran

Situation-Aware Smart Environment Modeling...................... 139
    Alencar Machado, Ana Marilza Pernas, Leandro Krug Wives,
    and José Palazzo Moreira de Oliveira

Semantic Web-Based Product Search 150
    Damir Vandic and Viorel Milea

News Recommendation Using Semantics
with the Bing-SF-IDF Approach 160
    Frederik Hogenboom, Michel Capelle, and Marnix Moerland

An Exploratory Study on Websites Quality Assessment 170
    Samira Si-saïd Cherfi, Anh Do Tuan, and Isabelle Comyn-Wattiau

A Hybrid Approach to Web Information System Modularization 180
    Jingang Zhou, Zuozhong Yang, Dazhe Zhao, and Jiren Liu

Using Fixed-Price Auctions for Selection in Communities
of Web Services.. 190
    Erbin Lim and Zakaria Maamar

DaSeM 2013 - Data Mining and Semantic Computing for Object Modeling

Preface to DaSEM 2013 203
    Yi Cai

Products Competitive Relationships Mining 205
    Jun Li, Tao Wang, Shuyue Hu, Qingchuan Zhao,
    and Huaqing Min

Exploring Set Recommendation from a Financial Perspective 216
    Yu Liu, Yi Cai, Shuyue Hu, Yifeng Shao, Tao Wang,
    and Huaqing Min

Exploring Users' Preference on Mobile Based on Customer Features 226
    Gang Yu, Zhiyan Wang, and Jiang Xue

SCME 2013 – 1st Symposium on Conceptual Modeling Education

Preface to SCME 2013... 235
    James Cheng and Il-Yeol Song

Former Students' Views on the Usefulness of Conceptual Modeling
Education.. 237
    Albert Tort, Antoni Olivé, and Joan Antoni Pastor

Teaching Conceptual Design Capture 247
    Karen C. Davis

PhD Symposium 2013

A Semantic DBMS Prototype 257
    Liu Chen and Ting Yu

Towards a Domain Specific Modeling Language for Agent-Based
Modeling of Land Use/Cover Change 267
    Cédric Grueau

The Role Concept for Relational Database Management Systems 277
    Tobias Jaekel

Store Review Spammer Detection Based on Review Relationship 287
    Qingxi Peng

Author Index 299

Glocal News: An Attempt to Visualize the Discovery of Localized Top Local News, Globally

Dimitris Spathis, Theofilos Mouratidis, Spyros Sioutas, and Athanasios Tsakalidis

Department of Informatics, Ionian University, Corfu, Greece
Department of Computer Engineering and Informatics, University of Patras, Patras, Greece
{p11spat,p11mour,sioutas}@ionio.gr, tsak@ceid.upatras.gr

Abstract. Glocal News is a web app, a mashup of Google News and Google Maps, which attempts to visualize top local news, globally, in 70 languages. The news headlines, which are displayed on an *infowindow*, are provided by the public Google News RSS. The algorithm, built in JavaScript, uses geocoding in order to extract the toponym from a given location and the local storage technique in order to store the news temporary on the user's browser.

Keywords: Data visualization, Location, News, Localization, Google News, Google Maps, Geocoding, Local Storage, HTML, CSS, Javascript.

1 Introduction

Current information landscape enables people to have access to huge amounts of information, frequently in semi-structured data, which cannot be processed by humans as it is, leading to a phenomenon commonly named as "information overload".

Users discover news of interest in two ways: searching and browsing. If they have something specific in mind, they type usually relevant keywords on search engines. On the other hand, when they don't have something to look for, they just browse for stuff that arouses their curiosity.

We tried to combine the above "methods", satisfying the searching "needs" with specific local news and the browsing "needs" making it pleasant and playful to drag and drop the pin in order to discover more news.

Until now, news are presented usually in a timeline or divided in categories such as Politics, Sports, and International. However, many news portals are gradually embracing the crowd-sourced web (e.g. CNN iReport), providing news discovery per location or neighborhood. That trend was our main inspiration.

Our project, www.glocalne.ws, is a web application described as a mashup [1,2] of Google News built on top of Google Maps. A mashup, is a web page, or web application, that uses and combines data, from two or more sources to create new services. The term implies easy, fast integration, frequently using open application programming interfaces (API) [3] and data sources to produce enriched results.

The field of mashups started to grow the last 5 years following the establishment of Web 2.0. Currently, there are several similar implementations out there, but they are

J. Parsons and D. Chiu (Eds.): ER Workshops 2013, LNCS 8697, pp. 1–6, 2014.

pretty niched, such as Trendsmap [4] which presents the most popular hashtags per location, or a project [5] showing BBC News on a map only for UK though.

The one that resembles our idea is Newsmap [6] by Marcos Weskamp, which shows Google News top news not on map but on a treemap, providing just the basic languages.

2   The Web App

2.1   Functionality

Our objective is to display the top five news of every place on earth, from the largest country to the tiniest village, adjusting the results by taking into account your language of preference.

Fig. 1. The Localization Menu

A given user, firstly, chooses his language from the dropdown menu Localization [Fig.1], secondly, drags the pin to the desired place [Fig.2]. The browser's zoom level adjusts dynamically the results on the window. So, the same coordinates represent different results, according to the abstraction level.

To elaborate on that, as the user zooms in, the results adjust automatically as follows: Country / State / Province / County / Municipality (roughly, due to the fact that many countries follow different administrative division policy).

2.2   Localization

Currently, we support approximately 70 languages. It is worth to note that for some bilingual countries, the user can choose between the two languages. E.g. in Belgium we provide both Dutch and French version. If we can't find results in the local language, we provide the respective ones in English.

Fig. 2. The German user interface showing France's top news

2.3 Potential Use

We imagine the prospective user as a tourist, a traveller planning a trip, a journalist, a businessman, a jetsetter, you name it. The aforementioned user is eager to discover news about his/her destination, directly, quickly, in one's native language.

Of course, that does not exclude the casual user who just wants to have a comprehensive view of the world happenings.

2.4 Technology

The web app is developed in HTML, CSS and Javascript. The Javascript algorithm, initially, removes unnecessary elements from the map, such as streets, leaving just the place names. Then it takes care of the zoom level, the geocoding [7], the local storage, the query, the presentation, the geolocation and the exceptions in case it cannot find news.

The local storage technique of HTML5 gives us the freedom of not using web servers. All data are loaded the moment the user's click fires the query link and are saved temporary on browser. The query that hits Google News [8] is the following:

```
https://news.google.com/news/feeds?pz=1&hl=' + localSto-
rage.hl + '&ned=' + localStorage.ned + '&q=' + query +
'&ie=UTF-8&output=rss
```

One of the most crucial parts of the algorithm is the reverse geocoding, where we convert the coordinates to place names:

```
getQuery::
//Swaps strings and numbers making a valid array derived
from searchTypes
var temp_types = ObjToArray(searchTypes);
//Detects available administrative levels (coun-
try,region,city etc...)
for (var i in results.reverse()) {
  for (var j in temp_types) {
    if (results[i].types[0] == temp_types[j]) {
                temp_types.splice(j, 1);
      var bounds = get-
Bounds(results[i].geometry.viewport);
      query_results.push({/*Data for names, administra-
tion levels and bounds*/});
    }
  }
}
//Orders the results as seen in seachTypes variables
query_results.sort(function (a, b) { return sear-
chTypes[a.type] - searchTypes[b.type] });
//Gets the right name according to zoom level
query = encodeURI(getName(query_results));
```

Of course, in order to form the query rightly, we have to take map viewports and administration levels into account:

```
getName::
//We get the map's viewport and then check for each ad-
ministrative level's viewport(written in "data" varia-
ble).
 //If it fits, we return that result to search for it at
Google news.
var s = size(map.getBounds().toSpan());
var i = 0;
while (size(data[i].bounds.toSpan()) > s && i + 1 < da-
ta.length) i++;
query_title = data[i].name;
```

Here you can see the way our code chooses the administration levels (mentioned in 2.1):

```
var searchTypes = {
    "country": 0, "administrative_area_level_1": 1, "ad-
ministrative_area_level_2": 2,
    "administrative_area_level_3": 3, "political": 4,
"locality": 5, "sublocality": 6
};
```

Finally, the results are presented on an *infowindow*, ready to be consumed by the end user's eyeballs:

```
displayFeed::
//Every query is kept in localstorage and it is accessed
with [set/get]Data() functions
var f = getData().filter(function (v) { return v.q ==
query })[0];
if (f == null || /*Expired*/) {
  var s = getData();

  feed = new google.feeds.Feed(_url());
  feed.setNumEntries(5);
  feed.load(function (result) {
  if (!result.error) {
    /*Load rss contents*/
  }
  else {
    infowindow.setContent("This location provides no news
currently");
  }
  var d = { /*Data*/ };
  /*Update data according to d*/
  setData(s);
  infowindow.open(marker.get('map'), marker);
```

2.5   Known Issues

At the core of geoparsing's difficulty are the many ambiguities present in natural language, including ambiguities related to toponyms. The type of ambiguity most relevant for geoparsing is termed geo/non-geo ambiguity [9]. For example, "Paris" can refer to "Paris, France", "Paris, Texas" but might also refer to the person "Paris Hilton".

We tried to overcome this ambiguity by forming the search query as follows: [City, County], but the displayed results were reduced. Understandable, due to the fact that e.g. an article can just refer to "Athens" instead of "Athens, Attica", or "Athens, Greece", reducing the redundancy. The above problem could be addressed with supervised machine learning methods.

3   Further Work

In order to improve the user experience, we are thinking of presenting the results into subsections such as: Entertainment, Sports, Technology, Politics etc. using probably a SOM [10,11] technique helping us clustering the relevant articles, keeping in mind the visualization [12] principles to avoid information overload. Also, the idea of solving the issue described on section 2.5, is on the roadmap. Another interesting area is the personalized news [13]. Google News provides that option to its users but since there is not an available API, we are still puzzled how we can integrate this extra feature.

References

1. Takemura, J., Sawires, A., Po, O.: Mashup Feeds: continuous queries over web services. In: SIGMOD 2007 Proceedings, pp. 1128–1130. ACM (2007)
2. Di Lorenzo, G., Hacid, H., Paik, H., Benatallah, B.: Data integration in mashups. ACM SIGMOD Record 38(1), 59–66 (2009)
3. Google Maps API V3, https://developers.google.com/maps/documentation/javascript/
4. Trendsmap, http://trendsmap.com
5. BBC lab project, http://dev.benedictoneill.com/bbc/
6. Newsmap, http://newsmap.jp/
7. Google Geocoding API, https://developers.google.com/maps/documentation/geocoding/
8. Google News RSS, http://news.google.com/?output=rss
9. Leidner, J., Lieberman, M.: Detecting geographical references in the form of place names and associated spatial natural language. SIGSPATIAL ACM 3(2), 5–11 (2011)
10. Rauber, A., Merkl, D.: Using Self-Organizing Maps to Organize Document Archives and to Characterize Subject Matters: How to Make a Map Tell the News of the World. In: Bench-Capon, T.J.M., Soda, G., Tjoa, A.M. (eds.) DEXA 1999. LNCS, vol. 1677, pp. 302–311. Springer, Heidelberg (1999)
11. Ong, T., Chen, H., Sung, W., Zhu, B.: Newsmap: a knowledge map for online news. Decision Support Systems 39(4), 583–597 (2005)
12. Rennison, E.: Galaxy of news: an approach to visualizing and understanding expansive news landscapes. In: UIST 1994 Proceedings, ACM Symposium on User Interface Software and Technology, pp. 3–12 (1994)
13. Das, A., Datar, M., Garg, A.: Google news personalization: scalable online collaborative filtering. In: WWW 2007 Proceedings of the 16th international conference on World Wide Web, pp. 271–280. ACM (2007)

Identifying Personality-Based Communities
in Social Networks

Eleanna Kafeza[1], Andreas Kanavos[2], Christos Makris[2], and Dickson Chiu[3]

[1] Athens University of Economics and Business, Greece
kafeza@aueb.gr
[2] Computer Engineering and Informatics Department, University of Patras, Greece
{kanavos,makri}@ceid.upatras.gr
[3] The University of Hong Kong, Hong Kong
dchiu88@hku.hk

Abstract. In this paper we present a novel algorithm for forming communities in a graph representing social relations as they emerge from the use of services like Twitter. The main idea centers in the careful use of features to characterize the members in the community, and in the hypothesis that well formed communities are those that designate diversity in the features of the participating members.

1 Introduction

The topic of the paper is to present a novel methodology in order to characterize interesting communities as they arise in social networks, such as those that are formed in Twitter. The novelty of our approach lies in the fact that we are looking for emerging communities, according to the diversity among the characters of the involved users.

Until now, most practices on message transmission are based on finding the influential users and try to use them to transmit a message. Moreover, recent work on data flow on social networks deals with the problem of predicting the information current. Our approach is different in the sense that we examine ways to "drive" the information within the network. We look for sub-networks that demonstrate a high degree of information flow and as a second step; we aim at using these networks for increasing information continuance.

There is a lot of work from different areas for creating communities from graphs. For a thorough survey, we propose [5]. In our approach we argue that communities in social media, e.g. Twitter, are more probable to contact information easily if they are not "biased" with respect to user personality. A balanced community can handle information flow quicker and deeper. Hence, here we divide the Twitter graph related to the personality of users which is extracted based on their behavior.

2 Related Work

Analysis in social networks has a long history, which is related to graph clustering algorithms, web searching algorithms, as well as bibliometrics; for a complete

J. Parsons and D. Chiu (Eds.): ER Workshops 2013, LNCS 8697, pp. 7–13, 2014.

review of this area one should consult [4], [5], [10], [12], [14] and [17]. The field is related to link analysis in the web with cornerstone the analysis of the significance of web pages in Google using the PageRank citation metric [3], the HITS algorithm proposed by Kleinberg [9] as well as their numerous variants proposed in [11]. PageRank employs a simple metric based on the importance of the incoming links while HITS uses two metrics emphasizing the dual role of a web page as a hub and as an authority for information. Both metrics have been improved in various forms and a related review can be found in [11].

Concerning community detection, various algorithms in literature have been proposed. It should be noted that HITS by itself if exploring non principal eigenvectors, can be used in order to compute communities. Concerning communities, the problem with which one can come across in bibliography, is related to graph partitioning. A breakthrough in the area is the algorithm proposed in [6], for identifying the edges lying between communities and their successive removal; a procedure that after some iterations leads to the isolation of the communities [6]. The majority of the algorithms proposed in the area are related to spectral partitioning techniques. Those are techniques that partition objects by using the eigenvectors of matrices, which form themselves in the specific set [8], [15], [18] and [19]. One should also mention techniques that use modularity, a metric that designates the density of links inside communities against the density outside communities [5], [13], with the most popular being the algorithm proposed by [2].

Besides finding emerging communities, estimating authorities has also attracted attention. In [1], they extracted several graph features such as the users' degree distribution, hubs and authority scores in order to model a user's relative importance. Other works in this area include Expertise Ranking [7] and [21], where they identified authorities using link analysis by considering the induced graph from interactions between users.

Interesting is the work presented in [20], which employs Latent Dirichlet Allocation and a variant of the PageRank algorithm that clusters according to topics and finds the authorities of each topic; the proposed metric is called Twitter-Rank. A method proposed in [16], though similar to TwitterRank, differs in the use of additional features, in the employment of clustering, and in its applicability in real-time scenarios since it can be easily implemented.

3   A Methodology for Identifying Personality-Based Communities in Social Networks

In our work we address the problem of identifying networks that can potential exhibit maximum flow of information regarding a subject matter. As already mentioned in most cases in literature authors deal with the problem of finding influential nodes, and there are several metrics developed to address this issue. Our approach is different in two aspects; first we identify influential networks and not individuals ones. Then we extract the networks related to a specific subject, and compute the influence based on user personality as extracted and computed by quantitative metrics retrieved by Social Networks.

Social Networks provide metrics to measure different aspects of user behavior. In this paper, we will use Twitter as a case study but our approach can be easily extended to any Social Network.

3.1   Basic Twitter Metrics

In this section we examine the basic metrics that we have exported from Twitter so as to extract users personality. Primarily, we can categorize users' tweets into two categories: direct tweets and indirect tweets:

- Direct tweets (D): Here we can find tweets that are produced by an author. This category comes from the option Compose new Tweet and by this, a user can potentially start a new conversation.
- Indirect tweets $(I1, I2)$: In this category, tweets come from another user and can take place with one of two following ways: when a user copies or forwards a specific tweet so as to spread it in his network (retweets) or in the second possible way, a user makes a comment to another tweet and as a matter of fact, a possible conversation may be started (conversations). More specifically, $I1$ represents the number of retweets of a user for a specific time interval and in contrast, $I2$ represents the number of times there actually was a conversation upon a tweet.

Other metrics we look into are:

- Number of followers (F): The number of users that follow a specific user.
- Frequency (FR): It calculates the frequency of users tweets. Hence this metric indicates how often an author posts tweets. The way to calculate the frequency is given as a set of time e.g. half an hour, how many times the user tweeted.
- Number Hashtag keywords (HK): These keywords are words starting with the symbol #. Under this symbol, anyone can put a specific tweet into a certain thematic category. These metrics count the number of hashtags a user has used upon a set of tweets that have occurred for a specific set of time.

Table 1. Twitter basic metrics

Metric	Sense/Meaning
F	Number of followers
D	Number of direct tweets
I1	Number of indirect tweets (retweets)
I2	Number of indirect tweets (conversations)
FR	Frequency of user's tweets
HK	Number of hashtag keywords

3.2   Using Metrics to Extract User Personality

Related to the above metrics, we identify users personality as it appears in Twitter. We have classified users in four basic categories based on their personality as perceived by their peers and as reflected by their behavior. We call them *personality traits*. A *personality trait* is a type of behavior exhibited by a Twitter user and can get one of the following values:

1. **Popular:** when a user is followed by many other users (e.g. followers).
2. **Energetic:** when a user posts tweets frequently. This means that this specific user is energetic and enjoys talking hence he/she tweets on a regular basis.
3. **Conversational:** when a user takes part in conversations either by commenting other people's posts or republishing them.
4. **Multi-systemic:** where a user has a high number of interests and likes to state his opinion in a variety of subjects.

Given the above basic behavioral characteristics that a user can show in any social network, we associate features in each one of them so as to have a qualitative insight.

An *atomic personality trait* for a user x, is a tuple $(F1, F2, F3, F4)$ where each F_i is defined as follows:

1. Atomic Popular ($F1$): the number of followers computed as F.
2. Atomic Energetic ($F2$): the number of direct tweets divided by time interval, computed as FR.
3. Atomic Conversational ($F3$): the number of retweets plus the number of conversations computed as $I1 + I2$.
4. Atomic Multi-systemic ($F4$): the number of hashtags found in a given set of tweets that occurs in a specific time interval, computed as HK.

Related to the above definitions, given a user of the Twitter x_i, the atomic personality trait is a tuple $(F1, F2, F3, F4)$ where each F_i, $1 \leq i \leq 4$, holds the degree that a user's personality is associated with each one of the personality traits. As a next step, we need to identify the dominant characteristics for each user. As a result, for each metric, we set a range of values such that for the characteristic F_i if the atomic values of F_i are within the given range, we characterize the user as having the corresponding behavior. For example, let us assume that we have the user Helen$_{14,3,2,1}$ and that the range for each F_i is set to (10-14, 1-5, 3-7,0-4); then Helen is Popular, Energetic as well as Multi-systemic.

Let P ={Popular ($p1$), Energetic ($p2$), Conversational ($p3$), Multi-systemic ($p4$)} be the set of personality traits and $x_{F1,F2,F3,F4}$ the atomic personality trait for the user x. Moreover, we define with $R_{R1,R2,R3,R4}$, a set of values that determine the dominance of personalities; then $color(x)$ is a tuple $(c1, c2, c3, c4)$ (personality tuple) such that c_i has the value p_i if $F_i \leq R_i$, for $1 \leq i \leq 4$.

3.3   The Community Extraction Algorithm

Based on the above we can now derive the personality traits of each user of the Twitter. We conceptualize Twitter as a graph where users are the nodes and we color each node of the graph related to user personality.

We map Twitter as a graph where each node is a user and there is an edge between two users if there is a relation between them i.e. one user follows the other or vice versa. We then associate each node with one of the 15 possible personality traits. Based on the above description of personality there are 4 possible personality traits and each user can have any of the $2^4 - 1$ possible values as his personality tuple. We use a breadth first approach to traverse the graph and for each node we use the definition of $color(x)$ to decide upon the color of each node/user.

After having decided upon the color/personality of each user, we define "personality balanced networks". A personality balances network is a network that contains at least one node of every possible personality tuple. Related to observations regarding the flow of information in human networks, we notice that balanced networks which are composed by users with different personality traits tend to demonstrate higher degrees of information flow. In our approach we create sub-graphs based on the coloring of the nodes. Given the initial Twitter graph, we traverse the graph using BFS until we find nodes from each one of the 15 personality tuples. The algorithm then extracts that sub-graph.

4   Experimental Evaluation and Results

We examined the validity of our approach through experiments. We then implemented the Twitter graph using Twitter4J, and have colored our graph according to our methodology and finally have extracted the personality-based community graph. Twitter4J is a Java library for the Twitter API, with which one can easily integrate a Java application with the Twitter service.

Firstly, we created a Twitter graph as follows: we made a query on Twitter on the subject of *#SocialNetworks* and we retrieved all the associated information regarding users and tweets for a time interval of 7 days ($01/07/2013 - 08/07/2013$).

We also defined the dominance of personality ranges as follows. Initially, we specified ranges of a user that has all the personality trait as follows; (15%, 35%, 35%, 25%). Consequently, we identified the users that satisfy the above ranges. As a next step, for the following more similar personality traits, we increased each particular range by (33%, 25%, 25%, 33%) respectively.

For example, suppose that the initial user has $(500, 2, 3, 6)$ and is characterized as Popular, Energetic, Conversational as well as Multi-systemic. Then a user in order to be characterized as Popular, Energetic, Conversational, he/she has to demonstrate this tuple $(750, 3, 4, < 8)$.

We use this approach to set ranges in order to incorporate the concept that these personality traits are inter-related. For example, a user with 1000 tweets is characterized as Popular, but also a user with 500 tweets and a number of retweets plus conversations is also characterized as Popular.

Our results show that the selected nodes are approximately the 3% of our graph for the time interval we use. Furthermore, the percentage of the number of all tweets that the users of this graph exchange divided by the total number of tweets for the given time is approximately 10%. Tweets consist of direct tweets, retweets, as well as conversational tweets.

5   Conclusions and Future Work

Our conclusions are that although the community graph was the 3% of the whole graph (number of community nodes divided by the number of total nodes in the graph), we had in this network almost 10% of tweets (direct, retweets, conversations) of the whole Twitter traffic. Hence we can conclude that our assumption of the personality based communities playing a dominant role in data traffic, has been verified.

This is a preliminary work. Further work is necessary to identify other personality traits, different clusters of networks and different ranges for dominant personalities. Moreover, this work could be extended to other Social Networks as well.

References

1. Agichtein, E., Castillo, C., Donato, D., Gionis, A., Mishne, G.: Finding high-quality content in social media. In: WSDM 2008, pp. 183–194 (2008)
2. Blondel, V.D., Guillaume, J.-L., Lambiotte, R., Lefebvre, E.: Fast unfolding of community hierarchies in large networks. Journal of Statistical Mechanics: Theory and Experiment P1000 (2008)
3. Brin, S., Page, L.: The PageRank Citation Ranking: Bringing Order to the Web. Stanford Digital Library (1998)
4. Carrington, P.J., Scott, J., Wasserman, S.: Models and Methods in Social Network Analysis. Cambridge University Press (2005)
5. Fortunato, S.: Community detection in graphs. Physics Reports 486, 75–174 (2010)
6. Girvan, M., Newman, M.E.J.: Community Structure in Social and Biological Networks. National Academy of Sciences 99(12), 7821–7826 (2002)
7. Jurczyk, P., Agichtein, E.: Discovering Authorities in Question Answer Communities by Using Link Analysis. In: CIKM, pp. 919–922 (2007)
8. Kernighan, B.W., Lin, S.: An Efficient Heuristic Procedure for Partitioning Graphs. The Bell System Technical Journal 49(1), 291–307 (1970)
9. Kleinberg, J.M.: Authoritative Sources in a Hyperlinked Environment. SODA 1998:668-677
10. Lancichinetti, A., Fortunato, S.: Community detection algorithms: A comparative analysis. Physical Review E80, 056117 (2009)
11. Langville, A.N., Meyer, C.D.: Google's PageRank and Beyond: The Science of Search Engine Rankings. Princeton University Press (2006)
12. Leskovec, J., Lang, K.J., Mahoney, M.W.: Empirical Comparison of Algorithms for Network Community Detection. In: WWW 2010, pp. 631–640 (2010)
13. Newman, M.E.J.: Fast algorithm for detecting community structure in networks. Phys. Rev. E 69, 066133 (2004)
14. Newman, M.E.J.: Networks: An Introduction. Oxford University Press (2010)
15. Ng, A.Y., Jordan, M.I., Weiss, Y.: On Spectral Clustering: Analysis and an algorithm. In: NIPS, pp. 849–856 (2001)

16. Pal, A., Counts, S.: Identifying topical authorities in microblogs. In: WSDM, pp. 45–54 (2011)
17. Scott, J.G.: Social Network Analysis: A Handbook. SAGE Publications Ltd (2000)
18. Shi, J., Malik, J.: Normalized Cuts and Image Segmentation, pp. 731–737 (1997)
19. Shi, J., Malik, J.: Normalized Cuts and Image Segmentation. IEEE Transactions on Pattern Analysis and Machine Intelligence 22(8), 888–905 (2000)
20. Weng, J., Lim, E.-P., Jiang, J., He, Q.: TwitterRank: Finding Topic-sensitive Influential Twitterers. In: WSDM 2010, pp. 261–270 (2010)
21. Zhang, J., Ackerman, M.S., Adamic, L.A.: Expertise Networks in Online Communities: Structure and Algorithms. In: WWW 2007, pp. 221–230 (2007)

Towards a Domain-Specific Conceptual Modeling Approach of Open Source CMS

Vassiliki Gkantouna[1], Zafeiria-Marina Ioannou[1], Athanasios Tsakalidis[1],
John Tsaknakis[2], and Giannis Tzimas[2]

[1] Department of Computer Engineering and Informatics, Faculty of Engineering,
University of Patras, Patras, Greece
[2] Department of Applied Informatics in Management & Economy, Faculty of Management and
Economics, Technological Educational Institute of Messolonghi, Messolonghi, Greece

Abstract. Staying tuned to the trends in a certain domain has extremely dynamic and potential applications in many areas. For example, business analysts need to know the current solutions used for attracting customers in order to decide on the most appropriate marketing strategy. Meanwhile, a respectable number of organizations today exploit their online presence to boost their profits. Particularly, they utilize Content Management Systems (CMS) as the core system to support their Web Applications (WAs) thanks to their efficiency for managing digital content. In this context, having the ability to discover commonly reusable patterns can be a valuable tool in the domain-specific development process. To this end, we propose a model-driven approach for modeling WAs developed using the Joomla! CMS utilizing reverse engineering (RE) and clustering techniques. When applied to a large number of applications, it enables hypertext architects to identify patterns and discover design solutions for WAs frameworks per topic.

Keywords: Data mining, conceptual modeling, content management system, Joomla!, clustering algorithm, document clustering.

1   Introduction

The worldwide expansion of the World Wide Web has led to a radical change in the way organizations offer information to the public. In an effort to adjust to the new challenges, an increasing number of businesses obtain an online presence. The use of CMS as the base platform for the development of their WA is rapidly increasing thanks to their efficiency to manage and publish digital content. Indeed, most CMS-based WAs can be realized with merely configuration of the CMS instead of software engineering from scratch enhancing this way WA's reusability and efficiency. Due to the traditional source-code-oriented development process of CMS, the configuration of a CMS for data-intensive WAs still remains complex and time consuming.

Simultaneously, Model-Driven Engineering (MDE) is a promising approach to software development and maintenance advocating the use of models as first-class citizens throughout the engineering lifecycle. Additionally, the integration of MDE

J. Parsons and D. Chiu (Eds.): ER Workshops 2013, LNCS 8697, pp. 14–19, 2014.

approaches with RE techniques can lead to high maintainability of the underlying system enabling developers to focus on the overall system architecture without paying attention on the implementation details [1,2,3].

Under this point of view, we propose a model-driven RE approach for the automatic extraction of the conceptual model of existing WAs developed using the widely used CMS, Joomla! [4], by applying mining techniques. The recovered models are specified by referring to the Web Modeling Language (WebML) [5]. By obtaining the conceptual model of a large number of Joomla!-based WAs related to a specific domain, we aim to identify commonly reusable patterns and discover potential design solutions per topic by utilizing mining techniques, as a next step. The remainder of this paper is organized as follows: Section 2 presents the Conceptual Modeling Approach in detail, while Section 3 provides concluding remarks and discusses future steps.

2   Conceptual Modeling Approach

In the context of this work, we refer to the conceptual model with the notion of the WebML Hypertext model [5], composed by the composition and the navigation model. The composition model specifies which pages compose the hypertext, and which content units make up a page. The key ingredients of WebML are pages, units, and links, organized into modularization constructs called areas and site views. Units are the atomic pieces of publishable content used to publish the information described in the data model and they are the building blocks of pages. Each unit is associated to one underlying entity, from which the content of the unit is computed. Pages are typically built by assembling several units of various kinds, and they are the actual interface elements delivered to the users. Page and units do not stand alone, but are linked to form a hypertext structure. Links express the possibility of navigating from one point to another one in the hypertext, and the passage of parameters from one unit to another unit required for the proper computation of the content of a page. The navigation model expresses how pages and content units are linked to form the hypertext.

In order to model Joomla! elements in WebML notation, we defined a set of WebML representations for pages and page components. Based on the fact that pages have a fixed structure composed by the central part, containing the main content specified by the particular component, and the peripheral parts displaying the content of the published modules, we defined the WebML representation of a Joomla! WA's page. It consists of two conjunctive nested pages (AND subpages), namely the Modules subpage, containing all the modules that lie within the page, and the Layout subpage, modeling the way the content is displayed to the users. We also define WebML representations for the Components and the Modules extensions. Components produce the major content of WAs and have one or more "views" that control how the content is displayed in the page's central part. Based on the way they publish content, we resulted in WebML representations consisting of a combination of content units, for every type of the available components. Modules are small blocks of content that can be displayed in various positions on the peripheral parts of a page. Again, we defined proper WebML representations for every module reflecting the module's functionality and the way it delivers the content to the user. Some typical examples are shown in Figures 1 (Fig.1).

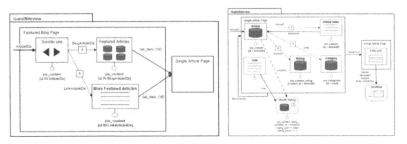

Fig. 1. Featured blog and single article WebML representations

2.1   The Reverse Engineering Process

The approach is oriented towards the recovery of the constitution and navigation models which in turn synthesize the WA's hypertext model. The composition model can be recovered by identifying specific structural elements (particular types of Joomla! extensions) in the HTML source code of a page followed by the mapping of these elements to their corresponding WebML representations. These elements are the components and modules indicative of the HTML page's layout structure. In the same spirit, the navigation model can be extracted by identifying the hyperlinks between HTML pages as well as the possible navigation flows between the structural components of the WA created by the navigation modules such as menus and breadcrumbs, followed by the mapping of the identified links to the corresponding WebML representations.

As a first step, HTML pages are captured by a web crawler in order to perform source code parsing. The parsing aims to identify such items in the source code that strongly imply the presence of specific Joomla! elements in that particular page. These items are the values of the class attribute of an HTML page which characterize the various structural elements, facilitating this way the identification of the published components and modules. We refer to these values as keywords. As a result, by parsing the HTML code of a page, we can identify the keywords it contains and this way to find out the included component and modules. For instance, the keyword describing a single article is the word "item-page" and the keyword for a login module is the word "userdata". Another aspect of WAs that must be considered is the modeling of the implying functionalities performed as a result of potential navigational flows. In WebML, this is modeled as operation units [5]. For this reason, we have examined the possible navigation "scenarios" that could imply a potential operation and model them as WebML operation units. For the identification of those scenarios, we searched again for specific keywords in the source code of webpages. For example, when a page contains an email icon, it is modeled as a page having a link to a sendmail unit. As a result, given the HTML code of a page, based on these keywords, we can mine the component used and all the displayed modules abstracting a view of the page's layout structure and behavior. In the following diagram, the RE process for mining of the composition and navigation model is presented.

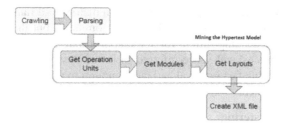

Fig. 2. The Reverse Engineering methodology for mining the WA's Hypertext model

2.2   Data Distribution

Regarding the recovery of the Data model, we could not obtain a representation of the WA's database schema since most WAs do not allow access to the underlying database. Nevertheless, we manage to capture the data distribution by applying an effective data mining technique on the content published by the HTML pages. More specifically, we have created a document containing the content published on a page for each page of the WA. These documents are given as input to a clustering tool consisting of a combination of two different clustering techniques, the Hierarchical Algorithm and the spherical k-means algorithm. The basic steps of the algorithm are [6]: Preprocessing of document collection in order to represent them in a more processable structure, Latent Semantic Indexing and Coarse Clustering in an attempt to generate an initial partition of documents, Agglomerative Hierarchical Clustering in order to reduce the number of the initial clusters (in case that the number is relatively large) and finally spherical k-means algorithm in order to enhance the quality of the produced clustering.

Preprocessing of the Text Collection
According to the bag-of-words model, each document is represented as a sequence of terms/words. To this end, each document is divided into a set of lexical units that cannot be further divided, called tokens. After document parsing, usually two kinds of feature reduction (or term pruning) are performed. The first one removes the stopwords while the second one involves Part-Of-Speech Tagging and lemmatization. Finally, only the unique lemmas of noun words are retained. Subsequently, according to the vector space model, each document is represented as a vector of m dimensions, where m is the number of unique lemmas. For each document the contribution of each lemma in its content representation is computed by using the TF-IDF weighting scheme. As a product of this representation, a matrix A of dimension m×n is produced, where m is the number of unique lemmas and n is the number of documents.

Latent Semantic Indexing
LSI is a well-established indexing and retrieval method for extracting hidden relationships between terms and concepts contained in large, unstructured collections of documents. The basic idea of the method lies in the projection of the documents vectors in a new, low-dimensional space obtained by the Singular Value Decomposition of

the term-document matrix A. The SVD of an m×n matrix A of rank r expresses A as a product of three simpler matrices, A=USV. LSI omits all but the k largest singular values in the above decomposition, for some appropriate k which will be the dimension of the low-dimensional space referred to in the description above. It should be small enough to enable fast retrieval and large enough to adequately capture the structure of the corpus. Then, $A=U_k S_k V_k$.

Coarse (initial) Clustering

In our clustering approach, we interpret the results of the LSI transformation of the initial A matrix as a form of fuzzy clustering and then we transform the fuzzy clustering to a hard-crisp clustering by assigning each document to exactly one cluster, the cluster where the document has the highest degree of participation. In this way, we produce an initial rough clustering of documents. Later these initial clusters are going to be reduced and furthermore re-organized in order to enhance their quality. In particular, based on the n×k matrix $V_k S_k$, produced by SVD, we interpret the k columns of the $V_k S_k$ matrix as a set of k clusters and the n rows as the documents. Each element (i, j) of the $V_k S_k$ matrix, defines the document i degree of participation to the cluster j. This fuzzy clustering is transformed to a crisp clustering by assigning each document to exactly one cluster, where the document has the highest degree of participation according to the values of the $V_k S_k$ matrix.

Hierarchical Clustering

In the proposed clustering method, an agglomerative hierarchical clustering algorithm is employed in an attempt to reduce the number of the initial clusters produced by the LSI and Fuzzy Clustering in the previous steps. To this end, the agglomerative hierarchical clustering algorithm starts assuming as initial clusters, the set of k clusters, where k is equal to the LSI dimension. At each step, the algorithm merges the two most similar clusters based on the UPGMA scheme. These steps need to be repeated until the desired number of clusters is obtained.

Spherical k-means Algorithm

The spherical k-means algorithm is a well-studied variant of classical k-means algorithm with cosine similarity as the selected distance measure. The motivation for applying the spherical k-means algorithm as the final step of our clustering approach is in order to enhance the quality and the precision of the clustering produced by the previous steps. Specifically, we utilize a refinement algorithm that uses local search in order to refine the clusters generated by spherical k-means.

Significant Terms

For the purpose of discovering significant terms from all the generated document clusters, we employ the cluster centroids that can be used in order to summarize the content of a cluster. Specifically, we extract as significant terms, the highly weighted terms of the document cluster centroids, i.e. all the terms having a weight above a given threshold.

In the end of the clustering phase, there is a predefined set of clusters and a set of significant terms representative of the concept of each cluster. We consider that the pages lying in the same cluster are referring to the same theme and we use the cluster's significant terms as the source attribute (the origin of a unit's content) in the WebML units representations.

2.3   Creation of the XML File

Based on the above, we compose the hypertext model of the target WA in its textual Extensible Markup Language (XML) syntax. The Joomla!-based WA is represented as a siteview containing a set of pages and operation units. Each page is comprised from two subjunctives nested pages, the Modules and the Layout pages modeling the modules and the component respectively identified in the specific page. Links connecting pages or content units model the WA navigation behavior.

3   Conclusions and Future Steps

In conclusion, we present an efficient RE approach for the automatic extraction of the conceptual models from existing WAs developed by Joomla! referring to the WebML notation. Having the source code as a starting point, we extract the composition and navigation model which eventually are combined to form the WA's hypertext model. For capturing the data distribution of the WA, we utilize a novel clustering method. A tool supporting the proposed methodology can be accessed at http://alkistis.ceid.upatras.gr/research/modeling. Obtaining the conceptual model of Joomla!-based WA, the next logical question that arises is the following: in which ways it can be utilized. This work is the first part of a larger project towards the identification of design patterns or potential recurrent design solutions that lie in the recovered hypertext model of Joomla!-based WAs within a specific domain [7]. We are now working on developing mining algorithms that can be efficiently applied in a large number of abstracted models in order to identify potential model clones.

References

1. Di Lucca, G.A., Fasolino, A.R., Tramontana, P.: Reverse engineering web applications: the ware approach. Journal of Software Maintenance and Evolution 16, 71–101 (2004)
2. Bernardi, M.L., Lucca, G.A.D., Distante, D.: The re-uwa approach to recover user centered conceptual models from web applications. International Journal on Software Tools for Technology Transfer 11(6), 485–501 (2009)
3. Weijun, S., Shixian, L., Xianming, L.: An approach for reverse engineering of web applications. In: International Symposium on Information Science and Engineering, vol. 2, pp. 98–102 (2008)
4. Joomla! Content Management System, http://www.joomla.org/
5. WebML modeling language, http://www.webml.org/webml/page1.do
6. Ioannou, Z.-M., Makris, C., Patrinos, G.P., Tzimas, G.: A Set of Novel Mining Tools for Efficient Biological Knowledge Discovery. Artificial Intelligence Review (2013)
7. Panagis, Y., Sakkopoulos, E., Sirmakessis, S., Tsakalidis, A., Tzimas, G.: Discovering Re-usable Design Solutions in Web Conceptual Schemas: Metrics and Methodology, pp. 545–556. ICWE (2005)

Preface to MoBiD 2013

Due to the enormous amount of data present and growing in the Web, there has been an increasing interest in incorporating the huge amount of external and unstructured data, normally referred as "Big Data", into traditional applications. This necessity has made that traditional database systems and processing need to evolve and accommodate them to this new situation. Two main ideas underneath this evolution are that new external and internal data (i) need to be stored in the cloud and (ii) offer a set of services to allow us to access, abstract, analyze, and visualize the data.

Therefore, this new conceptualization of cloud applications incorporating both internal and external Big Data requires new models and methods to accomplish their conceptual modeling phase. Thus, the objective of the First International Workshop on Modeling for Data-Intensive Computing (MoBiD'13) is to be an international forum for exchanging ideas on the latest and best proposals for the conceptual modeling issues surrounding this new data-driven paradigm with Big Data. Papers focusing on the application and the use of conceptual modeling approaches for Big Data, MapReduce, Hadoop and Hive, Big Data Analytics, social networking, security and privacy, data science, etc. will be highly encouraged. The workshop will be a forum for researchers and practitioners who are interested in the different facets related to the use of the conceptual modeling approaches for the development of this next generation of applications based on these Big Data.

The workshop has been announced in the main announcement venues in order to attract papers from different countries that are distributed all over the world. We have finally received 7 papers and the Program Committee have selected only 2 papers, making an acceptance rate of 28.5%. We also have an invited keynote on Challenges and Opportunities in the Evolving Data Web by George Papastefanatos.

We would like to express our gratitude to the Program Committee members for their hard work in reviewing papers, the authors for submitting their papers, and the ER 2013 organizing committee for all their support.

July 2013

David Gil
Carlos Blanco
Il-Yeol Song
Program Co-Chairs
MoBiD'13

Challenges and Opportunities in the Evolving Data Web[*]

George Papastefanatos

RC "ATHENA" \ IMIS
Athens, Greece
gpapas@imis.athena-innovation.gr

Abstract. The Data Web refers to the vast and rapidly increasing quantity of scientific, corporate, government and crowd-sourced data published in the form of Linked Open Data (LOD), encouraging the uniform representation of hetero-geneous data items on the web and the creation of interlinks between them. The growing availability of open linked datasets has brought forth significant new challenges regarding their proper preservation and the management of evolving information within linked datasets. In this paper, we focus on the evolution and preservation challenges related to publishing and maintaining evolving linked data. We present several insights regarding their proper modelling and querying and provide an overview of our current efforts towards a framework for managing the preservation of LOD.

Keywords: Data Web Evolution, Linked Data Preservation.

1   Introduction

Data Web refers to the vast and rapidly increasing quantity of scientific, corporate, government and crowd-sourced data published in the form of Linked Open Data (LOD). The Linked Data paradigm[1] provides the way for publishing and interlinking structured data on the web by offering appropriate standards and recommendations (e.g. SPARQL, RDF). At the core lies that data entities are published as web resources, which are uniquely identified with the use of URIs and interlinked in meaningful ways using typed links i.e., terms drawn from ontologies and vocabularies. In this regard, publication and consumption of information are actions that become federated and non-uniquely controlled within their environment. The most noteworthy advantage of the Data Web is that it records facts rather than documents. These facts become the basis for the discovery of new knowledge, which is not derivable from any individual data source, and thus help solving information needs that were not originally anticipated by their creators.

Given that data-aware practices have a huge potential to create additional value across several sectors, little attention has been devoted to the long-term accessibility and usability of the datasets comprising the Data Web. Linked datasets are subject to frequent changes in the encoded facts, in their structure or the data collection process

---

[*] Work supported by the EU project DIACHRON.

J. Parsons and D. Chiu (Eds.): ER Workshops 2013, LNCS 8697, pp. 23–28, 2014.
© Springer International Publishing Switzerland 2014

itself. Most changes are performed and managed under no centralized administration, eventually inducing several inconsistencies across interlinked datasets. Traditional web archiving and preservation practices handle individual datasets as digital objects, similarly to documents and multimedia, that are time stamped and "locked away" for future use. In contrast, we argue that LOD should be preserved by keeping them constantly accessible and integrated into a well-designed framework for evolving datasets that offers functionality for versioning, provenance tracking, change detection and quality control while at the same time provides efficient ways for querying the data both statically and across time. In this paper, we highlight the problems and the challenges related to the evolution of information published on the Data Web and present some prominent research directions and insights for the management of evolving LOD. We advocate the need of novel solutions for these challenges and present our current ongoing work towards a framework for the management of LOD evolution.

2   Challenges in the Management of Evolution in the Data Web

Most of the challenges related to the management of LOD evolution stem from the decentralized nature of publishing, curating and evolving interdependent datasets, with rich semantics and structural constraints, across multiple disparate sites. Traditional database versioning settings impose that data management and evolution are performed within a well-defined controlled environment where change operations and dependencies on data can be easily monitored and handled. On the other hand, web and digital preservation techniques assume that preservation subjects, such as web pages, are plain digital assets that are collected (usually via a crawling mechanism) and individually archived for future reference. In contrast with these two approaches, the Data Web poses new requirements for the management of evolution.

LOD Evolution Modeling: Unlike documents, LOD datasets are not only individual facts but represent real-world evolving entities with a certain structure for which additional constraints (e.g., name uniqueness) may hold. In addition, LOD come from different domains and use heterogeneous data models, including standard and/or ad hoc or proprietary formats. *This calls for appropriate methods for preserving across time a multitude of dimensions related to the internal structure of a dataset, its content and the semantics it carries as well as the context (e.g., authorship and provenance information, time validity, licencing information, etc.) under which it is published and the specific constraints holding.* Preservation should exhibit format-independence, data traceability and reproducibility and an overall common denomination for data that originate from different models. Reference schemes (URIs) must be properly designed such that unique identification is achieved not only across different sites but also across time taking into account different temporal and versioning aspects. Moreover, LOD may be interconnected through typed links when they refer to the same or related real-world entities. This calls for effective entity recognition and co-reference methods to rank LOD datasets according to their quality for guiding crawling and appraisal. It also stresses the need for preserving an entire network of interconnected LOD datasets, rather than individual ones, that may prove to be useful for future use and analysis.

LOD Change governance. Changes in linked datasets can occur at different granularity levels. At the dataset level, datasets are added, republished, renamed, or even disappear, without versioning or preservation control; at the schema level, ontologies and vocabularies may change and existing datasets must be repaired and validated to the new versions; finally, at the instance level data resources and properties are added, deleted or updated, while broken links between them decrease the quality of the published data. *Discovering LOD differences (deltas)[5] and representing them as first class citizens with structural, semantic, temporal and provenance information is vital in various tasks such as the synchronization of autonomously developed LOD versions, or visualizing the evolution history of a particular LOD dataset.* Building upon that, the ability of combining lower-level changes in order to describe higher-level complex ones is an essential requirement for providing rich semantics to any evolution management process. The higher the level of changes, the more context-dependent the issue becomes, as it is tied with factors such as the domain at hand, the design decisions, the underlying data, volume, dataset dynamicity and so on. These parameters come in combinations that create the need to study changes at different granularity levels. In order for changes to be detected and materialized on many levels, a formal and hierarchical representation model is required that allows for defining axiomatic, mathematically complete low-level LOD changes and at the same time provides a flexible mechanism for defining complex changes based on these [4].

LOD Synchronization. Unlike closed settings in which data changes are communicated via notification mechanisms, LOD evolution in the Data Web can be intermittently observed through crawling. In this respect, *high-level tools are required to detect the changes of evolving LOD datasets and repair their potential inconsistencies* as new real world entities are described or old ones are proven to be erroneous or even become obsolete. As the average change frequency in linked datasets is less than a week [2], synchronization operations, i.e., detection, propagation and repairing, across datasets cannot be manually performed but rather it requires a (semi-) automatic reaction that efficiently copes with the vast number, variety and frequency of changes. A prominent direction is the availability of a decentralized scalable publish-subscribe mechanism that can operate on parts or the global LOD space and offer monitoring and notification functionality enabling LOD synchronization across sites [6]. *This mechanism can guarantee that emerging changes are modeled according to a common vocabulary and propagated to all possibly affected datasets.*

LOD Uncertainty. As LOD usage is generalized, their quality may be compromised by various data imperfections (e.g., impreciseness, unreliability incompleteness) due to fundamental limitations of the underlying data acquisition infrastructures, the inherent ambiguity in the domain of interest, or even when privacy-preserving applications modify data by adding perturbations to it. Similarly, when LOD are produced by extracting structured information from text, or by entity resolution algorithms in sensor and social data, the results are approximate and uncertain. Uncertainty is a state of limited knowledge, where we cannot discern which alternative statements are true. In this respect, representing declaratively uncertainly and answering queries over probabilistic facts is a challenging problem not yet related to long-term LOD interpretability.

LOD Sustainability: Today, cloud technologies and infrastructures offer reasonable methods for protecting LOD archives from physical destruction, but this is no guarantee against the economic collapse of the organization that maintains the data. There has been a proliferation of data centres over the past years — many dedicated to the storage of research data gathered at public expense — but one wonders whether, by analogy with early libraries in human history, we are endangering our data by placing it in such centres without replication. The remote sites depend on continued public funding and there are signs that such centres are no more sustainable than early libraries. For this reason, distributed replication of LOD enhanced with temporal and provenance annotations can enable the long-term availability and minimize the risks of data loss.

LOD long term accessibility. LOD preservation mechanisms must enable the long-term accessibility of datasets and their meaningful exploration over time. As stated before, datasets with different time and schema constraints coexist and must be uniformly accessed, retrieved and combined. Longitudinal query capabilities across time must be offered such that data consumers can answer several types of queries, within a version or across sets of versions. Some typical examples of queries include:

- *Dataset versions*: Retrieve a list of all available versions of a given dataset. The list can either be exhaustive or filtered based on temporal, provenance or other metadata criteria.
- *Snapshot queries*: Retrieve a specific version(s) of a dataset or parts of it, filtered accordingly (e.g. specific version identifier, temporal criteria, etc.).
- *Longitudinal queries*: As above but with the complete timeline of the data. Temporal criteria can be applied to limit the timeline (specific versions or time periods), or successive versions.
- *Queries on Changes*: Retrieve changes between two concurrent versions of an entity (dataset, resource etc.). Limit results for specific type of changes, or for a specific part of the data (see partial dataset queries).
- *Join Queries on Changes and Data*: Retrieve datasets / parts of datasets that are affected by specific types of changes.

Considering the above, the benefits of evolution management can mainly be placed into two categories. The first one is concerned with quality control and maintenance. For instance, mishaps such as broken links or URI changes create inconsistencies and failures that are hardly feasible to overcome with no knowledge concerning the resources affected, their state of interconnectedness and the types of changes affecting them. The second one is concerned with data exploitation, as the evolution of data itself can provide valuable insights and shed light on the dynamics of the data, their domains and the operational aspects of the communities they are found in.

3   A Framework for Diachronic Linked Data

Current LOD lifecycle can be simplified into the following processes and stakeholders (Fig 1), i.e., data producers create and publish datasets, the curators aim at matchmaking and integrating data from multiple sources making it available as new added-value information, whereas the consumers operate on the published data by means of enriching their knowledge bases with external links and developing applications. To address the previously described challenges, our goal is to incorporate the preservation of evolving datasets into the data lifecycle and enable resources' diachronicity such that available open data can become tractable across time. Thus, in [3] we have proposed a distributed, service-based framework for the curation and preservation of LOD with the following essential functionality.

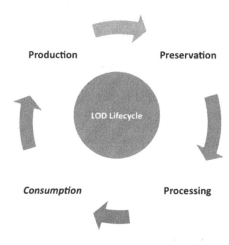

Fig. 1. Preservation as part of LOD lifecycle

Evolution Management. Modelling of evolving LOD is based on the assumption that a web resource can be captured with (a) a time-agnostic – diachronic - entity characterized by a set of immutable properties, such as the unique identification of this resource over time, and (b) a set of time-aware evolving entities corresponding to the time-specific instance of the resource. Both types of entities are identifiable and citable objects. In this way, the diachronic entity acts as a placeholder for invariant citation and reference, whereas evolving entities capture the dynamic nature, the different versions of the resource and carry all evolution semantics such as time and change information. Time information is captured by embedding temporal properties and time-aware links in the evolving entities at the time of data creation, allowing a one-step production and preservation.

Change detection. Changes are identified by pulling out and comparing snapshots, or by monitoring the actions of the user. The description of each change together with any superimposed information about the change annotates the evolving entities. Changes can trigger a notification mechanism that identify related resources and propagate the change to all possibly affected information resources.

Multiversion archiving. Each new "release" of the data is automatically archived at the time of creation, following a distributed approach for storing information. The archived data are replicated in several nodes in order to increase efficiency and guarantee the availability and preservation of information.

Longitudinal query capabilities. Questions are efficiently answered with complex conditions on the provenance and evolution of information objects. It will be possible to express snapshot queries on previous instances of the data and their relationships, and also pose longitudinal queries that cut across snapshots to give insight about the hows and whys of the current state of information.

Provenance support. Provenance information is recorded and captures the relationship among source and derived data along with any operations (e.g. SPARQL the query) that were involved in the derivations. This information enables or complements trust issues, interoperability between different sources, version control and licensing. Provenance metadata can capture dataset lineage and this way provide added value to the data themselves.

Adaptive focused crawling. Linked data are crawled and gathered from the Data Web regarding a specific domain (e.g., biological linked data), together with relevant background information that is required to put the data in context. The crawler will take into account the "preservation policies" provided by the data producers, will make decisions on which links to follow first, and will dynamically adapt its frontier accordingly.

4   Conclusions

In this paper, we have presented the challenges and requirements for the preservation and evolution management of datasets published in the form of LOD on the web. The growing availability of open linked datasets has brought forth significant new problems related to the distributed nature and decentralized evolution of LOD and has posed the need for novel efficient solutions for dealing with these problems. In this respect, we have highlighted some possible directions and presented our efforts towards a framework that captures several dimensions regarding the management of evolving information resources on the Data Web.

References

1. Bizer, C., Heath, T., Berners-Lee, T.: Linked Data – The Story So Far. Special. Issue on Linked Data. In: International Journal on Semantic Web and Information Systems (2009)
2. Umbrich, J., Hausenblas, M., Hogan, A., Polleres, A., Decker, S.: Towards Dataset Dynamics: Change Frequency of Linked Open Data Sources. In: LDOW 2010 (2010)
3. Auer, S., Dalamagas, T., Parkinson, H.E., Bancilhon, F., Flouris, G., Sacharidis, D., Buneman, P., Kotzinos, D., Stavrakas, Y., Christophides, V., Papastefanatos, G., Thiveos, K.: Diachronic linked data: towards long-term preservation of structured interrelated information. In: 1st Workshop on Open Data, WOD 2012 (2012)
4. Papastefanatos, G., Stavrakas, Y., Galani, T.: Capturing the history and change structure of evolving data. In: DBKDA (2013)
5. Papavasileiou, V., Flouris, G., Fundulaki, I., Kotzinos, D., Christophides, V.: High-level change detection in RDF(S) KBs. ACM Trans. Database Syst. 38(1), 1 (2013)
6. Umbrich, J., Villazón-Terrazas, B., Hausenblas, M.: Dataset dynamics compendium: A comparative study. In: COLD (2010)

Improving Massive Open Online Courses Analysis by Applying Modeling and Text Mining: A Case Study

Alejandro Maté, Elisa de Gregorio, José Cámara, and Juan Trujillo

Lucentia Research Group, Department of Software and Computing Systems,
University of Alicante, Spain
{amate,edg12,jmcamara,jtrujillo}@dlsi.ua.es

Abstract. The continuous increase in the number of open online courses has radically changed the traditional sectors of education during the last years. These new learning approaches are just impossible to being managed by using the traditional management methods. This is one of the main reasons to the failure of a big part of those courses. In this term article, we propose a big data modeling approach, considering information from a Big Data analysis perspective, finding out the most relevant indicators in order to guarantee the success of the course. This novel approach is driven along the paper using a case study of a course offered at our university. We describe the learning lesson in this work with the objective of providing general tools and indicator for courses overall. This will enable a better analysis and enhanced management of the courses in order to guarantee the success of them.

Keywords: business intelligence, analytics, MOOC, text mining.

1 Introduction

In recent years, the effect of the globalization along with the proliferation of open online courses has radically changed the traditional sectors of education. New technologies symbolise a big opportunity, although it is also required to face significant challenges to take full advantages of them [1].

More recently, a new kind of online course has appeared: the massive open online course (MOOC). A MOOC is an online course with the objective of interacting and promoting participation and open access via the web. Apart from the traditional resources such as books or texts, MOOCs provide video lectures, both off-line and on-line, and user forums that help to build an expert/professional community for the students and professors. These advantages have made that MOOCs quickly gain popularity, and thus they have been increasing their number of students exponentially during the last years.

MOOC courses can cover from simple courses which have between a few hundred and thousands of students and all the activities undertaken by them, to the most popular ones with more than 100,000 students (for instance, Game

J. Parsons and D. Chiu (Eds.): ER Workshops 2013, LNCS 8697, pp. 29–38, 2014.

Theory course [1] from Coursera [2] website and offered by Stanford university has reached 108,371 students enrolled a few days the start of the course). Some of the amazing numbers of one of the most popular websites in this new approach for education are 62 partners institutions, 313 total courses, 5 Languages, 4 Continents and it is now seeing around 1.4 million course enrollments each month. In addition, the quality of the data, not only at the level of the teachers but also the information provided by students is a new requirement in this new framework.

Besides the benefits of these new learning approaches, they also include new challenges and difficulties that render traditional course management methods inadequate for MOOC management. This needs novel approaches of inclusive delivery and it has to be tested with real students [2]. Among these new challenges, MOOC management faces a significant problem when trying to analyze the information of the interaction between students and the course. The dramatic number of simultaneous students interacting with the course creates a flood of data. For example, it is challenging to analyze if any subgroup of students coming from different parts of the world is struggling with certain course materials. Furthermore, the quality of the data provided, not only at the level of the teachers, but also the information provided by students, such as in their profile or at the user forums, is no longer guaranteed. This can lead to erroneous analysis and difficult course management.

This is the motivation that leads us to present this work not from an education perspective, but from a big data modeling approach. Big Data is characterized by 3 classical V's (or 4 if we consider the Veracity / quality of data). The classical 3 V's are volume, velocity and variety. Volume is the most common; especially in most popular courses where the interaction of students with their resources produces a huge volume of data. Velocity, in the sense of the growth and activity of the course, which can vary dramatically from one moment to the other, as students enroll from any part of the world as well as new courses appear. Finally, Variety is presented through the various demands required by each particular course (i.e. it could be required different amount of practical content, more or less media material, case studies to reinforce theoretical parts and the differences from the number of students enrolled in any course). In any case, it must exist common patterns.

Therefore, the main goal of this term article is to model MOOC information from a Big Data analysis perspective, finding out the most relevant indicators in order to guarantee the success of the course, and describing an analysis approach that can be applied to MOOCs in general. To this aim, we show the application of our approach to a case study from a MOOC taught and managed by the University of Alicante. Furthermore, we discuss our implementation and its particularities as well as its generalisability.

The remaining part of the paper is organized as follows. In Section 5, we provide a description of our approach to model the information required to

---

[1] https://class.coursera.org/gametheory-2012-002/class/index

[2] Coursera is an education company that partners with the top universities and organizations in the world to offer courses online for anyone to take, for free.

manage and analyze the course. Section 3 describes the characteristics of the data sources as well as the steps carried out to process and analyze the data. Next, in Section 4, we discuss the lessons learned as a result of our case study. Afterwards, in Section 5 we briefly describe the related work in the area of MOOCs. Finally, in Section 6 we draw the relevant conclusions and sketch future works.

2   MOOC Analysis and Modeling Process

In this section, we present the process followed to elicit and model the critical information from the MOOC named UniMOOC[3], as well as the results of such procedure. UniMOOC is a MOOC that currently has over unique 20000 students registered and focuses on entrepreneurship. The course includes several units and modules as well as a social network for students to interchange opinions. The overall process followed can be seen in Figure 1. First, user requirements are analyzed. Then, an initial multidimensional model is obtained. Finally, data is collected and analyzed, updating the multidimensional model on each iteration until the final model is obtained.

Our first step to tackle the analytical challenges of UniMOOC at the University of Alicante was to carry out several interviews with the organizers of this course. This provided us some abstract and high level information to about the goals and objectives of course managers, thus being able to derive a first set of indicators and create an initial version of the multidimensional model for analysis. The indicators obtained, which may be applicable to other online courses are as follows:

1. Increment in number of students
2. Dropout ratio
3. Recovery ratio of students
4. % Of active students
5. % Of students who fail the course
6. % Of students passing the exams without seeing the corresponding lessons
7. % Of students taking the course on a continuous or sequential pattern

According to these indicators, we created a multidimensional model to support their calculus and provide additional analysis capacities. The model allows the mapping from the indicators to DW elements making possible to generate the DW schema automatically. Our multidimensional model is composed of two analysis cubes: "Enrollment" and "Activity". The first one, "Enrollment", allows us to analyze if the characteristics of the students, such as country, interests and expectations present certain patterns. This multidimensional model[4] can be seen in Figure 2. The data sources available to populate this cube with data were composed by natural language answers gathered in an online form, to be crossed with student information from the server. The second cube, "Activity", allows us to analyze the interactions of the students with the course, thus

---

[3] UniMOOC can be accessed at `http://unimooc.com/landing/`.

[4] Attributes have been omitted due to lack of space.

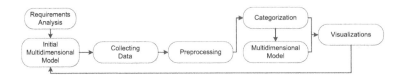

Fig. 1. Steps followed in the procedure of analysing data from a MOOC course

identifying abandonment points, materials which are mostly skipped by the students, or evaluating if altering the order of materials is obtaining better results than the previous order. The data sources to populate this cube were composed by server logs, database tables gathered in csv files, and data from an internal social network included within the course.

This multidimensional model was created by using the conceptual modeling proposal described in [3], where the information is organized according to Facts (center of analysis) and Dimensions (context of analysis) as shown in Figure 2.

In this Figure, we can see the center of the analysis (Fact) which is the "Enrollment" process. According to our data as well as our user analysis needs, there are several concepts related to enrollment that are relevant, and represent the context of analysis (Dimensions). First, we have the "Known from" dimension. This dimension gathers information about how a student knew about the course existence. According to the categorization process performed, we can differentiate between "Subtype" and "Type" aggregation levels. "Subtype" contains categories such as "newspaper" or "online", which can be further grouped into "Type", such as "news". Next, we have "Students". This dimension gathers the information regarding the different students who enroll in the course. As we were not interested in analyzing the personal data of individual students, we have grouped them by "Country".

Afterwards, we have "Interests" and "Expectations". The "Interests" dimension gathers the interests of the students when joining the course, whereas the "Expectations" dimension contains what the students expect to learn from the course. Finally, in order to be able to perform a time series analysis, we have the "Time" dimension, containing a standard hierarchy composed of "Day" that can be grouped into "Week", and then further into "Month" and "Year".

In addition to this cube, we created another cube to analyze the "Activity" of the students. This second cube shares some dimensions with the first one, i.e. "Student" and "Time". However, the information required is different, as knowing the country of the student suffices to analyze student preferences, but not for analyzing their interactions with the course. Furthermore, other dimensions had to be added. More specifically, the second cube includes the dimensions "Lesson", "Question", and "OrderUML". "Lesson" includes information about the lessons, modules and units that comprise the course. "Question" keeps track of the questions that compose self-evaluation activities and assessments. Finally, "OrderUML" is a special dimension included to satisfy the requirement of ana-

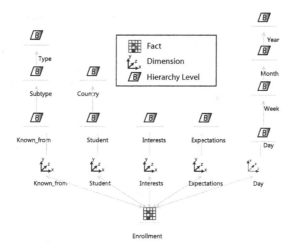

Fig. 2. MOOC Multidimensional modeling for the enrollment analysis

lyzing the order of "Unit/Module/Lesson" followed by the students when interacting with the course as opposed to the order proposed by the course itself.

These cube models allowed us to have a basis over which we could answer the questions posed by the MOOC decision makers for monitoring the MOOC. Furthermore, they were also used as patterns to automatically derive the data warehouse schema and provided the necessary scaffolding to perform more advanced analytics, such as data mining. However, the necessary data to populate these cubes was dispersed between several kinds of data sources, including unstructed data and inaccurate data. Thus, we had to analyze the data in detail, in order to obtain the information that we needed and also identifying potential changes in the analysis structure.

3   Data Analysis

In order to populate the initial multidimensional models, it was necessary to create a detailed list and analysis of the data sources available. As each source had its own characteristics, we had to evaluate its format and the quality of the data before loading it into the data warehouse. For these tasks, we used Pentaho Data Integration[5], which is an Extraction/Transformation/Loading (ETL) tool.

The first data source were the server logs that monitored the activity of the students. These server logs were saved in JSON[6] format, which is a list of pairs containing variables and values. These logs had to be parsed and integrated with the course information. As we focused strictly on gathering the answers of

---

[5] http://www.pentaho.com/explore/pentaho-data-integration/
[6] For more information see: http://www.json.org/.

the students, we linked each entry them with the corresponding elements in the multidimensional model.

Our second data source was in the form of structured server tables. These server tables were integrated within NoSQL database included in Google App Engine that supports the MOOC. Since we did not have direct access to the tables to query them, we got a copy of their contents in the form of csv files. Each of this csv files contained information about a certain element involved in the course, such as "Lessons", "Modules" or "Assessments', and required to be adequately integrated in order to obtain basic information, i.e. "Which Assessment corresponds to each Module?" or "What is the order of the Lessons in the course?".

It is noteworthy that, although it may be expected that server tables would be the easiest source to integrate, it was quite the opposite. First, when analyzing the information provided by students, we found out that even the information selected from predefined lists contained several errors. For example, some students selected their country but did not specify their city. Others, specified their city but did not select a country. Thus, we ended up with "Madrid" being in "Abjasia" according to the data available. In order to solve this problem, we included an additional external source to validate each pair city-country, and correct the inaccurate ones. Second, the information stored in server tables did not accurately reflect the state of the course when some interactions registered in server logs took place. For example, there were students who had interacted with lessons which were marked as not available, or that had followed a different lesson order than the currently established. In order to deal with these situations, we modified our multidimensional models, including an additional dimension, "OrderUML" which was presented in Section 2, as well as several attributes to include the missing information.

Finally, the third data source were course forms. Course forms were included in the course to gather students' expectations, interests and identifying where students heard about the course. The information was mostly gathered in the form of natural language answers. However, we found out that, in addition to being highly variable, the information stored was also highly inaccurate. For example, questions such as "Where did you know about the course?" could refer to a certain source by name or be as general as "Internet". Therefore, in order to solve this problem, we performed a text mining and categorization process, which is described throughout Sections 3.1 and 3.2.

An example of the ETL processes designed for cleaning and extracting information from these data sources can be seen in Figure 3. In this Figure, the relevant dates from activities and assessments captured in server logs are integrated into the analysis model. In order to perform this process, date data are extracted from the sources and then listed removing duplicates. Finally, additional data, such as month names, days of the year and so on are added to the flow before loading it into the analysis model.

The load of the initial data, and especially the analysis and processing of the different data sources, led us to the emergence of new elements that altered

Fig. 3. Excerpt of the relevant date list extraction

the structure of the analysis, thus requiring to repeatedly adapt and update the data modeling scheme. As it is common to discover new elements and relevant information as highly heterogeneous sources are explored, we adopted an iterative procedure to tackle this problem. This procedure can be seen in Figure 1. Initially, data are gathered from each data source. Then they are preprocessed according to its corresponding set of rules, i.e. regular expressions that ensure that data format is correct, null values filtered out, etc. Finally, data are visualized either directly, in a stand-alone way, to evaluate its quality or provide further understanding, or it is integrated within the multidimensional model, leading to a new version. Then, the new multidimensonal model is visualized in order to evaluate the result of the integration step. Afterwards, the cycle starts again, using the newly gained understanding to perform modifications on the procedure steps, i.e. ETL processes and natural language processes.

In the case of unstructured data, a categorization step is performed in order to provide some basic structure, and allow the integration with the rest of the data available. Most of the unstructured data involved in our analysis came from course forms. Although this source contained valuable information gathered from over 10200 students, it was necessary to understand its contents and manage its variability in order to obtain meaningful information. The processing of this unstructured data led to the iterative addition of the dimensions previously shown in Figure 2, and it is detailed in the following subsections.

3.1   Preprocessing and Text Mining

The information stored in the different fields within course forms was mainly textual and needed to be preprocessed in order to be evaluated. In this regard, we extracted the words most frequently used in each field. For this task, we transformed each string into a vector, by using "StringToWordVector" which is a filter that is built into Weka [4]. Weka is an open source toolbox containing a collection of machine learning algorithms developed at the University of Waikato.

As a result of the application of the "StringtoWordVector", we obtained a set of word occurrence frequencies, which described the words most commonly used by the students when filling the form. Using this information, we proceeded to the creation of categories.

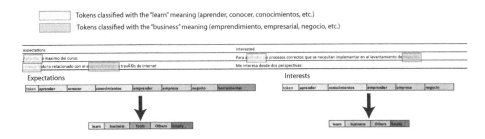

Fig. 4. Categorization of word occurrence for expectations and interests

3.2   Categories Creation

As we can appreciate in Figure 1 that represents the iterative schema followed in this work, once the procedure of word occurrence frequencies (preprocessing box according to the text mining) was finished, we evaluated the information obtained. As a result, we decided to categorize words according to the dimensions indicated in the model shown in Figure 2. Specifically, the "Known from" dimension presented a classification within different levels of abstraction. Therefore, we added an analysis hierarchy including types and subtypes. Afterwards, we modified the steps to automatically classify the information according to the semantical meaning of the different word occurrence (tokens) that appeared in the unstructured textual data gathered in course forms.

An example of this procedure showing the process for the expectations and interests dimensions of the enrollment modeling can be seen in Figure 4. We can appreciate on the left side the procedure where the tokens are extracted from the text. On the right side the categorization is done by grouping similar semantic meaning in natural language.

4   Lessons Learned

In this term article we have described the process followed to provide multidimensional analysis support in the case study of a MOOC at the University of Alicante. Initially, the project started with the creation of static models and direct data analysis. However, this approach was quickly dismissed due to several reasons. First, the lack of a clear direction had a dramatic effect, since we had to choose between a number of different data processing and analysis techniques without knowing beforehand if we would obtain any significant result, thus making time and effort futile in most cases. Second, the evaluation of results was challenging itself, since only clearly marked patterns could be identified as noteworthy. Third, the static models were continually being scrapped, as whenever the point of view on the data changed, the models did no longer fit.

Therefore, we scrapped this approach and started over again focusing on an iterative process. Having a clear point of view on the data, thanks to including domain knowledge and gathering a list of indicators, helped to determine which was the best way to integrate the variety of data sources that comprised all the information related to the course. Furthermore, this domain knowledge also allowed us to highlight the problem related to managing information uploaded by users, as even in the case of predefined lists it can be highly inaccurate.

In addition, since the course makes use of the Google App Engine platform employed by many online courses, we think that the set of indicators identified, as well as our approach, can be applied to online courses in general, thus enabling better analysis and better management of the courses.

Furthermore, we have also confirmed that traditional management and traditional basic analysis approaches are not applicable to MOOCs. The volume of the interactions between students and the course, as well as the amount of different sources and unstructured data dramatically increases the complexity of a traditional analysis, while at the same time limiting the knowledge that can be obtained from such analysis. Therefore, we consider that following an iterative process (customizable, adaptable and updateable), including early indicators that provide guidance about what to analyze and how to integrate the data, is compulsory. Otherwise, a lot of effort and time will be wasted, leading to a high probability of failure.

Finally, thanks to the analysis we have identified what modules are more popular, the presence of bots who repeat tests constantly, and the what tests are too complex for the students, among others.

5 Related Work

In this section we briefly cover the related work in the area of MOOC analytics and Big Data. Most of the works until now have been focused on analyzing the challenges and opportunities related to approaching MOOC analysis from a Big Data perspective. In [1] the authors express that this new situation poses a revolution in education, while the recent EdX initiative[5] by Harvard and MIT state "with an Internet connection, anyone anywhere in the world, can have (free) access to video lessons, online laboratories, quizzes". Next, [6] explains the challenges as well as the changes in higher education and international rankings of universities. In [7], the authors addressed similar targets as we do in this work. However none of these works cover the experimentation and implementation aspects. Finally, [8] presents a report of Big Data for Student Learning indicating new forms of assessment as well as the need of interconnected feedback loops among the diverse parts of the whole process (students, teachers, administrators and developers). They propose a Learning Registry open-source community for sharing social metadata, and have experimented with a number of organizations representing their social metadata using that schema. To the best of our knowledge all these previous work have not used a novel and dynamic architecture to face the Big Data analytics in education. This is the reason that lead us to go a further step to propose this novel approach to tackle the analysis problem for MOOCs.

6 Conclusions

In this term article we have presented a novel approach to model MOOC data from a big data perspective. As we discussed, the particularities of MOOCs compared with classical courses render traditional management and analysis approaches ineffective and, therefore, they require the application of more dynamic paradigms in order to be managed adequately. We have shown how applying a big data perspective can aid in the analysis of the variety of data available, ranging from server logs to student inputs, and in some cases including social network data. Furthermore, we have elicited a set of indicators that may be applied for managing other online courses and we have highlighted the key factors found while implementing the case study. There still are several challenges for MOOC management, since the amount of requirements can vary from one course to another. The compliance of those requirements and the capability to analyze the data according to them will be crucial to the success of the courses.

Our future work includes integrating the social network information, which was left outside the initial iteration, as well as consider additional sources of information outside the course.

Acknowledgments. This work has partially funded by the project GEODAS-BI (TIN2012-37493-C03-03) from the Ministry of Economy and Competitiveness (MINECO). Alejandro Maté is funded by a Vali+D grant (ACIF/2010/298). Elisa de Gregorio is funded by a FPI grant (BES-2011-043577). We would also like to thank the group at UniMOOC for their contributions.

References

1. Allison, C., Miller, A., Oliver, I., Michaelson, R., Tiropanis, T.: The web in education. Computer Networks 56(18), 3811–3824 (2012)
2. Baker, P.M., Bujak, K.R., DeMillo, R.: The evolving university: Disruptive change and institutional innovation. Procedia Computer Science 14, 330–335 (2012)
3. Lujan-Mora, S., Trujillo, J., Song, I.Y.: A uml profile for multidimensional modeling in data warehouses. Data and Knowledge Engineering 59(3), 725–769 (2006)
4. Witten, I.H., Frank, E., Hall, M.A.: Data Mining: Practical Machine Learning Tools and Techniques, 3rd edn., pp. 539–557. Morgan Kaufmann, Boston (2011)
5. Harvard, MIT, EdX: Edx courses (2012), http://www.edxonline.org
6. Brada, J.C., Bienkowski, W., Stanley, G.: The University in the Age of Globalization: Rankings, Resources and Reforms. Palgrave Macmillan (2012)
7. Schutlz, N.: Classes in the cloud. New Scientist 217(2905) (2013)
8. Bienkowski, M., Brecht, J., Klo, J.: The learning registry: building a foundation for learning resource analytics. In: LAK 2012, pp. 208–211. ACM (2012)

Functionality for Business Indicators
in Data Warehouse Requirements Engineering

Naveen Prakash and Hanu Bhardwaj

MRCE, Sector 43, Surajkund Badhkal Road, Faridabad 121001, India
praknav@hotmail.com,
bhardwajhanu@gmail.com

Abstract. Traditionally, data warehouse requirements engineering is oriented towards determining the information contents of the warehouse To Be. This has resulted in de-emphasized functional perspective of data warehouses. Consequently, it is difficult to specify functions needed for computing business indicators. Our approach aims to elicit needed business indicators from organizational decision makers. Thereafter, indicator hierarchies are built. Finally, we specify functionality using sequence diagrams and extended use case diagrams. Our use case diagrams allow for actor aggregation in addition to actor specialization. Further, we need to introduce the 'estimated from' relationship between use cases in addition to the extend and include relationships of UML. We illustrate our proposals with an example.

Keywords: Functionality, target, business indicator, indicator hierarchy, BI use case.

1 Introduction

In recent years, data warehouse requirements engineering has emphasized the determination of the information contents of the warehouse To Be. Indeed, all work in data warehouse requirements engineering known to the authors consider this aspect only. Consider the three life cycles described in [18]. The main task in the data base driven [9] and ER driven [10] life cycles is to restructure data bases and ER diagrams respectively to determine the required facts and dimensions. Goal oriented approaches [2, 3, 9, 17, 18] explore system/organizational goals and determine star schemas. [19] has introduced the notion of a target. Targets participate in two hierarchies, the relevance and fulfillment hierarchies. It has been shown that these hierarchies lead to determination of the information to be kept in the data warehouse To Be. In [19] the process of arriving at star schemas has been split into two parts (i) an 'early information' part where the information relevant to decision making is discovered and (ii) a 'late' part where the discovered information is structured as facts and dimensions.

Now, in concentrating on information discovery and structuring, data warehouse requirements engineering **de-emphasizes** an investigation into its functional aspect: what functions should be built for different stakeholders. We propose that one source of data warehouse functionality is business indicators. Computation of indicators in

J. Parsons and D. Chiu (Eds.): ER Workshops 2013, LNCS 8697, pp. 39–48, 2014.

the absence of well-defined mathematical functions was considered in [1] but no attempt was made to elicit the set of functions needed in a data warehouse. Even though performance indicator systems like Performance Pyramid [15] and Balanced Scorecard [11] for developing performance indicators exist, defining the right indicators remains a major issue [5, 7, 21].

Work on requirements engineering for data warehouse functionality starts once indicators are finalized by business people. The first step in the requirements engineering task is to elicit these. However, business indicators are dispersed [21] in an organization and involve many people. Thus, a method for discovering stakeholders and their indicators is crucial for elicitation.

In this paper, we propose an elicitation mechanism for business indicators and then consider the needed functionality. For this purpose, we use the notion of a target hierarchy defined in [19]. A target is an association of a set of **indicators** with an **aspect**. An aspect is a work unit or a work area. Targets are nodes in the target hierarchy and edges are *estimated from* relationship between nodes.

Our approach is in three steps, (a) elicitation of business indicators from positions occupied in organizational units, (b) determining sub-indicators needed to compute an indicator, and (c) identifying functional requirements for computing indicators from interaction and use case diagrams. Our use case diagrams include two features in addition to those found in UML use case diagrams. These are (a) actor aggregation and (b) the *estimated from* relationship between use cases.

In the next section we present our Indicator model and use it for eliciting indicators. Section 3 deals with functionality required to compute business indicators. Section 4 contains an example to illustrate our proposal. Section 5 contains related work and positions our work in the literature.

2   Eliciting *estimated from* Relationship

In this section, we define our Indicator Exchange Model and use this model as the basis for eliciting indicators and the indicator-sub indicator hierarchy.

2.1   The Indicator Exchange Model

Our model borrows the notions of *people* and *position* as well as the m:n relationship between these, from Organization Structure Metamodel, OSM [16]. This provides to us a basic set of stakeholders, from whom we will elicit indicators. The model is shown in Fig. 1. *People* are assigned *positions* which are held in *aspects*. Although there is an m:n relationship between *people* and *position*, we consider 1:1 in our paper, for reasons of simplicity. One *aspect* can have more than one *position*, as shown by the m:1 relationship shown in the figure. An *aspect* reflects the structural and behavioral properties of an organization. The *work unit* of Fig. 1 is a recognized association of *positions*, reflecting the organization structure. Thus *work unit* ISA *aspect*. It can be seen that *work unit* corresponds to the OSM notion of organization unit. *Work area* is a recognized association of *positions* charged with a certain organization task.

Accounts Department is an example of a work unit: it is a set of positions and defines a structural organization unit. Example of work area is Taxation: it is a set of positions associated to perform the task of tax computation and deduction.

Fig. 1 shows that there is an m:n relationship *interacts* between *aspects*; this models that an *aspect* interacts with another *aspect*.

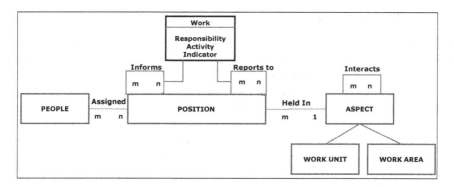

Fig. 1. The Indicator exchange model

Fig. 1 shows *position* as having two self loops, *Informs* and *Reports to*. The *informs* relationship says that a *position* keeps another *position* informed about the values of indicators. *Informs* enables us to focus on *positions* as sources of indicators. *Reports to* captures the formal lines of management. We assume that when a *position* *reports to* another, then there is a high probability of indicator exchange between them. As we will see, this provides us a good starting point for indicator exchange elicitation.

Both of these relationships have an associative class, *work*. *Work* has three attributes, *responsibility*, *activity* and *indicator*. Through this associative class, we model the fact that a *position reports to* or *informs* respectively *indicator* while performing a task.

The attribute *Responsibility* of *work* refers to the major categories of activities, carried out. We postulate these as Plan, Co-ordinate and Monitor. Activities are the tasks carried out. Thus, we can have a pair, *Plan Production*.

Let us represent an instance of *informs* as a triple, $<D_i, I_{ij}, D_j>$, where position D_i informs D_j about the set of indicators I_{ij}. Since D_j receives indicators from several sources, we can represent its information by the pair $<D_j, \{I_{1j}, I_{2j, ...} I_{nj} \}>$. Now, if we traverse informs in the reverse direction, then we get the receiver's view of indicators: what indicators is the receiving position expecting from its informers. The position D_j may expect indicator $EI_{1j}, EI_{2j, ...} EI_{nj}$ from its informers, $D_1, D_2, ... D_n$ respectively. Now, we can formulate a basic consistency check: the received information must be equal to the expected information. In other words, for D_j

$$\{I_{1j}, I_{2j, ...} I_{nj} \} = \{EI_{1j}, EI_{2j, ...} EI_{nj}\}$$

This equality does not guarantee completeness of informed indicators. This is because it is possible to miss an indicator from both the sender and the receiver points of view. However, it does guarantee that there is an agreement between both parties on the needed indicators. Further, it helps in elicitation when one party recognizes a missing indicator that the other party has omitted.

2.2 The Elicitation Process

We propose to start elicitation from the *reports to* relationship. Organizations often have a formal *reports to* relationship that is represented as an organization chart. The organization chart corresponds to *work units* interacting with other *work units*, shown in Fig. 1. This chart presents a starting set of our *aspects* and *positions* and is used to identify the dispersed *informs* amongst the different stakeholders. Elicitation consists of a number of steps as follows:

1. Obtain the positions and the *reports to* relationship between them from the organization chart, in a top-down left to right manner.
2. For each position, elicit its *informs* relationships.
3. For each <position1 – *'reports to'* position2> and<position1 –*'informs'* position2> , identify the indicators that position1 sends to position2.

The third step exploits the <*responsibility, activity*> attributes of *work* of Fig.1. For a position looking after a responsibility type, the activities and indicators reported for them are obtained, using the screen of Fig. 2.

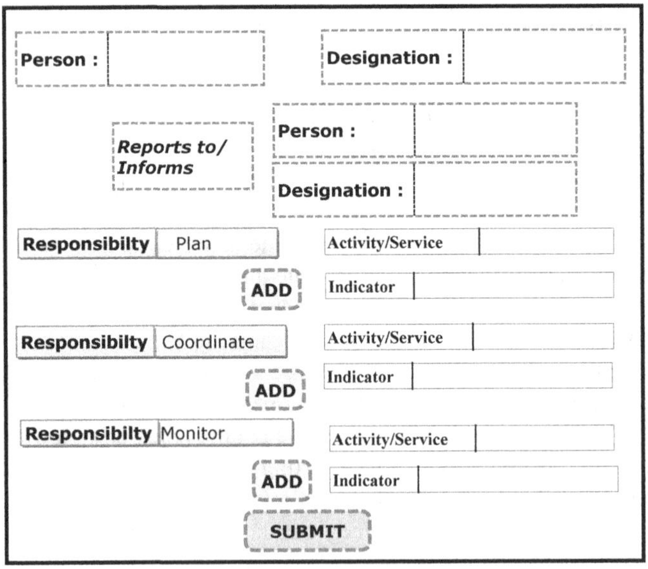

Fig. 2. Responsibility-Activity Details

Whereas the foregoing elicits those indicators that a position ***sends*** to others, our consistency check of section 2.1 needs indicators that a position ***expects*** from others. This is done by suitably modifying steps 1 to 3 and the screen of Fig. 2. For reasons of space, this is omitted. Indicator consistency check is performed for each position by partitioning the indicator set into received indicator set and expected indicator set and comparing these two sets.

In the final step we construct the indicator hierarchy. For every position, we display the indicators received and the indicators sent for each responsibility-activity. This position knows what is to be computed from what and builds the indicator sub-hierarchy. The total hierarchy is built by considering all positions. We have defined a number of validation checks that are the subject of another paper.

In real contexts, no common understanding of indicator name is likely. They may be referred to by different names; different people may use the same name to mean different indicators and so on. Therefore, we expect to have an enterprise-wide shared glossary or thesaurus.

3   Indicator Functionality

Let us now consider building use case and sequence diagrams for business indicator functionality. Since we introduce some additions in UML use case diagrams, we refer our diagrams as Business Indicator (BI) Use Case diagrams. First notice that *positions* become actors of our use case diagrams, and each position has its own use case. There are two additional properties as follows:

a. **Actor aggregation**: If an indicator goes into estimating the value of another, then the actor of the former is in the hierarchy of the latter. Thus, an actor 'is part of' another actor and we introduce the notion of aggregate actors in BI Use Case diagrams. Notice that UML provides for actor specialization/generalization and not for actor aggregation.

b. **Estimated from relationship between use cases**: Since an indicator is estimated from another sub indicator, the BI use case diagram must contain one use case for the composite indicator and another for the sub indicator. We now need to introduce a new relationship, *estimated from*, between use cases.

To understand the need for (b) above, consider the two UML relationships, extend and include:

a) extend - specifies that a use case extends the base use case. The base use case may stand alone, but under certain conditions, its behaviour may be extended by the other.

b) include - Specifies that the base use case explicitly incorporates the behaviour of another use case at a location specified by the base. The included use case never stands alone, but is only instantiated as part of some larger base that includes it.

The *estimated from* is a relationship between a base use case and an *estimated from* use case. Both use cases are capable of independent existence and have actors associated with them. The actor of the base use case interacts with the system and so does the actor of the *estimated from* use case. In this sense, the *estimated from* is different from UML's *include* relationship. It is also different from *extend* in that there is no extension of any behaviour. The indicator produced by the *estimated from* use case is used by the base use case.

There is no change in sequence diagrams and UML applies for us as well. Therefore, these diagrams are not elaborated here.

4   Example

We have applied the proposed technique to development of a data warehouse in our Institute. This warehouse was needed to make decisions about changes in the academic structure and teaching-learning processes. An organization chart of the Institute is available. It is in four levels and shows the Director, the Deans and various executive offices, the Heads of Departments, and the faculty members. Through various notifications of the Institute, we could determine the current incumbents of these positions.

Since the number of individuals and positions is rather large, for reasons of space we show a small part of the work. We started with the root of the hierarchy, namely, the Director. The Director was *reporting* to the Chairman, Board of Governors and *informing* to VP(PPC) and SVP. For the first 'informs' authority, namely, VP(PPC), the screen of Fig. 2 was proposed. The Director identified eight activities for Monitoring, five activities for Planning, as well as four Coordination activities. For reasons of brevity, the indicators identified under one Planning activity and two Monitoring activities are shown in Table 1.

Table 1. Indicators for Director-VP(PPC)

Responsibility	Activity	Indicator
Plan	Finance	Expenditure
		Receipts
Monitor	Admissions	Percentage of filled seats
	Results	Success Index
		Academic Performance Index

Thereafter, we moved in a left to right manner to the next level in the organization chart. We present below the result of interaction of the system with Dean Undergraduate Studies. The information is shown in Table 2.

Table 2. Dean UG Relationships

Name	Position	Reports to	Informs
Mamta	Dean Under Graduate	Director	
	Professor		HOD-Physics

A sampling of the indicators that the Dean reports to the Director is shown in Table 3.

Table 3. Indicators of Dean UG - Director

Respon-sibility	Activity	Indicator
Plan	Faculty Load allocation	Adequacy of faculty members
Monitor	Results	Engg. Success index, Science success index
		Engg. Academic Performance Index, Science Academic performance Index
Monitor	Admissions	Engg. Filled seats, Science filled seats

Now we moved to the next level of decision making, i.e the departments. We present in Table 4 the interaction done with Head of the Mechanical Engineering department. The Head reported six activities during her interaction with Director and ten activities during her interaction with Dean Undergraduate. Table 5 and 6 show Head - Director indicator exchange and Head - Dean UG indicator exchange respectively.

Table 4. Head's 'reports to'/'informs' relationships

Name	Position	Reports To	Informs
Smita	Head, Mech. Engg.	Director	Dean Undergraduate
			Dean Post Graduate
			Dean Industry Interaction
			Dean Students
	Professor		Self (HOD-ME)

Let us now illustrate the last step, construction of indicator hierarchy. For the root *position* Director, the first *responsibility-activity* 'Plan Finance' was picked up. The indicators 'Expenditure' and 'Receipts were displayed. This *responsibility activity* is absent in Table 3, and the corresponding indicators in Table 5 are displayed. The Director then establishes the indicator hierarchy, see Table 7. Now the next two responsibility-activities of Table 2 are picked up, their corresponding indicators are obtained and the hierarchy is built.

Table 5. Indicators of Head – Director

Responsi-bility	Activity	Indicator
Plan	Finance	Departmental Salary Expenditure, Student Training & Welfare Expenditure, Faculty & staff development Expenditure, Repair and maintenance Expenditure, Library Expenditure, Machinery & equipment Expenditure
		Departmental Fees Receipts, Sponsorship receipts, Consultancy receipts, Extension receipts

The foregoing builds only one level of the hierarchy. The full hierarchy is an assembly of many such. For example consider responsibility activity 'Monitor Results' of Dean UG, as in second row of Table 3. Following the procedure, we get sub indicators a) Departmental Success index, and b) Departmental Academic Performance Index, shown in Table 6.

Table 6. Indicators of Head – Dean UG

Responsibility	Activity	Indicator
Monitor	Results	Departmental Success index
		Departmental Academic Performance Index

A multi-level hierarchy is built by exploiting commonality of child and parent indicators. Thus we get, for example, Root : Success index; Level 1 : Engg. Success Index; Level 2 : Departmental Success Index.

We have found **two interesting observations** in our example study. These are as follows:

1. The use of the organization chart facilitates the discovery of *informs* relationship. When we tried not to use the organization chart then people and positions identification became completely ad-hoc. The organization chart provided to us a very good guide to initiate our work.

2. The *responsibility-activity* pair a) provides a guideline to elicit indicators. Our experience is that without this, it was difficult to provide guidance on where to look for indicators, b) while forming the indicator hierarchy, it provided a means to cut down on the search space of indicators to be considered as candidates for sub indicators.

Table 7. Indicator Hierarchy

Indicator	Sub Indicator
Expenditure	Departmental Salary Expenditure, Student Training & Welfare Expenditure, Faculty & staff development Expenditure, Repair and maintenance Expenditure, Library Expenditure, Machinery & equipment Expenditure
Receipts	Departmental Fees Receipts, Sponsorship receipts, Consultancy receipts, Extension receipts
Percentage of filled seats	Engg. Filled seats, Science filled seats
Success Index	Engg. Success index, Science success index
Academic Performance Index	Engg. Academic Performance Index, Science Academic performance Index

5   Related Work

In [1], business indicators have been divided into composite-component ones. The concern was to find ways by which composite indicators could be computed from their components. Our problem is that of eliciting indicators and finding suitable functions to be built in the proposed data warehouse. The manner of computation of [1] is then subsumed within the defined functions.

Elicitation of indicators is related to work on early requirement engineering. In [8] the approach of TROPOS [4] was used to model goal dependencies between stakeholders/actors. [8] used this to lay down goals and then associated decisions with goals. [12] model stakeholders as actors and these may be internal or external to the organization. Stakeholders have goals as their objectives and "delegate" goal achievement to one another.

In contrast, our proposal uses the *reports to/informs* relationship that is rather more general than the "supports goal achievement" dependency of TROPOS and [12]. Whereas our model allows us to define stakeholders, [8, 12] leave open the question of who are their stakeholders.

A number of UML based proposals exist for data warehouses. Prat et al [20] represent decision-maker information in a UML class diagram, thereby reusing transactional systems analysis methods. [6,14] extended UML using stereotypes, constraints and tagged values for representing security properties of multi dimensional structures. Our proposal is to extend UML use case diagrams with a view to representing the functionality to be provided.

[13] proposes UML use case for data warehouse design in an Analyst System diagram. They introduce a "uses" relationship between use cases that builds aggregates of use cases. A use case itself represents business process components. The differences between this approach and ours are

a) we define use case diagrams for identifying the business indicator functional capacity whereas use cases of Analyst system are for representing business processes,

b) our *estimated from* relationship forms an aggregation but for computing business indicator whereas the "uses" relationship forms process aggregation.

c) our actors are decision makers, real users of the data warehouse, who have business indicator needs whereas in [13] use cases are associated to analysts.

d) our actors enter into actor aggregation relationships which is not the case with [13].

6   Conclusion

Seeing the crucial role played by business indicators in decision making, our proposal is to consider these for data warehouse requirements engineering. On the one hand, this identifies the key indicators and on the other, the packaged functionality to be built.

Our proposal is to elicit indicators of different stakeholders in an organization through our indicator exchange model. Our elicitation technique exploits the organization chart of an organization as a starting point. Taking into account the hierarchical structure of indicators, we introduce the notion of actor aggregation and *estimated from* in use case diagrams.

In future, we wish to explore our process further. In particular, we examine issues in construction of the indicator hierarchy and also handling the m:n relationship between *people* and *position*.

References

1. Barone, D., Jiang, L., Amyot, D., Mylopoulos, J.: Composite Indicators for Business Intelligence. In: Jeusfeld, M., Delcambre, L., Ling, T.-W. (eds.) ER 2011. LNCS, vol. 6998, pp. 448–458. Springer, Heidelberg (2011)
2. Boehnlein, M.: Ulbrich vom Ende A.: Deriving initial Data Warehouse Structures from the Conceptual Data Models of the Underlying Operational Information Systems. In: Proc. of Workshop on Data Warehousing and OLAP (DOLAP), Kansas City, MO, USA (1999)
3. Bonifati, A., Cattaneo, F., Ceri, S., Fuggetta, A., Paraboschi, S.: Designing data marts for data warehouses. ACMTOSEM 10(4), 452–483 (2001)
4. Bresciani, P., Giorgini, P., Mylopoulos, L., Perini, A.: Tropos: An agent oriented software development Methodology. Journal Autonomous Agents and Multi-agent Systems 8, 203–236 (2004)
5. Chalmeta, R., Grangel, R.: Performance Measurement Systems for Virtual Enterprise Integration. International Journal of Computer Integrated Manufacturing, 73–84 (2005)
6. Fernández-Medina, E., Villarroel, J., Piattini, R., Trujillo, M., Developing, J.: Secure data warehouses with a UML extension. Information Systems 32(6), 826–856 (2007)
7. Frank, U., Heise, D., Kattenstroth, H., Schauer, H.: Designing and Utilizing Indicator Systems Within Enterprise Models – Outline of a Method. In: MobIS 2008, pp. 89–105 (2008)
8. Giorgini, P., Rizzi, S., Garzetti, M.: GRAnD: A goal oriented approach to requirement analysis in data warehouses. Decision Support Systems 45, 4–21 (2008)
9. Golfarelli, M., Rizzi, S.: Designing the Data Warehouse: Key Steps and Crucial Issues. Journal of Computer Science and Information Management 2(3) (1999)
10. Hüsemann, B., Lechtenbörger, J., Vossen, G.: Conceptual Data Warehouse Design. In: Proceedings of the International Workshop on Design and Management of Data Warehouses (DMDW 2000) Stockholm, Sweden, June 5-6 (2000)
11. Kaplan, R., Norton, D.: The Balanced Scorecard: Measures that Drive Performance. Harvard Businss Review 70(1), 71–79 (1992)
12. Kumar, M., Gosain, A., Singh, Y.: Stakeholders driven requirements engineering approach for data warehouse development. Journal of Information Processing Systems 6(3), 385–402 (2010)
13. List, B., Schiefer, J., Tjoa, A.M.: Process-Oriented Requirement Analysis Supporting the#11Data Warehouse Design Process - A Use Case Driven Approach. In: Ibrahim, M., Küng, J., Revell, N. (eds.) DEXA 2000. LNCS, vol. 1873, pp. 593–603. Springer, Heidelberg (2000)
14. Luján-Mora, S., Trujillo, J., Song, I.: A UML profile for multidimensional modeling in data warehouses. Data & Knowledge Engineering 59(3), 725–769 (2006)
15. Lynch, R.L., Cross, K.F.: Measure Up!: Yardsticks for Continuous Imrpovement. Wiley, Blackwell (1991)
16. Organization Structure Metamodel (OSM), 2nd Initial Submission, OMG Document bmi/2006-11-02 (2006)
17. Prakash, N., Singh, Y., Gosain, A.: Informational Scenarios for Data Warehouse Requirements Elicitation. In: Atzeni, P., Chu, W., Lu, H., Zhou, S., Ling, T.-W. (eds.) ER 2004. LNCS, vol. 3288, pp. 205–216. Springer, Heidelberg (2004)
18. Prakash, N., Gosain, A.: An Approach to Engineering the Requirements of Data Warehouses. Requirements Engineering Journal 13(1), 49–72 (2008)
19. Prakash, N., Bhardwaj, H.: Early Information Requirements Engineering for Target Driven Data Warehouse Development. In: Sandkuhl, K., Seigerroth, U., Stirna, J. (eds.) PoEM 2012. LNBIP, vol. 134, pp. 188–202. Springer, Heidelberg (2012)
20. Prat, N., Akoka, J., Comyn-Attiau, I.: A UML-based data warehouse design method. Decision Support Systems 42(3), 1449–1473 (2006)
21. Shanks, G., Sharma, R., Seddon, P., Reynolds, P.: Business Analytics and Competitive Advantage: A Review and Research Agenda. In: 21st Australasia Conference on Information Systems, pp. 1–11 (2010)

Preface to RIGiM 2013

Colette Rolland[1], Lin Liu[2], Jennifer Horkoff[3], and Eric Yu[4]

[1] Université Paris 1 Panthéon - Sorbonne, France
[2] Tsinghua University, China
[3] University of Trento, Italy
[4] University of Toronto, Canada

The use of intentional concepts, the notion of "goal" in particular, has been prominent in recent approaches to requirements engineering, producing a body of work focusing on Goal-Oriented Requirements Engineering (GORE). RIGiM (Requirements Intentions and Goals in Conceptual Modeling) aims to provide a forum for discussing the interplay between requirements engineering and conceptual modeling, and in particular, to investigate how goal- and intention-driven approaches help in conceptualising purposeful systems. What are the upcoming modelling challenges and issues in GORE? What are the unresolved open questions? What lessons are there to be learnt from industrial experiences? What empirical data are there to support the cost-benefit analysis when adopting GORE methods? Are there applications domains or types of project settings for which goals and intentional approaches are particularly suitable or not suitable? What degree of formalization, automation or interactivity is feasible and appropriate for what types of participants during requirements engineering?

This year, RIGiM includes three high-quality accepted papers:

- Clotilde Rohleder, Jing Lin, Indra Kusuma and Gülru Özkan. Requirements Engineering in Business Analytics for Innovation and Product Lifecycle Management
- Christophe Gnaho, Farida Semmak and Regine Laleau. Modeling the Impact of Non-Functional Requirements on Functional Requirements
- Naveen Prakash, Deepak Kumar Sharma, Deepika Prakash and Dheerendra Singh. A Framework for Business Rules Requirements

Each of the submitted papers went through a thorough review process with three reviews from our program committee. We thank authors and reviewers for their valuable contributions.

Requirements Engineering in Business Analytics for Innovation and Product Lifecycle Management

Clotilde Rohleder[1], Jing Lin[2], Indra Kusumah[3], and Gülru Özkan[4]

[1] University of Appl. Sc. Constance, Germany
clotilde.rohleder@htwg-konstanz.de
[2] Siemens SISW, Nuremberg, Germany
jinglin@siemens.com
[3] RTT Real Time Technology AG, Munich, Germany
Indra.kusumah@rtt.com
[4] Clemson University, Clemson, South Carolina, USA
gulruo@clemson.edu

Abstract. Considering Requirements Engineering (RE) in business analytics, involving market oriented management, computer science and statistics, may be valuable for managing innovation in Product Lifecycle Management (PLM). RE and business analytics can help maximize the value of corporate product information throughout the value chain starting with innovation management. Innovation and PLM must address 1) big data, 2) development of well-defined business goals and principles, 3) cost/benefit analysis, 4) continuous change management, and 5) statistical and report science. This paper is a positioning note that addresses some business case considerations for analytics project involving PLM data, patents, and innovations. We describe a number of research challenges in RE that addresses business analytics when high PLM data should be turned into a successful market oriented innovation management strategy. We provide a draft on how to address these research challenges.

1 Introduction

PLM is "the process of managing the entire lifecycle of a product from its conception, through design and manufacture, to service and disposal. PLM integrates people, data, processes and business systems and provides a product information backbone for companies and their extended enterprise." [23]. Product Lifecycle Management (PLM) generally employs an integrated set of business tools to streamline the mission-critical processes across a product's lifecycle, maximizing the value of information for the product information throughout the value chain. This lifecycle starts with ideation – the solicitation, incubation, filtering and selection of an idea as shown in Fig. 1.

Fig. 1. Process of innovation management within PLM

J. Parsons and D. Chiu (Eds.): ER Workshops 2013, LNCS 8697, pp. 51–58, 2014.
© Springer International Publishing Switzerland 2014

Throughout this process (see Fig. 1), and on into commercialization or institutiona-lization, a huge amount of information (often referred to as intellectual property) must be captured and managed with respect to the content and as they relate to the decision making processes. PLM world is driven by the utilization of vast amount of data called big data and processes to guide decision-making.

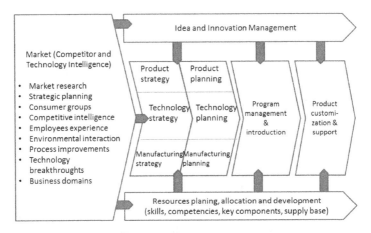

Fig. 2. Relevant PLM data for business analytics

While many departments interact with each other to solidify innovation manage-ment by manufacturing new products, they have to face the challenge of synthesizing and analyzing the amount of market oriented information and data (Fig. 2) [18]: pa-tents, market survey, competitors data, substitute products, laws, norms, ecological, quality, user/customer and technical requirements and specifications, CAD (computer aided design) data, bill of material, CAE data (computer aided engineering), CAM (computer aided manufacturing) data, test, prototypes, sales and marketing informa-tion, etc. Enterprise servers processed about 9.57 zettabytes of data globally in 2008, of which PLM data was a substantial part [22]. Industrial organizations recognize the importance of using this data as a strategic asset. Some organizations include analyt-ics to improve the quality of customer experience by linking various divisions and business units that customers intends to connect with. Others analyze data to "predict customers' behavior, make recommendations for future purchases or offer discounts to promote long term loyalty." [2]. It is therefore worthwhile discuss how business analytics and data mining research community could help make the PLM vast amounts of data more useful in business contexts. This note is organized as follows: (1) context of PLM and its characteristics, (2) need for considering RE in innovation and the wish to enrich the SIEMENS PLM Tool by RE oriented innovation enablers, (3) assumption that RE helps PLM in innovation issues, (4) research challenges and first draft of research plan.

2   The Context: Product Lifecycle Management (PLM)

PLM requires dealing with big data (lifecycle data of products). We base on our industrial experience and consider the product structure of a car, specifically a limousine, which has approximately 120.000 occurrences. Almost each occurrence has CAD models, drawings, manufacturing information, specific metadata and ERP related information (business data such as supplier, cost, etc.). Revisions and variants of that car will increase the amount of data exponentially. PLM data are heterogeneous: In the field of innovation and PLM, the granularity of the data among heterogeneous sources also varies widely. Most of time, the sources are multi-site, multiplatform and at an aggregate level. Most of the data are available online. PLM processes are very complex. These include idea generation through filtering and selection. Complexity arises from ideas originating throughout the business and from many external sources, and people interacting and communicating with each other and sharing information to pursue these ideas. The process complexity is due to high levels of data and complicated production processes and systems involved, as well as a large number of decision makers. There are a number of people from various departments, handling data from diverse software systems, applied in different workflow types (manual, automated, serial, parallel) from multiple product development stages.

3   The Need for Innovation: Innovate or Perish and the Wish to Enrich Teamcenter© PLM with Innovation Enablers

Innovation is at the top of the executive agendas today across many industries, especially in the consumer and packaged goods industries. With tens of thousands of products launched annually, and the competition now being on a truly global scale, companies must differentiate their products by more than just price and promotional activities if they are to gain a share of the consumer's wallet. They must create products that offer unique and novel consumer value. A lack of innovation will result in the inability to differentiate their products from their competitors and will ultimately lead to market commoditization, declining margins and reduced product profitability. Till now, SIEMENS SISW's module named Teamcenter Reporting and Analytics© measures and visualizes the quality and efficiency of PLM processes. There is no requirements engineering and predictive action associated with this tool for innovation management. Teamcenter Reporting and Analytics© enable user to navigate a hierarchy of information, display information about selected objects, open an editor, or display properties. The module guaranteed user to reuse and repeat most processes and operations. The supported Teamcenter© application is to design reports from analytics to extract specific types of data from the Teamcenter© database. We wish to enrich Teamcenter© with innovation enablers. Our research results should show how to put the innovation process of taking an original idea and converting it into measurable business value to an organization within PLM. This should be achieved by the commercialization of the idea into a product or service that can be taken to market.

In addition, it could be achieved by the institutionalization of an idea, like a method or process that enables the company to achieve higher productivity and quality at lower total cost.

4   Assumption that RE in Business Analytics Can Contribute to Innovation Management within PLM

The tendency is that the decision makers of PLM fields are more networked (linked) in order to achieve higher efficiency and effectiveness that leads to an accelerated level of innovation for the company. While innovation is advantageous for companies, decision makers have to make use of the vast amount of data and information generated through an innovation process. Automation of collection and processing of this data can lead to more effective utilization of it. The effectiveness of automation of collection and processing of the innovation data would benefit innovations in automotive industry as well. For example, during the design of a new limousine mentioned in section 2, the innovation embedded into the design involves not only creativity from the design department, but also data and feedback from the product development, marketing and sales departments. The sales department who is able to collect data directly from the customer is able to provide valuable input during the design of the new (and innovative) limousine. Fig. 3 shows where RE in business analytics should be applied in Innovation and PLM. Organizations include analytics to improve the quality of customer experience by linking various divisions and business units that customers intends to connect with [2]. Others analyze data to predict customers 'behavior, make recommendations for future purchases or offer discounts to promote long term loyalty. According to [3] [4], data is analyzed in order to provide companies with analytical insights used to refine internal processes, promote safety, and highlight operational issues and feedback through controlling on strategy. But few researchers have reported strategies for the use of big data for innovation and PLM.

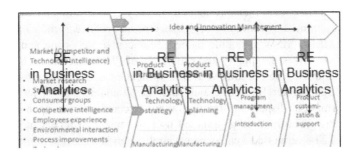

Fig. 3. RE in Business Analytics for Innovation and PLM

5   Some RE Research Challenges and Objectives

The first challenge is to perform RE in business analytics with big PLM data for innovation management. [5] reported forensics practices where they covered irregularities in financial data, including errors, duplicates and omissions, and investigated them via analytics. We cannot apply the forensics approach to the PLM and innovation management domains as the business analytics in the forensics have different goals. In PLM, the goal is not to identify irregularities and to find the source of the anomalies but rather to capture new opportunities for innovation management. The second challenge is to manage RE in business Analytics on Online PLM Data. The third challenge is that RE in business analytics has to be done with heterogeneous PLM Data Sources. The fourth challenge is that RE in business analytics will have to deal with very complex PLM processes for innovation management.

6   Draft of a Research Plan

The way how we want to address the research challenges is as follows: we will perform our research using analytical modeling methodologies and aim to provide validation of our research work examining industrial projects in the automotive field using SIEMENS Licenses (PLM Teamcenter©). We intend to perform research in this area in cooperation with researchers from Clemson University as well as University Paris 1 Pantheon Sorbonne. The collaborators that will work on this research together are with the following organizations and institutions: SIEMENS SISW, Nuremberg, Germany, RTT AG, Munich, Germany, Automotive Project Jaguar, University of Applied Sciences Constance, Germany, Centre de Recherche en Informatique of University Paris 1 – Panthéon – Sorbonne, France, Clemson University, South Carolina, USA.

Research objectives: Our focus is to explain how RE in business analytics can be applied to the field of PLM and how business analytics impacts PLM innovation variants. Through having an understanding of this impact we will explain how RE in system business analytics can be modeled and expressed to the PLM customer for innovation management.

Methodology: We will use a business analytics model for PLM to achieve effective results on the innovation embedded into a new product. We will express RE in business analytics through a model that supports the user to select and to visualize the relevant PLM data for innovation. We will investigate how the current goal oriented requirements (GORE) representation models can be used for our objectives. We should first consider the functional as well as the non-functional requirements for an adequate innovation. Some researches [1], [6], [7], [11], [10], [12], [25], [26] provide representation models that address functional and non-functional requirements. We will investigate if and how intentional oriented requirements representation, used to represent the PLM variants requirements on an intentional level [14, 15, 16, 17, 18, 19, 20. 21], could be completed and extended by business analytics concepts for innovation management. Additionally, the legal framework is very important for innovation issues. Our approach should not only consider current research approaches for

ISO [8] and Quality Standards integration [18] [10] but also the patent laws [24]. Patenting is one of the most important ways to protect company's core business concepts and intellectual proprietary technologies. Analyzing large volume of patent data is needed to innovate products in adequacy with the market and to develop strategies for intellectual property (IP), R&D, and marketing. Cost prioritization issues [13] will also be considered.

Learning from business analytics for RE: Based on our model to be developed, we aim at developing a product innovation process that considers the business analytics results inside RE for a final innovation product. The method and results from our approach should be generalizable to all PLM systems. Therefore, our objectives are to develop a solution that helps decision makers to:

- visualize, quantify and evaluate business analytics data,
- select the relevant business analytics data and apply business analytics mining,
- show the impact of business analytics on innovation variants,
- use this business analytics information to build the right innovation product,
- save time and effort in building and validating derived innovation products, and
- provide a business analytics quality control to improve adequacy between market requirements and innovation product

After describing this PLM analytics model we will provide an overview of current results, their applied experiences, and future research work related to the currents results.

7   Conclusion

In this paper, we emphasize the need to consider RE in business analytics role in PLM. There is a need to utilize the PLM data strategically in maximizing the value of corporate product information throughout the value chain starting with innovation management. We reported the challenge of performing RE in business analytics on innovation and PLM field because of the characteristics of this field, e.g. big data, definition of business goals and principles like cost/benefit analysis combined with continuous change management in order to nurture the portfolio management with innovation management. Our paper addresses some business cases for analytics project involving PLM data and patent data and aim to outline the requirements with business analytics when high volume of data should be turned into successful products through effective innovation management strategies. The data mining research community provides the business analytics area with tools and methodologies needed to approach. We need to include this in RE and PLM innovation data in a scientific, practical, and economic manner. RE in Business analytics applied on innovation and product lifecycle steps that involve statistical analysis of the information embedded data to achieve practical interpretations, understanding of the marginal business value of the information, and economic considerations such as costs of storing, cleansing, visualizing, and analyzing increasingly big data sets aims to increase the effectiveness of PLM decisions. RE in business analytics on PLM data is expected to drive higher efficiency, profitability, and competitiveness and result in successful and market oriented positioning strategy.

References

[1] Chung, L., Nixon, B.A., Yu, E.: Dealing with Change: An approach Using Non-functional Requirements. Requirements Engineering Journal, 238–260 (1996) Proceedings of the Second Internation Symposium on Requirements Engineering, York, England. Springer Verlag London Limited

[2] Davenport, T.H., Mule, L.D., Lucker, J.: Know what your customers want before they do. Harvard Business Review (December 2011)

[3] Guszcza, J., Lucker, J.: Beyond the numbers: Analytics as a strategic capability. Deloitte Review (2011)

[4] Guszcza, J., Lucker, J.: A delicate balance: Organizational barriers to evidence-based management. Deloitte Review (2012)

[5] Hans, S., Swineheart, G.: Finding the needle – using forensic analytics to understand what happened – and what might happen. Deloitte (2011)

[6] González-Baixauli, B.: Visual Variability Analysis for Goal Models. In: Requirements Engineering Conf., pp. 198–207 (2004)

[7] González-Baixauli, B., Laguna, M.A.: Sampaio do Prado Leite J.C.: A Meta-model to Support Visual Variability Analysis. In: First International Workshop on Variability Modelling of Software-intensive Systems, Limerick, Ireland (January 2007)

[8] International Standards Organization, ISO9126, Quality Management Systems Requirements (2000)

[9] Kazhamiakin, R., Pistore, M., Roveri, M.: A Framework for Integrating Business Processes and Business Requirements. In: 8th IEEE International Enterprise Distributed Object Computing Conference (EDOC 2004), pp. 9–20 (2004)

[10] Kemmerer, S.J.: STEP, the grand experience, National Institute of Standards and Technology, special publication 939 (1999)

[11] Lapouchnian, A., Yu, Y.: Mylopoulos J., Liaskos S., Sampaio do Prado Leite J.C.: From stakeholder goals to high-variability software design, ftp.cs.toronto.edu/csrg-technicalreports/509. Tech. rep., University of Toronto (2005)

[12] Mylopoulos, J., Chung, L., Nixon, B.: Representing and Using Non-Functional Requirements: A Process-Oriented Approach. IEEE Trans. on Software Engineering 18(6), 483–497 (1992)

[13] Regnell, B., Höst, M., Berntsson Svensson, R.: A Quality Performance Model for Cost-Benefit Analysis of Non-Functional Requirement Applied to the Mobile Handset Domain. In: Sawyer, P., Heymans, P. (eds.) REFSQ 2007. LNCS, vol. 4542, pp. 277–291. Springer, Heidelberg (2007)

[14] Rohleder, C.: Representing Non-Functional Requirements on Services – A Case Study. In: COMPSAC 2012, Trustworthy Software Systems for the Digital Society, Izmir, Turkey, July 16-20 (2012)

[15] Rohleder, C.: Quality Product Derivation: A Case Study for Quality Control at Siemens. In: 8th WSEAS (World Scientific and Engineering Academy and Society) Best Paper Award International Conference on Software Engineering, Parallel and Distributed Systems (SEPADS 2009), pp. 51–56. Cambridge, UK (February 2009)

[16] Rohleder, C., Marhold, C., Salinesi, C., Doerr, J.: Quality Data Model and Quality Control in the Product Lifecycle Management. In: PLM 2009, International Conference on Product Lifecycle Management, Bath, United Kingdom (July 2009)

[17] Rohleder, C.: Visualizing the Impact of Non-Functional Requirements on Variants - A Case Study. In: 16th IEEE International Requirements Engineering Conference, Workshop REV 2008, Barcelona, Spain (September 2008)

[18] Rohleder, C., Ling, J., Kusumah, I., Ozkan, G.: Business Analytics in Innovation and Product Lifecycle Management. In: IEEE Research Challenges on Information Sciences Conference, Paris (2013)

[19] Rohleder, C., Marhold, C., Salinesi, C., Doerr, J.: Clarifying Non-Functional Requirements to Improve User Acceptance – Experience at Siemens. In: REFSQ Requirements Engineering: Foundation for Software Quality, Amsterdam, Netherland (June 2009)

[20] Rohleder, C.: Representing Variants Including Quality Attributes. IPSI Transaction Journal, Transaction on Internet Research 4(1), 1820–4503 (2008)

[21] Rohleder, C.: Requirements Management using Positioning Requirements in Enterprise System Projects. Issues in Information Systems VIII(2), 152–157 (2006)

[22] Short, J.E., Bohn, R.E., Baru, C.: How much information? 2010 report on enterprise server information. Global Information Industry Center, UC San Diego (2011)

[23] Saaksvuori, A.: Product Lifecycle Management, Springer (2005), ISBN 3540257314

[24] Tseng, Y.-H., Lin, C.-J., Lin, Y.-I.: Text mining techniques for patent analysis. Inf. Process. Manage. 43, 1216–1247 (2007)

[25] Van Lamsweerde, A., Dairmont, R., Massonet, P.: Goal Directed Elaboration of Requirements for a Meeting Scheduler: Problems and Lessons Learnt. In: Proc. of IEEE RE 1995 – 2nd Int. Symp. On Requirements Engineering, pp. 194–204. IEEE Computer Society, York (1995)

[26] Yu, E.: Towards Modelling and Reasoning Support for Early-Phase Requirements Engineering. In: Proceedings of the 3rd IEEE Int. Symp. on Requirements Engineering (RE 1997), January 6-8, pp. 226–235. IEEE Computer Society, Washington D.C (1997)

Modeling the Impact of Non-functional Requirements on Functional Requirements

Christophe Gnaho[1,2], Farida Semmak[1], and Regine Laleau[1]

[1] Laboratoire Algorithmique, Complexité et Logique, Université Paris Est,
61 av du général de Gaulle, 94010 Créteil cedex, France
{semmak,laleau}@u-pec.fr
[2] Université Paris Descartes, 45 rue des Saints-pères, 75006 Paris, France
christophe.gnaho@parisdescartes.fr

Abstract. To develop quality software and systems, both functional and non-functional requirements need to be taken into account at the same level of abstraction; and must be traced throughout the development cycle. *The concept of goal has been widely used and adopted to represent functional and non-functional requirements. However the issue of the impact of non-functional requirements on functional requirements has been rarely addressed. The aim of this paper is to propose a first contribution to this issue.*

Keywords: Non-Functional Requirements, Goal-oriented requirements modelling, dependencies FR-NFR.

1 Introduction

A system is determined by both its functional and non-functional requirements. Non-Functional Requirements (NFRs) express qualities of the system to be developed such as efficiency, accuracy, security and so on [1], [4], [6], [9]. Modelling techniques of Functional Requirements (FRs) are significantly more developed than those used for NFRs [4], [7], [11], [13]. However, several works in NFR domain have tried to address interesting issues such as elicitation, expression, dependency, and prioritization [16]. Issues around NFR dependencies are many and varied; but the important works have focused on relationships between NFRs and software architectures or software designs [2,], [5], [10].

In this paper, we investigate the relationship between non-functional requirements and functional requirements. We believe that non-functional requirements must be integrated much earlier, at the same level of abstraction than functional requirements. In particular, we think that emphasizing the impact of non-functional requirements on functional requirements would be beneficial for the evaluation of alternatives and conflicts. Functional requirements are represented with concepts of the KAOS goal model and non-functional are represented with concepts inspired and adapted from NFR Framework. In particular, we have adapted the concept of contribution and added concepts related to the impact aspects.

J. Parsons and D. Chiu (Eds.): ER Workshops 2013, LNCS 8697, pp. 59–67, 2014.

The rest of the paper is organized as follows. Section 2 presents the related work Section 3 presents the proposed approach. Section 4 concludes with some remarks about the results and future works.

2   Related Work

Among many requirements engineering methods, two goal oriented approaches were the first to deal with NFRs in more depth: the KAOS approach and the NFR framework.

KAOS addresses both functional and non functional requirements as goals [6], [13], [14]. It identifies two types of goals: behavioural and soft goals. Goals are formalized in terms of operators such as *Achieve*, *Maintain* and *Avoid* and some temporal operators. The graphical language makes the differentiation between functional and non-functional goals. The operationalized goals can be described in terms of constraints. Other works on the KAOS approach treat the non-functional requirements at the design level or when building the system architecture [10], [15].

The NFR framework emphasises on Non-Functional Requirements (NFRs) [3], NFRs are represented in terms of very abstract goals called *Softgoals*. A *softgoal* is refined into other *softgoals*. When *softgoals* have been sufficiently refined, *operationalizing softgoals* representing design techniques for achieving them are identified and implemented in the target system. The NFR framework proposed several types of interdependencies to make explicit the influences (positive or negative) between non-functional goals.

The works published by Chung and Supakkul extended the NFR framework for representing and integrating NFRs in the UML use case model. Details about this framework named 'the goal-oriented and Use Case Driven Analysis and Design Process' are clearly presented in [12].

The approach proposed by Cysneiros in [5] is also based on the NFR framework. It provides a very interesting and complete process to elicit non functional goals, analyze their interdependencies and trace them to functional conceptual models. NFRs are analyzed using the NFR Framework and *operationalizing softgoals* are expressed into class and interaction diagrams.

Similar to the NFR framework and the Cysneiros approach, we claim the idea to define non-functional requirements at the highest level of abstraction. However, in those two approaches, the non-functional requirements are integrated in conceptual models and design models. Thus, the main difference between our proposal and the two approaches is that we attempt to explicitly define how non-functional requirements can impact functional requirements. In other words, we propose to model non-functional and functional requirements in parallel during the early requirements engineering phase so impact from the former ones on the latter ones can be evaluated.

3   The Proposed Approach

The proposed approach is based on KAOS and the NFR Framework, two approaches largely recognized and used in requirements engineering over the past decade. As shown in Figure 1, this approach provides three main steps. In the first step, functional and non-functional requirements are specified in two separate goal models. Then, the impact of the non functional requirements on functional ones are analyzed and described. In the last step, a final integrated goal model is obtained. It describes the impact of non-functional requirements on functional ones.

Functional requirements are represented with concepts of the KAOS goal model and non-functional are represented with concepts inspired and adapted from NFR Framework. In particular, we have adapted the concept of contribution and added some concepts related to the impact aspects.

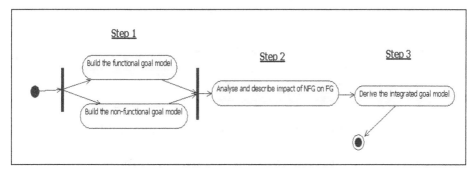

Fig. 1. Overview of the proposed approach

We will illustrate the approach in the next section using an extract of the Cycab case study, the Cycab localization component. A Cycab is a new mode of transport designed for restricted access zones: historic, city center, airport, etc. It has fully automated driving capabilities and is controlled by embedded electronics [17].

3.1   Abstract Goal Concept

Figure 2 gives an overview of the concepts for building hierarchies of functional and non-functional goals.

Functional and non-functional requirements are represented as abstract goals, which are recursively refined into sub-goals, thanks to the AND/OR refinement mechanism. Figure 2 focuses on the non-functional concepts. A non-functional goal that cannot be further refined is called an elementary non-functional goal (meta-class **Elementary NFG**). Thus, when all the abstract non-functional goals are refined into a set of elementary goals, we need to find and express solutions that satisfied them. These solutions will be presented in the following sub-section.

3.2   The Concept of 'Contribution'

The concept of contribution is used to describe the alternative solutions to satisfy elementary non-functional goals. Unlike in the NFR Framework, this concept is used exclusively for elementary non-functional requirements.

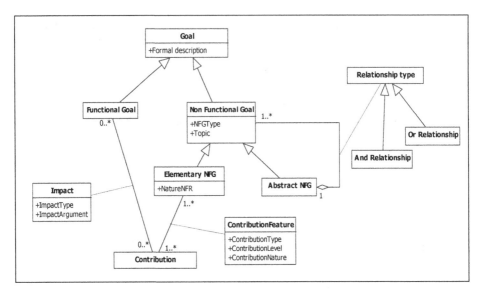

Fig. 2. Functional Goal and non-functional goal meta-model

Thus, a *contribution* (meta-class **Contribution**) captures a possible solution to satisfy an elementary non-functional goal. It expresses the way by which an elementary non-functional goal could be achieved.

For example, the sub-goal *Availability [Localization Data]* in Figure 3 can be considered as an elementary goal. In order to achieve it, two alternative solutions can be considered: *to use a redundant localization component or to combine GPS with indoor positioning system.*

The characteristics of a *contribution* are captured in Figure 2 by the association class **Contribution Feature** which provides three properties: **Contribution Type, Contribution Level and Contribution Nature**

The property **Contribution Type** specifies whether the contribution is **positive** or **negative**. A positive (or negative) contribution helps (or prevents) to the satisfaction of an elementary non functional goal.

As we said, several solutions can contribute to the same elementary goal, but at different levels. For example, *use large storage space* may better contribute (positively) to the goal *GoodStorageSpace [Localization Data]* than *use a compressed format*. The level of contribution is captured thanks to the property **Contribution Level,** which allows us to associate to the type of contribution (positive or negative), a level that can range from very high to low. Basically, this property can take four values: *very high, high, moderate and low*. This concept is closed to the concepts *make, help, break and hurt*, which are used in the NFR Framework, but with two main differences. First, we use the same values for positive and negative contribution while the NFR Framework uses *make* and *help* for positive contribution and *break* and *hurt* for negative. Secondly, we have a larger range of values which allows for a more nuanced. We think that this would facilitate the choice between several conflicting solutions. For example, we could neglect the contributions that have a *low* level, or in case of a negative contribution, we could quickly identify areas of conflict or obstacles.

The property **ContributionNature** specifies whether the contribution is **explicit** or **induced**.

For example, *Using a compressed format* is a positive and explicit contribution to the elementary goal *GoodStorageSpace [localization data]* because it is explicitly stated and considered to be helpful. However, compressing localization data would prevent the satisfaction of the non-functional elementary goal *GoodResponseTime [localization data]* by slowing down access to localization data. Thus, this contribution which is explicitly stated to satisfy the *GoodStorageSpace*, induce a negative contribution to *GoodResponseTime*. It is important to note that a contribution must at least once positively help to the satisfaction of a non-functional goal. If this is not the case, its presence in the model cannot be justified.

An explicit contribution is graphically represented by a solid line and an induced contribution is graphically represented by dashes. The type of the contribution is represented together with its level by a "+ (level)" or "– (level)" sign on the link.

3.3   The Concept of 'Impact'

Recall that the specificity of our approach is to consider non-functional goals together with functional goals from the early requirements engineering phase. After analysing and describing all the potential impacts in the step 2 of our process (see Figure 1), they are evaluated in step 3 and decisions are made in order to choose from among the possible solutions, the best one for the target system. As a result, we obtain a new goal model (the integrated goal model) that integrates functional and non-functional requirements.

Thus, we introduce the concept of **Impact**, which is represented in the meta-model as an association class between a contribution and a functional goal. It is characterized by two main properties: **impactType** and **impactArgument**.

The **impacType** property may have two possible values: *positive* or *negative*. A positive impact means that the contribution may positively impact the achievement of the related functional goal. In other words, the choice of this contribution can guarantee, that the target system perform the corresponding function with the expected quality. A negative impact means that the contribution may have a negative impact on the achievement of the related functional goal. The choice of this contribution does not guarantee that the target system will provide the service with all the qualities expected. In some case, it will be necessary to find the best compromise.

The **impactArgument** property is intended to capture some arguments or rationales. It is generally used to argue for or against some decisions.

In order to illustrate the concept of impact, let us come back to the example of Figure 3. The hierarchy of functional goals is represented on the left and the hierarchy of non-functional goals is represented on the right (see step 1 of the process).

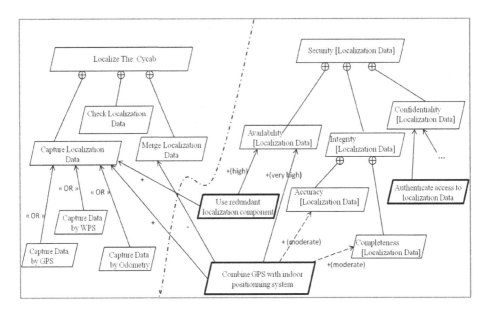

Fig. 3. Impacts between non functional goals and functional goals

According to the functional goals hierarchy, the localization of the Cycab is performed by capturing data giving its position, checking these data and merging them in order to obtain the Cycab position. The root goal *Localize the Cycab* is then refined into three sub-goals: *Capture Localization Data*, *Check Localization Data* and *Merge Localization Data*.

In parallel, we develop a hierarchy of non functional goals in order to specify the quality properties related to this case.

Thus, the goal *Security [Localization Data]* is refined into three sub-goals (according to the **AND refinement**): *Availability [Localization Data], Integrity [Localization Data]*, and *Confidentiality [Localization Data]*. In order to guarantee the availability of localization data, two solutions can be considered: *to use a redundant localization component or to combine GPS with indoor positioning system*. These two contributions contribute positively and explicitly, but in addition, they have an impact on the functional goal *Capture localization data*.

An argument (**impactArgument**) for the impact of the first contribution on the capture of localization data could be *the increase of the resilience of the target system*, while for the second; we could say that *it ensures reliable and accurate position outdoor and indoor, even if GPS signal is lost*.

Finally, the example also shows a negative impact between the contribution *to combine GPS with indoor positioning system* and the functional sub-goal *Merge localization data*. An argument against this impact is that *this contribution may increase the complexity of the merge algorithm and therefore degrade the performance of the system*.

From now, we can consider that all the possible solutions to satisfy the non-functional goals are identified and expressed and the impact of those solutions on functional goals are described (see step1 and step2 of the process). The hierarchy of non-functional goals thus represents a set of competing alternative solutions, which may affect positively or negatively the functional goals.

Remember that, due to the nature of non-functional goals, we are not always able to guarantee their total satisfaction. Therefore, the next step (step 3 of the process) is to select among the competing solutions, those that are most optimal for the system to be developed. This selection process is based on the analysis of interactions between contributions, the analysis of impacts on functional goals and also on the stake-holders' constraints. For example, having identified and expressed two possible con-tributions to satisfy the availability of localization data (see Figure 3), we have to discuss and choose the most optimal contribution for the target system. In this case, we think that the contribution *Combine GPS with indoor positioning system* is the most solution for two main reasons. First, it also induces positive contribution to the non-functional goals *Accuracy [Localization data]* and *Completeness [Localization data]*. Secondly, it has a positive impact on the functional goal *Capture Localization Data* because it ensures overall position even if GPS signal is lost. This positive im-pact should be reflected in the functional goals model and thereby needs some changes in the hierarchy of goals. The implication here is a constraint on the three refinement links of the sub-goal *Capture Localization Data*. Indeed, the sub-goal *Capture Data by GPS* is mandatory and must be combined with at least one of the other two, which are considered as indoor positioning systems. At the end, we obtain a new functional goal hierarchy that is shown in Figure 4.

The analysis and treatment of *impact* relationships could be related to aspects of variability discussed in some works.

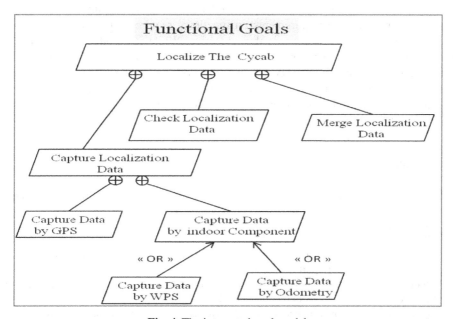

Fig. 4. The integrated goal model

Moreover, analysing non-functional goals can lead to the identification of new functional goals. To illustrate this, consider the contribution *Authenticate access to localization data* in Figure 3, which contributes positively to the non-function goal *Confidentiality [Localization Data]*. As this contribution specifies something the system should do, it is considered as a functional goal that must be integrated with the existing functional goals.

Finally, some contributions do not directly have impact on functional goals but generate constraints on the target system components. This is the case for example of the contribution *Using a compressed format, which* requires a constraint on the format of the localization data. This constraint must be taken into account when implementing the localization component. Requirements traceability is not discussed in this paper; it is the subject of another ongoing work.

To summarize, we argue that non-functional goals may have impact on functional goals, which can be expressed in different manners. Indeed, in the present state of our work, we have shown that non-functional goals may have an impact on the choices and decisions that are taken when refining functional goals and when transforming them into target systems. In addition, analyzing non-functional goals can lead to the identification of new functional goals, which must be integrated with the existing functional goal hierarchy. Finally, some contributions do not directly have impact on functional goals but generate constraints on the system components, which must be taken into account later, for instance during the implementation phase.

4   Conclusion

In this paper, we have presented an approach that allows analysing and expressing the impact of non functional requirements on functional requirements. This work therefore represents a first step towards this objective. While it introduces and demonstrates the approach, a number of works are ongoing. First, we are improving and completing the current result. Second, we are working on the bridge between requirements models and specification models and also on traceability aspects. Finally, we plan to combine requirements models with formal ones in order to check consistency properties.

References

1. Chung, L., do Prado Leite, J.C.S.P.: On Non-Functional Requirements in Software Engineering. In: Borgida, A.T., Chaudhri, V.K., Giorgini, P., Yu, E.S. (eds.) Conceptual Modeling: Foundations and Applications. LNCS, vol. 5600, pp. 363–379. Springer, Heidelberg (2009)
2. Ameller, D., Ayala, C., Cabot, J., Franch, X.: Non-Functional Requirements in Software Architecture Practice. Report ESSI-TR-12-1 (2012)
3. Chung, L., Nixon, B.A., Yu, E., Mylopoulos, J.: Non-functional Requirements in Software Engineering. Kluwer, Academic Publishers (2000)
4. Pohl, K.: Requirements Engineering: Fundamentals, Principles and Techniques. Springer

5. Cysneiros, L.N., Leite, J.C.S.P.: Non-functional Requirements: From Elicitation to Conceptual Models. IEEE Transactions on Software Engineering 30(5), 328–350 (2004)
6. Dardenne, A., van Lamsweerde, A., Fickas, S.: Goal-oriented Requirements Acquisition. Science of Computer Programming 20(1-2), 3–50 (1993)
7. Glinz, M.: On Non-Functional Requirements. In: Proceedings of the 15th IEEE International Requirements Engineering Conference (2007)
8. IEEE Standard Computer dictionary: a compilation of IEEE standard computer glossaries (1990)
9. ISO/IEC 9126-1:2001(E) Software engineering - product quality, Part 1: Quality Model (2001)
10. Jani, D., Vanderveken, D., Perry, D.E.: Deriving Architecture Specifications from KAOS Specifications: A Research Case Study. In: Morrison, R., Oquendo, F. (eds.) EWSA 2005. LNCS, vol. 3527, pp. 185–202. Springer, Heidelberg (2005)
11. Kotonya, G., Sommerville, I.: Requirements Engineering: Processes and Techniques. John Wiley & Sons (1998)
12. Chung, L., Supakkul, S.: Representing NFRs and FRs: A Goal-Oriented and Use Case Driven Approach. In: Dosch, W., Lee, R.Y., Wu, C. (eds.) SERA 2004. LNCS, vol. 3647, pp. 29–41. Springer, Heidelberg (2006)
13. van Lamsweerde, A.: Goal-oriented Requirements Engineering: A guided tour. Proc. of the 5th Int. Symposium on Requirements Engineering, Toronto (2001)
14. van Lamsweerde, A.: Requirements Engineering: From System Goals to UML Models to Software Specifications. Wiley (2009)
15. van Lamsweerde, A.: From System Goals to Software Architecture. In: Bernardo, M., Inverardi, P. (eds.) SFM 2003. LNCS, vol. 2804, pp. 25–43. Springer, Heidelberg (2003)
16. Paech, B., Kerkow, D.: Non-functional Requirements Engineering – Quality is essential. In: Proc. of the 10th International Workshop on Requirements Engineering: Foundations for Software Quality – REFSQ 2004 (2004)
17. Parent, M.: Automated public vehicle: a first step towards the automatic highway. In: The Proc. of the World Congress on Intelligent transport systems (1997)

A Framework for Business Rules

Naveen Prakash[1], Deepak Kumar Sharma[1], Deepika Prakash[2], and Dheerendra Singh[3]

[1]MRCE, Sector 43, SurajkundBadhkal Road, Faridabad 121001, India
praknav@hotmail.com
masterdeepak12@gmail.com
[2]Department of Computer Engineering, DTU, New Delhi-110042, India
dpka.prakash@gmail.com
[3]Department of Computer Science, SUSCET, TangoriMohali, India
professordsingh@gmail.com

Abstract. The subject of business rules is complex. We propose a 4-dimensional framework to better understand, communicate, and realize such rules in organizations and application systems. Our 4-dimensions are **domain**, that considers the role of business rules in business; **system** for properties of business rule management systems; **application** platform to understand support for business rules applications; and **representation** for expressing business rules. We derive these from work of the Business Rules Group, namely, the Business Rules Manifesto, Business Motivation Model, and Semantics of Business Vocabulary and business Rules, SBVR. We characterize our research position in terms of this framework.

Keywords: Business rules, BRG Manifesto, Business Motivation Model, Semantics of Business Vocabulary and business Rules, business rule management.

1 Introduction

Business rules have been have been the subject of intense investigation in the past. It was shown that business rules can be obtained by forward and reverse engineering. In the former case, business rules are requirements [7] [11] that systems must embody and therefore obtaining business rules falls under the ambit of requirements engineering. In the latter case, researchers have argued that existing operational systems are the best sources [5] of business rules because these systems reflect the latest business rules.

The **business-oriented view** of business rules was reflected in the Business Rule Manifesto [1] of the Business Rules Group, BRG. This manifesto promotes the notion of a business rule as a first class concept. The basic idea is that business rules are primary requirements, independent of processes and procedures, represent deliberate knowledge, and are declarative in nature. Business rules should arise from knowledgeable business people and there is need for tools to help in formulation, validation, and management of business rules.

J. Parsons and D. Chiu (Eds.): ER Workshops 2013, LNCS 8697, pp. 68–73, 2014.

BRG has also put in the public domain additional reports like the Business Motivation Model BMM [9], Semantics of Business Vocabulary and Business Rules, SBVR [8]. These use the central notions of the Manifesto.

It seems to us that Business Rules is a complex subject and it would be helpful to deal with it from different dimensions to better understand, communicate and realize such rules in organizations or systems. Towards this end, we propose a 4-dimensional framework derived largely from the Business Rules Manifesto. Some aspects of our framework are derived from BMM and SBVR as well.

The **business dimension** deals with the role of business rules in organizations. This is in accordance with BRG view that business rules belong to businesses and not to system/technical people. Business rules are considered as directives to govern and guide courses of actions of business [9], as statements that [1][14]define and constrain various aspects of business, assert business structure[13] and influence and control the behavior of a business [8]. The business rules management system or **system dimension** for brevity, deals with to the formulation, elicitation, validation, storage and evolution of business rules. Thus, it provides support for business people to develop their business rules. This corresponds to the 'tools' of the Manifesto (see sub article 9.2). The application platform or **application dimension** for short, deals with support for business rules applications. An application is a subset of the business that is captured in software systems. Thus, we are concerned here with characteristics of platforms that deal with enactment of business rules in functions and process models. Lastly, **the representation dimension** deals with the expression of business rules in various forms. A representation is a means of expressing business rules used in the system and application dimensions for rules formulation and execution respectively.

We see that the four dimensions taken together provide a view of a business rule in terms of its origins (business), its formulation and definition (system), its expression (representation) and its deployment (application). In this sense, these dimensions constitute a framework for understanding business rules.

In Table 1, we show which article and sub-article the Business Rules Manifesto maps to which dimension of our framework.

Table 1. The Dimensions and BR Manifesto

Dimension	Article/sub article of BR Manifesto
Business	4.7, 7.1 to 7.3, 8.1 to 8.3
System	4.1, 6.1, 8.1, 10.3
Representation	4.1, 4.5, 5.1 to 5.3
Application	6.2 to 6.4, 10.3,10.4

Notice that some articles of the Manifesto are missing. These are of a general explanatory nature, for example, sub article 1.1 that says, "Rules are first class citizens of the requirements world"; sub article 4.2 that states "if something cannot be expressed, then it is not a rule"; and sub article 4.3 which says "a set of statements is declarative only if the set has no implicit sequencing".

We now consider each dimension of the framework in turn.

2   The Business Dimension

The Business Rules Manifesto when combined with the Business Motivation Model, BMM, of BRG gives us additional information about the business dimension. Whereas the Manifesto gives us "Principles of Rule Independence" [1], in BMM [9], the idea is to propose concepts for business governance and their inter relationships.

BMM organizes businesses in terms of Ends and Means. Ends are Vision, Goals and Objectives. For Means, BMM introduces three broad concepts, Mission, Courses of Action and Directives. Missions are means to achieve visions, courses of actions achieve goals, and directives achieve objectives. Directives govern courses of action and there are two kinds of Directives namely, business policy and **business rules**. Following this, we get **two attributes along the business dimension**, namely, Guides and Contributes. Guides takes on values from Courses of Action. It is multi valued and contains one or more courses of action that it guides. Similarly, Contributes contains one or more objectives to which it contributes. The first two rows of Table 2 show these attributes. The table contains two additional attributes, Role and Cost directly obtained from the Manifesto. Role identifies whether the business rule is a *main* rule or an *exception*. It is single valued. Cost contains one or more business opportunities that are lost due to the rule.

Table 2. Attributes of the Business Dimension

S. No.	Attribute	Value	Manifesto Reference
1.	Guides	SET{Course of action}	8.1
2.	Contributes	SET{Objective}	8.1
3.	Role	{Main, Exception}	4.7, 7.1, 7.2, 7.3
4.	Cost	SET{Lost opportunity}	8.2, 8.3

As an example of a business rule along the business dimension consider the rule of a library of an Institute that "It is necessary that a student or staff member is registered as a borrower". This guides the *courses of action*, register borrower and issue book; contributes to the *objective*, Easy availability to Institute members; the role is as a *main* rule; and the *lost opportunity* is that our library cannot participate in a network of libraries.

3   Application Dimension

The application dimension, see Table 3, tells us the properties of the application platforms on which business rule applications run. The first issue is about the manner in which business rules are executed. This can be through a rule engine[2], as a service,[3,4] or as a procedure[12].

If the application system supports traceability then the result of every rule is traceable to the objective it contributes to or the course of action it guides.

Table 3. Attributes of the Application Platform Dimension

Attribute	Value	Manifesto Reference
Execution	{Rule engine, Service, Procedure}	6.2, 6.4
Traceability	{Total, Objective, Course of action, None}	6.3
Evolution	Boolean	10.4
Portable	Boolean	10.3, 10.4

Traceability is *total* when it considers both objective and course of action; *objective* traces back to objectives; *course of action* traces back to courses of action; and traceability has the value *none* otherwise. The attribute, evolution, specifies whether the business rules management system allows changes in legacy rules or not. Lastly, portability refers to the ability to move the application from one hardware/software platform to another.

4   The Representation Dimension

This dimension tells us the audience of the representation system, its form and the nature of business rule enforcement available. The attributes of this dimension are in Table 4.

The first attribute is the nature of the audience. Broadly speaking, there are two of these, business and technical people respectively. For business people the essential requirement is that rules should be declarative whereas for technical people, the representation should provide 'main' rule and all 'coping' mechanisms like errors, and compensations. Further, technical people may like to associate the role responsible for rule enforcement with a rule.

Table 4. Attributes of the Representation Dimension

Attribute	Value	Manifesto Reference
Audience	{Business, Technical}	4.1
Form	{Graphical, Logic based, Natural Language, Implication, Event}	4.1 5.1,5.2,5.3
Guidance	SET (Necessity, Obligation)	4.5
Practicability	SET(Automated, Manual)	None

The second attribute is the **form** of the representation. This attribute is single valued. Perhaps only the last two values of the second column need explanation. Implication refers to the IF-THEN [2,8] form of rules whereas event refers to the WHEN-IF-THEN form and its variants [6] . The attribute, **guidance**, is multi valued. For obligation, six enforcement levels exist in SBVR, ranging from *strict* to *guideline*. The last attribute, **practicability**, follows from SBVR. P-type may be automated or manual. We did not find any article in the Manifesto that relates to this.

5   The System Dimension

In the system dimension, we specify the nature of systems needed to support the management of business rules. The first row of Table 5 specifies the type of business rules management support:

1. Decisional: In [10], business rules management takes the form of a data warehouse system that maintains information needed to decide whether a business rules is appropriate or not. That is, the initial formulation and subsequent management of business rules is a decision-making problem.
2. Elicitation: If one assumes that business rules definition is external to a system, then the major task is to elicit rules and check for consistency. It is necessary her to maintain a repository of rules so that rule evolution is handled.

This aspect is not considered by the Manifesto (also not by BMM or SBVR).

The second row of the table specifies the user of the rules management system, business people or technical ones. It is multi-valued. The third row is about whether the rules management system supports rules evolution or not. If the system supports this then it is adaptable otherwise it is fixed.

Table 5. Attributes of the System Dimension

Attribute	Value	Manifesto Article
Type	{Decisional, Elicitation}	None
User	SET{Business , Technical}	4.1
Evolution	{Fixed, adaptable}	6.1
Traceability	{Total, Objective, Course of action, None}	8.1
Portable	Boolean	10.3

The fourth attribute is traceability. If the system supports traceability then every rule is traced back to the objective it contributes to or the course of action it guides. Traceability is *total* when it considers both objective and course of action; *objective* rules trace back to objectives; *course of action* when it traces back to courses of action; and it is *none* otherwise. Lastly, portability refers to the ability to organize and store rules independent of the underlying hardware or software systems. It is Boolean valued.

The rules management system described in [10] has attributes < Type = Decisional; User = Technical; Evolution = Adaptable, Traceable = False>.

6   Conclusion

We have proposed a 4-dimensional framework for understanding business rules based on our study of Business Rules Manifesto, Business Motivation Model and SBVR. The four dimensions capture business rules from the perspective of the business where they originate; system that formulates, manages and stores rules; representation that expresses rules; and application that deals with the characteristics of the application platform.

We are developing a business rules management system and our interest is developing an approach to capture, represent, and manage business rules for business people. Our work addresses the Business, Representation and System Dimensions of our framework. The representation dimension is < Audience = Business, Form = implication, Guidance = {necessity, obligation}, Practicability = {Automated, Manual}>. The system dimension is < Type = elicitation, User = business, Evolution = Fixed, Traceability = {Courses of action}, Portability = False}>

References

1. Ross, R.G. (ed.): Business Rules Group. Business Rules Manifesto The Principles of Rule Independence, Version 2.0 (November 1, 2003),
   http://www.BusinessRulesGroup.org
2. Gaweł, B., Skalna, I.: Model driven architecture and classification of Business rules modeling languages. In: Conference on Computer Science and Information Systems (2012)
3. Camlon, H.: Asuncion1, Maria-Eugenia Iacob2, and Marten J. van Sinderen.: Towards a flexible service integration through separation of business rules. In: IEEE International Enterprise Distributed Object Computing Conference (2010)
4. Friedman-Hill, E.: Jess in Action: Rule-Based Systems in Java., Manning Publications Co. (2003)
5. Gang, X.: Business Rule Extraction from Legacy system Using Dependence-Cache Slicing. In: The 1st International Conference on Information Science and Engineering, pp. 4214–4218 (2009)
6. Hanson, E.N., Widom, J.: An Overview of Production Rules in Database Systems. Knowledge Engineering Review, 121–143 (1993)
7. Kardasis, P., Loucopoulos, P.: Expressing and organizing business rules. Information and Software Technology 46, 701–718 (2004)
8. OMG., Semantics of Business Vocabulary and Business Rules (SBVR)., v1.0 (2008),
   http://www.omg.org/spec/SBVR/1.0/PDF
9. OMG, Business Motivation Model., V1.1 (2011), available at
   http://www.omg.org/spec/BMM/1.1/
10. Prakash, D., Gupta, D.: Eliciting Data Warehouse Contents for Policy Enforcement Rules. In: Communicated in IJISMD (2013)
11. Rosca, D., Greenspan, S., Feblowitz, M., Wild, C.: A Decision Making Methodology in Support of the Business Rules Lifecycle, 236–246 (1997)
12. Sriganesh, S., Ramanathan, C.: Externalizing Business Rules from Business Processes for Model Based Testing. In: IEEE Proceding of ICIT 2012 (2012)
13. Skersys, T., Tutkute, L., Butleris, R.: The Enrichment of BPMN Business Process Model with SBVR Business Vocabulary and Rules. In: 34th International Conference Information Technology Interface, June 25-28 (2012)

Preface to SeCoGIS 2013

Recent advances in information technology have changed the way geographical data were originally produced and made available. Nowadays, the use of Geographic Information Systems (GIS) is not reserved anymore to the specialized user. GISs are emerging as a common information infrastructure, which penetrates into more and more aspects of our society. The technological drift implies a profound change in mentality, with a deep impact on the way geographical data needs to be conceptualized. New methodological and data engineering challenges must be confronted by GIS researchers in the near future in order to accommodate new users' requirements for new applications.

The SeCoGIS workshop intends to bring together researchers, developers, users, and practitioners with an interest in all semantic and conceptual issues in GISs. The aim is to stimulate discussions on the integration of conceptual modeling and semantics into various web applications dealing with spatio-temporally referenced data and how this benefits end-users. The workshop provides a forum for original research contributions and practical experiences of conceptual modeling and semantic web technologies for GIS, fostering interdisciplinary discussions in all aspects of these two fields and highlighting future trends in this area. The workshop is organized in a way to stimulate interaction amongst the participants.

This edition of the workshop received 15 submissions, from which the Program Committee selected 6 high quality papers, corresponding to an acceptance rate of 40%. The authors of the accepted papers are world-wide distributed, making SeCoGIS a truly international workshop. The accepted papers were organized in three sessions. The first one contains a keynote speaker. The next ones contain three papers each. The second session is about semantic issues of geographic data modeling. The third one is about conceptual modeling of geographic applications.

We would like to express our gratitude to the Program Committee members for their qualified work in reviewing papers, the authors for considering SeCoGIS as a forum to publish their research, and the ER 2013 organizers for all their support.

July 2013

Mir Abolfazl Mostafavi
Esteban Zimanyi
Program Co-Chairs SeCoGIS 2013

Integration of Heterogeneous Spatial Databases for Disaster Management

Imen Bizid[1,2], Sami Faiz[1], Patrice Boursier[2],
and Jawahir Che Mustapha Yusuf[3]

[1] Laboratoire LTSIRS, BP 37 Le Belvedere 1002, Tunis, Tunisia
[2] Laboratoire L3i, University of La Rochelle, Pole Sciences et Technologies
Avenue M. Crepeau, La Rochelle, France
[3] UniKL-Malaysian Institute of Information Technology, University 2,
Kuala Lumpur, Malaysia

Abstract. The response phase in a disaster case is often considered to be the most critical in terms of saving lives and dealing with irreversible damage. The timely provision of geospatial information is crucial in the decision-making process. Thus, there is a need for the integration of heterogeneous spatial databases which are inherently distributed and created under different projects by various organizations. The integration of all relevant data for timely decision making is a challenging task due to syntactic, schematic and semantic heterogeneity. This paper aims to propose a framework for the integration of heterogeneous spatial databases using novel approaches, such as web services and ontologies. We focus on providing solutions for the three levels of heterogeneity, in order to be able to interrogate the content of the different databases conveniently. Based on the proposed framework, we implemented a use case using heterogeneous data belonging to La Rochelle city in France.

Keywords: Heterogeneous Spatial Databases, Data Integration, Disaster Management, Ontologies.

1 Introduction

Disaster management is a scope of great relevance as it aims to reduce the negative impact and consequences of a disaster and to provide a timely and clear rescue plan. Proposing powerful tools to generate efficient strategies for the decision makers gives rise to the delivery of disaster relief in the right moment. Two types of disasters are of interest natural and man-made. Natural disasters often strike without warning, such as earthquakes, tsunamis and tornados. Man-made disasters include every action due to technological hazards, sociological hazards or transportation hazards among others. Despite the difference between these two categories in specifics and complexity, both instances can cause irreversible damage if the rescue plan is not executed at time. In order to effectively manage such disasters, it is important to coordinate between the police, Red Cross, and other first responders to work together and extract the needed information to

J. Parsons and D. Chiu (Eds.): ER Workshops 2013, LNCS 8697, pp. 77–86, 2014.
© Springer International Publishing Switzerland 2014

maintain a rescue plan. However, the data stored in these distinct heterogeneous sources located in different departments, are maintained under heterogeneous formats, structures and are not semantically rich enough to express the emergency responders ' needs. Experience suggests that the bottlenecks of emergency responses are, in most cases, the difficulties in making intelligent search and integration of heterogeneous geospatial information stocked in different departments [1]. This paper has been working on the heterogeneity levels that can block emergency responders to automate the search of geospatial data stored in different spatial databases. Although there were many works that all address important pieces of the major challenge to automatically search geospatial information from heterogeneous spatial databases, many issues still remain to be solved to fully realize this goal. This paper is structured as follows: In section 2, we describe the three heterogeneity levels. In section 3, we present briefly the recent progress made on the integration of heterogeneous spatial databases, Section 4 proposes a new solution represented in a framework dealing with the three heterogeneity levels. In section 5, we describe the different interoperability modules designed in our framework. Afterward, we analyze the evaluation results related to the framework in Section 6. Finally, we present our conclusions in section 7.

2   Spatial Databases Heterogeneity Levels

Each emergency response community has developed its own database using its personalized infrastructure and its own requirements. Hence, in order to maintain a rescue plan, emergency responders have to interrogate at the same time the overall data stored in heterogeneous databases through complex queries. This gives rise to the problem of access to the required information in a critical time. As mentioned in [2,3] that illustrate databases heterogeneity through three levels, i.e., semantic schematic and syntactic.

Syntactic heterogeneity refers to data format differences and problems related to the implementation of databases in different storage paradigms: relational or object orientated, and the geometric representation of objects: raster or vector. Many organizations contributing in a disaster case rely on a range of storage solutions. However, some organizations are motivated to make their data accessible through Open Geospatial Consortium (OGC) formats that provide syntactically unified formats and services such as Geography Markup Language (GML) [4] and Web Feature Service (WFS) [5].

Schematic heterogeneity regards the differences in data models between emergency communities. Each spatial database schema reflects an abstracted view of data related to one community. Therefore, different hierarchical and classification structures are used by each community to refer to identical or similar objects. Schematic heterogeneity can be classified into three main schemes:

- • Entity versus Entity, i.e., the same entity can exist in two different databases with different name or structure;
- • Attribute versus Attribute, i.e., an attribute related to a class in one database can exist in another class related to another database;

 — • Entity versus Attribute, i.e., a class in one database can be designed as an attribute in another database.

Semantic heterogeneity can be divided into two types: the *naming hetero-geneity* and the *cognitive heterogeneity*. The naming heterogeneity arises when the same data objects are named in a different manner or when different seman-tic data objects are named identically. The cognitive heterogeneity refers to the different domains assigned to each organization. Each community has different cognitive views of a word, which means that they describe similar real word objects from different perspectives.

It is against these complex backdrops that our paper applies. Hence, we offer a comprehensive approach providing an access to the whole information consis-tently and quickly.

3   Related Works

The integration of heterogeneous databases constitutes an old challenge for com-puter information systems communities; it has been extensively studied in the literature. Therefore, various approaches have been proposed that we divide into two broad categories; traditional approaches and novel approaches. For the first category, two main approaches can be cited: the virtualized approaches that include the *Federated Databases* approach [6] and the *Mediator / Wrapper* ap-proach [7], and the *Data Warehouse* (or materialized) approach [8,9]. Novel approaches deal with interoperability issues, and include *Web Services* [10], *On-tologies* [11,12] and *Semantic Web* approaches [13]. Due to the large volumes of spatial data, the complexity of handling and analysing data and its importance in various domains, different researchers working on geographical information systems all over the world have focused on the adaption of the existing inte-gration solutions to spatial databases. Thus, by using different techniques that integrate the spatial component, new solutions have been proposed, such as *Spatial Data Warehouse, Federated Spatial Databases, Geo-web services, Spatial Data Infrastructure* (SDI) [14] among others.

Table 1. The interoperability position of the different integration approaches

Approaches	Syntactic	Schematic	Semantic
Spatial datawarehouses		X	
Federated Spatial Databases	X	X	
Mediation systems	X	X	
Spatial Data Infrastructure	X		
Geo-Web Services	X		
Ontologies		X	X
Semantic Web	X		X

Traditional and innovative approaches presented in Table 1 provide partial solutions for the integration of heterogeneous spatial databases; they only afford one or two interoperability levels and most of them do not support the specication of the data semantics. However, the area related to heterogeneous databases and disaster management is still asking for new solutions and approaches.

Currently, there exist some software packages, such as ArcGIS[1] and Sahana[2], that are used in real disaster scenarios in order to help emergency actors. However, they do not take into account the semantic interoperability and the entities and naming conventions in different databases are duplicated, ambiguous and imprecise. Hence, urgent solutions are required in order to solve these ambiguities that result from the heterogeneous spatial databases stored in diverse organizations.

4   A Hybrid Approach for Providing Intelligent Search in a Disaster Framework

The previous sections have introduced the different heterogeneity levels that could block emergency responders when they query various heterogeneous spatial databases. In response to these difficulties, we design a conceptual framework using Geo-web services and ontology based data integration approach to support the three heterogeneity levels. This framework is based on SOA (Service-Oriented Architecture), which is composed of a service provider, a service broker, and a client service as shown in Figure 1.

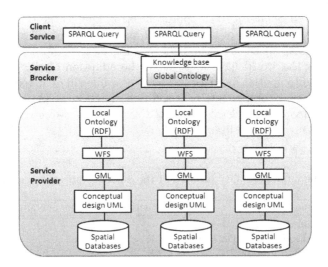

Fig. 1. The framework architecture

---

[1] http://www.esri.com
[2] http://sahanafoundation.org

Service Provider affords the syntactic interoperability, the data models are conceptualized in UML[3] (Unified Modeling Language) and converted afterward into GML (Geographic Markup Language) for sharing data. OGC WFSs (Web Feature Services) were used for publishing feature-level data from heterogeneous databases. For the schematic and semantic interoperability, two types of mappings are required: information source to local ontology mapping and local ontologies to global ontology mapping. Information source to local ontology mapping is obtained by translating GML data to RDF (Resource Description Framework) using an automatic conversion system. Local ontologies to global ontology mapping is used for merging the different local ontologies built into one global ontology.

Service Broker is the main component of the architecture that contains the global ontology, a mapping directory, and a binding technique to apply the ontology hybrid approach by connecting the local ontology to the global ontology. The global ontology is used to create mappings of equivalent classes and attributes in the local ontologies. Hence, it describes the global model that represents local ontologies. **Client Service** employs the RDF SPARQL query language to query the global ontology that contains all the properties defined in the different local ones. The results of SPARQL queries will be presented in a map using Google Visualization API and SPARQL (SPARQL Protocol and RDF Query Language) proxy.

5   The Framework Modules

In this section, we explain the two modules developed in our framework in order to ensure the three interoperability levels. Firstly, we describe the syntactic interoperability module that includes the conversion of the UML models into GML and the integration of these GML models into web feature services. Then, we analyze the schematic and semantic module used to build the different local ontologies and to merge them into a global one.

5.1   Syntactic Interoperability Module

This module deals with the syntactic heterogeneity problems. it contains an automatic converter from UML application schema to a common GML format. The application schema is expressed in UML, and the chosen exchange format is GML. A set of conversion rules have been identified and implemented in a tool named Shapechange that reads UML class diagrams and writes corresponding GML code. Therefore, in order to ensure the GML conversion, we have firstly to conceptualize the different UML models for each spatial database. Then, the UML application schemas have to be converted into XMI representations. Once the XMI documents have been designed using UML, conversion to GML schema specified by the OGC can be done easily by defining some conversion rules.

---

[3] http://www.uml.org

The UML to GML Application Schema mapping tool supports this conversion automatically. After standardizing the different databases into GML files, they are published and integrated in WFS.

5.2 Schematic and Semantic Interoperability Module

In our framework, we opt to use the hybrid ontology approach for its various advantages [12]. In order to apply this approach, two types of mappings are required: information source to local ontology mapping and local ontologies to global ontology mapping.

Information Source to Local Ontology Mapping. The local ontologies corresponding to each database are built using two languages, RDF (Resource Description Framework) and OWL (Web Ontology Language) for representing triples and modeling the relations between them. Such a representation is obtained by using the GML2RDF automated conversion system [15]. Each entity in the database is represented by its own configuration which contains a list of all the attributes. The following steps present briefly the building of the different local ontologies:

- • Each spatial database is separately converted into its local ontology.
- • Each entity in the database is converted to the class name of the local ontology. Each component related to a class is described using a set of triples. This triple comprises three parts: subject, predicate, and object.
- • The subject is the result of the conversion of each class instance in the dataset.
- • The predicate is the conversion result of each non-prime attribute. It expresses a relationship between the subject and the object.
- • The object is obtained by converting each attribute value corresponding to an attribute.
- • If two classes C1 and C2 take part in formal corresponding relationships, then class C2 will be declared as the subclass of class C1. The foreign key relationship between the classes is shown as the predicate where C2 will be the domain.

Local Ontologies to Global Ontology Mapping. After building the different local ontologies, we have to map them in order to determine the semantic and schematic correspondences between the concepts of two ontologies. If two concepts correspond, then they mean the same thing or closely related things. The mapping process proposed in our research is based on the two approaches presented below.

N-Grams match [16] is a method used to compute lexical similarity between two words. Generally, the N-Grams algorithm takes as input two strings and computes the number of common substrings between them. An n-gram is a sequence of n characters; for each string, the set of all possible n-grams, are computed. Then, a pre-processing step is executed to normalize both strings. The third step is to extract the n-grams from each string. Finally, the algorithm counts the matching percentage of the two strings.

Synonym match [17] is a technique for detecting semantic similarity between two words. In many cases, two strings may appear as different words but may represent the same meaning in a particular domain. To identify such semantically related words, we use the ontology and lexical database Wordnet.

Ontology Matching Steps. To map the local ontologies and merge them into a global one, all the possible combinations of local ontologies should be detected and mentioned in a list. Then, we extract and match the different classes in each local ontology.

Class Name matching. The different classes are represented in prefixes. Hence, we extract all the names of classes from there without considering the predifined prefixes list. Then, we apply the class name match, each class in the first local ontology is paired with all other entities in the second one. The N-Grams and the Synonym match scores are used to validate each step. So, the N-Grams score should be greater than a threshold and the Synonym match returns a boolean result synonym (1) or not synonym (0). If the matching result is validated by the N-Grams or the Synonym match, then we can proceed to next matching steps using the same approaches and techniques.

Attribute Type matching. This step is executed only if the previous one was validated by one matching approach. At this stage, the attribute type of the matching class is extracted from the list created for each class name containing the attributes name and their corresponding types. This list is obtained by the extraction of the attributes name from the predicate. The data type attribute is paired in such a way that one data type attribute related to a class in one local ontology is matched with all the data types of the second class in the other local ontology. If two types of attributes related to one pair are detected as similar then we proceed to the next step to compare their related names.

Attribute Name matching. This phase could be employed only if the pair of attribute names that will be matched have the same data types. In this case, the attributes of the matching entity names are executed.

Attribute Value matching. Until now, this approach is relatively susceptible to homonym-like pairs of strings: although syntactically very similar, they could mean entirely different things, N-Grams and Synonym match will give them a high similarity score. To deal with this problem, we apply an attribute value match. This matching is executed only if the attribute name matching of one pair was validated, then three instances related to each attribute are matched to detect if the two classes are similar or not. Moreover, this solution is extensible and we could make an attribute-class matching, relations matching and many others using the same principle.

Local Ontologies Merging. To merge the different local ontologies, we analyze the matching results using algorithm 1. If two classes are matched as similar, then one of these classes will be added to the global ontology. Else, the two classes are saved in the global ontology. The same method is applied for the couple attribute-class and attribute- attribute merging.

Algorithm 1. Merging local ontologies

Require: ListOntologieN3 *listOnt*;
  for (int i = 0; i < listOnt.size-1 ; i=i+2) **do**
    ListClassMatching = matching(*listOnt*[i],*listOnt*[i+1])
    for (int j = 0; j < ListClassMatching.size-1 ; j++) **do**
      if *classmatching*[j][2] = true **then**
        if (!*GlobalOntology*.contains(*classmatching*[j][0])) **then**
          GlobalOntology.add(*classmatching*[j][0])
        end if
      else
        if (!*GlobalOntology*.contains(*classmatching*[j][0])) **then**
          GlobalOntology.add(*classmatching*[j][0])
        end if
        if (!*GlobalOntology*.contains(*classmatching*[j][1])) **then**
          GlobalOntology.add(*classmatching*[j][1])
        end if
      end if
    end for
  end for
  return *GlobalOntology*

After constructing our global ontology, we need to store it in an ontology server to be able to query it. Therefore, we stored the resulting global ontology in the joseki[4] ontology server.

6   Experiments and Results

Based on the proposed framework, we have implemented a prototype for providing automatic search from heterogeneous datasets in a disaster case. Therefore, we have used three heterogeneous datasets belonging to La Rochelle city in France. The first one represents the office of mayor data stored in KML files, the second one contains the emergency service data stored in MIF files and the third dataset belongs to the police service data stored in Shapefiles. Then, we designed the different UML models conceptualized for each dataset using Rational Rose Software.

The Unisys XMI tool is used to store the different UML models in a single XMI document. At that time, conversion to GML schema specified by the OGC can be done easily using the UML to GML mapping tool Shapechange[5]. To integrate

---

[4] http://www.joseki.org
[5] http://www.shapechange.net/

the different GML files, we use OGC web services specially WFS. Thus, we use Geoserver 2.2.1 and the GML plugin to publish the generated GML datasets. To build the local ontologies for each dataset, a conversion program named GML2RDF is used which makes use of two predeveloped open source APIs for parsing GML files and handling the creation of the RDF models. The GeoTools API is used for reading the data from GML files, and the Jena API is used to contain the converted RDF data in a memory model and eventually write the data into a N3 file. Similarly, the Jena semantic web framework for java is integrated in our application to access ontology definitions, analyze the WordNet thesaurus and to realize the different necessary mappings. To evaluate the mapping approaches applied in our framework, we visualize the different results provided by the mapping algorithm. Hence, these different results are analyzed using our three datasets and 90% of them are matched correctly. A spatial ontology server was developed based on Joseki to support the global ontology N3 file and to interrogate it using SPARQL forms. The query results are displayed into a satellite image using Google Maps API. Our experiments yield to promising results and show that, with the implemented prototype, it is possible to directly search geospatial information from heterogeneous sources using our framework. Therefore, to deliver the needed information in a short time, we only have to interogate our global ontology using a simple query that returns the response as a map.

7   Conclusion and Future Work

In this paper, we propose a framework for the integration of heterogeneous spatial databases that enables emergency responders to easily query spatial heterogeneous databases and facilitates the automatic search of geospatial information in order to make quick and correct decisions and prompt actions. Our framework uses novel techniques maintained under SOA architecture to deal with three major tasks: Syntactic interoperability is analyzed by adopting GML as a common language; Schematic (Structural) interoperability is construed by the ontology mapping process and Semantic interoperability is assured by using the hybrid ontology approach.

Furthermore, by the extensible and autonomy characters hidden behind the ontology approach and OGC web services many interesting functionalities can be added. We plan to treat information from texts and comments posted in social networks. This will be helpful in the case of a lack of information.

References

1. Zhang, C., Zhao, T., Li, W.: Automatic search of geospatial features for disaster and emergency management. International Journal Applied Earth Observation and Geoinformation 12(6), 409–418 (2010)
2. Bishr, Y.: Overcoming the semantic and other barriers to gis interoperability. International Journal of Geographical Information Science 12(4), 299–314 (1998)
3. Stuckenschmidt, H., Harmelen, F.: Sharing on the Semantic Web. Springer, Heidelberg (2005)

4. Cox, S., Daisey, P., Lake, R., Portele, C., Whiteside, A.: Opengis geography markup language (gml) implementation specification, version 3.0 (2003)
5. Zhang, C., Li, W.: The roles of web feature and web map services in real time geospatial data sharing for time-critical applications. Cartography and Geographic Information Science 32(4), 269 (2005)
6. Heimbigner, D., McLeod, D.: A federated architecture for information management. ACM Transactions on Office Information Systems 3(3), 253–278 (1985)
7. Leclercq, E., Benslimane, D., Yetongnon, K.: Amun: An object oriented model for cooperative spatial information systems. In: Proceedings of the 1997 IEEE Knowledge and Data Englishineering Exchange Workshop. IEEE Computer Society, Washington, DC (1997)
8. Inmon, W.H.: Building the Data Warehouse. John Wiley & Sons, Inc., New York (1992)
9. Kimball, R.: The Data Warehouse Toolkit: Practical Techniques for Building Dimensional Data Warehouses. John Wiley (1996)
10. Zhang, S., Gan, J., Miao, L., Lv, G., Huang, J.: Study on gml spatial interoperability based on web service. In: Proceedings of the 31st Annual International Computer Software and Applications Conference, vol. 1, pp. 649–656. IEEE Computer Society, Washington, DC (2007)
11. Xu, W., Zlatanova, S.: Ontologies for disaster management response geomatics solutions for disaster management. In: Li, J., Zlatanova, S., Fabbri, A.G. (eds.) Geomatics Solutions for Disaster Management. Lecture Notes in Geoinformation and Cartography, pp. 185–200. Springer, Heidelberg (2007)
12. Mustapha, Y.J., Mohd Su'ud, M., Boursier, P.: Analyzing the ontology approaches and the formation of open ontology model: A step for organisational ontology employment. In: Semaparo: The Fifth International Conference on Advances in Semantic Processing, Lisbon, Portugal, pp. 6–13 (2011)
13. Zhang, C., Li, W., Zhao, T.: Geospatial data sharing based on geospatial semantic web technologies. Journal of Spatial Science 52(2), 35–49 (2007)
14. Maguire, D.J., Longley, P.A.: The emergence of geoportals and their role in spatial data infrastructures. Computers, Environment and Urban Systems 29(1), 3–14 (2005)
15. Bulen, A., Carter, J., Varanka, D.: A program for the conversion of the national map data from proprietary format to resource description framework (rdf). Technical Report U.S. Geological Survey Open-File Report 2011–1142., U.S. Department of the Interior (2011)
16. Cavnar, W., Trenkle, J.M.: N-gram based text categorization. In: Proceeding of 3rd Annual Symposium on Document Analysis and Information Retrieval, Las Vegas, pp. 161–175 (1994)
17. Lin, F., Sandkuhl, K.: A survey of exploiting wordnet in ontology matching. In: Bramer, M. (ed.) Artificial Intelligence and Practice II, vol. 276, pp. 341–350. Springer, Heidelberg (2008)

An Ontology for Submarine Feature Representation on Charts

Jingya Yan[1,2], Eric Guilbert[2], and Eric Saux[1]

[1] Naval Academy Research Institute, GIS group
Lanvéoc-Poulmic, CC600, 29240 Brest Cedex 9, France
yjytt59@gmail.com

[2] Département des Sciences Géomatiques, Pavillon Louis-Jacques-Casault,
Université Laval, Québec (Québec) G1V 0A6, Canada
eric.guilbert@scg.ulaval.ca

Abstract. A landform is a subjective individuation of a part of a terrain. Landform recognition is a difficult task because its definition usually relies on a qualitative and fuzzy description. Achieving automatic recognition of landforms requires a formal definition of the landforms properties and their modelling. In the maritime domain, the International Hydrographic Organisation published a standard terminology of undersea feature names which formalises a set of definition mainly for naming and communication purpose. This terminology is here used as a starting point for the definition of an ontology of undersea features and their automatic classification from a terrain model. First, an ontology of undersea features is built. The ontology is composed of an application domain ontology describing the main properties and relationships between features and a representation ontology deals with representation on a chart where features are portrayed by soundings and isobaths. A database model was generated from the ontology. Geometrical properties describing the feature shape are computed from soundings and isobaths and are used for feature classification. An example of automatic classification on a nautical chart is presented and results and on-going research are discussed.

Keywords: Geographical domain ontology, Landform classification, Nautical chart, Digital terrain modelling.

1 Introduction

On nautical charts, undersea features are portrayed by sets of soundings (depth points) and isobaths (depth contours) from which the map reader can interpret landforms. As defined by [1], "a landform is a part of the Earth's surface that is characteristically apprehended as a unitary thing or object because of its particular shape". However describing its shape is a subjective task as a landform is inherently vague. Shape and boundary are defined qualitatively and their appreciation depends on the context or the cultural knowledge of people. Establishing a list of landform types is therefore not a trivial task. Existing landform classifications usually provide an end-user terminology for the need of a community.

J. Parsons and D. Chiu (Eds.): ER Workshops 2013, LNCS 8697, pp. 87–96, 2014.

In the maritime domain, the International Hydrographic Organisation (IHO) has published a nomenclature of undersea features which provides a standard terminology for the naming of undersea features on charts and in publications [2]. The objective of this research is to generate a submarine feature classification so that features can be identified automatically from the seafloor representation. Such tool can assist both the cartographer and the map reader in selecting or visualising important features and evaluating the quality of a chart. An ontology of undersea features is designed and an application implementing the concepts is developed. The ontology is divided into two parts. The Application Domain Ontology built directly from the IHO terminology, organises and describes the properties of the features, forming a hierarchy of concepts. The Phenomenological Domain Ontology describes the concepts for representing the seafloor on the chart. Concepts from the ADO are translated so that each feature corresponds to a set of soundings and isobaths and its properties are extracted from the terrain model. A database model is then derived and is implemented in a triplestore database.

This paper first reviews existing works on landform classification and ontologies. Section 3 presents the ADO and PDO detailing how features are classified on the chart. Section 4 presents the database model and discusses classification results obtained from bathymetric data. The last section presents conclusions and directions for future work.

2   Ontologies of Landforms

2.1   Landform Classification

Landforms characteristics being by essence fuzzy and scale dependent [3], their description can vary easily according to people's perception and experience. Landform classification in that case is rather a problem of defining formal specifications that correspond to verbal descriptions for the purpose of communication within a community [4]. Existing work in this domain consists in the establishment of a core reference or a domain ontology collecting and formalising knowledge gathered from experts. Major sources of landform taxonomy are provided by spatial data standards such as SDTS and by national mapping agencies such as the IGN-E in Spain [5] and the Ordnance Survey in the UK[1]. Proposed ontologies rely on several ontologies including a topographic ontology and a hydrologic ontology. They provide formal qualitative properties and relations between features. However classification requires the assessment of geometrical properties such as height, length or area and so the definition of some quantitative descriptors. Existing work in this direction mostly relates to identifying specific landforms such as valley [6], bay [7] and reef [8].

In the maritime domain, the IHO is the international body engaged in defining standards in order to advance maritime safety. In order to build a common frame for the naming of undersea features, the IHO defined a terminology of

---

[1] http://www.ordnancesurvey.co.uk/oswebsite/ontology/

undersea feature names [2]. The purpose of the document is to set a standard for communication (the terminology is available in several languages) and for the denomination of undersea features (with a guideline for naming features). Although this document is only a terminology with definitions in natural language, it defines a standard, classifies more terms and provides more precise definitions than the Geo-Wordnet[2] database or USGS's SDTS[3]. Therefore this document provides a uniform view of undersea features solving most semantic difficulties [9] and is used as a base for the definition of the ontology of submarine features.

2.2   The Geographical Ontology Framework

Conceptualising knowledge for a specific application is done by gathering specific knowledge from a domain and by integrating concepts from higher level ontologies. In order to represent geographic objects from the real world to computer language, [10] introduced a five-universe paradigm. The physical and cognitive universes contain real world phenomena and their representation in the human mind. The logical universe provides explicit ontologies formalising the cognitive universe. The representation universe deals with the description of geographical elements from the logical universe and contains ontologies conceptualising the elements according to the type of representation (e.g. field or object model). Finally, the implementation universe describes algorithms and data structures as implemented in the application.

In order to organise information on geographic worlds into ontologies, [10] considered a multiple-ontology approach where knowledge is shared between the logical universe and the representation universe. [10] defined first the Application Domain Ontology (ADO), concerned with describing specific subjects and tasks, in the logical universe. It is composed of two kinds of ontology: a subject ontology describing the vocabulary related to a generic domain, and a task ontology describing a task or application within a specialisation domain. Second, the Phenomenological Domain Ontology (PDO) in the representation universe manages different properties of the geographical phenomena in the GIS. It is composed of method and measurement ontologies. A method ontology defines a set of algorithms and data structures, and a measurement ontology describes the physical process of recording a geographical phenomenon. Both universes are defined separately. Different representations can be defined for one application or one representation used for different applications. The connection between both ontologies is made by semantic mediators.

3   An Ontology of Undersea Features

Following Fonseca's framework, the undersea feature ontology can be divided into two parts (Figure 1). Concepts that belong to the maritime domain are part of the logical universe. The subject ontology conceptualises knowledge about

---

[2] http://geowordnet.semanticmatching.org/
[3] http://mcmcweb.er.usgs.gov/sdts/

submarine features and is mostly derived from the IHO terminology. The subject ontology describes any activity that requires or analyses seafloor information. In the context of this work, nautical charts being mainly designed for navigation purpose, the task ontology would logically be related to navigation and route planning.

The representation universe is concerned with the representation of undersea features on the nautical chart. The method ontology focuses on terrain representation techniques including objects on the chart (soundings, isobaths) and operations handling these objects (isobath extraction, generalisation operations) as well as operations matching features from the ADO to the PDO. The measurement ontology refers to data collection techniques (e.g. echo sounding, LIDAR).

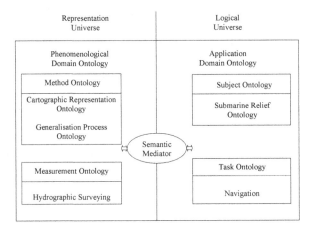

Fig. 1. Phenomenological and application domain ontologies of undersea features

This work focuses on the characterisation of undersea features and their representation. Task and measurement ontologies require knowledge about data acquisition or maritime navigation and so are not addressed. The next section presents the subject ontology by defining the properties required to describe undersea features. Section 3.2 describes the method ontology and presents how features from the subject ontology are represented in the method ontology. Ontologies also include information such as value restrictions (e.g. depth values range) and specification of logical relationships between concepts (e.g. each morphological feature must include at least one isobath or a sounding).

3.1   The Subject Ontology

Building the domain ontology is done in two steps. First, properties and relationships characterising each of the 46 features are identified by analysing the definitions and extracting keywords corresponding to feature characteristics.

Second, these characteristics are organised into different concepts (composition, shape) describing the feature properties and relationships (mereological, topological, taxonomic). At the end of the process, a hierarchy of features is defined. IHO features correspond to the most specialised concepts and are at the bottom of the hierarchy, inheriting from one or several more generalised concepts such as depression (a feature which is lower than its surrounding) or prominence (a feature which is higher than its surrounding). The hierarchical structure provides several levels of semantic precision which can be adjusted according to the accuracy of the input data or to the required precision of the description. For example, although a large number of features are part of the ocean floor, a detailed description is not needed on an offshore navigation chart as they cannot be portrayed precisely on a large scale map.

Figure 2 shows the structure of the subject ontology. A full description of properties, relationships and concepts involved at top level and application level is given in [11]. Properties describing the features are the composition (e.g. rock, sand), the depth level and the shape properties. The depth level relates features with parts of the seafloor at different range of depths and having different geomorphological properties.

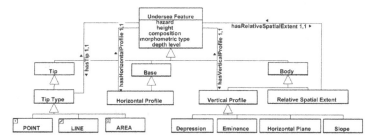

Fig. 2. Concepts describing undersea features

In order to describe the feature shape, the feature can be divided into three parts: its body, tip and base. The body is described by the feature height, vertical profile and relative spatial extent. The vertical profile defines the overall shape (peak, ridge, plane area) which includes the morphometric class as well as the type of slope (steep, gentle, horizontal). The relative spatial extent indicates if a feature is relatively large or small. The tip concept applies to eminences and depressions and describes the shape of the extremity. For example, a summit can be sharp (like a pinnacle) or flat (like a plateau). Finally, the base is described by the horizontal profile (e.g. elongated, circular).

3.2   The Method Ontology

The method ontology formalises the way submarine features are represented on the chart. It includes concepts and rules defined by hydrographic offices [12,13]. Four main concepts (chart, isobath, sounding and feature) are defined together with their spatial relationships and properties (Figure 3). The chart concept mostly includes metadata about the scale and the symbology. Isobaths and soundings are the elements portraying the seafloor. A sounding is defined by a depth and a position. Soundings are also classified into different classes according to their importance in characterising features that are relevant to navigation [11]. An isobath is defined by a line and its depth. Topological relationships between soundings and isobaths are also recorded.

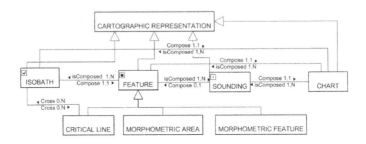

Fig. 3. Chart elements defined in the method ontology

The chart feature concept corresponds to the representation of an undersea feature from the subject ontology. As mentioned in section 2.1, classification is scale dependent and is based on fuzzy characteristics. In the context of representation on a chart, a feature is portrayed by a set of soundings and isobaths that the reader can interpret. For example, a reef feature is represented by a sounding which is close to the sea level, representing a hazard and an isobath containing the sounding. The method ontology also defines operations extracting the isobaths from a set of soundings and cartographic generalisation operations (e.g. selection, filtering) adapting the chart elements to the scale.

4   Implementation

4.1   System Design

Both ADO and PDO ontologies[4] were built in the Protégé 4.2 platform and exported into a RDF file. Figure 4 is an extract of the undersea feature ontology. The ontological model was then integrated in Virtuoso. It can function as a web application server as well as a host for data-driven web services. Virtuoso offers a triplestore database that is a purpose-built database for the storage and retrieval of triples in RDF terminology in the form of *subject-predicate-object* expressions. Triplestore is in coherence with the current emphasis on development of native stores since their performance are optimised for the storage and retrieval of triples. Information or knowledge is accessible via SPARQL. The Jena API was used to read from and write to the RDF graph. An example of such a RDF

---

[4] www.dropbox.com/s/2hssg1cty1dvfji/undersea.owl

graph is proposed in figure 5. The *Hill* concept, defined in the IHO terminology, inherits from the *HillFeature* and the *PointFeature* concepts and describes a feature having a point tip. The *HillFeature* concept is a generalisation of different concepts which differ by the type of tip and their possible location.

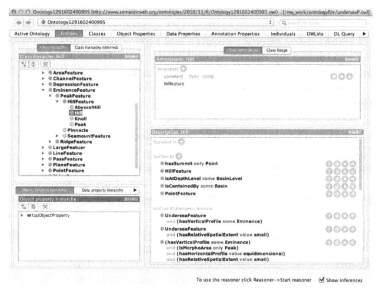

Fig. 4. Extract of the ADO in Protégé: the Hill concept

A triplestore is also built for the storage of the bathymetric data of a chart (soundings, isobaths, undersea features). Its schema is generated by the ontological triplestore. Predicates in this database connect data together (e.g. isobath *I belongs to* feature *F*) and data with concepts (e.g. isobath *I is an instance of* the isobath concept). Finally, the ontological and data knowledge are connected to the geographical information system. As our information system was initially developed in C++ language, Java Native Interface (JNI) is used to connect Java (i.e. Jena) and C++.

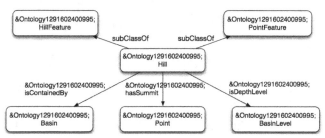

Fig. 5. Graph associated to the RDF/XML description of the Hill concept

4.2   Results

The model was tested on a set of soundings provided by the French Hydrographic Office for a large scale map (1:12500) of a coastal area. Isobaths were extracted with a 1 metre vertical interval by interpolation. A first step before feature classification is their identification. On such a chart, cartographers and readers mostly make use of isobaths to delineate hazards and navigation routes. Therefore, features are characterised by one or several isobaths at the same depth marking their boundary [14]. A current limitation of this approach is that only depressions and prominences are considered. The method extracts features based on depth variations between adjacent isobaths and yields a feature tree providing topological relationships between features (adjacency and inclusion). Relationships between isobaths and soundings are defined by a constrained Delaunay triangulation.

Only features that inherit from the prominence and depression concepts are classified as they are the only ones identified on the chart. Shape properties are computed from the soundings and isobaths composing a feature. Base properties are computed from the boundary contours. The tip is defined by starting from the highest or deepest sounding and by adding neighbouring triangles to extract the largest possible horizontal surface. Figure 6 presents a set of classified features. Figure 6A shows leaves of the feature tree, i.e. feature which do not contain any other features. Figure 6B shows features at the top of the hierarchy. The hierarchy of feature concepts defined in the ADO was used as a decision tree to reach the highest level of precision. Seven types of feature (peak feature, reef, bank, shoal, pit, channel and basin feature) were identified and characterised (Table 1). The first four features are prominences and three of them are defined in the IHO terminology. The last three are depressions and are not in the terminology because in shallow areas, noticeable features are mainly features which represent a danger for navigation. A channel corresponds to an elongated depression. The largest one, shown on Figure 6B, indicates a navigation route. Others are indeed contained by the first one.

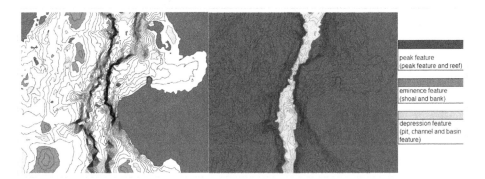

peak feature
(peak feature and reef)

eminence feature
(shoal and bank)

depression feature
(pit, channel and basin feature)

Fig. 6. Results of undersea features characterization. The colour figure with more details of undersea features is accessible on line[6].

Table 1. Undersea features (features defined in the IHO terminology in bold)

Peak feature	Reef	Bank	Shoal	Pit	Channel	Basin feature	Total
25	6	4	9	34	6	17	101

5   Conclusion

This paper introduced an ontology of undersea features for landform classification. The concepts were implemented into a cartographic application to enrich the bathymetric database for purpose of cartographic and model generalisation. The ontology is divided into an application domain, defining the feature properties, and a phenomenological domain, addressing their representation on a chart. On top of the IHO definitions, general concepts were added to provide a description at different precisions. These general concepts are useful for the representation because on one side, the bathymetric database usually does not contain enough data for a full characterisation of all features and on the other side, the amount of details is adapted to the scale and the purpose of the chart.

All concepts defined in the ontology have not been implemented yet. Only features that are bounded by one or several isobaths are identified. Due to the inherent vagueness of landforms, delineating undersea features with a crisp boundary is subjective however it corresponds to the representation that is given on the chart and provides a rigorous definition for shape properties. Further work can be done by representing features by one or several soundings (e.g. a seamount where only the summit is marked) or by dealing with plane features. In such cases, features are not represented on the chart with a crisp boundary and therefore vagueness has to be taken into account in the position and computation of geometric properties [15]. As the level of complexity would increase greatly with the number of feature concepts involved, the decision tree may be pruned according to the type of chart (large or small scale, coastal or offshore navigation) to limit the number of features considered.

This work is part of a larger project on the cartographic and model generalisation of the seafloor for nautical chart production. Therefore the next step is the integration of cartographic rules and generalisation constraints and operators in the method ontology. The feature ontology may also be extended by adding more information about relevance to navigation: some prominences are already marked as hazards, channels can also be marked as navigation routes to be preserved. Based on this knowledge, the application shall be able to infer plans for automatic processing and to evaluate the quality of the generalised data.

Acknowledgments. The work presented in this paper is funded by the Consulate General of France in Hong Kong and the Région Bretagne in France under grant 0211/ ARE 09011/00026102 and partly by grant A-PK56. The authors wish to thank the "Service Hydrographique et Océanographique de la Marine" in France for their cartographic data.

---

[6] https://dl.dropboxusercontent.com/u/85206736/results-1.eps

References

1. Mark, D.M., Smith, B.: A science of topography: From qualitative ontology to digital representations. In: Bishop, M.P., Shroder, J.F. (eds.) Geographic Information Science and Mountain Geomorphology, pp. 75–100. Praxis Publishing (2004)
2. International Hydrographic Organization: Standardization of undersea feature names, 4th edn. International Hydrographic Bureau, Monaco (2008)
3. Chaudhry, O., Mackaness, W.: Creating mountains out of mole hills: Automatic identification of hills and ranges using morphometric analysis. Transactions in GIS 12(5), 567–589 (2008)
4. Smith, B., Mark, D.M.: Do mountains exist? towards an ontology of landforms. Environment and Planning B: Planning and Design 30(3) (2003)
5. Gómez-Pérez, A., Ramos, J., Rodríguez-Pascual, A., Vilches-Blázquez, L.: The IGN-E case: Integrating through a hidden ontology. In: Ruas, A., Gold, C. (eds.) Headway in Spatial Data Handling, pp. 417–435. Springer (2008)
6. Straumann, R.K., Purves, R.S.: Computation and elicitation of valleyness. Spatial cognition and computation 11(2), 178–204 (2011)
7. Feng, C.C., Bittner, T.: Ontology-based qualitative feature analysis: Bays as a case study. Transactions in GIS 14(4), 547–568 (2010)
8. Duce, S.: Towards an ontology for reef islands. In: Janowicz, K., Raubal, M., Levashkin, S. (eds.) GeoS 2009. LNCS, vol. 5892, pp. 175–187. Springer, Heidelberg (2009)
9. Bittner, T., Donnelly, M., Winter, S.: Ontology and semantic interoperability. In: Large-Scale 3D Data Integration, pp. 139–160 (2005)
10. Fonseca, F.T.: Ontology-driven geographic information systems. PhD thesis, The University of Maine (2001)
11. Yan, J., Guilbert, E., Saux, E.: An ontology of the submarine relief for analysis and representation on nautical charts. The Cartographic Journal (to appear)
12. National Oceanic and Atmospheric Administration, U.S. Department of Commerce: Nautical Chart User's Manual (1997)
13. Service Hydrographique et Océanographique de la Marine: Etude d'aide à la préparation des cartes marines – étude de faisabilité: Partie 2 Conception détaillée des traitements (1995)
14. Guilbert, E.: Multi-level representation of terrain features on a contour map. Geoinformatica 17(2), 301–324 (2013)
15. Bittner, T.: Vagueness and the trade-off between the classification and delineation of geographic regions: an ontological analysis. International Journal of Geographical Information Science 25(5), 825–850 (2011)

A Human-Enhanced Framework
for Assessing Open Geo-spatial Data

Roula Karam and Michele Melchiori

Dept. of Information Engineering University of Brescia
Via Branze, 38 - 25123 Brescia, Italy
roulakaramm@gmail.com, melchior@ing.unibs.it

Abstract. With the advent of collaborative Web 2.0, spatial data creation is no more exclusively in the hands of professionals. For example, linked open data (LOD) promotes a new paradigm for online and freely accessible spatial information. Noteworthy initiatives in this direction are Geonames and OpenStreetMap. Moreover, as cities are continuously changing and growing, Points of Interest (POIs) are no more historical and their descriptions have to be updated frequently. One appropriate solution is to encourage participation of voluntary on-site experts to the process of information gathering and updating. In this context, we propose a human-enhanced framework, based on linked data principles and technologies, and devoted to collect, organize and rank user-generated corrections and completions in order to improve the accuracy and completeness of Geo-spatial LOD. Metrics have been defined for both human contributors and contents in order to estimate their reliability. The generated data introduces an additional linked data layer for hosting the revised version of the original datasets.

Keywords: Geo-spatial Web, Linked Data, Location-based Applications, Model-driven Approach, Human Computation, Crowdsourcing.

1 Introduction

Current popularity of Location-Based Services (LBS) is fueling a growing interest for Web geo-spatial data sources. Well known examples of very large geo-spatial datasets are Foursquare, Google Places and OpenStreetMap. Recently, some geo-spatial data sources have published their content as linked open data (LOD). For example, the LinkedGeoData initiative is based on the content of OpenStreetMap to make it available as RDF knowledge base according to the linked data (LD) principles. Publishing geographical data as LD is motivated by many advantages in terms of accessibility and interoperability of the sources, such as: (i) making datasets accessible by non-proprietary languages and tools (e.g., SPARQL, GeoSPARQL[1], RDF Browsers, Geo LD Browser [3]); (ii) introducing formal semantics to make data machine processable; (iii) enriching data with links to external resources (e.g., DBpedia) to set cooperating relationships

---

[1] http://www.opengeo-spatial.org/standards/geosparql

J. Parsons and D. Chiu (Eds.): ER Workshops 2013, LNCS 8697, pp. 97–106, 2014.
© Springer International Publishing Switzerland 2014

among data sources; (iv) allowing to query/browse multiple data sources in a combined way. On the other hand, geo-spatial data suffer from two known drawbacks: variable quality and description conflicts. The first one concerns updating, completeness and data accuracy. The second one concerns possible inconsistent descriptions for the same Points of Interest (POI) from different sources as cities are growing and new POIs can appear or their features can change. With reference to quality, geographic data providers such as Geonames and OpenStreetMap make available simple models for improving data from users' feedbacks. Concerning conflicts in descriptions, some techniques have been studied to catch conflicting descriptions for the same POI and integrate them [10,14]. However, these automatic techniques are not completely effective and are usually not helpful if the information is incorrect or missing in all sources. Feedbacks from users that have knowledge or physical presence in the considered place are therefore valuable contributions to the data quality. In general, we can say that pushing the user in the life cycle of geographic data is fundamental for describing the urban environments.

In this paper, we describe a *provider independent* framework to collect, organize and rank user-generated corrections and completions for improving accuracy and completeness of geo-spatial Linked data that in a preliminary version has been presented in [11]. Within such framework, the user has different roles as contributor (on-site volunteer and paid expert). Metrics have been defined to evaluate both contributors and the user-generated content. Moreover, validated and ranked user-provided corrections and completions are published as LOD. A repository for such data is maintained separately from the original data sources and can be queried jointly with them [4]. The paper outline is the following. In Section 2, the problem of conflicts is introduced by a simple, but real example. In Section 3, some relevant literature and approaches about conflicts in Geo data, data quality and users contribution are discussed; Section 4 presents the requirements and the conceptual model of the framework; Section 5 introduces how we assess the quality of the users' contributions; Section 6 describes the settings for some evaluation perspectives. Finally, in Section 7 we conclude with some remarks and future directions.

2   Conflicts in POI Descriptions

The problems of data quality and specifically of conflicts in POI descriptions may concern different aspects of the description as in the following example. Let us consider a user's request to find the nearest hotel to her current position, submitted to two different geo-data providers (e.g., Google Maps and Microsoft Bing). The answers obtained by the providers may present various conflicts, as described in [10]. Different levels of heterogeneities (both in the underlying data and in the representation), can be identified at cartographic, syntactic, structural, semantic and geographic levels. For example, they provide slightly different positions for it on the maps (e.g., approx. 100 meters). The hotel could be named "Hotel Maxim" in the first answer and "Maxim" in the second one and there are other differences in the (semantic) details of the descriptions (e.g., website, telephone number, menu, etc.). Besides, the hotel is represented with two different cartographic symbols or icons on different base-maps (cartographic). Another type of heterogeneity could concern differences in the positioning of the same POI. Usually, these differences are related to the adopted positioning technique that can have different levels of precision. As a consequence, this may lead to imprecise results for the geo-coding function. Differences in POI names can be related to spatial databases that lack of frequent updating. Details about POIs can be different among providers due to lack of updates as well as missing some common agreements about representation formats for email addresses, websites/URL, facilities, etc.

3   Related Work

Literature and approaches about conflict management in data integration, quality assessment of LOD and Volunteered Geographic Information (VGI) are relevant to our discussion.

Conflict in geo-spatial data. Inspired by the works of [12] and [9], we proposed a general solution in [10] to integrate POI descriptions with presence of conflicts. The work in [13], classifies different types of conflicts (conspicuous/ inconspicuous) and presents some detection/resolution strategies to assist humans for image annotation.

User contribution to data quality. As emphasized also in [5,8], LD practices give a contribution to the quality of data because of: (i) the adoption of shared vocabularies which makes explicit the semantics of the data and therefore increases the possibilities to understand and check it, and (ii) the presence of links makes it possible to check the consistency of data across different sources. Considering the domain of geo data, in order to obtain high quality links between POIs and photos retrieved by social media, the UrbanMatch application is proposed in [5].

Quality evaluation in crowdsourcing. Crowdsourcing, for example Amazon Mechanical Turk (https://www.mturk.com/) is an example such a type of platforms, requires new strategies to evaluate involved workers as well as their outputs. A main motivation for this, is the sparsity of contributions that have a severe impact on the content quality which is assured, for example, by means of aggregation and reputation evaluation. In crowdsourcing processes, quality control has to be considered inorder to filter noisy or ambiguous information and extract the high qualified reliable one. Some authors had studied the quality issue in crowdsourcing as cited in [16,15], where the quality control implies users' credibility weight based on their mobility patterns, past contributions (trustworthiness/reputation score).

Quality evaluation in volunteered geographic information. The discussion presented in [7] deals with the quality of volunteered geographic information (VGI). In particular, this interesting work presents three alternative approaches for assessing quality of VGI contributions with merits and limits: social, crowdsourcing and geographic. Actually, our work is based on the first and the second one. Other works, like [6] compare VGI data collections with professional one a given territory to perform a comparative quality analysis. The authors in [2] had surveyed many volunteered open geo-knowledge bases and discussed the issue of their quality. This work had also inspired us to elaborate their point by: (i) introducing two types of users as producers of spatial feedbacks (expert volunteers and paid), and (ii) assessing users and their activities to have more reliable and precise information based on the user reputation.

4   Design of the Human-Enhanced Framework

4.1   Requirements

The purpose of the proposed framework is to maintain an organized user-generated collection of feedbacks about geo-spatial linked data published by LOD sources. The collection includes corrections generated and validated by users, complementary information and conflict resolutions. According to a conceptual perspective, this data constitutes an additional *linked corrections layer* in the architecture of geo-spatial linked data. The main motivations for the proposed framework are: (i) introducing more sophisticated and provider-independent models for collecting and evaluating user-generated feedbacks than the ones currently offered by geo-spatial linked data providers and (ii) dealing with conflicts in descriptions offered by different providers. Basic requirements of the framework consider that the new data collection has to be complementary to the existing sources and compliant to the LD practices as described below:

- The *linked corrections layer* is published as LOD like the original data. This means that, each updated POI description includes as well the original URI(s) that can be resolved to access the original POI descriptions.
- The *linked corrections layer* constitutes a mediation layer built over the original sources and linked to them.
- Applications and users can browse this layer from any RDF data browser and query it using SPARQL or GeoSPARQL languages.

Corrections, complementary information and conflict resolutions stored in the data model as discussed in the following section, are generated and evaluated based on the users activities (volunteers and paid ones). Conflicts in POIs descriptions can be detected by automatic procedures [10], or they can be reported by users, and in some cases can be solved automatically too. If this is not possible, they are submitted to users who are competent about the geographical area of the relevant POI. Voluntary and paid users have different roles in the framework. A voluntary contributor is a user that has a direct knowledge about the POI or geo-entity she is providing information about (e.g., on-site expert), and she acts to share her knowledge and improve the quality of the datasets (e.g., as for Tripadvisor users' feedbacks). A paid user performs human computation

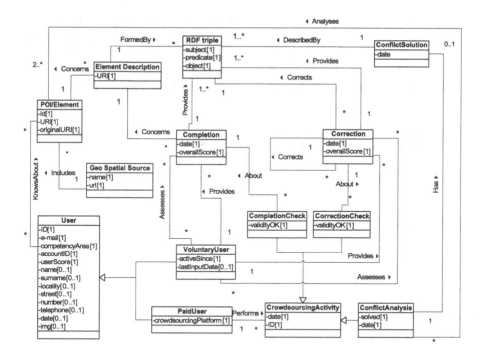

Fig. 1. Data Model

tasks on the collected data, more precisely she verifies the consistency of information uploaded by the voluntary users. The human computation tasks can be performed through a game with a purpose (GWAP) engagement and rewarding model [1] or a crowdsourcing platform where the user is rewarded monetarily.

4.2   Description of the Data Model

The data model of the framework is shown in Fig. 1. It describes the data requirements to process the users' submissions and evaluations. A `User` is specialized as `VoluntaryUser` and `PaidUser`. Both have a *CompetencyArea* that allows to establish competency about POIs. The competency can also be declared directly by a user (*KnowsAbout* association). A `POI/Element` has a *URI* and represents a POI or an Element that has received some feedback. A `POI/Element Description` is the description of a POI/Element according to a given source. It maintains the *originalURI* in the data source and is formed by the set of RDF triples describing it in the source. A `VoluntaryUser` provides a `Completion` or a `Correction` as RDF triple to complete/correct a POI Description. A `Correction` can also be introduced to correct another `Correction` considered incorrect by a peer user. The latter has an important role in evaluating any update or change as positive or negative, (i.e., a `Completion` or a `Correction`) provided by another user, through the *Assesses* associations. These evaluations are used to calculate an overall evaluation of the change and of the voluntary users, as explained in

Section 6. A change is also analyzed by a `PaidUser` who expressed its validity
or negates it by performing a `CompletionAnalysis` or a `CorrectionAnalysis`.
A `ConflictAnalysis` is performed by a `PaidUser` and concerns a conflict that
cannot be solved automatically among the descriptions of a given POI/Element.
The result of this analysis can provide a `ConflictSolution` in terms of a set of
RDF triples.

5   Estimating the Quality of the User Contributions

As user' contributions are central in the proposed approach, both users and
their modifications have to be evaluated to filter spammers and biased corrections thus improving their data quality. First of all, we evaluate each contributor
and her changes with appropriate *scores*. Secondly, we propose a simple measure of users' agreement to estimate the overall quality of the output data. It
worths mentioning that *quantitative* metrics based on *objective measurement*
(e.g., Single Scoring Algorithm, etc.) and *qualitative* metrics based on *subjective
measurement* are essential to the quality control of geo-spatial data. The optimal
solution is to combine both assessments and make any measurement as a multi-
level effort. A plan for monitoring data quality must integrate both technology
and human experience.

5.1   Scoring of Activities and Users

A user's score is stored in the *userScore* attribute of the `User` class (see Fig. 1).
The score calculation is based on: (i) the history of activities performed by
the user and (ii) the history of activities other users performed on these user's
changes. The user's score is used to evaluate her trustworthiness or reputation
and is consequently considered also for evaluating the changes she proposes. An
activity provides a positive or negative indication about a change, as shown in
Table 1. A weight is associated for each considered activity based on its relative
importance in the evaluation process. The default weights listed in the table
reflect the subjective measures we have assigned to each activity based on some
preliminary experimentation. The score of a user U_j is evaluated by adapting
a formula proposed for information retrieval queries with positive and negative
feedback [17].

$$userScore_{U_j} = \alpha_U * \frac{POS_j}{n_{pos_j}} - \beta_U * \frac{NEG_j}{n_{neg_j}} \in [-2, +2] \tag{1}$$

where POS_j and NEG_j are weighted sums of performed activities a_i concerning
the user U_j:

$$POS_j = \sum_i count(a_i) * w_{a_i} \tag{2}$$

where $count(a_i)$ is the number of occurrences of a_i of positive type. NEG_j
is defined similarly. The α_U and β_U are coefficients to determine the relative
importance of negative and positive components of the score. $0 \leq \alpha_U, \beta_U \leq 1$

Table 1. User activities considered for scoring

User Activity a_i	Type	Weight w_{a_i} (default)
Correction/Completion validated (by Paid-User)	+	2
Correction/Completion not validated (by Paid-User)	-	0
Correction/Completion with a majority of Neg.assessments (for V-User)	-	1.5
Correction/Completion with a majority of Pos.assessments (for V-User)	+	1.5
Positive assessment received for the user change (by another V-Peer)	+	0.6
Negative assessment received for the user change (by another V-Peer)	-	0.4
Assessment produced (by the V-User)	+	0.1
Correction made on the user change (by another V-Peer)	-	0.5

where:
V-User is a Volunteer who makes the change,
V-Peer is another Volunteer who assesses the change made by the V-User.

and $\alpha_U + \beta_U = 1$. n_{pos_j} and n_{neg_j} are the total number of occurrences of activities of positive, resp. negative, type concerning the user U_j.

A change C_k proposed by the user U_j is evaluated as followed. Firstly, a community score is assigned according to the users' assessments about C_k.

$$communityScore_{C_k} = 4 * (\alpha_C * \frac{POS_k}{n_{pos_k}} - \beta_C * \frac{NEG_k}{n_{neg_k}}) \qquad (3)$$

The community score ranges in $[-2, +2]$. POS_k and NEG_k are defined as for the user score but considering only assessment activities for the change C_k. The coefficients α_C and β_C followed the same constraints defined for α_U and β_U. Secondly, a overall score is defined for C_k, as:

$$overallScore_{C_k} = \alpha_O * communityScore_{C_k} + \beta_C * userScore_{U_j} \qquad (4)$$

The coefficients α_C and β_C define the relative weighting of the scores of C_k and U_j. Moreover, they follow the same constraints as in the previous definitions.

5.2 Agreement Measure

Furthermore, we propose a measure for users' agreement as an estimator of the overall quality of changes. This measure is based on evaluating the coherence of the corrections submitted and validated for a given RDF triple in a given time interval. This agreement score could be adopted between a volunteer user and his peer or between a volunteer and a paid user. We consider a subset $\{D_{i1}, .., D_{in}\}$ of the POI descriptions receiving corrections in a given time interval $[t_1, t_2]$. According to the data model presented in Sect. 4.2, a correction specifies an RDF triple in order to correct another RDF triple associated with the description. For each description D_j in $\{D_{i1}, .., D_{in}\}$, we consider every triple r_{jk} associated with D_j, produced in the interval $[t_1, t_2]$ that has received at least one correction. An agglomerative hierarchical clustering procedure is applied to the set of RDF triple $corr(r_{jk})$ that corrects r_{jk} in order to get one or more clusters C_{jl}. Therefore, each cluster is formed by corrections that are considered coherent for the same triple. As similarity measures are used in the clustering procedure, we rely on standard metrics provided by the SILK link discovery tool[2] also discussed in. Specific standard metrics have to be used for data when we dealt with the geographic positions. The agreement on corrections on $\{D_{i1}, .., D_{in}\}$ is defined as:

$$corrAgreement_{[t_1,t_2]}(\{D_{i1}, .., D_{in}\}) = \frac{|\{r_{jk}\}|}{|\{Cj_l\}|} \qquad (5)$$

Ideally, this coefficient is 1 when all the corrections concerning each triple r_k are coherent. In this case, for each r_k, its corrections are recognized as similar and all of them are grouped into the same cluster. On the contrary, values of $corrAgreement_{[\cdot]}(\cdot)$ that are less than 1 indicate a higher number of clusters, which means a lower coherence between corrections. This may denote the presence of malicious and/or wrong corrections among voluntary users for the same POI.

6   Evaluation Perspectives

In this section, we discuss some evaluation perspectives we are following in order to: i) assess the ability of our approach to give meaningful results for the end user; ii) verify the usability for both contributors and end users in such system. Unfortunately, as far as we know, no test sets are available for the collections of user's feedbacks in multi-provider geo-spatial data domain so most of the evaluations will be performed after the implementation of a prototype.

- Evaluation of the offered functionalities compared to other tools for quality assurance of open geo-spatial data sets. Specifically, we distinguish between tools that rely completely on users (e.g., OpenStreetBug[3] and Skobbler[4]. And those with error detection capabilities (e.g., KeepRight[5]). Our framework offers more advanced management and evaluation metrics of user feedbacks w.r.t. these tools and it could exploit the output of the automatic tools in order to discover inconsistencies to be submitted as corrections for users.
- Evaluation of completeness and accuracy of the produced data. Output from a set of contributors who perform activities as volunteers and paid ones are collected. Then, two possible experimentations can be performed: (i) comparison of the results, ranked according to the scoring metrics (Sect. 5), with the content of the original reliable data sets. The comparison is performed as per a set of standard spatial data quality parameters as listed in [6]; (ii) considering a limited portion of territory, a group of users that are experts about this territory can assess according to the framework some selected POIs. The feedbacks are ranked according to the scoring metrics and the result is compared with a manually produced ranking.

---

[2] http://wifo5-03.informatik.uni-mannheim.de/bizer/silk/
[3] http://openstreetbugs.schokokeks.org/
[4] http://www.skobbler.com/
[5] http://keepright.at/

- Evaluation of the usability concerning the different roles of users and based on the system workflow of users activities and interface.
- Evaluation of the data coherence. The purpose is to test the robustness of the metrics described in Sect. 5 for such type of sabotage. We simulate some malicious users (noisy or spammers) by performing some activities (i.e., inserting wrong contributions) to damage the data set.

7 Conclusions and Future Work

Improving the data quality of large data sets by the public GIS participation is challenging but essential for maintaining up-to-date geo-spatial data sources. In this paper, we described a framework for managing and providing a collection of updated data published by linked open data sources. The collection is built by paid and volunteered contributions to resolve conflicts for each POI or update/improve its description. A scoring mechanism has been introduced for evaluating both users and their changes. With such kind of evaluation, as mentioned in Sections 4 and 5, we had considered some critical implications of crowdsourcing, such as the reliability of contributors after ranking them based on their scores. In future work, we will extend the model to include the timeliness of the contributions. Our framework will be finalized with the definition of an ontology for the published data. We are adopting for this task the methodology proposed by the authors of GeoLinkedData in [18] that focuses in particular on vocabularies reuse. Other planned work includes continuing the implementation of the framework as well as performing some quantitative evaluations for the different use cases as discussed in Section 6.

References

1. von Ahn, L.: Games with a purpose. IEEE Computer Magazine 39(6), 92–94 (2006)
2. Ballatore, A., Wislon, D.C., Bertolotto, M.: A survey of volunteered open geoknowledge bases in the semantic web. In: Pasi, G., Bordogna, G., Jain, L.C. (eds.) Quality Issues in the Management of Web Information, vol. 50, pp. 93–120. Springer, Heidelberg (1977)
3. Becker, C., Bizer, C.: Dbpedia mobile: A location-enabled linked data browser. In: Bizer, C., Heath, T., Idehen, K., Berners-Lee, T. (eds.) LDOW. CEUR Workshop Proceedings, vol. 369. CEUR-WS.org (2008)
4. Bianchini, D., De Antonellis, V., Melchiori, M.: A Linked Data Perspective for Effective Exploration of Web APIs Repositories. In: Daniel, F., Dolog, P., Li, Q. (eds.) ICWE 2013. LNCS, vol. 7977, pp. 506–509. Springer, Heidelberg (2013)
5. Celino, I., Contessa, S., Corubolo, M., Dell'Aglio, D., Valle, E.D., Fumeo, S., Krüger, T., Krüger, T.: Urbanmatch - linking and improving smart cities data. In: LDOW (2012)
6. Girres, J.-F., Touya, G.: Quality Assessment of the French OpenStreetMap Dataset. Transactions in GIS 14(4), 435–459 (2010)
7. Goodchild, M.F., Li, L.: Assuring the quality of volunteered geographic information. Spatial Statistics 1(0), 110–120 (2012)

8. Heath, T., Bizer, C.: Linked Data: Evolving the Web into a Global Data Space. In: Synthesis Lectures on the Semantic Web. Morgan & Claypool Publishers (2011)

9. Jang, S.-G., Kim, T.J.: Modeling an interoperable multimodal travel guide system using the iso 19100 series of international standards. In: Proceedings of the 14th Annual ACM International Symposium on Advances in Geographic Information Systems, GIS 2006, pp. 115–122. ACM, New York (2006)

10. Karam, R., Favetta, F., Laurini, R., Chamoun, R.K.: Uncertain geoinformation representation and reasoning: A use case in lbs integration. In: Proceedings of the 2010 Workshops on Database and Expert Systems Applications, DEXA 2010, pp. 313–317. IEEE Computer Society, Washington, DC (2010)

11. Karam, R., Melchiori, M.: Improving geo-spatial linked data with the wisdom of the crowds. In: Proceedings of the Joint EDBT/ICDT 2013 Workshops, EDBT 2013, pp. 68–74. ACM, New York (2013)

12. Laurini, R.: Pre-consensus ontologies and urban databases. In: Teller, J., Lee, J.R., Roussey, C. (eds.) Ontologies for Urban Development, vol. 61, pp. 27–36. Springer, Heidelberg (2007)

13. Lee, C.-Y., Soo, V.-W.: The conflict detection and resolution in knowledge merging for image annotation. Information Processing & Management 42(4), 1030–1055 (2006)

14. Martins, B.: A supervised machine learning approach for duplicate detection over gazetteer records. In: Claramunt, C., Levashkin, S., Bertolotto, M. (eds.) GeoS 2011. LNCS, vol. 6631, pp. 34–51. Springer, Heidelberg (2011)

15. Mashhadi, A.J., Capra, L.: Quality control for real-time ubiquitous crowdsourcing. In: Proceedings of the 2nd International Workshop on Ubiquitous Crowdsouring, UbiCrowd 2011, pp. 5–8. ACM, New York (2011)

16. Nowak, S., Rüger, S.: How reliable are annotations via crowdsourcing: a study about inter-annotator agreement for multi-label image annotation. In: Proceedings of the International Conference on Multimedia Information Retrieval, MIR 2010, pp. 557–566. ACM, New York (2010)

17. Rocchio, J.J.: The SMART Retrieval System - Experiments in Automatic Document Processing. In: Relevance Feedback in Information Retrieval, Prentice Hall, Englewood (1971)

18. Vilches-Blázquez, L.M., Villazón-Terrazas, B., Saquicela, V., de León, A., Corcho, O., Gómez-Pérez, A.: Geolinked data and inspire through an application case. In: Proceedings of the 18th SIGSPATIAL International Conference on Advances in Geographic Information Systems, GIS 2010, pp. 446–449. ACM, New York (2010)

Supporting Disaster Management with Real-Time-CPAR Platform

Mohamed Bakillah[1,2] and Steve H.L. Liang[2]

[1] Institute of GIScience, Heidelberg University, Heidelberg, Germany
[2] Department of Geomatics Engineering, University of Calgary, Alberta, Canada

Abstract. Disaster management requires that various geospatial data producers and users collaborate in an ad hoc manner, despite their different backgrounds and contexts. While semantic interoperability is meant to support meaningful sharing of geospatial data, semantic interoperability approaches that were designed for static and closed environments, or that do not address the particularities of geospatial data, are not suitable for supporting disaster management. In this paper, we present the Real-Time-CPAR prototype for enabling real time semantic interoperability in ad hoc network of geospatial databases that can answer the needs of disaster management. The prototype comprises four main services for discovering coalitions of geospatial databases; semantic enrichment; semantic reconciliation of heterogeneous databases and propagation of geospatial queries. We demonstrate how this tool can contribute to disaster management.

Keywords: Ad hoc networks, Disaster management, Real time systems, Semantic interoperability.

1 Introduction

When populated regions are affected by natural of human disasters, emergency authorities need real time information about the material damages, available resources and their geographical location (Goodchild 2006). An interoperable platform for accessing heterogeneous data could support this need. Semantic interoperability is a major challenge in GIScience and disaster management (Cutter 2003). Semantic interoperability is the knowledge-level interoperability that provides databases with the ability to resolve semantic heterogeneities arising from differences in the meaning of concepts (Park and Ram 2004). Several semantic interoperability frameworks for the geospatial domain have been proposed (Bishr 1998; Kuhn 2003; Lutz et al. 2003; Bian and Hu 2007; Staub et al. 2008). In ad hoc networks, the databases that have to interoperate are not known in advance. Semantic interoperability approaches that were dedicated to a limited number of sources are not appropriate for distributed environments such as ad hoc networks, due to their thigh coupling and their lack of flexibility (Tsou and Buttenfield 2002). Also, existing semantic interoperability frameworks that are designed for dynamic environment such as peer-to-peer networks are based on poor knowledge representations that are not complex enough to deal with geospatial concepts. Frameworks for interoperability in the geospatial domain do not

J. Parsons and D. Chiu (Eds.): ER Workshops 2013, LNCS 8697, pp. 107–116, 2014.

integrate the capacities that are required to deal with the dynamicity of networks, such as performing semantic matching at run-time, or using different interoperability strategies when requirements are changing. This paper presents the Real Time CPAR prototype for real time semantic interoperability in ad hoc networks or geospatial databases. Real Time CPAR addresses both requirements of the geospatial domain and of dynamic, ad hoc networks. This prototype's major components are the following: a service for the discovering and formation of coalitions of geospatial databases to support geocollaboration; a service for semantic enrichment; a service for automating the semantic reconciliation process that is suitable for geospatial concepts, and a service for propagating geospatial queries to relevant nodes of the network. We demonstrate that the prototype is useful for supporting disaster management tasks.

2   Moving from Semantic Interoperability to Real Time Semantic Interoperability in Ad Hoc Networks of Geospatial Databases

While there are many semantic interoperability approaches, new problems arise when we consider ad hoc networks of geospatial databases, in opposition to "traditional" semantic interoperability. Geospatial databases that were developed by different communities are affected by semantic heterogeneities. We must solve heterogeneities caused by thematic differences, but also by different representations of the spatial and temporal features of concepts. Resolving semantic heterogeneities requires addressing two complementary issues: representing semantics of geospatial data, and discovering semantic relationships between geospatial concepts. Ontologies are used to represent semantics of data. Ontologies are composed of concepts, relations, properties and axioms that represent a domain of interest (Agarwal 2005). Fonseca et al. (2002) have proposed the ontology-driven geographic information system (ODGIS) to resolve heterogeneity of geographic data. Ontologies are components that describe the view of a given geospatial information community (GIC). By browsing through ontologies, the users access information available in the embedded knowledge of the system. This approach is suitable for a limited number of sources only. Also, ontologies alone are not the complete solution, since they are themselves semantically heterogeneous and their degree of semantic explicitness is varying. In the ontology development process, some knowledge is left implicit. For instance, geospatial concepts are often described by definitions (e.g., "floodplain is a meadow that is adjacent to a river"), which cannot be easily and straightforwardly exploited to automatically compare concepts, since they are not formalized. Other implicit knowledge about geospatial concepts include the context of the concept (e.g., river in the context of flooding or dryness), and dependencies between features of concepts (e.g., the geometrical representation of a river is related to its width). Leaving knowledge implicit makes differences in meaning undetectable. A comprehensive representation of semantics is required.

Discovering semantic relationships among geospatial concepts is the goal of semantic mapping. Many semantic mapping frameworks aim at discovering quantitative relationships (a semantic similarity value), and few aim at discovering qualitative relationships (equivalence, inclusion, overlap, etc.). Some semantic similarity frameworks are dedicated to compare geospatial concepts (see Schwering 2008). Nevertheless, these models do not consider semantics of spatial and temporal features in a separated manner. For example, the G-Match model (Hess et al. 2007) considers that two geospatial concepts with different geometric primitives (e.g., point vs. line) are geometrically different and two geospatial concepts having the same geometric primitive are geometrically equivalent. However, the same geometrical primitive (e.g. surface, for the concept house) may represent two different parts of the same object (e.g., roof and foundation). In the broader domain of semantic matching, existing approaches often integrate several matching techniques, which were classified by Euzenat and Shvaiko (2007). Among those approaches, none use the dependencies between the features of a concept as valuable structure to discover semantic mappings. In addition, the resolution of semantic heterogeneities is not the only issue that must be addressed to ensure real time semantic interoperability in dynamic and open environments. Because of the large number of sources, we cannot assume that users know which sources are relevant to their needs. Therefore, a solution to structure the network (at the semantic level) into groups of databases is needed. Such a semantic structure would support discovery of relevant sources, and propagation of users' queries to these sources. While there exist semantic grouping approaches for networks (e.g., Montanelli and Castano 2008), these approaches were developed for generic peer-to-peer systems and are not adapted to geospatial domain. In addition, we need to consider that the groups that are formed in the network are dynamic; as a result, the semantic interoperability process must constantly adapt to the changes. While some semantic interoperability frameworks dedicated to dynamic environments exist (e.g., Keeney et al. 2006), they focus on automatic semantic mapping but do not address the need for adapting the interoperability solution to current changes of the network.

3   Requirements Related to Disaster Management

In comparison to static situations, the tasks related to disaster management impose more constraints on semantic interoperability processes (Goodchild 2006). Table 1 provides some examples of tasks that may take place during the different phases of the disaster management cycle.

We have identified the characteristics that should guide the development of a semantic interoperability approach suitable for disaster management: (1) Organisms that

Table 1. Example of tasks related to disaster management

Disaster management phase	Task example
Response	Coordinate the allocation of rescue personnel; localise logistical support and resources
Recovery	Produce maps of damages to infrastructures
Reconstruction	Monitor land use; Identify building characteristics and occupancy
Preparation	Produce risk maps; Determine potential evacuation plans

must collaborate are not known in advance; no common agreement on knowledge representation can be assumed, and semantic heterogeneity is high between their geospatial databases; (2) Actors of disaster management must be able to form collaborative groups for short-lived needs; (3) Actors of disaster management must obtain fast, up-to-date, but accurate response to their queries; (4) To ensure effective communication, conflicts on the meaning of shared data must be detected and resolved rapidly; (5) Actors of disaster management must access static data (e.g., information on building occupancy, demographic data) and dynamic, operational data (water levels, damage detection, meteorological conditions). In the following, we present the architecture of the Real Time CPAR prototype to address the above requirements.

4   Architecture of the Real Time C-PAR Prototype

An ad hoc network is an open network where nodes (often representing wireless devices, mobiles, geospatial databases, etc.) can move freely, enter or leave the network. The Real Time CPAR (Coalition-Propagation-Augmentation-Reconciliation) prototype's architecture (Fig. 1) comprises the services required to achieve real time semantic interoperability in ad hoc networks of geospatial databases.

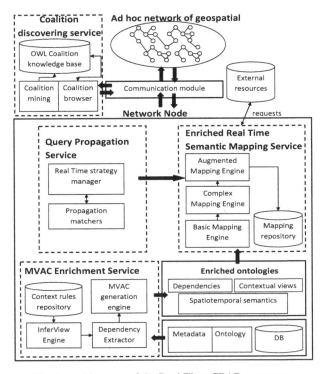

Fig. 1. Architecture of the Real Time CPAR prototype

Each node holds a geospatial database and an OWL ontology, plus the following:

(1) an OWL description of the database's context. The context is defined by (a) the geographical location covered by the entities stored in the database; (b) the time period during which these entities existed; (c) the domain described by the database (road network, demography, etc.); (d) the role of the database (monitor water levels, describe buildings, etc.). The purpose of the context description is to support the discovering and formation of coalitions of geospatial databases that have similar contexts, and the propagation of geospatial queries to the relevant nodes of the network.
(2) a list of queries that the node had previously answered. This list is called the memory. It is useful for propagation of geospatial queries.
A node has access to the four following services:

Geospatial Database Coalition Discovering Service. This service is responsible for the discovery of groups of nodes which users may collaborate toward a common goal. These groups are called *coalitions of geospatial databases*. This service is implemented as an autonomous node in the network which other nodes can request. The discovering of coalitions is enabled by a coalition mining algorithm that uses network analysis techniques to find nodes that may act as central attractor for other nodes. For example, a node may be an attractor node when its database's context is more general than the contexts of several other nodes' databases. This coalition mining algorithm resolves semantic heterogeneity conflicts between contexts. The geospatial database coalition management service also comprises a coalition browser where users can visualize a dynamic hierarchy of existing coalitions in the network. Coalitions support collaboration but also facilitate the discovery of relevant sources. Details on the group discovery approach are in (Bakillah and Liang 2012).

Multi-View Augmented Concept (MVAC) Enrichment Service. This service is responsible for enriching the semantics of the ontologies that describe geospatial databases. This service addresses the problem of poor knowledge representation. It is a fundamental issue for improving semantic interoperability because the more the semantics of data is complete, the more users of different databases can resolve semantic conflicts and avoid misinterpretation of shared data. Existing definitions of concepts are not always sufficient to represent all the semantic richness of geospatial concepts. In addition, semantics may be implicit (not formalized). We have previously proposed a new model for representing concepts, namely, the Multi-View Augmented concept (MVAC). In this concept model, each view represents the definition of the concept under a specific context, and the concept is augmented with the implicit dependencies that can be discovered between its features (properties and relations) with rule mining techniques. An example of such dependency is between the spatial property *altitude* and the thematic property *flooding risk*: Altitude (*land*, *low*)→ *Flooding Risk* (*land*, *high*). The MVAC component takes as input the ontologies and generates ontologies with MVAC concepts through the following steps: (1) extract the possible contexts with pattern detection; (2) extract a view for each context, and (3) augment the concepts with dependencies. The description of the MVAC tool is provided in (Bakillah et al. 2012a).

G-MAP Enriched Real Time Semantic Mapping Service. The semantic mapping service takes as input the MVAC concepts and automatically computes qualitative semantic relations among them (equivalence, inclusion, overlap, disjoint). The semantic mappings depend on the chosen context. This means that a user can select the most appropriate context to its situation and the semantic mapping service uses the definition of the concept valid in that context. The advantage is a context-dependent semantic interoperability solution tailored to user's needs. In addition, the semantic relations are decomposed according to the spatial, temporal and thematic dimensions. The global semantic relation between two concepts is obtained by merging the three dimensions. The other contribution of this semantic mapping approach is its augmented matching feature. The augmented semantic mapping reasoning engine takes as input the semantic mappings computed by the basic semantic mapping reasoning engine and tries to improve it by running a structural matcher that compares dependencies of MVAC concepts. The automatic computation of semantic mappings is ensured by logic inference rules. The reasoning process is based on the verification by the reasoning engine that all conditions stated in a mapping rule for a semantic relation to be true are verified. Details on this semantic mapping approach are provided in (Bakillah and Mostafavi 2010).

Query Propagation Component. This service resolves the problem of determining to which nodes this query should be sent in order to obtain the required data. The result is an oriented graph, where nodes are the selected databases and directed arcs are paths along which the query is routed. The distinction of our approach with respect to other query propagation approaches (e.g., Montanelli and Castano 2008) is that it does not rely on existing semantic mappings between ontologies. Therefore, the propagation graph only determines the minimal number of databases that should be mapped, reducing the cost of the semantic mapping. With the strategy manager, the user can select three different propagation strategies:

(1) The coalition-based strategy uses coalitions to send a query to set of databases, based on a comparison of the query's context with the context of coalitions.

(2) The context-based strategy determines the propagation graph according to context similarity between the query and the databases' contexts; it is intended to be used inside the scope of a single coalition.

(3) The collective memory-based strategy uses the knowledge that users of databases have about queries that were previously answered to forward queries to relevant databases. Queries are forwarded to databases that have successfully processed similar queries in the past.

For each strategy, the strategy manager deploys different matchers for comparing contexts, queries and coalitions. The approach for query propagation is detailed in Bakillah et al. (2012b).

5   Real-Time CPAR Prototype for Disaster Management

The objective of the REAL-TIME CPAR prototype is to search and discover geospatial databases that can form relevant coalitions, improve the semantics of data with the MVAC model, and find the concepts that are relevant to a given geospatial query. The architecture has three main components: the Coalition Discovering and Visualization component, the MVAC Generation and Visualization component, and G-MAP Semantic Mapping component. The data used to demonstrate the approach come from various sources, including the National Topographic Database of Canada (NTDB), the Quebec Topographic Database (BDTQ), data sets on disasters (flooding, earthquakes and tornados) in North America, and the Topographic and Administrative

Database of Quebec (BDTA). We have developed a set of geospatial database's context descriptions, ontologies for databases, and instances, using OWL ontology language, based on specifications of the above data sets. The spatial and temporal descriptors of concepts were defined manually based on textual definitions of concepts. We demonstrate the prototype with a scenario where a user searches for *watercourses that are near a given residential area*, in order to *assess flooding risk in diverse regions of North America in the last decade*. First, the user runs the coalition-discovering component that displays the resulting coalitions in a Coalition Tree. The Coalition Tree allows the user to browse the list of coalitions according to a taxonomic classification based in the chosen features: role, domain, geographical location and temporal validity period. The coalition-discovering component integrates a coalition-mining algorithm based on network analysis. In this example, the coalitions are classified according to the role feature (Figure 2).

Fig. 2. The results of the coalition discovering service

The hierarchy of roles is build by classifying all roles of coalitions according to is-a (subsumption) relation between roles. For instance, the category "*coalitions for disaster management*" includes the category "*coalitions for flooding management*". The coalitions serve as a basis for supporting collaboration, but also for facilitating the search of relevant geospatial databases. Notably, the coalitions partition the network in a way that supports query propagation. The query is composed of a concept and of the context of the query. For example, the following query is about the concept "flooding risk zone," in the geographical location "Canada," during the time period 2010-2011, with "hydrography" as domain and "produce risk map" as a function:

```
<owl:Class rdf:ID="FloodingRiskZone"/>
```

```
<owlx:ObjectProperty owlx:name="InGeographicalLocation">
        <owlx:domain owlx:class="FloodingRiskZone"/>
        <owlx:range owlx:class="Canada"/>
</owlx:ObjectProperty>
<owlx:ObjectProperty owlx:name="TimePeriodBegin">
        <owlx:domain owlx:class="FloodingRiskZone"/>
        <owlx:range owlx:class="2010"/>
</owlx:ObjectProperty>
<owlx:ObjectProperty owlx:name="TimePeriodEnd">
        <owlx:domain owlx:class="FloodingRiskZone"/>
        <owlx:range owlx:class="2011"/>
</owlx:ObjectProperty>
<owlx:ObjectProperty owlx:name="InDomain">
        <owlx:domain owlx:class="FloodingRiskZone"/>
        <owlx:range owlx:class="Hydrography"/>
</owlx:ObjectProperty>
<owlx:ObjectProperty owlx:name="Function">
        <owlx:domain owlx:class="FloodingRiskZone"/>
        <owlx:range owlx:class="ProduceRiskMap"/>
</owlx:ObjectProperty>
```

The propagation graph is displayed as a tree where the databases that were selected are identified. The databases that are closer to the graph's root are considered as more relevant, because their context is semantically closer to the query. For example, the DB20 is a database about hydrological disaster in the Quebec province, while DB6 is the Natural Risk Database for Canada, which also contains data on other types of disasters. The propagation graph is a tree because the query propagation algorithm avoid cycles by removing nodes that have already received the query. When the user has identified the relevant sources of the network as determined by the query propagation service, before he or she submits a query to the databases, the MVAC tool generates MVAC concepts from databases' ontologies of the coalition. The MVAC tool allows to visualise the MVAC representation of the query concept (ex: *watercourse*) and select the relevant view according to context, for example, "*flooded*", which is a situational context (upper part of Figure 3). It also displays the dependencies that augment the concept, for example function(watercourse, navigable)→ is-a(watercourse, sea route) and water level(watercourse, high)→ runoff(watercourse, continuous). The G-MAP produces mappings according to the view selected by the user, making this matching tool more flexible. The G-MAP tool shows the concepts that were matched with the query concept watercourse as a tree were nodes are databases and sub-nodes are matched concepts (bottom left of Figure 3). When a user selects a matched concept, the G-MAP tool displays the thematic, spatial, and temporal components of the mappings, as well as the spatiotemporal conflicts that were detected during the mapping process. For instance, while the concept *stream* matches the concept *watercourse*, *stream* may not be a relevant concept for the user, considering that the spatial extent of *stream* represents the bed of the stream, while the spatial extent of the query concept *watercourse* represents the flooded area. The geometries of watercourses and streams objects stored in respective geospatial databases are therefore not comparable. This is a conflict that existing semantic mapping tools do not explicitly detect but that is fundamental for the correct interpretation of shared geospatial data. Additionally, the G-MAP tool displays the elements of MVAC that were matched with the augmented mapping functionality (augmentation impact), for example, the match between sea route and shipping lane.

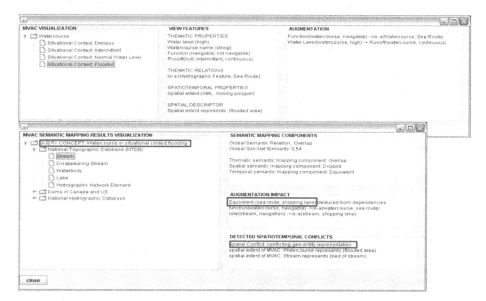

Fig. 3. The semantic enrichment and real time semantic mapping services

5   Conclusion

In this paper, it was explained that real time semantic interoperability is a critical issue for disaster management. A prototype for a real time semantic interoperability in ad hoc networks of geospatial databases was proposed. This prototype, called Real Time CPAR, integrates the services required to address both constraints posed by geospatial semantics and constraints posed by dynamic, decentralized environments such as ad hoc networks. The prototype includes services for the formation of coalitions of geospatial databases, semantic enrichment service, an augmented real time semantic mapping process that consider space, time and theme as distinctive components, and a multi-strategy real time query propagation approach. The combination of these four services in the prototype ensures meaningful sharing of geospatial data in real time. The prototype demonstrates the ability to reduce risks of misinterpretation of shared data in a disaster management situation where reliability of information and respect of time constraints are crucial.

References

1. Agarwal, P.: Ontological Considerations in GIScience. Int. Journal of Geographical Information Science 19(5), 501–536 (2005)
2. Bakillah, M., Mostafavi, M.A., Brodeur, J.: Multi-View Augmented Concept in Support of Geospatial Data Retrieval. Journal of Earth Science and Engineering 1, 57–70 (2012a)
3. Bakillah, M., Mostafavi, M.A., Liang, S.H.L.: Real Time Query Propagation in Ad Hoc Networks of Geospatial Databases wit Lightweight Coordination Calculus. Journal of Networks and Computer Applications (2012b) (to appear)
4. Bakillah, M., Liang, S.H.L.: Discovering Sensor Services with Social Network Analysis and Expanded SQWRL Querying. In: Di Martino, S., Peron, A., Tezuka, T. (eds.) W2GIS 2012. LNCS, vol. 7236, pp. 221–238. Springer, Heidelberg (2012)
5. Bakillah, M., Mostafavi, M.A.: G-Map Semantic Mapping Approach to Improve Semantic Interoperability of Distributed Geospatial Web Services. In: Trujillo, J., et al. (eds.) ER 2010. LNCS, vol. 6413, pp. 12–22. Springer, Heidelberg (2010)
6. Bian, L., Hu, S.: Identifying Components for Interoperable Process Models using Concept Lattice and Semantic Reference System. Int. Journal of Geographical Information Science 21(9), 1009–1032 (2007)
7. Bishr, Y.: Overcoming the Semantic and other Barriers to GIS Interoperability. Int. Journal of Geographical Information Science 12(4), 299–314 (1998)
8. Cutter, S.L.: GI Science, Disasters, and Emergency Management. Transactions in GIS 7(4), 439–445 (2003)
9. Euzenat, J., Shvaiko, P.: Ontology Matching. Springer, Heidelberg (2007)
10. Fonseca, F.T., Egenhofer, M.J., Agouris, P., Câmara, G.: Using Ontologies for Integrated Geographic Information Systems. Transactions in GIS 6(3), 231–257 (2002)
11. Goodchild, M.F.: GIS and Disasters: Planning for Catastrophe. Computers, Environment and Urban Systems 30(3), 227–229 (2006)
12. Keeney, J., Lewis, D., O'Sullivan, D., Roelens, A., Wade, V., Boran, A., Richardson, R.: Runtime Semantic Interoperability for Gathering Ontology-based Network Context. In: 10th IEEE/IFIP Network Operations and Management Symposium, pp. 56–65 (2006)
13. Khambatti, M., Ryu, K.D., Dasgupta, P.: Peer-to-peer Communities: Formation and Discovery. In: 14th IASTED Conference on Parallel and Distributed Computing Systems (PDCS), Cambridge, Massachusetts, pp. 166–173 (2002)
14. Kuhn, W.: Semantic Reference System. Int. Journal of Geographical Information Science 17(5), 405–409 (2003)
15. Lutz, M., Riedemann, C., Probst, F.: A Classification Framework for Approaches to Achieving Semantic Interoperability between GI Web Services. In: Kuhn, W., Worboys, M.F., Timpf, S. (eds.) COSIT 2003. LNCS, vol. 2825, pp. 186–203. Springer, Heidelberg (2003)
16. Montanelli, S., Castano, S.: Semantically Routing Queries in Peer-based System: the H-LINK Approach. The Knowledge Engineering Review 23, 51–72 (2008)
17. Park, J., Ram, S.: Information Systems Interoperability: What Lies Beneath? ACM Transactions on Information Systems 22(4), 595–632 (2004)
18. Schwering, A.: Approaches to Semantic Similarity Measurement for Geo-Spatial Data: A Survey. Transactions in GIS 12(1), 5–29 (2008)
19. Staub, P., Gnägi, H.R., Morf, A.: Semantic Interoperability through the Definition of Conceptual Model Transformations. Transactions in GIS 12(2), 193–207 (2008)
20. Tsou, M.-H., Buttenfield, B.P.: A Dynamic Architecture for Distributing Geographic Information Services. Transactions in GIS 6(4), 355–381 (2002)

A Semantic Web Approach for Geodata Discovery

Helbert Arenas, Benjamin Harbelot, and Christophe Cruz

Laboratoire Le2i, UMR-6302 CNRS,Departement Informatique,
University of Burgundy, 7 Boulevard Docteur Petitjean, 21078 Dijon, France
{helbert.arenas,benjamin.harbelot}@checksem.fr,
christophe.cruz@u-bourgogne.fr
http://checksem.u-bourgogne.fr/www/

Abstract. Currently, vast amounts of geospatial information are offered through OGC's services. However this information has limited formal semantics. The most common method to search for a dataset consists in matching keywords to metadata elements. By adding semantics to available descriptions we could use modern inference and reasoning mechanisms currently available in the Semantic Web. In this paper we present a novel architecture currently in development in which we use state of the art triplestores as the backend of a CSW service. In our approach, each metadata record is considered an instance of a given class in a domain ontology. Our architecture also adds a spatial dataset of features with toponym values. These additions allow us to provide advance searches based on 1) Instance to class matching, 2) Class to class subsuming relationships, 3) Spatial relationships resulting from comparing the bounding box of a metadata record with our toponym spatial dataset.

Keywords: Semantic Web,ontologies, geodata discovery, catalogues, OGC services.

1 Introduction

Currently there is a vast amount of spatial information available on the web though services such as WFS, WMS or SOS to mention some. This information allows scientists to perform complex analysis. Goodwin (2005) used the term *smart queries* to describe analysis that combine heterogeneous datasources in order to solve complex problems [1]. Our field of interest is the use of heterogeneous datasources to perform spatio-temporal *smart queries* using Semantic Web tools. In previous work [2] we presented our research on spatio-temporal operators, using local data repositories. The next logical step in the evolution of our work is to integrate it to the SDI (Spatial Data Infrastracture). The term SDI was first introduced by the U.S. National Research Council in 1993. It refers to a set of technologies, policies and agreements designed to allow the sharing of spatial information and resources between institutions [3]. The Spatial Data Infrastructure has a service oriented architecture. In such infrastructure, functionalities such as storage and data search are carried out through Web services.

J. Parsons and D. Chiu (Eds.): ER Workshops 2013, LNCS 8697, pp. 117–126, 2014.
© Springer International Publishing Switzerland 2014

The typical work flow involves: 1) The discovery of a data source, 2) The download of relevant geo spatial data, 3) The use of appropriate analytical methods and 4) The visualization of the results on a suitable map.

In order to integrate our work with the SDI we need to find and retrieve pertinent online datasets. OGC has introduced a standard for catalogue services called CSW. A server implementing this standard has access to a metadata repository. It allows the search of spatial data or web services using open criteria (i.e. free text as a search in a search engine) or using more specific criteria (title, coordinate system, data type, etc.). Servers implementing CSW are also able to: synchronize their content with other catalogues, add, modify or delete metadata records. They are also able to harvest metadata from other OGC services [4]. Like other OGC standards CSW implements *OWS Common*, which describes basic features shared by all of them. These common elements are basic parameters and data structures used in the request or response from web service operations. The standardization proposed through OWS Common serves as support for the interoperability of OGC web services [5].

Our broad goal is to implement *smart queries* using data repositories available in the SDI. The use of the different services involved in a SDI raise several semantic challenges. Most semantic problems arise due to the lack of significant content descriptions. As a consequence the resulting ambiguities are then propagated throughout the process of data [6]. The discovery of datasets is currently done though OGC CSW. However the search of records is done using a string matching process, not considering the semantics of the metadata information [7]. Greatly improved results would be obtained if catalogue services are able to use the hierarchical relationships between elements and concepts achieving in this way semantic interoperability [8]. Fortunately, nowadays there are tools in the field of semantic web, like Sesame, Jena, SPARQL/GeoSPARQL and diverse triplestores, that offer storage, query and retrieval capabilities of information with semantic annotations. In this paper we present our work on the storage and retrieval of metadata records using a triplestore. We developed a proof of concept CSW service that is able to retrieve metadata records by mapping a subset of CQL operators to SPARQL/GeoSPARQL. In section 2 we describe other works in this field. In section 3 we describe our implementation. Finally we present our conclusions and future work in section 4.

2   Related Research

Catalogues are a core component of the Spatial Data Infrastructure. The most used catalogue specification is the one proposed by the OGC: CSW. A service implementing CSW handles descriptions of datasets and services, formatted as ISO 19115:2003. The descriptions include information regarding the extent, quality, spatial and temporal characteristics as well as the distribution rights of a given dataset. A CSW service handles its requests and responses using the HTTP protocol using the GET and POST method [8].

Previous researchers have identified limitations on traditional CSW services. The string matching process as the only query option is mentioned in [9] [7] and [8]. In these works authors explore options to add semantic capabilities to CSW overcoming this limitation.

In [8] the author describes the CSW limitations by evaluating GeoNetwork, a popular open source CSW implementation. The author identifies three ways in which it is possible to add semantic annotations to the CSW: 1) By associating keywords to concepts using the *getCapabilities* response. 2) By adding a link in the GeoNetwork client interface to a ontology browser. In this way the user instead of using keywords, would be able to utilize the hierarchical structure to identify the topic that best suits her interest. 3) Adding ontologies as an extension package using ebRIM. The author concludes that the third option is the most suitable.

Yue et al. (2006) extend the ebRIM CSW specification by: 1) adding new classes based on existing ebRIM classes; and 2) adding Slots to existing classes, thus creating new attributes. As a result they are able to store richer metadata records in the catalogue. The authors identified two possible options to implement a search functionality: 1) create an external component without further modification of the CSW schemas; 2) modify the CSW adding semantic functionalities to the existing CSW schemas. In this research they choose for the first option [9]. Yue et al. (2011) extends this work, adding further development in the field of geoservices [7].

A different approach is used by [10]. In this research the goal is to provide access to data stored in CSW as Linked Data. In order to achieve this goal the authors developed CSW2LD, a middle layer on top of a conventional CSW based server. It allows the server to mimic other Linked Data sources and publish metadata records. CSW2LD wraps the following CSW requests: *GetCapabilities*, *GetRecords* and *GetRecordById*.

A very interesting work in progress is described in [11]. This is a website describing a proposal by a team from the GeoNetwork developer community. The authors intend to perform a major change in GeoNetwork, allowing it to store metadata as RDF facts stored in a RDF repository. They intent to use SPARQL/GeoSPARQL to retrieve data. The website describe technical characteristics of GeoNetwork and mentions fields that require work in order to implement the project. Currently the constraints that filter the search are encoded using an OGC standard based on CQL [12][13]. As indicated in [11] a CSW implementation that uses a triplestore needs to map the constraints to SPARQL/GeoSPARQL which are current W3C recommendations [14][15]. However there is scarce research on this topic. By the time we wrote this paper, there was no further development in this project and the website was last updated by the end of October of 2012.

In the next section we describe how we deal with some of the challenges already identified by previous researchers.

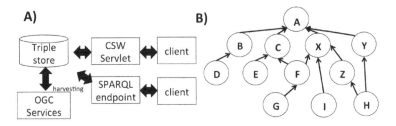

Fig. 1. A)Proposed CSW architecture (The triple store works as a metadata reposi-tory). B)Dummy domain class ontology.

3   Implementation

The complete implementation of the CSW standard is not a trivial task. By implementing the whole standard, a CSW would be able to manage a wide range of elements for metadata records and respond to the queries using multiple formats. However the number of queryable elements that must be implemented in a service of this nature is small. A CSW must implement query operations to at least the 15 classic Dublin Core metadata terms. It should also be able to respond to queries using the *csw:SummaryRecord* format [16].

In order to provide semantic capabilities to catalogue, we decided to de-velop a proof of concept CSW implementation using only the minimum ele-ments and operations. Figure 1A depicts the architecture we are using. We use a Parliament triplestore as our data repository connected to a Java servlet. Our servlet transforms 1) requests from clients into queries processable by the triplestore, and 2) the triplestore response into a xml document that follows the *csw:SummaryRecord* format.

Our goal is to implement a CSW able to:1) Retrieve records based on an ontology class taxonomy; and 2) Retrieve records based on spatial relationships with elements with toponym values (For instance records located *within* the element known as "Burgundy").

In order to take advantage of the spatial capabilities of our triplestore we must use *geo:SpatialObject* as a superclass and *geo:Feature* as its immediate sub-class. Then we are able to use spatial operators in all the instances of the class *geo:Feature* and its subclasses [15]. In our implementation we create two main subclasses of *geo:Feature*: *MetadataRecord* and *ToponymUnit*. All the required Dublin core elements are associated with the class *MetadataRecord*. Additional elements are linked to *dc:Publisher* and *dc:Description*. The class *ToponymU-nit* represents spatial elements with toponymic values in our ontology. Both *ToponymUnit* and *MetadataRecord* implement the property *geo:hasGeometry* which links to a geometry element, which itself can be linked to a WKT spatial representation (*sf:wktliteral*) with the property *geo:asWKT*. Figure 2 depicts the created classes, properties and relationships.

Knowledge stored in domain ontologies can be used by creating subclasses of *MetadataRecord*. The knowledge represented in the relationships between the

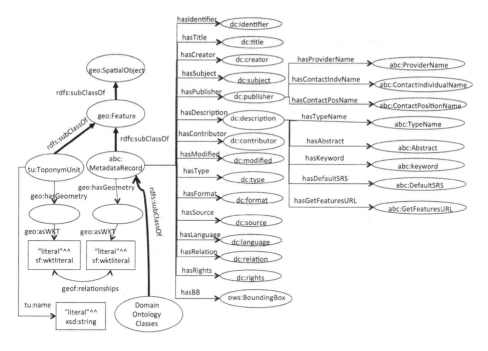

Fig. 2. Proposed ontology and relationship with external domain ontologies

classes can easily be added to the queries. We propose to map each metadata record as an instance of a given domain ontology class. To achieve this goal, we plan to harvest keywords from existing metadata elements, such as *keywords*, *abstract*, *title*, etc, and use this information to find the most suitable class based on specifications of the domain ontology. We propose to use a method based on research conducted by Werner et al. (2012) [17]. This part of the system is still in development. Figure 1B depicts a dummy ontology with a taxonomy of classes. Using the dummy ontology, if the user requests for metadata records of class *C*, due to the class relationship, the system would also return instances of classes *E*, *F*, and *G*.

The metadata records in our research were created by harvesting a set WFS services. We use a custom made tool, developed with Java. Our tool submits a *GetCapabilities* request to a WFS, and parses the response in order to identify relevant elements. Currently we harvest the following elements: a) provider Name, b) contact individual name, c) contact position name, d) type Name, e) abstract, f) keywords, g) default spatial representation system, h) the URL of the *GetFeatures* request, and i) the bounding box of the dataset. Being this a proof of concept application we considered these to be enough elements.

To feed our ontology with toponymic elements we are importing datasets available in vector format. We want to use global datasets of administrative units (Countries, provinces, states, etc.). Brigham et al.(2011) evaluated three global datasets: 1) GAUL, developed by FAO and the European Commision,

2) GADM, developed by the University of California, Berkeley and the International Rice Research Institute, and 3) UNSALB, developed by the United Nations Geographic Information Group. They concluded that GAUL showed better completeness and accuracy[18]. We intended to use the GAUL dataset for evaluation purposes. However, by the time of writing this paper, our request was still on process. In the meantime we are using an alternative provided by Esri and DeLorme Publishing Company, Inc. under a Creative Commons Attribution-Noncommercial-Share Alike 3.0 United States License. This dataset depicts the subnational and national boundaries updated with 2011 information [19]. We plan to update our toponym dataset as soon as a better dataset is available.

The most used CSW request is *GetRecords*. A typical request includes a set of pairs of the form (*parameter=value*). The CSW server filters out results that do not meet the criteria specified in the parameter *constraint*. These constraints are encoded using OGC compliant syntax based on CQL.

In our implementation we submit *GetRecords* requests. Our server application parses the request and extracts the value for the *constraint*. We encode our constraint using a subset of the OGC specification, to which we have added elements to describe *instanceOf* relationships. The user can link multiple constraints using the operator AND. We also allow the use of an optional boolean element NOT, to indicate that elements matching certain criteria, should be removed from query results. Our servlet reads the constraint and maps it to suitable SPARQL/GeoSPARQL syntax. The mapping is done using a Java application developed by us. Currently our application supports the following predicates:

- *PropertyIsInstanceOf* To constrain the class membership. This is a custom property, not included in the OGC specification.
- *PropertyIsEqualTo* To compare queryable metadata elements to text strings.
- *PropertyIsLike* To make partial comparisons between queryable metadata elements and text strings.
- *Within* To specify that the bounding box of the metadata record must be inside a given toponym unit.
- *Intersect* The bounding box of the metadata record should intersect the geometry of the toponym unit.
- *DWithin* To define a buffer zone around a given toponym unit and compare it with the bounding box of a metadata record.

Currently, we are using Parliament as our triplestore. We decided to use Parliament due to its good performace, supported capabilities and its open source nature. Parliament support for GeoSPARQL includes multiple functions and operators allowing users to perform complex spatial queries. Once installed it allows users to access it though an HTTP SPARQL endpoint [20] [21]. Our implementation interacts with Parliament using Java with Jena libraries.

Next we show examples of constraints.The original constraints follow the OGC XML filter specification, however they are not fully compliant because of our add ons (InstanceOf, ToponymUnit). The constraints are mapped to SPARQL/GeoSPARQL using a java application.

Example 1. Metadata records corresponding to ontology domain class *A*.

```
<PropertyIsInstanceOf>
  <PropertyName>a</PropertyName>
  <OntClass>xyz:A</OntClass>
</PropertyIsInstanceOf>
```

```
SELECT ?metadatarecord
 WHERE {
?metadataRecord a abc:MetadataRecord.
?metadataRecord a xyz:A. }
```

The namespace *abc:* links to our implemented ontology. Class *xyz:A* is part of our Dummy ontology, and is a subclass of *abc:MetadataRecord*. The results of this query will include the instances of *xyz:A* as well as instances of all its subclasses.

Example 2. Metadata records corresponding to ontology domain class *B*, that include the word *water* among their keywords.

```
<and>
    <PropertyIsInstanceOf>
      <PropertyName>a</PropertyName>
      <OntClass>xyz:B</OntClass>
    </PropertyIsInstanceOf>
    <PropertyIsLike wildCard="*" singleChar="#" escapeChar="!">
      <PropertyName>abc:keyword</PropertyName>
      <Literal>water</Literal>
    </PropertyIsLike>
</and>
```

```
SELECT ?metadatarecord
 WHERE {
?metadataRecord a abc:MetadataRecord.
?metadataRecord a xyz:B.
?metadataRecord abc:hasDescription ?description.
?description abc:haskeyword ?element_keyword.
?element_keyword abc:hasLiteral ?literal_keyword.
FILTER(regex(?literal_keyword,"water","i")) }
```

The maping of the second condition requires further processing. *abc:Metadata Record* is linked to *dc:description* by the property *abc:hasDescription*, which itself is linked to *abc:keyword* through the property *abc:haskeyword*. This element itself is linked to a literal that contains the string containing the keyword. We use the function *regex()* to search for the word *water* as a substring of the keywords.

Example 3. Retrieve metadata records that are members of ontology domain class *C.*The bounding boxes of the records should be located within the toponym unit *France*.

```
<and>
    <PropertyIsInstanceOf>
      <PropertyName>a</PropertyName>
      <OntClass>xyz:C</OntClass>
    </PropertyIsInstanceOf>
    <Within>
      <PropertyName>geo:asWKT</PropertyName>
      <ToponymUnit>tu:France</ToponymUnit>
    </Within>
</and>
```

```
SELECT ?metadatarecord
 WHERE {
?metadataRecord a abc:MetadataRecord.
?metadataRecord a xyz:C.
?metadataRecord geo:hasGeometry ?boundingbox.
?boundingbox geo:asWKT ?boundingbox_wkt.
tu:France geo:hasGeometry ?France_geometry.
?France_geometry geo:asWKT ?France_wkt.
FILTER(geof:sfWithin(?boundingbox_wkt,?France_wkt)) }
```

We use *geo:asWKT* to represent the geometry of the selected metadata records. The namespace *tu:* links to an ontology containing our toponym elements. The filter *Within* is interpreted by the servlet as an spatial operation between the bounding box of the metadata record and the geometry of toponym unit. After obtaining the wkt literal representation of the geometry, the spatial comparisons are obtained using the funtion *geof:sfWithin* inside the *FILTER*.

Example 4. Retrieve metadata records whose bounding boxes are located within 100km from France, overlaping Germany.

```
<and>
    <DWithin>
      <PropertyName>geo:asWKT</PropertyName>
      <ToponymUnit>tu:France</ToponymUnit>
      <Distance unit="http://www.uomdict.com/uom.html#meters">
      100000</Distance>
    </DWithin>
    <Intersect>
      <PropertyName>geo:asWKT</PropertyName>
      <ToponymUnit>tu:Germany</ToponymUnit>
    </Intersect>
</and>
```

```
SELECT ?metadatarecord
 WHERE {
```

```
?metadataRecord a abc:MetadataRecord.
?metadataRecord geo:hasGeometry ?boundingbox.
?boundingbox geo:asWKT ?boundingbox_wkt.
tu:France geo:hasGeometry ?France_geometry.
?France_geometry geo:asWKT ?France_wkt.
tu:Germany geo:hasGeometry ?Germany_geometry.
?Germany_geometry geo:asWKT ?Germany_wkt.
BIND(geof:buffer(France_wkt,100000,units:m) as France_buff_wkt)
FILTER(geof:sfIntersects(?boundingbox_wkt,?France_buff_wkt))
FILTER(geof:sfIntersects(?boundingbox_wkt,?Germany_wkt)) }
```

In this example we use a buffer function available in our triplestore. The operator *DWithin* indicates the servlet that it needs create a new wkt literal using the parameter values with the function *geof:buffer*. The resulting literal is added to the query using the *BIND* form. This query uses two filters, one for each spatial constraint.

4 Conclusions

In this paper we are implementing a basic catalogue, so we are not dealing with the real spatial features (streets, roads, etc.). However by using an external domain ontology and having the URL of the WFS *GetFeatures* request, we are able to easily identify a dataset and add it to a *smart query*.

Our research shows that mapping between OGC filter specification and SPARQL is not complicated. However, in order to take advantage of additional elements such as a domain ontology and toponym units, it would be necessary to develop a graphic interface on the client application, to reduce syntax errors.

The triple store implements its own SPARQL endpoint allowing users to directly access the metadata information bypassing the CSW. However, most of the human users would prefer a CSW interface.

We implemented a proof of concept CSW. Our results look promising. However, further research in this field should consider collaborating with larger open source efforts such as GeoNetwork. Particularly interesting for us, is the project proposed in [11].

Our SPARQL/GeoSPARQL queries are not optimized, further research is necessary to improve performance for automatically created queries.

Acknowledgements. This research is supported by: 1) Conseil régional de Bourgogne. 2) Direction Générale de l'Armement, see: http://www.defense. gouv.fr/dga/

References

1. Goodwin, J.: What have ontologies ever done for us - potential applications at a national mapping agency. In: OWL: Experiences and Directions (OWLED) (2005)
2. Harbelot, B., Arenas, H., Cruz, C.: The spatio-temporal semantics from a perdurantism perspective. In: Proceedings of the Fifth International Conference on Advanced Geographic Information Systems, Applications, and Services GEOProcessing (February-March 2013)
3. ESRI: GIS Best Practices: Spatial Data Infrastructure (SDI) (2010)
4. Nebert, D., Whiteside, A., Vetranos, P.: Catalogue services specification (2007)
5. Whiteside, A.: Web services common specification (2005)
6. Janowicz, K., Schade, S., Broring, A., Kebler, C., Maue, P., Stasch, C.: Semantic enablement for spatial data infrastructures. Transactions in GIS 14(2), 111–129 (2010)
7. Yue, P., Gong, J., Di, L., He, L., Wei, Y.: Integrating semantic web technologies and geospatial catalog services for geospatial information discovery and processing in cyberinfrastructure. GeoInformatica 15, 273–303 (2011), doi:10.1007/s10707-009-0096-1
8. Gwenzi, J.: Enhancing spatial web seach with semantic web technology and metadata visualization (2010)
9. Yue, P., Di, L., Yang, W., Yu, G., Zhao, P.: Path planning for chaining geospatial web services. In: Carswell, J.D., Tezuka, T. (eds.) W2GIS 2006. LNCS, vol. 4295, pp. 214–226. Springer, Heidelberg (2006)
10. Lopez-Pellicer, F.J., Florczyk, A., Renteria-Aguaviva, W., Nogueras-Iso, J., Muro-Medrano, P.R.: CSW2LD: a Linked Data frontend for CSW (2010)
11. Pigot, S.: Using rdf as metadata storage (2012), http://trac.osgeo.org/geonetwork/wiki/rdfstore (accessed on May 2013)
12. OSGeo: CQL (2012), http://docs.geotools.org/latest/userguide/library/cql/cql.html (accessed on November 2012)
13. Vretanos, P.A.: Filter encoding implementation specification (2005) (accessed on May 2013)
14. DuCharme, B.: Learning SPARQL. O'Reilly Media, Inc. (July 2011)
15. Kolas, D., Batle, R.: GeoSPARQL user guide (2012), http://ontolog.cim3.net/file/work/SOCoP/Educational/GeoSPARQLUserGuide.docx (accessed on May 2013)
16. OGC: Make a really basic catalog service for the web, csw (2011), http://www.ogcnetwork.net/node/630 (accessed on May 2013)
17. Werner, D., Cruz, C., Nicolle, C.: Ontology-based recommender system of economic articles. In: WEBIST, pp. 725–728 (2012)
18. Brighman, C., Gilbert, S., Xu, Q.: Open Geospatial Data: An Assesment of Global Boundary Datasets (2011), http://maps.worldbank.org/content/article/open-geospatial-data-assessment-global-boundary-datasets (accessed on May 2013)
19. Esri, D.: World administrative units (2011), http://resources.arcgis.com/content/data-maps/10.0/world (accessed on May 2013)
20. Emmons, I.: Parliament User Guide. Raytheon BBN Technologies (2012)
21. Battle, R., Kolas, D.: Enabling the geospatial semantic web with parliament and GeoSPARQL. Semantic Web (2012)

Mob-Warehouse: A Semantic Approach for Mobility Analysis with a Trajectory Data Warehouse

Ricardo Wagner[1], José Antonio Fernandes de Macedo[1], Alessandra Raffaetà[2],
Chiara Renso[3], Alessandro Roncato[2], and Roberto Trasarti[3]

[1] Universidade Federal do Ceará, Brazil
[2] Ca' Foscari University of Venice, Italy
[3] ISTI-CNR, Italy

Abstract. The effective analysis and understanding of huge amount of mobility data have been a hot research topic in the last few years. In this paper, we introduce *Mob-Warehouse*, a Trajectory Data Warehouse which goes a step further to the state of the art on mobility analysis since it models trajectories enriched with semantics. The unit of movement is the (spatio-temporal) point endowed with several semantic dimensions including the activity, the transportation means and the mobility patterns. This model allows us to answer the classical Why, Who, When, Where, What, How questions providing an aggregated view of different aspects of the user movements, no longer limited to space and time. We briefly present an experiment of *Mob-Warehouse* on a real dataset.

1 Introduction

With the incredible availability of mobile devices equipped with geographical localization services, it has become economical and technically feasible to collect a huge amount of moving object traces in real life. Many interesting applications may take advantage of such data performing analysis on the moving objects. For example, in a traffic management system, traffic jams may be determined by mining movement patterns of groups of cars. Similarly, in a zoology application, the analysis of a group of bird trajectories can help explaining their migration patterns. However, trajectory data as they are collected by mobile devices are usually represented as a set of triples (latitude, longitude, timestamp), lacking other non spatio-temporal information like why objects move and other contextual semantic information. These non spatio-temporal aspects are key factors for the real success and deployment of the trajectory analysis results in any application scenario.

Semantic enrichment of mobility data refers to the process of integrating domain knowledge with trajectory data. In other words, the spatio-temporal points forming the trajectory need to be linked to application domain data giving rise to what is called *semantic trajectories*. How can semantic trajectories be useful for application analysis? Let us assume that we have a trajectory dataset about

J. Parsons and D. Chiu (Eds.): ER Workshops 2013, LNCS 8697, pp. 127–136, 2014.
© Springer International Publishing Switzerland 2014

people moving around a city, and we want to answer the following query: *Which is the average distance traveled by people using public transportation to visit at least one cultural attraction?* In this scenario, we should integrate each trajectory relative to some user with city's points of interest and their categories (like "cultural attraction") where the user stops, and with the transportation means used by the moving user. Then, we should compute the average distance for all trajectories satisfying the required conditions. Other queries may need not only domain knowledge integrated into trajectory data, but also the capability to combine complex analysis methods with the trajectory dataset. For example, the query *Which are the car trajectories belonging to a traffic congestion where the average speed inside this congestion is less than 30 km/h?* Here we use the notion of traffic congestion which is not native in spatio-temporal data, but can be computed with trajectory mining algorithms. Again, we need to combine different non spatio-temporal aspects like traffic jams with pure spatio-temporal components like the speed of the car, and then aggregate to compute the average velocity. The combination and aggregation of these different aspects on large trajectory datasets can be handled by a Trajectory Data Warehouse (TDW).

Traditional DW techniques and current analytic tools do not satisfy the requisites for a TDW, since the representation and aggregation of trajectories require the capability of modeling and aggregating varied and interrelated data types, such as geometries, context information and spatio-temporal objects. Consequently, despite several proposals, there is still no consensus about how trajectories should be modeled multidimensionally and organized in different levels of aggregation in a DW, and about what functionality such DWs should support [11]. For example, in [7] a data model for storing measures related to trajectories is presented, focusing on the efficient approximation of aggregates. The same data model has been adopted in [6], to evaluate design solutions that integrate moving object databases (MOD) and DW. In [9] such a framework has been used to examine traffic data, in combination with tools for the visual analysis of spatio-temporal data. Other proposals extend spatial Data Warehouses to include in the model a temporal dimension for dynamic spatial data (e.g, [3]). In [5] two modeling approaches are proposed, both based on design patterns, for devising trajectory data schemas for relational and multidimensional environment. The main limitation of the mentioned approaches is the fact that they do not deal with *semantic trajectories*, but simply with sequences of spatio-temporal points.

Substantial research has been conducted on providing methods and prototype systems for enriching trajectories with domain knowledge like points of interest visited by the users, transportation means, user activities and annotations [8]. The model CONSTAnT [1] proposes a conceptual model for semantic trajectories, but with no specific reference to a data warehouse model. Nevertheless, CONSTAnT model inspired our current work in combining spatio-temporal and semantic aspects in a general concept of semantic trajectory.

Given this context, we propose a comprehensive TDW model for mobility called *Mob-Warehouse*, enriching trajectory data with domain knowledge. In particular, the model is based on the so called 5W1H (Who, Where, When,

What, Why, How) framework [13]. This is a well-known approach for getting the complete story on a subject, often mentioned in journalism, research, and police investigations. In our case, we intend to use this framework for specifying contextual information on trajectories and analyze the different aspects of the "mobility story" that the user "is writing" with his/her tracks. It will also guide the specification of the ETL process, which integrates trajectory data and domain application data. We developed a prototype implementation of the model and we experiment it in a case study consisting of a large dataset of car trajectories.

This paper is organized as follows. Section 2 introduces some basic concepts like trajectories and semantic trajectories. Section 3 briefly describes the 5W1H model and presents the conceptual model of *Mob-Warehouse*. Section 4 discusses the case study and shows some interesting queries that Mob-Warehouse allows to answer. Section 5 draws some conclusions.

2   Preliminaries

Several works in the literature address the analysis of trajectory data. Even the definition of a trajectory can have several variants. A trajectory can be defined as a representation of the spatio-temporal evolution of a moving object. However, since trajectories are usually collected by means of position-enabled devices, the notion of trajectory has to deal with the concept of *sampling*. Here we call *raw trajectory* the discrete representation of a trajectory as a sequence of spatio-temporal points or *samples* as collected by the device.

Definition 1 (Raw Trajectory). *A trajectory T is an ordered list of spatio-temporal points or* samples $p_1, p_2, p_3, \ldots, p_n$. *Each* $p_i = (id, x_i, y_i, t_i)$ *where id is the identifier of the trajectory, x_i, y_i are the geographical coordinates of the sampled point and t_i is the timestamp in which the point has been collected, with $t_1 < t_2 < t_3 < \ldots < t_n$.*

From a raw trajectory it is possible to infer a number of properties of a trajectory like the speed, the acceleration and the traveled distance. However, some other aspects are missing like the places visited by the object, or the performed activities. The concept of semantic trajectory has been proposed as a way to overcome the lack of semantics characterizing raw trajectories. A well known definition of semantic trajectory relies on the "stop and move" approach: a trajectory is segmented into parts where the object is stopped (the "stop") and the parts where the object is changing his/her position (the "move") [10]. This approach evolved to the more general definition of *episodes* to represent segments of a trajectory complying to some predicate representing the semantics of that segment, like the transportation mean, the goal or activity [8]. A further evolution towards this direction brought to the definition of a conceptual model for semantic trajectories as proposed in [1] where several contextual aspects contribute to create the concept of semantic trajectory. Formally:

Definition 2 (Semantic Trajectory). *A semantic trajectory is a trajectory that has been enhanced with annotations and/or one or several complementary segmentations.*

3   Mob-Warehouse

This section introduces the Mob-Warehouse model which is organized around the notion of semantic trajectory where different aspects contribute to describe the context.

As already discussed, raw trajectories are, by nature, semantically poor and they have to be enriched with domain knowledge in order to achieve better understanding of moving objects behavior. In the literature, to the best of our knowledge, no systematic and comprehensible method for accomplishing this task exists. Thus, we need a basic framework for describing object's movement, which provides a minimal set of information that is expressive enough for helping analyzing object behavior.

3.1   The 5W1H Model

In this research, we propose the use of a narrative method as a conduit for systematically explaining the context involving a moving object trajectory. To this end, we resort to the six narrative questions, which were first mentioned in the poem Six Honest Serving Men [4], coined by the mnemonic 5W1H. The basic idea of this approach is to apply six narrative questions of *Who, What, When, Where, Why* and *How* to provide a consistent amount of understanding of the context of a circumstance. The 5W1H framework has been recurrently used by journalists as a guide for narrating a fact.

Each narrative question of the 5W1H model is mapped to a specific trajectory feature. In this way, we describe an object (*Who*) moving by a transportation means and/or having a certain behavior (*How*), performing an activity (*What*), for a certain reason (*Why*), at a given time (*When*) and place (*Where*).

Using this narrative approach, we may increase the level of semantic information into our model allowing to perform more meaningful queries about moving object habits. Below, we discuss the correlation of each question with trajectory features:

Who: This addresses the identification of a moving object, which is easily answered in case all objects are identified by the tracking system.

Where: This concerns the place where the trajectory point is located. Having the georeferenced location of each trajectory point, we may associate the latitude and longitude with a set of points of interest.

When: This question refers to the time extent related with trajectory points. This question is necessary to associate sampled points with specific calendar events, week periods, at different levels of details.

What: This question refers to what a moving object is doing, what task it is trying to perform or achieve. Clearly, answering this question is a challenge

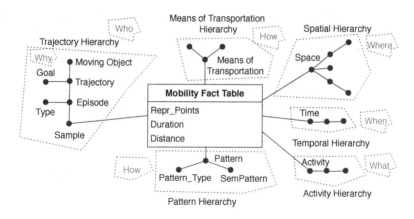

Fig. 1. TDW Conceptual model

since we should infer from each trajectory point the corresponding activity. This process could be facilitated using the information provided by other questions.

Why: This represents the motivation for traveling. This is an issue since this is so deeply rooted into the moving entity intent.

How: This question identifies both the way the object is moving, like the transportation means, and the behavior like belonging to a traffic congestion. Answering to this question could be challenging: when trajectories use multi-modal transportation means, identifying the transportation means could be far to be trivial. Moreover, mining algorithms have to be used to extract meaningful behavior: trajectories can be associated with one or more patterns depending on the fact the trajectory *entails* or satisfies the behavior.

3.2   The TDW Conceptual Model

Following the 5W1H Model we define a TDW conceptual model with six dimensions, as illustrated in Fig. 1. First, two dimensions represent space and time and they correspond respectively to the *Where* and *When* questions of the 5W1H Model. With respect to [6,9] here the spatial domain can be structured according to the application requirements, providing the user with a greater flexibility. The spatial hierarchy is no longer restricted to consist of simple regular grids, the user can define hierarchies of regions with ad-hoc shapes. While a hierarchy of regular grids can be used to analyze objects that can move freely in the space, hierarchies with ad-hoc shapes are useful for objects whose movements are constrained, such as objects that can only move along a road network (e.g., cars). Moreover, Voronoi tessellation can be employed in order to build hierarchies of regions based on the actual distribution of the points forming the trajectories. This kind of partitioning turns out to be particularly suited for highlighting the directions of the trajectory movement.

In [6,9] a third dimension named *object group* represents features of the objects under analysis. Here we call this dimension *Trajectory*, as it becomes a central component of our model and it is used to represent the trajectory of the moving objects. At the base granularity it represents a single sample (id, x, y, t) belonging to the trajectory identified by id. The hierarchy having *Sample* as a root mixes together semantic and geometric features. A sample belongs to an *episode*, which can be classified according to its *Type* (e.g., a *stop* or a *move*) and it is grouped into a *Trajectory*. Each *Trajectory* is associated not only with the *Moving object* but also to a *Goal*, which is the main objective of such a trajectory. This dimension allows one to model *Who* is performing the action (the moving object) and the attribute *goal* answers the question *Why*. A fourth dimension, called *Activity*, states the activity the object is doing in a certain sample. This allows one to describe in a very detailed manner *What* is going on at the different samples of a trajectory. We can build a hierarchy of activities which classifies properly the variety of things an object can perform. Usually this hierarchy is application dependent hence in the general model it is not specified and should be instantiated case by case depending on the application requirements. Then the dimension *Means of Transportation* represents which transportation means the object is using for the movement. The last dimension, called *Pattern*, collects the patterns mined from the data under analysis. In this way we can directly relate trajectories to the patterns they belong to. An example of hierarchy on this dimension could be: each pattern is associated with its *Type*, such as cluster, frequent pattern, flock, and with a *Semantic Pattern*, which expresses the interpretation of such a pattern. For instance, in [2] to compute the movements of commuters in the city of Milan a clustering algorithm is applied to the trajectories of the moving objects. We can store these mined clusters in Mob-Warehouse as follows. Each cluster c_i is represented as a row in the dimension table *Patterns*: the identifier of the cluster is the primary key, the attribute *Semantic Pattern* can state *north-east commuters*, to point out that the semantic interpretation of cluster c_i is a group of people moving from North to East whereas the attribute *Pattern_type* assumes *cluster* as value. The latter two dimensions express the concept of *How* the movement is performed.

The fact table stores measures concerning the samples of the trajectories. Differently from [6,9] where at the minimum granularity data were already aggregated, in this paper we want to record the detailed information to give the user the flexibility to analyze the behavior according to various points of view: at the minimum granularity we store information related to a single sample of a trajectory, specifying the kind of activity is doing, the means of transportation is using, the patterns, the space and time it belongs to. Then by aggregating according to the described hierarchies we can recover also properties concerning the whole trajectory or groups of trajectories satisfying certain conditions.

In the fact table we store measures related to a given sample $s = \langle id, x, y, t \rangle$

- *Repr_Points* is a spatio-temporal measure containing the spatial and temporal component of the sample, i.e., (id, x, y, t);
- *Duration* is the time spent to reach the sample from the previous point of the same trajectory in the same granule. It is set to 0, if this is the first point of the trajectory in such a granule;

– *Distance* is the traveled distance from the previous point to the sample of the trajectory in the same granule. It is set to 0, if this is the first point of the trajectory in such a granule.

As far as the aggregate functions are concerned, for the measures *Duration* and *Distance*, we use the *distributive* function *sum*: super-aggregates are computed by summing up the sub-aggregates at finer granularities. On the other hand, the aggregate function for the measure *Repr_points* can be defined in different ways according to the application requirements. The simplest way is to use the *union* operator to join together the points satisfying given conditions. Differently one can return a bounding box enclosing all the points or compress the points removing the ones which are spatio-temporally similar. For our experiments in Section 4 we will assume the union operator.

4   Experiments

Here we present a real case study using a trajectory dataset of people traveling by car in Milan (Italy), during one week in April 2007. The dataset contains tracks of 16,946 cars and 48,906 trajectories for a total of 1,806,293 points. We start describing the ETL process designed for building the Mob-Warehouse. Next, we present some queries that help analyzing people behavior in Milan city.

ETL Process. Although the description of the ETL process is not the main focus of this paper, we discuss briefly here the steps performed to populate Mob-Warehouse. The ETL process includes a semantic enrichment step, whose goal is to associate semantic information from the application domain with the trajectory data. Clearly, the semantic enrichment step is application dependent and may be very complex. Here, we adopted a quite simple semantic enrichment approach sufficient to illustrate the underlying idea and to show that the model is powerful enough to perform interesting analyses.

An important preprocessing task consists in transforming the GPS samples (id, x, y, t) into trajectories. The first step of such process is called *trajectory segmentation*, where the main goal is to split the samples into groups of related elements. We assume that trajectories end at three o'clock in the morning. The next step is the *stop identification*, where each sample must be classified as a move or a stop. This is done by means of a speed-based approach [12]. In our experiment, when the distance and the time difference between two consecutive samples are below the thresholds of 100 meters and 20 minutes, the second point is labeled as a stop. Otherwise, it is considered as a move. Hence a trajectory can be viewed as an alternation of a stop and a move.

The **spatial dimension** (space_dim) was populated using data extracted from the Open Street Map project[1] covering the city of Milan. Each kind of spatial object like streets, neighborhoods, districts, municipalities, states, countries and points of interest (POI) are represented as geometries. While streets are represented with linestrings, the other spatial objects are represented with points,

---

[1] http://www.openstreetmap.org

polygons or multipolygons. Moreover, the POI is also described by its category in a specific text attribute (poi_category). The **temporal dimension** (time_dim) is populated by using the temporal component of trajectory samples, which are copied to the temporal hierarchy lowest level. Higher levels (day of the week, month, year) are built by aggregating lower levels. The **trajectory dimension** (traj_dim) is populated, at its lowest granularity with trajectory samples. Higher levels of the trajectory hierarchy are populated with the episodes, which could be a *begin*, an *end*, a *stop*, or a *move*. We distinguished two special kinds of stops, namely *Home* and *Work*. To identify them, we compute the most frequent locations and we assigned the first most frequent to *Home* and the second most frequent to *Work*. The **activity dimension** (activity_dim) is populated with 12 predefined activities derived from a transportation research survey performed in the context of the project DataSIM[2]. Clearly, the approach is parametric with respect to the list of possible activities and can be changed depending on the application requirements. The **transportation means** dimension is not instantiated since we use only data describing car movements. The **pattern dimension** is populated with the mined patterns (clustering, frequent patterns, and flock detection) from the Milan trajectory dataset. For instance, in [2] a clustering algorithm is applied to extract groups of trajectories ending in a similar place. The identifier of each cluster is stored into the pattern dimension and it is associated with the samples of the trajectories belonging to such a cluster. Moreover, the attribute *SemPattern* specifies a semantic interpretation of the cluster, when it is known.

Queries Evaluation. Mob-Warehouse can be queried for analyzing people behavior in Milan city. We next discuss two examples. The first query aims at understanding what people usually do after leaving home, by finding *the most frequent activity after home*. Considering the 5W1H, such query uses the *What* perspective. For answering this query, we created a view, called *stopsAtHome*, to represent when a person is at home, i.e. his/her stops at home.

```
SELECT ac.category, COUNT(*)
FROM points_fact pf, traj_dim tr, activity_dim ac, stopsAtHome stops
  WHERE (join conditions) AND tr.trajectory = stops.trajectory
  AND tr.episode = stops.episode + 2 AND ac.category <> 'HOME'
GROUP BY ac.category ORDER BY 2 DESC;
```

where `join conditions` consists of equalities between the foreign keys in the fact tables and the corresponding primary keys in the dimension tables. The attribute `episode` contains a progressive number identifying the segments composing a trajectory. Hence the condition `tr.episode = stops.episode + 2` states that we look for the first stop after 'HOME'.

The result of this query is reported in the table below. We notice that the prevalent activity is *Working*. The second most frequent is *Leisure*, i.e., going for leisure activities like jogging in a park. At the third position we find *Services* like

---

[2] http://www.datasim-fp7.com

visiting a doctor or a bank. The low number of education activities is probably due to few POIs related to education.

Variants of the same query may be used to find activities after work or before home/work by only modifying the view.

Activity	After Home
Working	6401
Leisure activities	1866
Services	1403
Shopping	593
Sports	523
Eating	473
Social activities	434
Education	63
Religion	40

The second query aims at exploring the *When*, *Why*, *Where* and *Who* perspectives by *finding the users and their time spent traveling from home to work*. Below, we show the query used to answer this question. We use, in this query, a view, called *firstWorkStop*, to select the timestamp of the first sample, after leaving home, having as activity Work and classified as a stop.

```
SELECT traj_dim.trajectory, SUM(points_fact.duration) AS time
   FROM points_fact, traj_dim, activity_dim, time_dim
   WHERE (join conditions) AND
   ((traj_dim.episode_type = 'BEGIN' AND activity_dim.category = 'HOME')
      OR (traj_dim.episode_type <> 'BEGIN'))
   AND time_dim.minute <= firstWorkStop(traj_dim.trajectory)
GROUP BY traj_dim.trajectory;
```

The result of this query is a list of users with the duration of their travel from home to work. The effective values are not worth to be presented. We just mention that there is a high variability in the durations (from less than one hour to several hours). This deserves a further deeper analysis to properly understand what happens in travels with longer durations.

5   Conclusion and Future Work

We presented Mob-Warehouse, a semantic-enhanced warehouse for trajectories. The main contribution is the introduction of a model where the spatio-temporal component of trajectory data is properly integrated with context related information like transportation means, performed activities and mobility patterns. The key idea is to consider the spatio-temporal point sampled by a device as the lowest granularity to which semantic information is linked. We followed the 5W1H model to describe the context where objects move. This allows us to express a wide range of queries, involving the questions Who, What, Why, When, Where and How. Due to lack of space we only briefly sketched some experiments performed with Mob-Warehouse on a real dataset of trajectories. Future works include the development of a more sophisticated ETL process to enrich raw trajectory data with contextual information and the definition of more complex aggregate functions for the measure *Repr_Points*, like *representative trajectories*.

Acknowledgments. We acknowledge European Projects SEEK Marie Curie Action N. 295179, DATASIM FET N. 270833, the national research project PON TETRis (no. PON01 00451) for partially supporting this work.

References

1. Bogorny, V., Renso, C., de Aquino, A.R., de Lucca Siqueira, F., Alvares, L.O.: CONSTAnT – A Conceptual Data Model for Semantic Trajectories of Moving Objects. Transactions in GIS 18(1), 66–88 (2014)
2. Giannotti, F., Nanni, M., Pedreschi, D., Pinelli, F., Renso, C., Rinzivillo, S., Trasarti, R.: Unveiling the complexity of human mobility by querying and mining massive trajectory data. VLDB J. 20(5), 695–719 (2011)
3. Gómez, L.I., Kuijpers, B., Vaisman, A.A.: A data model and query language for spatio-temporal decision support. GeoInformatica 15(3), 455–496 (2011)
4. Kipling. Six Honest Serving Men Poem, http://www.kipling.org.uk/poems_serving.htm (accessed: June 5, 2013)
5. Leal, B., de Macêdo, J.A.F., Times, V.C., Casanova, M.A., Vidal, V.M.P., de Carvalho, M.T.M.: From Conceptual Modeling to Logical Representation of Trajectories in DBMS-OR and DW Systems. JIDM 2(3), 463–478 (2011)
6. Marketos, G., Frentzos, E., Ntoutsi, I., Pelekis, N., Raffaetà, A., Theodoridis, Y.: Building Real World Trajectory Warehouses. In: Proc. of MobiDE, pp. 8–15 (2008)
7. Orlando, S., Orsini, R., Raffaetà, A., Roncato, A., Silvestri, C.: Trajectory Data Warehouses: Design and Implementation Issues. Journal of Computing Science and Engineering 1(2), 240–261 (2007)
8. Parent, C., Spaccapietra, S., Renso, C., Andrienko, G., Andrienko, N., Bogorny, V., Damiani, M.L., Gkoulalas-Divanis, A., Macedo, J.A., Pelekis, N., Theodoridis, Y., Yan, Z.: Semantic Trajectories Modeling and Analysis. ACM Computing Surveys 45(4), 42 (2013)
9. Raffaetà, A., Leonardi, L., Marketos, G., Andrienko, G., Andrienko, N., Frentzos, E., Giatrakos, N., Orlando, S., Pelekis, N., Roncato, A., Silvestri, C.: Visual Mobility Analysis using T-Warehouse. J. of Data Warehousing and Mining 7(1), 1–23 (2011)
10. Spaccapietra, S., Parent, C., Damiani, M.L., de Macedo, J.A., Porto, F., Vangenot, C.: A conceptual view on trajectories. Data & Knowledge Engineering 65(1), 126–146 (2008)
11. Vaisman, A., Zimányi, E.: What Is Spatio-Temporal Data Warehousing? In: Pedersen, T.B., Mohania, M.K., Tjoa, A.M. (eds.) DaWaK 2009. LNCS, vol. 5691, pp. 9–23. Springer, Heidelberg (2009)
12. Yan, Z.: Towards Semantic Trajectory Data Analysis: A Conceptual and Computational Approach. In: VLDB PhD Workshop (2009)
13. Yang, L., Hu, Z., Long, J., Guo, T.: 5W1H-based Conceptual Modeling Framework for Domain Ontology and Its Application on STPO. In: Proc. of SKG, pp. 203–206. IEEE (2011)

Preface to WISM 2013

The international workshop on Web Information Systems Modeling (WISM) aims to discuss the most recent developments in the field of model-driven design of Web Information Systems (WIS). This is the tenth edition of the workshop, after ninth successful editions organized in Florence (2012), Brussels (2011), Vancouver (2010), Amsterdam (2009), Barcelona (2008), Trondheim (2007), Luxembourg (2006), Sydney (2005), and Riga (2004).

The invited paper by Machado et al. addresses the adaptation aspect in ubiquitous computing. For this purpose, it proposes a system model for recommending situation-aware actions to users. The model makes use of a situation ontology to describe the system states and SWRL rules to specify the state transitions. The proposed solution is validated based on a use case that recommends personalized actions in a residential home-care environment.

The first regular paper by Vandic and Milea considers two current problems in Web product search: the lack of Web product data aggregation and the missing of Web-wide parametric search. To address these issues the authors propose the Semantic Web Enhanced Product Search (SWEPS) framework. The framework revolves around a product ontology and contains three modules: information integration, knowledge management, and search engine. Several evaluation strategies are explored for each of the SWEPS modules.

The second paper by Hogenboom et al. tackles the topic of news recommendation on the Web. The existing SF-IDF algorithm, which is the TF-IDF algorithm applied to senses instead of terms, is extended to account for named entities, which are usually not represented in a semantic lexicon. For this purpose, the authors make use of the Bing page counts, resulting in the Bing-SF-IDF recommender. The new recommender significantly outperforms both the TF-IDF and SF-IDF recommenders on the F1-measure.

The third paper by Cherfi et al. aims to map existing Web quality metrics to the ISO/IEC 9126 standard for software quality characteristics. The results show that existing metrics largely cover all the standard characteristics and most metrics can be evaluated only when the Web application is online. The prolific activity in this field seem to suggest that the current quality standards need to be updated and some quality factors (e.g., security) need to be better supported by metrics.

The fourth paper by Zhou et al. investigates how to modularize Web information systems in order to deal with the complexity of these systems. The proposed solution is a hybrid classloader: one for the business modules using the Open Services Gateway initiative (OSGi) bundles and one for the traditional Web application components. The approach is successfully tested and used in an industrial setting.

The fifth and last paper, by Lim and Maamar considers the problem of determining the service with the highest level of Quality of Service (QoS) given a fixed price that the user is willing to pay. A fixed price second-QoS sealed auction protocol is used to select the desired Web service. The client is able to express its preferences by means of an utility function. The effectiveness of the approach is demonstrated by using a real-world data set.

We do hope that the above topics on modeling Web Information Systems have triggered the reader's interest to have a closer look at the workshop proceedings. Last, we would also like to thank all the authors, reviewers, participants, and ER 2013 workshop chairs for their input and support of the workshop.

November 2013   Flavius Frasincar
                                                Geert-Jan Houben
                                                Philippe Thiran

Situation-Aware Smart Environment Modeling

Alencar Machado[1,3], Ana Marilza Pernas[2], Leandro Krug Wives[4],
and José Palazzo Moreira de Oliveira[3]

[1] Politécnico, Universidade Federal de Santa Maria, Santa Maria, Brazil
[2] UFPEL, Universidade Federal de Pelotas, Pelotas, Brazil
[3] UFRGS – Instituto de Informática, PPGC, Porto Alegre, Brazil
alencar.comp@gmail.com, marilza@inf.ufpel.edu.br
{wives,palazzo}@inf.ufrgs.br

Abstract. The term ubiquitous smart system is utilized to characterize applications that are able to perceive the user context and properly react, according to the occurrence of specific events. Lately, several solutions have been developed in order to propose new approaches focused on ubiquitous computing, in general, not exploring a general model that could be broadly applied and calibrated respecting the context of interests of specific ubiquitous applications. In this sense the objective of this work is to propose a system model and functioning that is capable of recommending situation-aware actions to users, implemented in a Situation as a Service way. The system enables customized behavior, depending on user's situation, which is the main research challenge considering that a number of context elements have to be evaluated. A use-case shows how ubiquitous applications can automatically define the user situations and recommend personalized actions within a residential home-care scenario.

Keywords: Home-Care Environments, Ubiquitous Applications, Situation-awareness, Ontologies.

1   Introduction

With an increasing life expectancy, world population is showing an aging problem. Dementia or decreased ability to perform daily activities makes this population subject to a decreased quality of life. This degenerative illness does not determine a mandatory hospitalization, but makes the patient dependent and in need of basic home-care support. One solution to support this kind of person's needs is centered in automating their residential environment, since it is where they spend most of their time. In this sense, the home as an Ambient Intelligent Environment is becoming an important research field for home care [1].

Adaptation and situation awareness walk together in different kinds of applications. Situation awareness does not necessarily imply adaptation, but an adaptive system, in general, need to be aware about the occurrence of specific events and properly react to them. Among a variety of systems that propose to present a situation aware character, this work shows a case study in the specific domain of ubiquitous applications to home-care environments. In this research, ubiquitous applications are software applications

J. Parsons and D. Chiu (Eds.): ER Workshops 2013, LNCS 8697, pp. 139–149, 2014.

that reactively request triggering actions (web services) due to the situations detected (SWRL rules) in the environment, altering their behavior due to the existing contextual information. This area is critical as systems are developed generically and need to be deployed in specific homes with particular characteristics with a variety of particularities that should be taken into account. This deployment must be supported by a semi-automated process in order to scale to hundreds or thousands of residences.

A number of researches have been done on the development of ubiquitous applications [2]. In general, these works are not focused on a general model, which could be broadly applied and calibrated respecting the context of interests of specific ubiquitous applications. In this sense, our objective is to propose a system model and functioning that is capable of recommending situation-aware actions to users, developed to behave in a Situation as a Service way.

In our work, the system presents a reactive character to the situations faced by the user. To support this behavior, it is necessary to distinguish several particularities of the user's routine. The system must also be able to suggest certain adaptation actions according to a specific situation, presenting alternatives to help in the process of reaching the final goal in the ambient assisted living.

This paper is organized as follows. Next section presents a solution to support adaptive situations in the system explaining the models to context data, the relevant events and situations. Following we present a case study, explaining the Situation as a Service middleware developed and showing its operation in an application scenario. We finalize the paper with conclusions and future works.

2   Related Works

According to Sadri [2] adaptation is a key feature to ubiquitous applications, personalization being one of the most significant promises for Ambient Intelligence. In the last years, many efforts focused on the development of context-aware systems have been proposed. In a manner that is similar to our work, these approaches use ontologies to model the context and its underlying dimensions to evaluate interactions among people. Recent researches [4] show that the use of ontologies to model environments and to describe existing knowledge facilitates the semi-automation process of situations. In a situation aware environment, a situation is defined as a set of contextual characteristics that are invariable in a defined time interval [7]. It corresponds to the set of semantic relationships that are valid for a given instant or that are stable on a time interval. An event in situation-aware systems consists on occurrences in the environment, resulted from a direct user action or not, which will determine the system's reaction. Different types of events can be defined and, depending on the event, a new situation can be started. The detailed explanation about these concepts may be found at Pernas et al.   (2012).[17]

Some works are related to situations and scenarios, like the one presented in Kokar et al. [3], in which the authors use adaptive scenarios to represent and model situations. A context-aware and ontology-based recommender system is presented in [6]. It takes into account the user situation, i.e., if the user is at home, in the office or driving his/her car. However, they only describe the design of the system, and do not formalize the concept of situations and don't give details about the situation model. Our work goes further as we specify formalism to model situations, to be aware of them and to suggest actions in a situation-aware environment.

3   Situation-Awareness Model

In a situation aware environment, a situation is defined as a set of contextual characteristics that are invariable in a defined time interval [7]. It corresponds to the set of semantic relationships that are valid for a given instant or that are stable on a given time interval. To us, a situation is treated as a set of state variables, which identifies a specific user/ambient state, i.e., a situation. For instance, a generic scenario could represent *a person sitting in the living room at 11h15 AM, watching television, to whom a drug for diabetes is scheduled to be taken at 12h00 AM*, the person sitting in the living room is a situation. The person will be at this same situation for a specific time, and this situation will be changed when an event occurs, for example, it is *12h00 AM and the drug was taken by the person.*

According to O'Brien [5], some key information must be included in the instance definition of situations in order for a system to be able to detect situations:

- A list of events that may participate in situation detection;
- The context in which the situation detection is relevant;
- The semantic conditions that must be satisfied;
- The conditions and the associated events [8].

Consequently, we will first explore the underlying context of a home-care environment and explain how it can be modeled. Then we present the events that can occur before and during situation detection and how they can be expressed. To finish, we present our semantic representation of a situation.

3.1   Modeling Underlying Contexts

To perform situation-aware adaptation in a home-care environment a situation-aware system has to detect different user's situations at any time. This implies storing, managing and being aware of a large amount of contextual elements (e.g., user location, surrounding resources and so on), which have to be well structured to allow the identification of the current user's situation.

To do that, we develop separated models, each one representing a specific set of contextual elements. We identify three sets of contextual elements: (i) data related to the user profile, represented as the User Model; (ii) data about the application domain, represented as the Personal Health Model; and (iii) data related to the context that surround the user, represented as the Environmental Model.

These components are represented by specific ontologies, defined in OWL language [9]. In the following, we first explain how each one of these models is internally structured and which kind of contextual elements are stored on them. Then, we present an approach to deal with situation analyses and selection of adaptive actions.

- **User Model.** Comprehends the user ontology, and stores the user's preferences (level of awareness) and interests [10]. This ontology is very important in order to recommend actions in specific situations, since the system has to know each user´s particularities in order to correctly recommend good (and not bad) actions. For example, if some user is affected by chronic diseases hypertension and diabetes, and the system detects that their vital signs are bad, so the system has to be aware about which action should be recommended.
- **Personal Health Model.** It relates to the personal health ontology, storing information about the health care provider, the caregiver, and the user´s health conditions, among others. In particular, it ensures chronic disease management for helping applications to make decisions about which actions are more appropriate to perform on each situation. Examples of such ontologies can be found in [11].
- **Environmental Model.** It is responsible for storing and managing contextual elements related to the user's environmental context (see Figure 1). For the moment, it is composed by two ontologies: location and devices ontologies. The location ontology allows the system to filter information according to users proximity (if in the living room, or kitchen, for example) allowing inference about the more correct action to be executed. The device ontology contains information about the patients device, which helps filtering information accordingly to each device´s properties. In this work, devices are objects that publish their functionality through Web services. A composition of Web services comprehends an action and the execution of an action by the system can adapt the environment accordingly to a given situation.

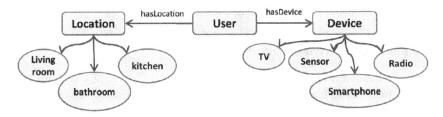

Fig. 1. Ontologies located in the Environmental Model

3.2   Modeling Relevant Events

In a situation-aware system, several types of events can be identified and defined. According to the event, a new situation can be started. Therefore, we can define an event as a quick occurrence in a situation, which will determine the system's reaction.

In our approach, we take into account two types of events: internal and external. The concepts of internal and external events are defined in the theory of Situation Calculus [12], where the distinction between them is that internal events are governed by occurrence axioms, while external events are not. An external event could be the change of a computer device or the kind of network connection being used. This kind of event can be identified by changing the value of one or more state variables. An internal event could be detected by the result of successive state variable changes or the change of one specific state variable. Therefore, they have to be treated by internal axioms.

Events have a time instant during which they occur. The conditions for raising one event are defined by its constraints, which represent an expression that may contain other situations or events. Events are represented by the syntax shown in (1). Some examples of monitored events are presented in Table 1, stating the event itself, the classification type and the relevant context to be stored in the aforementioned server models.

$$Event = \{EventName; EventType; Constraints; TimeStamp; RelevantContext\} \qquad (1)$$

Table 1. Examples of events

Event	Type	Relevant context
E1: time to take the drug ("user unmedicated" situation starts)	Internal	user_id, timestamp, sensor_location, device near
E2: Location has changed	External	new_location, new_dispositive near
E3: user warns that he has took the drug by interacting with a smart tv ("user medicated situation" starts)	External	*Ctxt E1, Ctxt E2*
E4: abnormal heart beats detected, pulse rate and user moves through various places in home ("user agitated" situation starts)	Internal	*Ctxt E1, sensor_heartBeats, sensor_pulse, sensor_pedometer*

3.3   Modeling Situations

We consider a situation as an interpretation of a set of contextual elements, relating each one of them in order to provide some information valid in a specific time interval. Thus, modeling situations implies analyzing users´ contextual elements taking into account the time dimension. In Figure 2 we show how the previously described context models can be related, focusing on the user and with the intent to discover the user situation.

Each kind of event and contextual elements group configured in the system identifies a corresponding situation. In Table 2 we show examples of situations that can be represented by the proposed model, including the group of events related to the situation and the recommended actions. The situations are explained in a higher level of abstraction, to provide a better understanding.

To internally model these situations, we propose a situation aware ontology to represent the activities and situations experienced by the user while performing a daily task. This high level ontology obtains data from the contextual models described before and applies rules to discover the activity and situation that is currently being experienced by the user.

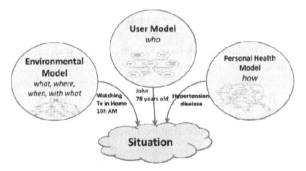

Fig. 2. Relation among context models to express a situation

Table 2. Examples of situations

Situation	Events	Adaptive Actions
User is unmedi-cated (need to take some drug)	Events like *E1*, *E3*.	The system identifies the user's location and the nearest device that can interact with him and warn him (audibly or visually) to take an specific drug.
User is agitated	Events like *E4*.	The system will check into the Personal Health Model whether this situation affects the user (illness). If so, it will search the information in this model for a preventive action, which for instance could be playing some music through some device or even notifying a health care pro-vider.

To propose this ontology we investigate other situation ontologies in the literature in order to reuse their concepts and turn the ontology development more flexible. Some examples are defined in [13] and [14] and they particularly appear to be more flexible and may be applied in different contexts. They are very similar, and [14] states that the essential difference is that they incorporate space-temporal relation types that are different from the alternative designs proposed by [13], which is known as the SAWA ontology (Situation Awareness Assistant). The ontology defined in [14] is focused in a domain where the dimension of time is very relevant: road traffic. Thus, the authors define specialized concepts to deal with time. In [13] the interest is to build an ontology that is generic in nature, and applicable to a wide variety of prob-lem domains through the redefinition of the domain knowledge used.

After studying these ontologies we conclude that, for situations in home care Am-bient Intelligence, the ontology presented in [14] was more interesting, but with some modifications to represent activities' relations. However, some concepts in [13] are important too. Thus, in Figure 3 we present the fusion of these two ontologies, in order to better fit our proposal. Thus, activity corresponds to the Relation concept defined in [13], because we define the relations among objects as daily activities. Thus, we opted to simplify the ontology specializing this concept. Here, a Situation is the product of a user (corresponding to the concept Object in [13] and [14]), performing an Activity.

Activity represents daily activities like breakfasting, watching television, reading newspaper or doing exercises. Comparing to Situations, an Activity is more generic and can be applied to different users in different times. However, the Situation can be valid only in a specific time interval. So, to represent this valid period of time we apply the concept of lifespan, which is also important for the problem of activating reactive situations by events from different sources (see Figure 3). The concept of lifespan was borrowed from [8], where it is defined as a time interval when the situation is relevant (or valid). According to [8], a lifespan is limited by the occurrence of an initiator and a terminator. Still, a situation can have more than one lifespan in the same time, defined by two initiators and two terminators. A lifespan has a location in time, which is represented by an abstract ontology of time, like OWL-Time [15].

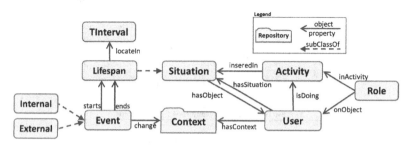

Fig. 3. The situation ontology

In this model, events of interest are identified by ubiquitous applications, thus while designing these applications.

The user context, i.e., the attributes of a home environment (location, device, sensors, profile) are represented in Figure 3 as a repository because these concepts and properties are imported from the three server models presented in subsection 3.1: User Model; Personal Heath Model and Environmental Model.

For instance, if we want to state that "A user is watching television", "She is at living room", and "She needs to take her drug for hypertension at 10:00 am", the instantiated situation, defined here in SWRL[1], is presented in (2). The discovered situation has, internally, its lifespan and will represent specific actions in the intelligence environment.

S0: User (x?)∧ isTask (?x, watching_tv) ∧ haslocation(?x, living_room)

takeDrug(?x, 10) ∧ Time(?y) ∧ swrlb:greaterThan (?y, 10) → hasSitua- (2)

tion(?x, unMedicated)

In the next section we present our case study, which is called a Situation as a Service middleware, showing how the contextual elements are obtained and internally managed.

---

[1] http://www.w3.org/Submission/SWRL/.

4   The Situation as a Service Middleware

Systems for Ambient Intelligence focused on smart home-care should support the users' mobility and provide adequate services to their needs. Resources embedded in the environment are finely suited for reasons of cost and performance. To enable these features, we developed a middleware which provides the management of *SItuations as a* Service (SIaaS) for pervasive applications in Ambient Intelligence [16].

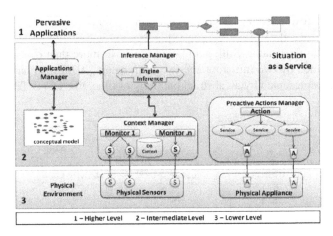

Fig. 4. Architecture for Pervasive Application

The **Intermediate Level (2)** shown in Figure 4 contains the semantic model, described in section 3, together with the situation rules and the relevant events that must be detected. This Intermediate Level consists on a software layer (SIaaS middleware), developed to provide a stable and secure environment for applications interesting on performing pervasive actions in the SIaaS. It registers the pervasive applications acquired to the user´s residency (Application Manager). Also notifies these applications whenever an event of interest has become true (through the Inference Manager component). Besides, this layer monitors the environment and provides contextualized information according to the interest stated by each pervasive application (through the Context Manager), which, in turns, must subscribe to this middle-ware in order to be informed.

In this sense, this layer links the physical environment and the ubiquitous applications, and it is connected to the physical world through Web services that publish the functionality of corresponding devices and sensors (i.e., the appliances shown in Figure 4). This link is established and managed by the Proactive Actions Manager. It is important to state that the objective of this level is to provide a homogeneous vision of heterogeneous data from the different sources (Web services), allowing the access, distribution, integration, and fusion of multiple applications in different domains [16].

4.1   Case Study

Here we show a practical execution of how the SIaaS could identify a user situation in the following fictitious scenario: *"John is a 78 years old citizen that is involved in some diseases associated with aging as diabetes, hypertension and lightweight de-mentia. John observes that he constantly forgets to take his drugs, and this fact is causing deterioration in treating his chronic diseases, mainly diabetes and hyperten-sion, which can lead to a Cerebral Vascular Accident (CVA). Thus, John buys a solu-tion (i.e., a pervasive application for managing medications) to control the schedule of the drugs he has to take and to interact with him through his surrounding physical environment to aid him remembering to take those drugs."*

The purchased solution comprises a pervasive application (namely pervAppMedi-cation) for managing drugs administration and its events of interest corresponds to the user in an "unmedicated situation" (i.e., an internal event) that is defined by the fol-lowing rule:

EVENT A: User (x?) ∧ Drug (?d) ∧ takeDrug(?x, ?d) ∧ userTakeDrugTime(x?,10)   Time(?y)

   ∧ swrlb:greaterThan (?y, 10) → hasSituation(?x, unMedicated)

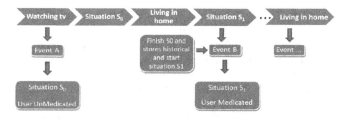

Fig. 5. Lifetime of the SIaaS

As shown in Figure 5, during John´s daily activities, the following situation could be detected: *"It is 10h00 AM and John is watching TV in his living room. As he is being treated for hypertension, he needs to be medicated at this exactly time (10h00 AM). Then, the event (Event A) becomes true and this condition triggers the "unmedi-cated situation".* The pervAppMedication is signaled and it freezes the program being shown in his television and plays an audible warn and shows a picture with the fol-lowing phrase*: "Mr John, it is time to take your medication XXX for hypertension. After taking this medication, press ´ok´."* Immediately John goes to the medicine box and takes drug XXX, ingests it and presses the *"OK" button (witch is the external Event B), stating that he took the necessary medicament".* This is the end of the "un-medicated situation".

5   Conclusions and Future Works

This paper proposes an ambient intelligent approach to deal with ubiquitous home-care environment, taking into account the detected patient situation to select the cor-rect actions to be taken in a reactive way. As our main contribution, we propose a model to describe the patient's context, with relevant events and situations. We also present an approach to analyze this information to execute relevant actions regarding the current user situation. At the end of this work we present a case study in Situation as a Service middleware, showing how is a daily operation of the proposed situation-aware system. This operation aims to be more consistent with users, considering their needs, actions, tasks and even devices. A conceptual model was developed [16] to be reused in several applications to improve interoperability. The model offers stronger semantic relations between the environment and the pervasive application. Our goal is to design models to describe an automated residential environment totally controlled by a middleware. Currently we are developing tests on the situation detection capability over a real and automated environment.

References

1. Chan, M., Campo, E., Esteve, D., Fourniols, J.Y.: Smart homes - Current Features and Future Perspectives. Maturitas 64(2), 90–97 (2009)
2. Sadri, F.: Ambient Intelligence: A survery. ACM Computing Surverys (CSUR) 43(4), 36–66 (2011)
3. Kokar, M.M., Matheus, C.J., Baclawski, K.: Ontology-based situation awareness. Journal of Information Fusion 10(1), 83–98 (2009)
4. Bettini, C., Brdiczkab, O., Henricksen, K., Indulskad, J., Nicklase, D., Ranaganatha, R.D.: A survey of Context Modelling and Reasoning Techniques. Pervasive and Mobile Computing, 161–180 (2010)
5. O'Brien, P.: An Ontology for Mobile Situation Aware Systems. Australasian Journal of Information Systems 15(2), 45–72 (2009)
6. Rack, C., Arbanowski, S., Steglich, S.: Context-aware, ontology-based recommendations. In: International Symposium on Applications and the Internet Workshops, SAINT Workshops, p. 7 (2006)
7. Weißenberg, N., Gartmann, R., Voisard, A.: An Ontology-Based Approach to Personalized Situation-Aware Mobile Service Supply. Journal of GeoInformatica 10, 55–90 (2006)
8. Adi, A., Botzer, D., Etzion, O.: The Situation Manager Component of Amit - Active Middleware Technology. In: Halevy, A.Y., Gal, A. (eds.) NGITS 2002. LNCS, vol. 2382, pp. 158–168. Springer, Heidelberg (2002)
9. McGuinness, D.L., van Harmelen, F.: OWL web ontology language overview. W3C recommendation (2004)
10. Preuveneers, D., et al.: Towards an Extensible Context Ontology for Ambient Intelligence. In: Markopoulos, P., Eggen, B., Aarts, E., Crowley, J.L. (eds.) EUSAI 2004. LNCS, vol. 3295, pp. 148–159. Springer, Heidelberg (2004)
11. Iqbal, A.M., Shepher, M., Adibi, S.S.R.: An Ontology-Based Electronic Medical Record for Chronic Disease Management. In: Proceedings of International Conference on Systems Science, pp. 1–10 (2011)
12. Mccarthy, J.: Actions and Other Events in Situation Calculus. In: Proceedings of the 8th International Conference on Principles of Knowledge Representation and Reasoning, pp. 615–628. Morgan Kaufmann Publishers (2002)
13. Matheus, C., Kokar, M., Baclawski, K., Letkowski, J., Call, C., Hinman, M., Salermo, J., Boulware, D.: SAWA: An Assistant for Higher-Level Fusion and Situation Awareness. In: Proc. of SPIE Multisensor, Multisource Information Fusion: Architectures, Algorithms, and Applications, pp. 75–85 (2005)

14. Baumgartner, N., Gottesheim, W., Mitsch, S., Retschitzegger, W., Schwinger, W.: BeAware! Situation awareness, the ontology-driven way. Data & Knowledge Engineering 69, 1181–1193 (2010)
15. Hobbs, J., Pan, F.: Time ontology in OWL. W3C working draft (2006), http://www.w3.org/TR/owl-time (last accessed June 29, 2013)
16. Machado, A., Pernas, A.M., Augustin, I., Thom, L.H., Wives, L.K., de Oliveira, P.M.: Situation as a key for proactive actions in Ambient Assisted Living. In: 15th International Conference on Enterprise Information Systems (ICEIS), Angers, France, July 4-7 (2013)
17. Pernas, A.M., Diaz, A.D., Motz, R., Palazzo, M., Oliveira, J.: Enriching adaptation in e-learning systems through a situation-aware ontology network. Interactive Technology and Smart Education 9(2), 1 (2012)

Semantic Web-Based Product Search

Damir Vandic and Viorel Milea

Erasmus University Rotterdam
P.O. Box 1738, 3000 DR Rotterdam, The Netherlands
{vandic,milea}@ese.eur.nl

Abstract. Product search on the Web has become increasingly popular for consumers to find products of interest. This paper proposes SWEPS, a platform inspired by concepts from the Semantic Web, for the purpose of effective and efficient product search. The proposed platform consists of modules that are responsible for the retrieval, integration, aggregation, and presentation of product information on the Web. The main goal is to reduce the consumer effort when searching and browsing for desired products. In order to test the viability of the proposed approach, we also present an adequate evaluation methodology for the proposed platform.

1 Introduction

Over the last few years, online product search has become very popular among consumers. According to a recent projection from Forrester Research, e-commerce spending in the United States will hit approximately $262 billion this year [16], which is an 13.4% increase compared to last year ($231 billion in 2012). Predictions for the future also show us that e-commerce will continue to play an important role, as Forrester Research predicts that in 2017, online spending will reach $370 billion (approximately a 10% compound annual growth rate from 2012). One of the reasons behind this growth is the increase in product specificity and consumer preference variation. Another reason is that the product search space on the Web has grown, as traditional stores without a Web shop are increasingly starting to offer their services also on the Web.

Although it is predicted that e-commerce will continue to grow, the current state of product search on the Web is characterized by several issues that can restrict this growth. First, most product search engines cannot properly deal with synonyms and homonyms. Second, there is no adequate support for multiple languages. Most importantly, the aggregation of Web-wide information is seldom done. These symptoms are present when we analyze the way consumers search for products on the Web. They keep switching back and forth from search results in order to compare, for example, prices of a certain product. Consumers would benefit from one unified view that displays such aggregated product information. Third, there is no parametric Web-wide product search available. Consumers cannot use queries like 'all televisions that (1) have a screen size of 100 inch, (2) support a wireless Internet connection, and (3) have an average energy consumption lower than 60 watt'.

J. Parsons and D. Chiu (Eds.): ER Workshops 2013, LNCS 8697, pp. 150–159, 2014.
© Springer International Publishing Switzerland 2014

Nowadays, there are several Web shops that offer local, as opposed to Web-wide, parametric product search. In this case, the user does employ parametric search in order to find the products that match specific criteria. However, this search is executed only over products that are available in a Web shop. Google Products, Overstock.com, and Shopzilla.com are three well-known applications of this type of product search engines. These search engines expect to receive the data from Web shops in a customized format. The downside of this approach is that every search engine has its own standard that needs to be obeyed by Web shops. It is highly unlikely that a product search engine of this type will cover most of the Web shops on the Web.

A possible solution to this problem can be the realization of the Semantic Web. In that case, the Web shops would not have to customize their data for each product search engine. This is because the Semantic Web extends the current Web in a way that enables machines to understand Web content. Allowing machines to understand concepts like persons, companies, products, etc., facilitates automatic aggregation of information over resources. For instance, consider that a Web page only describes the battery life of a mobile phone and another Web page describes just the color. If a computer can understand that 'battery life' and 'color' are properties of a mobile phone, and it can identify that the two Web pages are about the same resource (a specific mobile phone), then it can aggregate this information as describing one product and its properties.

Semantic annotations can provide users with search benefits [8,14]. The reason for this advantage is that data can be aggregated in one place. Consequently, users do not have to switch back and forth from result page to search results page. Furthermore, with semantic annotations it is possible to build more intelligent product search engines and user interfaces, as systems are then able to reason about products and their properties. For example, a search engine in such a setting is able to sort products based on properties with qualitative values, if the relationships between these qualitative values is known (e.g., Internet speed with values 'GPRS', '3G', 'HSDPA', and '4G'). Besides direct search benefits, semantic annotations can result in indirect search benefits. For example, they can allow intelligent agents, e.g., agents aiming at comparing products or performing automatic trading, to perform their tasks better.

In this paper, we propose the Semantic Web Enhanced Product Search framework (SWEPS), which addresses some of the issues that traditional product search engines are currently facing. From a high level point-of-view, SWEPS can be viewed as a framework with three main modules. The Information Integration module is responsible for the input of raw data and the output of structured information. The Knowledge Management module is used for the management of the framework domain ontology and the collected product information data. The Search Engine module provides search interfaces that optimally make use of the available semantic product information.

This paper paper is organized as follows. We discuss the related work in Sect. 2. Next, in Sect. 3, we explain the three different modules of the SWEPS framework in detail and discuss our evaluation methodology. Last, we provide a summary of this paper and indicate further directions for this research in Sect. 4.

2   Related Work

A vocabulary that has recently gained popularity is the schema.org vocabulary [5], proposed in 2011 by Bing, Google, Yahoo!, and Yandex. This is a very broad vocabulary that can be used both with the RDFa Lite and Microdata formats. Schema.org is a result of joint effort of the previously mentioned four companies, which means they all understand and support this vocabulary. With this vocabulary, the search engines aim to have a broad shared vocabulary that focuses on popular Web concepts. This means that it is by no means an effort to have an ontology of 'everything' or an ontology that is very specialized in one domain.

A more formal ontology is the GoodRelations ontology [12], developed and maintained by Martin Hepp since 2002. It is a highly standardized vocabulary that not only can describe product data, but also company data and product offerings. This ontology aims to specify all aspects that come into play in the domain of e-commerce. For example, it supports statements to depict time frames for which an offering is valid. Fortunately, in 2012, the schema.org team announced that GoodRelations has been integrated in their vocabulary, which means that schema.org can now be used to describe more granular product information [5]. Although GoodRelations defines concepts that can be used to describe product classes, i.e., their hierarchy and the associated product properties, the actual product classes, such as 'Phone' or 'Television', are not defined. The SWEPS framework not only provides a starting point of several product models in the domain of consumer electronics, but it also defines a Knowledge Management module that can be used to easily update or add new product information.

There are several studies that have investigated emerging Semantic Web search engine vocabularies and their application for the purpose of product information retrieval, aggregation, and presentation [7,10,18]. The authors of [10] present a general discussion on taxonomies, i.e., how they help us realize the full power of e-commerce, the future issues, and how the industry looks at this phenomenon. In [7], the authors argue that due to the many 'standards' in e-commerce (e.g., GoodRelations, UNSPSC, e-cl@ss, etc.), no consensus has been reached in the business-to-business market. They propose an approach that integrates the different standards and initiatives by means of ontology mapping. Nowadays, as stated previously, there is no need for such a solution, as four popular search engines have adopted a vocabulary (schema.org) that supports one main e-commerce ontology, i.e., GoodRelations. However, the fact remains that Web publishers can make mistakes in their annotations and can make use of other ontologies than schema.org. We argue that we still need to address this possibility, but not using an 'eager' ontology-integration based approach, where the mapping is done before the data collection process. Because GoodRelations can now be considered as the most important ontology for e-commerce, it is better to focus on approaches that instantiate on the fly product information and offerings in the GoodRelations ontology or a derivative of this ontology.

An overview of information extraction techniques that are useful in the context of SWEPS is given in [13]. As part of the information extraction task, we proposed effective entity-resolution algorithms for product descriptions retrieval in previous studies [2,3]. Furthermore, we investigated how one can classify newly found product descriptions to existing product classes [1,17]. For the Search Engine module, we focus on enhancing multi-faceted interfaces by effectively making use of the available semantics. Multifaceted search, also sometimes referred to as 'guided navigation', is a popular interaction paradigm that allows users to navigate through multidimensional data. One of the main uses of multifaceted search is in the domain of e-commerce, i.e., Web shops. It is being employed to solve the parametric product search problem for Web shops that have collected local offerings and product information. For example, in a Web shop the user might enter a query like 'samsung, gps' in order to search for a Samsung phone that has built-in GPS capabilities. After showing the initial result set, most Web shopping interfaces display the facets of the products in the result set, which can be used to further drill down into the results set. In the SWEPS framework, we aim for a user interface that effectively makes use of the semantics to improve the product search effectiveness and efficiency. For more details on multi-faceted search interfaces, we refer the reader to [9,11].

3   The SWEPS Framework

The SWEPS framework describes the modules that are used to process (possibly semantically annotated) Web pages, and provide an effective, user-friendly product search engine. Furthermore, it closely defines how these different components interact with each other. A high-level overview of the SWEPS framework is given in Fig. 1. Here we can observe the architecture of the SWEPS framework, which, as mentioned previously, consists of three modules: the Information Integration, the Knowledge Management, and the Search Engine module.

3.1   Semantic Database

All three modules are either indirectly or directly dependent on the Semantic Database. This database encapsulates the SWEPS ontology and the corresponding instance data (e.g., product instances and product offerings). The SWEPS ontology, which is used as the central ontology in the SWEPS framework, makes use of the GoodRelations ontology, and because GoodRelations does not have inference support for units of measurement, also the MUO ontology [4]. Fig. 2 shows an example of product information that is represented in the SWEPS Semantic Database. As one can notice, in order to make our ontology compatible with the used ontologies, the SWEPS ontology classes are subclasses of the corresponding classes either from the MUO or GoodRelations ontology.

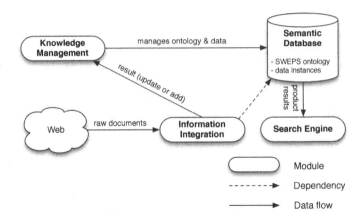

Fig. 1. An overview of the SWEPS framework. It shows us that the framework consists of three modules: Information Integration, Knowledge Management, and Search Engine.

For the implementation of the Semantic Database, we propose a hybrid approach. Because the algorithms in the Search Engine module need fast access to the product information (including aggregation support), we use a NoSQL database, i.e., MongoDB, to store the instances (e.g., product data). Because for some tasks reasoning is needed, such as the conversion between units of measurements, we also store the data in an RDF store with reasoning capabilities. For this purpose, we use the Jena framework with the TDB back-end for the storage and querying.

3.2   Information Integration

The Information Integration module is responsible for determining whether information obtained from the Web (e.g., product information, product offerings, etc.) has to be considered as an update to an existing entity (i.e., an RDF product instance) or the construction of a new entity. The information coming from the Web can be unstructured or structured (using any Semantic Web vocabulary). Fig. 3 shows a more detailed view of this module. One can notice that the module consists of three types of operations, i.e., classification, entity resolution, and RDF instantiation. As we can see in Fig. 1, the results of the Information Integration module (i.e., the 'RDF Instantiation' process) are passed on to the Knowledge Management module, which, in short, is responsible for persisting the result to the Semantic Database. The input for the 'Classification' process is either a set of key/value pairs or a set of RDF statements. The output of the 'RDF Instantiation' process is an RDF object with meta-data that indicates whether it concerns an insert or an update.

The flow of the Information Integration module is defined as following. When a document, structured or unstructured, enters the module, it first needs to be

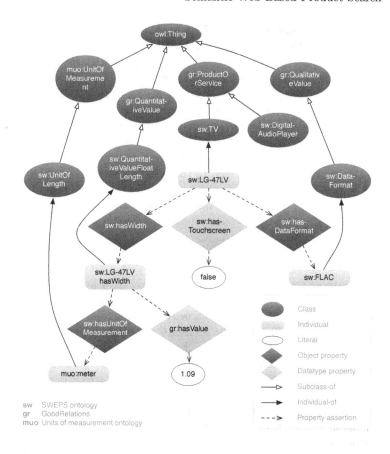

Fig. 2. An example of product information modeled using the SWEPS ontology. This graph shows an RDF representation of a TV from LG, with no touch screen, that supports the FLAC audio data format and that has a width of 1.09 meter.

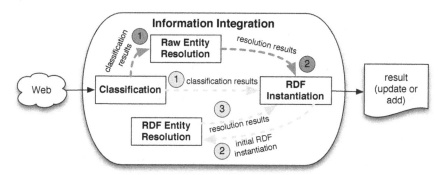

Fig. 3. A closer look at the Information Integration module

classified, i.e., which class from the SWEPS ontology should be considered in the instantiation process. Next, depending on whether we are processing structured or unstructured documents, we proceed to the proper entity resolution process. If we are dealing with an unstructured document, we execute the 'Raw Entity Resolution' process. This process passes its results on to the 'RDF Instantiation' process, which in turn constructs a new result that encodes whether we are dealing with an insert or an update. If the document is structured (i.e., annotated), we use a different entity resolution process, called the 'RDF Entity Resolution' process. This process first asks the 'RDF Instantiation' to create a valid RDF instance of the correct type (identified in the previous step). This RDF instance is then used to perform the entity resolution. We have proposed several solutions for two processes of the Information Integration module, i.e., the classification process [1,17] and the 'Raw Entity Resolution' process [2,3].

3.3 Knowledge Management

This module is mostly used for providing user interfaces for various tasks that concern the management of the Semantic Database. Given the results of the Information Integration module, the Knowledge Management module provides a user interface that can be used to semi-automatically process this result by persisting it to the Semantic Database. For example, if the result of the Information Integration module was an update, e.g., a Web page is encountered that describes more properties of the iPhone 5 than currently present in the database, the user can easily verify the update and once checked, commit it to the database. It is important to note that the Knowledge Management module is not responsible for identifying whether a product instance is already present in the database, that is the responsibility of the Information Integration module.

Besides providing a user interface for processing the results of the Information Integration module, the Knowledge Management module also enables users to manage the SWEPS ontology (e.g., the product classes and their properties). This process is also semi-automatic, i.e., the users can load a Web page that contains key/value pairs (representing product information) and the system will try to recognize new properties and their associated range (e.g., integer, float, qualitative value, etc.). The system can also recognize new qualitative values for existing, known properties. For example, it might be the case that for the property 'screen resolution' only the qualitative value 'Full-HD' is known, while there are also other values, such as '720p', which need to be added.

3.4 Search Engine

The Search Engine module encapsulates information retrieval algorithms that are specifically tailored for product search, and a multi-faceted product search interface that makes use of the semantics of the product data in order to improve the effectiveness and efficiency of product search. An important problem of multifaceted search is the selection of facets that should be displayed for each query. Because products have so many attributes that could be displayed as facets,

Web shops usually have some static business logic to display certain facets for each result set. Although this works for local Web shops that do not have many product categories, the creation of the business logic is a time consuming process and is not appropriate for Web-wide product search. In literature, the optimal selection of facets that minimizes the number of drill-downs is referred to as the *facet selection* problem, which can be expressed as the optimization of a hyperactive media link generation process [6]. For this module, we propose new algorithms for the facet selection problem in product search and we distinguish between two types of tasks, i.e., exact product search, and fuzzy product search.

In the situation of exact product search, users know exactly the characteristics of their desired product and we assume that such a product actually exists. We aim to investigate to what extent users are employing the optimal drill-down with a fixed list of facets and how this is affected if we use a facet optimization algorithm. We hypothesize that a user interface with dynamic facet selection, where the order and grouping of facets is optimally arranged depending on the query, will result in shorter and more effective search sessions compared to faceted search engines that are not dynamic. In the literature, we can find algorithms for the facet selection problem [15]. However, as our initial experimental results showed, these algorithms are not adequate in the context of product information facets. One of the reasons is that these algorithms rely on data assumptions that do not hold for product data. For example, with traditional faceted interfaces, there is often no sensible ranking of product results, while it is assumed that such a ranking exists.

The desired product does not exist in the case of fuzzy product search, i.e., the consumers need to find the 'closest' product that matches the characteristics of the original target product. For example, the user might be looking for a phone that has Wi-Fi, supports 4G, and has a full-HD screen of at least 4 inches. Currently there are no services available where the user can indicate the relative importance of these attributes and where the search results are ranked according to these importances. For instance, if there is no phone that matches these criteria, but there is one with support for 3G, then that phone might be suggested. In order to achieve this, we need to understand the underlying semantics of each attribute value, i.e., that 3G is closer to 4G instead of GPRS (a slower type wireless connection).

3.5   Evaluation

Several evaluation techniques can be used to assess the performance of the different framework components as well as the overall system performance. The Information Integrator module can be evaluated by analyzing the performance of the individual processes. Each of the Information Integration processes, i.e., classification, entity resolution, and instantiation, is evaluated using the precision, recall, accuracy, and specificity measures. The Knowledge Management module can be evaluated by performing interviews with users, in order to asses to what extent the system is easy to use and effective in reaching its goal. For the Search Engine module we propose to setup two experiments. In the first experiment, users are asked to search for a product with specific characteristics, using our search interface and an existing static faceted product search engine. In this experiment we measure the time and number of drill-downs. For the second experiment, we place users in the same context but change the task, i.e., instead of finding a product that exactly matches a particular set of characteristics, the users need to find the *closest* matching product.

Last, we should evaluate if the goal of the platform is achieved, namely to provide users more precise product search in more databases and but in less time. For this purpose an external pool of users should be asked to perform specific queries using our system as well as regular Web product search (e.g., Google product search, Shopzilla.com, Shopping.com, etc.). One example of such a query task can be: 'all Nokia phones that cost less than 300 Euro and have excellent reviews'. We propose to evaluate the efficiency of the two approaches, the SWEPS approach versus the traditional Web product search. For this purpose we have to measure and compare the time needed to retrieve the desired product using each of these two approaches. We also measure the precision, recall, accuracy, and specificity of the returned product results. In addition, by means of questionnaires, we propose to gather and compare the user's degree of satisfaction in interacting with each of these two systems.

4   Conclusion

In this paper we have identified the shortcomings of the current state of product search on the Web. One of the important issues is that there is no aggregation across multiple Web sites. Another issue is that there is no Web-wide parametric search possible, i.e., a user cannot specify his or her query very precisely. To address these issues, we propose the Semantic Web Enhanced Product Search framework (SWEPS). The SWEPS framework can be used to enhance the online product search effectiveness and efficiency.

The core of the SWEPS framework consists of three modules: the Information Integration module, the Knowledge Management module, and the Search Engine module. The Information Integration module is responsible for the processing of raw input data and the production of structured information. This structured information is semi-automatically managed using the Knowledge Management module. This module is also used for the management of the framework domain ontology. The Search Engine module provides a faceted search interface that optimally makes use of the available semantic product information.

Acknowledgment. Damir Vandic is sponsored by the NWO Mosaic project 017.007.142: Semantic Web Enhanced Product Search (SWEPS).

References

1. Aanen, S.S., Nederstigt, L.J., Vandić, D., Fräsincar, F.: SCHEMA - An Algorithm for Automated Product Taxonomy Mapping in E-commerce. In: Simperl, E., Cimiano, P., Polleres, A., Corcho, O., Presutti, V. (eds.) ESWC 2012. LNCS, vol. 7295, pp. 300–314. Springer, Heidelberg (2012)

2. de Bakker, M., Frasincar, F., Vandic, D.: A Hybrid Model Words-Driven Approach for Web Product Duplicate Detection. In: Salinesi, C., Norrie, M.C., Pastor, Ó. (eds.) CAiSE 2013. LNCS, vol. 7908, pp. 149–161. Springer, Heidelberg (2013)

3. de Bakker, M., Frasincar, F., Vandic, D., Kaymak, U.: Model Words-Driven Approaches for Duplicate Detection on the Web. In: 28th Symposium on Applied Computing (SAC 2013), pp. 717–723. ACM (2013)

4. Berrueta, D., Polo, L.: MUO | An Ontology to Represent Units of Measurement in RDF (2009), `http://goo.gl/fDsuk`

5. Bing, Google, Yahoo! and Yandex: Schema.org (2013), `http://schema.org/`

6. Brusilovsky, P.: Adaptive Hypermedia. User Modeling and User-Adapted Interaction 11(1), 87–110 (2001)

7. Corcho, O., G_omez-P_erez, A., et al.: Solving Integration Problems of E-commerce Standards and Initiatives Through Ontological Mappings. In: Workshop on E-Business and Intelligent Web (IJCAI 2001), pp. 1–10. Citeseer (2001)

8. Cuadrado, A.F., de la Torre, E.V.: SIS: Semantic Intelligent Search Engine from Heterogeneous Information Sources Applied to E-commerce. In: GI Jahrestagung (2), pp. 700–705 (2008)

9. English, J., Hearst, M., Sinha, R., Swearingen, K., Yee, K.: Hierarchical faceted metadata in site search interfaces. In: Human Factors in Computing Systems (CHI 2002), pp. 628–639. ACM (2002)

10. Fensel, D., McGuiness, D., Schulten, E., Ng, W., Lim, G., Yan, G.: Ontologies and electronic commerce. IEEE Intelligent Systems 16(1), 8–14 (2001)

11. Hearst, M., Elliott, A., English, J., Sinha, R., Swearingen, K., Yee, K.: Finding the flow in web site search. Communications of the ACM 45(9), 42–49 (2002)

12. Hepp, M.: GoodRelations: An Ontology for Describing Products and Services Offers on the Web. In: Gangemi, A., Euzenat, J. (eds.) EKAW 2008. LNCS (LNAI), vol. 5268, pp. 329–346. Springer, Heidelberg (2008)

13. Hogenboom, F., Frasincar, F., Kaymak, U.: An Overview of Approaches to Extract Information from Natural Language Corpora. In: Tenth Dutch-Belgian Information Retrieval Workshop (DIR 2010), pp. 69–70 (2010)

14. Kim, W., Choi, D., Park, S.: Intelligent product information search framework based on the semantic web. In: 3rd International Semantic Web Conference (ISWC 2004). pp. 7–11 (2004)

15. Liberman, S., Lempel, R.: Approximately Optimal Facet Selection. In: 27th Annual ACM Symposium on Applied Computing (SAC 2012), pp. 702–708. ACM (2012)

16. Babej, M.E.: Forrester: U.S. E-Commerce to Rise 13% This Year (2013), `http://goo.gl/zNa4n`

17. Nederstigt, L.J., Aanen, S.S., Vandić, D., Fräsincar, F.: An Automatic Approach for Mapping Product Taxonomies in E-Commerce Systems. In: Ralyté, J., Franch, X., Brinkkemper, S., Wrycza, S. (eds.) CAiSE 2012. LNCS, vol. 7328, pp. 334–349. Springer, Heidelberg (2012)

18. Vandic, D., van Dam, J.W., Frasincar, F.: Faceted Product Search Powered by the Semantic Web. Decision Support Systems 53(3), 425–437 (2012)

News Recommendation Using Semantics with the Bing-SF-IDF Approach

Frederik Hogenboom, Michel Capelle, and Marnix Moerland

Erasmus University Rotterdam
P.O. Box 1738, 3000 DR Rotterdam, The Netherlands
fhogenboom@ese.eur.nl,
{michelcapelle,marnix.moerland}@gmail.com

Abstract. Traditionally, content-based news recommendation is performed by means of the cosine similarity and the TF-IDF weighting scheme for terms occurring in news messages and user profiles. Semantics-driven variants like SF-IDF additionally take into account term meaning by exploiting synsets from semantic lexicons. However, semantics-based weighting techniques are not able to handle – often crucial – named entities, which are often not present in semantic lexicons. Hence, we extend SF-IDF by also employing named entity similarities using Bing page counts. Our proposed method, Bing-SF-IDF, outperforms TF-IDF and its semantics-driven variants in terms of F_1-scores and kappa statistics.

1 Introduction

The Web is an increasingly important source of information, which is mostly posted in the form of news. However, today's users are confronted with an overload of information, and hence, many recommendation methods have been developed that aid in filtering and structuring information based on user preferences or characteristics (captured in user profiles). Traditionally, such content-based recommender systems are based on term frequencies. A commonly used measure is the Term Frequency – Inverse Document Frequency (TF-IDF) [16]. When employing user profiles, these can be translated into vectors of TF-IDF weights. With a measure like cosine similarity, one can calculate the interestingness of a new item. For this, TF-IDF weights are computed on every term within a document.

TF-IDF-based systems do not consider the text semantics, which could be added by using Web ontologies. A drawback of ontologies is that they are domain dependent, and hence require continuous maintenance. Alternatively, one could employ synonym sets (synsets) from general semantic lexicons (e.g., WordNet [8]). In earlier work [5], we introduced the Synset Frequency – Inverse Document Frequency (SF-IDF) measure, operating on WordNet synsets instead of terms. We evaluated SF-IDF against TF-IDF and against an other semantics-based alternative, Semantic Similarity (SS), and demonstrated the benefits of considering synsets.

J. Parsons and D. Chiu (Eds.): ER Workshops 2013, LNCS 8697, pp. 160–169, 2014.

Generally, news articles are linked to many named entities. These could provide crucial information when constructing user profiles, yet when performing synset-based recommendation, they are often not considered. One could enhance existing semantics-based recommendation methods like SF-IDF by employing similarities based on page counts gathered by Web search engines, such as Google or Bing, thus avoiding the use of domain dependent ontologies. Our current endeavors contribute to the state-of-the-art by extending SF-IDF by additionally considering named entity similarities using Bing page counts. The proposed recommendation method, Bing-SF-IDF, as well as SF-IDF and several semantic lexicon-driven similarity methods are implemented and evaluated.

The remainder of this paper is organized as follows. First, we discuss related work in Section 2. Next, we introduce the semantics-driven Bing-SF-IDF news recommender in Section 3. Subsequently, we evaluate our performance in Section 4. Last, we draw conclusions and provide some directions for future work in Section 5.

2   Preliminaries

In the field of recommender systems, many different profile-based recommender systems have been developed. Their main difference lies in the implemented similarity measures for calculating news item and user profile similarities.

2.1   TF-IDF

The de facto standard of similarity measures found in literature is TF-IDF, combined with cosine similarities [14]. The TF-IDF method consists of two parts, i.e., term frequency $tf(t, d)$ and inverse document frequency $idf(t, d)$. It operates on terms T in documents D and measures the number of occurrences n of term $t \in T$ in document $d \in D$, expressed as a fraction of the total number of occurrences of all k terms in document d:

$$tf(t, d) = \frac{n_{t,d}}{\sum_k n_{k,d}} .$$

(1)

The inverse document frequency expresses the occurrence of a term t in a set of documents D and is defined as:

$$idf(t, d) = \log \frac{|D|}{|\{d : t \in d\}|} ,$$

(2)

where $|D|$ is the total amount of documents in the set of documents to compare, and $d : t \in d$ represents the amount of documents containing term t. Next, $T(t, d)$ is obtained by multiplying $tf(t, d)$ and $idf(t, d)$:

$$T(t, d) = tf(t, d) \times idf(t, d) .$$

(3)

Subsequently, for every term t in document d, the TF-IDF value is computed and stored in a vector $A(d)$. This computation is performed for all documents in D. Then, we obtain the similarity between a set of terms from news item d_u and user profile d_r using the cosine similarity measure:

$$sim_T(d_u, d_r) = \frac{A(d_u) \cdot A(d_r)}{||A(d_u)|| \times ||A(d_r)||} . \tag{4}$$

After every unread news document has been assigned a similarity value (with respect to the user profile), all unread news items with similarities higher than a cut-off value are recommended to the user.

2.2 SF-IDF

One of the main drawbacks of TF-IDF is that semantics are not considered. This causes synonyms to be mistakenly counted as separate terms, and homonyms as one term. Therefore, semantics-based similarity measures have been proposed, such as the Synset Frequency – Inverse Document Frequency (SF-IDF) [5], i.e., a TF-IDF variant which makes use of synonym sets (synsets) from a semantic lexicon (e.g., WordNet [8]) instead of terms. These synsets are obtained after a word sense disambiguation procedure. When replacing term t by synset s, the SF-IDF formulas are:

$$sf(s, d) = \frac{n_{s,d}}{\sum_k n_{k,d}} , \tag{5}$$

$$idf(s, d) = \log \frac{|D|}{|\{d : s \in d\}|} , \tag{6}$$

$$S(s, d) = sf(s, d) \times idf(s, d) , \tag{7}$$

$$sim_S(d_u, d_r) = \frac{A(d_u) \cdot A(d_r)}{||A(d_u)|| \times ||A(d_r)||} . \tag{8}$$

News item recommendation is subsequently performed in a similar manner as for the TF-IDF method, using the cosine similarity measure and a cut-off value.

2.3 Semantic Similarity

The Semantic Similarity (SS) method [5] compares synsets from unread news items with those of the user profile by employing pairs between the elements of the two sets with a common part-of-speech (i.e., they elements share a linguistic category such as a verb or a noun). We define $V = U \times R$, i.e., the Cartesian product of U and R containing all possible combinations of synsets from the unread news item d_u, referred to as U, and the union of synsets from the user profile d_r, denoted by R. Here u_k and r_l denote synsets from the unread news item and user profile, and k and l are the number of available synsets. A subset of V containing all the combinations with common parts-of-speech is defined as $W = \{(u, r) \in V : POS(u) = POS(r)\}$, where $POS(u)$ and $POS(r)$ describe the part-of-speech of synsets u and r in the unread news item and user profile, respectively.

For every combination in W, a similarity rank is computed. This rank measures the semantic distance between synsets u and r when represented as nodes in a hierarchy of 'is-a' relationships:

$$sim_{SS}(W) = \frac{\sum\limits_{(u,r) \in W} sim(u,r)}{|W|} . \tag{9}$$

Here, $sim(u,r)$ denotes the similarity rank between the synsets u and r, and the number of combinations between the synsets from the unread news item and the user profile is denoted by $|W|$. Again, similar to TF-IDF and SF-IDF, the ranks which are higher than a specific cut-off value are recommended to the user.

The similarity rank $sim(u,r)$ can be computed in various ways. Some make use of the information content (the negative logarithm of the sum of all probabilities of all the words in the synset). For instance, the Jiang & Conrath [11] measure uses the information content of both the synsets and the lowest common subsumer, while Lin's measure [13] makes use of the logarithms of the chances of appearance of both nodes and the lowest common subsumer. Resnik's measure [15] on the other hand maximizes the information content of the lowest common subsumer of the two nodes. The Leacock & Chodorow [12] and Wu & Palmer [18] measures on the other hand make use of the path length between the nodes. The path length is either the shortest path between the two nodes (Leacock & Chodorow) or the depth from a node to the top node (Wu & Palmer).

2.4   Enhancements

Recent studies have shown that the more a pair of entities co-occur on Web sites, the more likely it is that there is a similarity between both entities [3]. Therefore, one could enhance existing semantics-based recommendation methods, such as SF-IDF and SS, by (additionally) employing similarities based on page counts gathered by Web search engines, such as Google or Bing.

3   Bing-SF-IDF Recommendation

Like most semantics-based news recommendation methods, Bing-SF-IDF operates on a user profile, containing all currently read news items. For each unread news item, a similarity score between the news article and the user profile is computed. In case a similarity score exceeds a predefined cut-off value, the corresponding news item is recommended. In essence, the Bing-SF-IDF similarity score is a weighted average of two similarity scores. The Bing component expresses similarities between named entities, whereas SF-IDF measures the similarities between synsets.

The Bing similarity score takes into account the named entities that do not occur in a semantic lexicon, by deriving them from news articles through a named entity recognizer. For this, we consider an unread news item d_u and user profile d_r, which can be described respectively using two sets of named entities, i.e.,

$U = \{u_1, u_2, \ldots, u_k\}$, $R = \{r_1, r_2, \ldots, r_l\}$. Here, u_i (where $1 \leq i \leq k$) represents a named entity in the unread news item U, r_j (where $1 \leq j \leq l$) describes a named entity in the user profile R, and k and l are the number of named entities in the unread news item and in the user profile, respectively.

Next, we construct a vector $V = U \times R$ containing all possible pairs of named entities from the unread news item d_u and the user profile d_r. Then, between-pair similarity is measured using search engine page counts, i.e., the number of Web pages found by the Bing Web search engine containing a named entity or a pair of named entities. For every pair (u, r) in V we compute the page rank-based Point-Wise Mutual Information (PMI) co-occurrence similarity measure [4], which we define as:

$$sim_{PMI}(u, r) = \log \frac{\frac{c(u,r)}{N}}{\frac{c(u)}{N} \times \frac{c(r)}{N}} , \qquad (10)$$

where $c(u, r)$ denotes the page count for the pair (u, r) of named entities. Moreover, $c(u)$ and $c(r)$ are the page counts for the named entities u from the unread news item and r from the user profile, respectively, and N is the amount of Web pages indexed by Bing ($\sim$15 billion).

Last, the Bing similarity score is defined as the average of the PMI similarity scores over all named entity pairs:

$$sim_B(V) = \frac{\sum\limits_{(u,r) \in V} sim_{PMI}(u, r)}{|V|} . \qquad (11)$$

Next, we can combine the Bing score sim_B and SF-IDF similarity score sim_S for every unread news item d_u and user profile d_r. We employ min-max normalization between 0 and 1 on both sets of similarity scores, and subsequently take the weighted average of these scores:

$$\overline{sim}_B(d_u, d_r) = \frac{sim_B(d_u, d_r) - \min\limits_{u} sim_B(d_u, d_r)}{\max\limits_{u} sim_B(d_u, d_r) - \min\limits_{u} sim_B(d_u, d_r)} , \qquad (12)$$

$$\overline{sim}_S(d_u, d_r) = \frac{sim_S(d_u, d_r) - \min\limits_{u} sim_S(d_u, d_r)}{\max\limits_{u} sim_S(d_u, d_r) - \min\limits_{u} sim_S(d_u, d_r)} , \qquad (13)$$

$$sim_{BS}(d_u, d_r) = \alpha \times \overline{sim}_B(d_u, d_r) + (1 - \alpha) \times \overline{sim}_S(d_u, d_r) . \qquad (14)$$

Here, weight α is optimized during testing on a training set. All the unread news items which have a similarity score that exceeds the predefined cut-off value are recommended to the user.

Our framework is implemented as an extension to the Ceryx [5] plugin of the Hermes News Portal (HNP) [9]. The Java-based HNP operates based on user profiles and processes news items from RSS feeds, while making use of an expert-created OWL domain ontology. News items are classified using the GATE natural language processing software [7] and the WordNet [8] semantic lexicon. The semantics-based methods make use of the Stanford Log-Linear Part-of-Speech Tagger [17], Lesk Word Sense Disambiguation [10], and the Alias-i's

LingPipe 4.1.0 [1] Named Entity Recognizer. Page counts are collected with the Bing API 2.0 [2].

4   Evaluation

For our evaluation of the performance of Bing-SF-IDF compared against its alternatives, we collected 100 news articles from a Reuters news feed on technology companies. Although the set of articles appears to be rather small, the limited number of articles is motivated by the fact that subsequent annotation steps require a lot of effort from the annotators, and hence for now we suffice with 100 annotated news articles. In our experiments, three experts classified these articles based on eight given topics. Out of these user ratings, a user profile was constructed for every topic using a minimum inter-annotator agreement (IAA) of 66% The overall agreement was on average 90%. For each topic, the result set is split proportionally into a training set (60%) for creating the user profile and a test set (40%) for evaluation.

4.1   Experimental Set-Up

In order to evaluate our proposed recommendation method, we compare the performance to the performance of the TF-IDF [16], SF-IDF [5], and five SS recommendation methods [11,12,13,15,18] in terms of F_1 (i.e., the harmonic mean of precision and recall scores) and kappa statistics [6] (measuring whether the proposed classification is better than a random guess), which are the norm in this context. We additionally report on accuracy, precision, recall, sensitivity, and specificity. Moreover, we analyze graphs of F_1 and kappa statistics over the full range of cut-off values and assess the significance of the results using a one-tailed two-sample paired Student t-test with a level of 95% significance. Last, we optimize the α-value used in Bing-SF-IDF using a genetic algorithm, which aims to maximize F_1-scores. The genetic algorithm is executed with a population of 150, a mutation probability of 0.1, elitism of 50, and a maximum number of 25 generations.

4.2   Experimental Results

The average performance for each recommender is displayed in Table 1. From this, we can conclude that Bing-SF-IDF outperforms all recommenders, and demonstrates to be a substantial improvement over SF-IDF method which served as a basis for our proposed extension. Also, the Jiang & Conrath recommender shows good overall performance. The graphs in Figures 1(a) and 1(b) provide a closer look into the F_1-scores and kappa statistics for all cut-off values and support these findings. Figure 1(a) shows that for high cut-off values (i.e., above 0.3), Bing-SF-IDF outperforms all other recommenders in terms of F_1. For the other recommendation methods, performances do not differ a lot within the

Table 1. Average test results for Bing-SF-IDF (BS), SF-IDF (S), Jiang & Conrath (J&C), Leacock & Chodorow (L&C), Lin (L), Resnik (R), Wu & Palmer (W&P), and TF-IDF (T)

	Acc.	Prec.	Rec.	F_1	Sens.	Spec.	Kappa
BS	0.81	0.69	0.53	0.58	0.53	0.91	0.46
S	0.65	0.68	0.43	0.37	0.37	0.76	0.32
J&C	0.72	0.73	0.48	0.45	0.47	0.82	0.31
L&C	0.55	0.44	0.58	0.39	0.58	0.54	0.11
L	0.51	0.38	0.53	0.34	0.53	0.51	0.03
R	0.60	0.55	0.57	0.42	0.57	0.61	0.17
W&P	0.57	0.46	0.59	0.40	0.59	0.55	0.13
T	0.75	0.83	0.44	0.45	0.43	0.88	0.34

high range of cut-off values. For low cut-off values, on the other hand, TF-IDF performs best.

The kappa statistic, which is plotted in Figure 1(b), measures whether the proposed classifications are better than random guessing. Positive scores (better than random) are preferred over negative scores (worse than random) or scores of exactly 0 (same as random). The Bing-SF-IDF recommender scores a higher kappa statistic than the other recommenders for high cut-off values, indicating that the Bing-SF-IDF recommender seems to have more classification power than the others. Also, TF-IDF and the semantics-based SF-IDF and Jiang & Conrath SS methods show good performance.

The statistical significance of the results is assessed in Tables 2 and 3. We can deduce that Bing-SF-IDF significantly outperforms all other approaches in terms of F_1-scores and kappa statistics. Also, TF-IDF performs well, as it significantly outperforms SF-IDF and all SS methods when it comes to kappa statistics, yet it

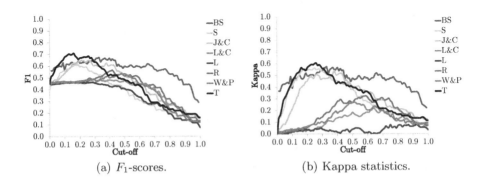

(a) F_1-scores.　　　　　　　　　　(b) Kappa statistics.

Fig. 1. F_1-scores and kappa statistics measured for the Bing-SF-IDF (BS), SF-IDF (S), Jiang & Conrath (J&C), Leacock & Chodorow (L&C), Lin (L), Resnik (R), Wu & Palmer (W&P), and TF-IDF (T) recommenders for various cut-off values

Table 2. One-tailed two-sample paired Student t-test p-values for the F_1-measure averages for the Bing-SF-IDF (BS), SF-IDF (S), Jiang & Conrath (J&C), Leacock & Chodorow (L&C), Lin (L), Resnik (R), Wu & Palmer (W&P), and TF-IDF (T) recommenders ($H_0 : \mu_{column} = \mu_{row}$, $H_1 : \mu_{column} > \mu_{row}$, $\alpha = 0.05$)

	BS	S	J&C	L&C	L	R	W&P	T
BS		1.00	1.00	1.00	1.00	1.00	1.00	1.00
S	0.00		0.00	0.03	1.00	0.00	0.01	0.00
J&C	0.00	1.00		1.00	1.00	1.00	1.00	0.59
L&C	0.00	0.97	0.00		1.00	0.00	0.07	0.00
L	0.00	0.00	0.00	0.00		0.00	0.00	0.00
R	0.00	1.00	0.00	1.00	1.00		1.00	0.01
W&P	0.00	0.99	0.00	0.93	1.00	0.00		0.00
T	0.00	1.00	0.41	1.00	1.00	0.99	1.00	

Table 3. One-tailed two-sample paired Student t-test p-values for the kappa statistic averages for the Bing-SF-IDF (BS), SF-IDF (S), Jiang & Conrath (J&C), Leacock & Chodorow (L&C), Lin (L), Resnik (R), Wu & Palmer (W&P), and TF-IDF (T) recommenders ($H_0 : \mu_{column} = \mu_{row}$, $H_1 : \mu_{column} > \mu_{row}$, $\alpha = 0.05$)

	BS	S	J&C	L&C	L	R	W&P	T
BS		1.00	1.00	1.00	1.00	1.00	1.00	1.00
S	0.00		0.56	1.00	1.00	1.00	1.00	0.00
J&C	0.00	0.44		1.00	1.00	1.00	1.00	0.00
L&C	0.00	0.00	0.00		1.00	0.00	0.00	0.00
L	0.00	0.00	0.00	0.00		0.00	0.00	0.00
R	0.00	0.00	0.00	1.00	1.00		1.00	0.00
W&P	0.00	0.00	0.00	1.00	1.00	0.00		0.00
T	0.00	1.00	1.00	1.00	1.00	1.00	1.00	

does not significantly outperform the Jiang & Conrath SS method in terms of F_1. SF-IDF merely outperforms one recommender in terms of F_1 (Lin SS), but seems to do better in terms of kappa statistics. The worst performing recommendation method overall is Lin SS, which is significantly outperformed by all methods on both measures.

Last, an evaluation of the optimized α-values for all cut-off values leads to various insights. For Bing-SF-IDF, scores are weighted using an average optimized α of 0.52 (with a standard deviation of 0.29). Hence, a substantial weight is given to both the Bing similarities and the synsets, underlining the importance of both proposed extensions. Worth noting is that the higher the cut-off, the higher the value of α. This indicates that Bing similarities become more important when a high precision is required. For lower cut-off values, i.e., when the focus is more on high recall, named entities seem less relevant and synsets alone are more than adequate for recommending news items.

5 Conclusions

In general, news recommendation is performed using the cosine similarity and the term-based TF-IDF weighting scheme. However, semantics-driven methods, which take into account term meaning, are able to handle news information in a better way. Such methods exploit semantic lexicon synsets and the cosine similarity (SF-IDF) or make use of semantic similarities (SS). However, they do not take into account named entities, which are usually not present in semantic lexicons.

Hence, we extended the state-of-the-art SF-IDF recommendation method by also taking into account named entities using Bing page counts. Our proposed method, Bing-SF-IDF, has been implemented in Ceryx, an extension to the Hermes news personalization service. Our evaluation on 100 financial news messages and 8 topics showed that Bing-SF-IDF significantly outperforms TF-IDF as well as other semantic methods with respect to F_1-scores and kappa statistics.

The discussed recommenders are based on synsets from a single semantic lexicon. However, this still creates a dependency on the information available in such lexicons. Therefore, as future work, we would like to investigate a way to combine multiple semantic lexicons. Moreover, it would be worthwhile to explore the possibilities of employing semantic relations from semantic lexicons, or to perform additional analysis on similar Bing-based named entity extensions to other recommendation methods, such as SS.

Acknowledgment. The authors are partially supported by the NWO Physical Sciences Free Competition project 612.001.009: Financial Events Recognition in News for Algorithmic Trading (FERNAT) and the Dutch national program COMMIT.

References

1. Alias-i: LingPipe 4.1.0 (2008), From: http://alias-i.com/lingpipe
2. Bing: Bing API 2.0 (2012), http://www.bing.com/developers/s/APIBasics.html
3. Bollegala, D., Matsuo, Y., Ishizuka, M.: Measuring Semantic Similarity between Words Using Web Search Engines. In: 16th Int. Conf. on World Wide Web (WWW 2007), pp. 757–766. ACM (2007)
4. Bouma, G.: Normalized (Pointwise) Mutual Information in Collocation Extraction. In: Chiarcos, C., de Castilho, R.E., Stede, M. (eds.) Biennial GSCL Conf. 2009 (GSCL 2009), pp. 31–40. Gunter Narr Verlag, Tübingen (2009)
5. Capelle, M., Moerland, M., Frasincar, F., Hogenboom, F.: Semantics-Based News Recommendation. In: 2nd Int. Conf. on Web Intelligence, Mining and Semantics (WIMS 2012). ACM (2012)
6. Cohen, J.: A Coefficient of Agreement for Nominal Scales. Educational and Psychological Measurement 20(1), 37–46 (1960)
7. Cunningham, H., Maynard, D., Bontcheva, K., Tablan, V.: GATE: A Framework and Graphical Development Environment for Robust NLP Tools and Applications. In: 40th Anniversary Meeting of the Association for Computational Linguistics (ACL 2002), pp. 168–175. Association for Computational Linguistics (2002)

8. Fellbaum, C.: WordNet: An Electronic Lexical Database. MIT Press (1998)
9. Frasincar, F., Borsje, J., Levering, L.: A Semantic Web-Based Approach for Building Personalized News Services. Int. J. E-Business Research 5(3), 35–53 (2009)
10. Jensen, A.S., Boss, N.S.: Textual Similarity: Comparing Texts in Order to Discover How Closely They Discuss the Same Topics. Bachelor's Thesis, Technical University of Denmark (2008)
11. Jiang, J.J., Conrath, D.W.: Semantic Similarity Based on Corpus Statistics and Lexical Taxonomy. In: 10th Int. Conf. on Research in Computational Linguistics (ROCLING 1997), pp. 19–33 (1997)
12. Leacock, C., Chodorow, M.: Combining Local Context and WordNet Similarity for Word Sense Identification. In: WordNet: An Electronic Lexical Database, pp. 265–283. MIT Press (1998)
13. Lin, D.: An Information-Theoretic Definition of Similarity. In: 15th Int. Conf. on Machine Learning (ICML 1998), pp. 296–304. Morgan Kaufmann (1998)
14. Moens, M.-F.: Information Extraction: Algorithms and Prospects in a Retrieval Context. Springer (2006)
15. Resnik, P.: Using Information Content to Evaluate Semantic Similarity in a Taxonomy. In: 14th Int. Joint Conf. on Artificial Intelligence (IJCAI 1995), pp. 448–453. Morgan Kaufmann (1995)
16. Salton, G., Buckley, C.: Term-Weighting Approaches in Automatic Text Retrieval. Information Processing and Management 24(5), 513–523 (1988)
17. Toutanova, K., Klein, D., Manning, C.D., Singer, Y.: Feature-Rich Part-of-Speech Tagging with a Cyclic Dependency Network. In: Human Language Technology Conf. of the North American Chapter of the Association for Computational Linguistics (HLTNAACL 2003), pp. 252–259 (2003)
18. Wu, Z., Palmer, M.S.: Verb Semantics and Lexical Selection. In: 32nd Annual Meeting of the Association for Computational Linguistics (ACL 1994), pp. 133–138. Association for Computational Linguistics (1994)

An Exploratory Study on Websites Quality Assessment

Samira Si-saïd Cherfi[1], Anh Do Tuan[1], and Isabelle Comyn-Wattiau[2]

[1] CEDRIC-CNAM, Paris, France
[2] CEDRIC-CNAM & ESSEC Business School, France
{samira.cherfi,wattiau}@cnam.fr,
dtanh@ioit.ac.vn

Abstract. The website of a company may be a real and sustainable competitive advantage. However, the quality of web applications does not increase as well as their rapid development. In software engineering many quality models were proposed. Research on website quality is prolific. State-of-the-arts on website quality have already been published. However, due to the productivity of this research field, this paper proposes an update of this literature in order to be able to sketch future research avenues on website quality. We analyze how the current approaches cover the large spectrum of web application quality factors. This paper aims at checking whether the main metrics proposed by researchers can be mapped towards ISO 9126 quality sub-characteristics and how this mapping covers the six main characteristics.

Keywords: quality, model, metrics, website quality, quality assessment.

1 Introduction

Hundreds of new websites are created every day. Existing ones are updated heavily and rapidly. Thanks to Netcraft market-share analysis, we know that the number of websites exceeded 56 million prior to December 2004. The size of the World Wide Web is estimated at around 13 billion web pages (www.worldwidewebsize.com). Building a website is performed by more and more professional developers. However, many websites are still produced by amateurs [1]. A website of a company may be a real and sustainable competitive advantage [2]. Moreover, the quality of the website heavily impacts the customer confidence. However, the quality of websites does not develop as well as their rapid development. Many developers did not realize that web applications have specific characteristics and requirements, considerably different from that of traditional software. The consequences are that nearly 25% web projects failed.

In software engineering, many quality models were proposed. Some of them became international standards, such as ISO 9126 [3] or, more recently ISO 25010 [4]. The ISO 9126 quality model classifies software quality in a set of six characteristics, and twenty seven sub-characteristics.

Research on website quality is prolific. It led to the definition of specific criteria, frameworks, and experiments. State-of-the-arts of the research on website quality have already been published. However, due to the productivity of this field, we argue

J. Parsons and D. Chiu (Eds.): ER Workshops 2013, LNCS 8697, pp. 170–179, 2014.
© Springer International Publishing Switzerland 2014

that it is necessary to update this literature in order to be able to sketch future research avenues on website quality.

This paper aims at checking whether the main metrics proposed by researchers can be mapped towards ISO 9126 quality sub-characteristics and thus it analyses how this mapping covers the six main characteristics. Section 2 defines and reviews website quality. Section 3 is dedicated to a state-of-the-art on measures and metrics specific to website quality. Section 4 synthesizes our analysis on how the current approaches cover the website quality factors. Finally, some conclusions and perspectives are provided in Section 5.

2   Website Quality

This section aims to provide an aggregate view of existing literature proposed to evaluate and ensure website quality. Metrics are presented in Section 3.

2.1   ISO and other Standards

To the best of our knowledge, there is no specific standard for websites quality. However, websites are specific software applications. Therefore quality standards of software can be applied to web applications.

ISO 9126 introduced in 1991 addresses the following subjects: quality model, external metrics, internal metrics, and quality in use metrics. It was an extension of previous works done by McCall [5], Boehm [6] and others. The first part of this standard is the quality model. The latter organizes the topic into six dimensions called characteristics. Each characteristic is refined into sub-characteristics. ISO/IEC 9126 contains 21 sub-characteristics. As an example, the usability is the degree to which a product or system can be used by specified users to achieve specified goals with effectiveness, efficiency and satisfaction in a specified context of use. It contains appropriateness, recognizability and other sub-characteristics. Each quality sub-characteristic is further divided into attributes. An attribute is an entity which can be verified or measured in the software product. However, attributes are not defined in the standard as they vary between different software products. They are measured by means of metrics. As an example, maturity, a sub-characteristic of reliability, may be measured by lack of cohesion in methods. ISO/IEC 9126, proposed in 1991 evolved into ISO/IEC 9126 for software product quality and ISO/IEC 14598 for software product evaluation. ISO/IEC later worked on SQuaRE (Software product Quality Requirements and Evaluation).

2.2   Website Quality Models

According to [7], a web application is a software system based on technologies and standards of the World Wide Web Consortium (W3C) that provides web specific resources such as content and services through a user interface, the web browser. Web applications have application-related, usage-related, development-related and evolution-related characteristics. In application-related characteristics, when developing websites, one has to consider not only functionality but equally address content, hypertext and presentation aspects. A comprehensive quality model is proposed in [8].

It considers five dimensions, i.e. correctness, presentation, content, navigation, and interaction. [9] proposes the Web Quality Model (WQM) which structures the characteristics, according to three dimensions: features, quality characteristics, and life cycle processes. [10] proposes a conceptual model called 2QCV3Q to evaluate website quality based on seven dimensions: who, what, why, when, where, how, and with what means and devices. Let us mention also QEM [11], WebQEM [12], WebQModel [13], WAQE [14], etc. This list is not exhaustive. It only illustrates the proliferation of such models, due to the recent interest of researchers in this specific field of software quality.

2.3   Website Quality Evaluation Methods

Distinctions are made between user-focused and expert-focused evaluation methods. Some methods are focused on certain quality characteristics such as usability [15]. It combines the inspection by an expert and empirical testing through panels of users. Authors in [16] present five studies comparing user-focused evaluation methods. They compare the methods according to the role of users in the evaluation and the context of the evaluation. They can use very different techniques, such as questionnaires, eye-tracking methods, etc. Some authors proposed interesting approaches for evaluating quality based on Analytical Hierarchy Process to aggregate website quality metrics value [17]. [18] used fuzzy sets to evaluate web site quality. A probabilistic approach was proposed in [19].

2.4   Web Quality Evaluation Tools

Besides methods, authors also developed tools for demonstrating and operationalizing their approaches. Various tools for evaluating the quality of websites have been developed. For example the tool described in [19] is composed of several modules: a measurement module using static and dynamic analysis, a probability function generation, and a Bayes network edition. [20] also developed a tool named QualWeb Evaluator for evaluating the accessibility criterion.

A tool evaluating the usability was proposed in [21]. It combines a HTML parser, a browser emulator, a site crawler tool, a metrics computation tool, and an analysis tool. [22] describes a tool for testing reliability of web applications. It emulates an unlimited number of users for testing its fault tolerance. An open source tool was proposed in [23] to automate websites testing. Accessibility is the sub-characteristic which is best covered by these tools. TAW [24] is one of these tools. It detects a list of problems classified according to four categories: Perceivable, Operable, Understandable and Robust. WAVE [25] provides the user with reports using icons, structures and texts to help find errors in a website. PowerMapper [26] provides a collection of tools to detect errors concerning broken links, browser compatibility, accessibility etc. It is based on WCAG standards (Web Content Accessibility, W3C organization). Link Popularity [27] measures the total number of websites that link to this site. WebQual [28] which assesses the usability, information, and service interaction quality of e-commerce websites.

This is only a partial list of tools. However, let us notice that all these tools measure external quality characteristics, when web applications are in use. To the best of our knowledge, there is no specific tool to measure external quality of websites during their design and development enabling prediction of quality.

3   Web Application Quality Metrics

The benefits obtained from quality measurement in the software engineering field led to its adoption in many other fields. In order to objectively evaluate the quality of websites, suitable quality metrics have to be defined. We start by clarifying the vocabulary related to quality characteristics. Below is a brief description of some ISO/IEC 9126 characteristics and their sub-characteristics. Due to space limitations, we chose to deal only with the 21 original sub-characteristics of ISO.

— Functionality is the degree to which a product or system provides functions that meet stated and implied needs when used under specified conditions. It is decomposed into Suitability, Accuracy, Interoperability, and Security.
— Efficacy is the performance relative to the amount of resources used under stated conditions. It is divided into Time behavior and Resource utilization.
— Usability is the degree to which a product can be used to achieve given goals. It is decomposed into Understandability, Learnability, Operability, and Attractiveness.
— Reliability is the degree to which a system, a product or a component performs a set of functions under precise conditions for a given period of time. It is composed of Maturity, Fault tolerance, and Recoverability.
— Maintainability is the ability of the system to fit new requirements. It is decomposed into Analyzability, Modifiability, Changeability and Testability.
— Portability measures the effort needed to transfer a system from hardware, software or other operational platform or usage environment to another. Its sub-characteristics are Adaptability, Installability, Replaceability and Conformance.

We notice that these descriptions remain vague and do not give indications on how to measure them. This argues in favor of defining metrics to evaluate these factors. We have analyzed 108 metrics from literature and classified them according to the above six quality characteristics and their sub-characteristics. We present below an analysis of each characteristic. Then we present a more global analysis in Section 4.

Functionality helps verifying whether the website provides its intended functionalities. If we consider its sub-characteristics, we notice that some of them are more prone to automatic evaluation than others. For example, suitability is more likely to be assessed by surveys and questionnaires. We could however consider that adequacy of image size or the possibility of horizontal scrolling could increase suitability and thus define an automatic way to measure this sub-characteristic. Moreover we found no metric taking into account user profiles. Literature about web metrics, in general, lacks considering usage context, except perhaps e-commerce websites that have benefited from specific contributions [30]. Table 1 presents an excerpt of our classification of web application metrics.

Table 1. An extract of web metrics

FUNCTIONALITY	Suitability	Accuracy	Interoperability	Security	Reference
Presence of site name in title		x			[29]
Adaptability of layouts	x	x	x		[8]
Number of broken links					[11],[8], [30], [17]
Lack of cohesion (LCOM)			x		[31]
EFFICACY	Time behavior		Resource utilization		
Number of in links			x		[32]
Download time	x				[31]
Average server response time	x				[17]
Total number of submit relationships	x		x		[34]
Data exchanged over nb of server pages	x		x		[21]
USABILITY	Understandability	Learnability	Operability	Attractiveness	
Local coherence	x	x			[33]
Author citation				x	[35]
Emphasized body word count	x	x		x	[21]
e-mail contact presence				x	[12]
Number of tables	x	x		x	[37]
RELIABILITY	Maturity	Fault tolerance	Recoverability		
Responding methods (RFC)	x	x			[31]
Avg server response time		x	x		[17]
Frequency of updates	x	x	x		[12]
Number of broken links	x	x	x		[12], [8], [30], [17]
Html warnings per page	x				[29]
Number of HTML errors	x				[8]
MAINTAINABILITY	Analyzability	Changeability	Stability	Testability	
Lack of cohesion (LCOM)	x	x		x	[31]
Responding methods (RFC)			x	x	[31]
Script size	x	x	x	x	[38]
Design optimization	x	x		x	[17]
Total number of form pages	x	x	x	x	[34]
PORTABILITY	Adaptability	Installability	Replaceability	Conformance	
Download time		x			[33]
Reusability	x		x		[34]
Number of in Links(connectivity)	x	x	x		[36]
Number of panes	x	x	x	x	[12]
Adaptability of layouts	x	x			[8]

Efficacy measures time and resource consuming. As a web page interaction requires programs execution (calculation, displaying texts, images etc.) and data transfer, it is rather easy to define quality metrics. However, developers are more accustomed with run time measurement than with static analysis. This is probably why few metrics have been defined. There is a need for more effort on defining accurate and suitable metrics for efficacy that could be evaluated early in the development process.

The usability of a website has a direct impact on its acceptability and success. It addresses quality from the user point of view leading generally to a subjective evaluation. Objective evaluations based on metrics rely on assumptions on user perception. For example, we generally assume that emphasized body words positively impact user perception. We noticed that measuring Usability often implies concentrating on application properties enhancing efficiency and effectiveness of navigation. This led to a variety of metrics exploiting within or inter pages links. Many other metrics rely on visual perception of pages exploiting properties such as font's variety, existence of images etc. Usability also encompasses the ease of understanding of pages. Such characteristic requires semantic-based measurements such as local consistency of pages or global consistency of the website. We also analyzed the distribution of metrics among the sub characteristics of usability. We notice that Understandability totalizes nearly 40% of the metrics.

Reliability is often defined as "The probability of failure-free operation for a specified time in a specified environment for a specified purpose" [39]. Among metrics measuring reliability there are those relying on run time testing, such as 'Mean time to failure' or 'Mean time to repair'. We have not collected such metrics in our study since we are more interested in measuring quality during analysis and design. Many metrics such as those based on existence of textual description for images are specific to websites. However, web developers also reuse metrics from software engineering. Authors in [40] propose a variety of metrics that can be applied in the context of web applications reliability. Among others, they showed that modules with high complexity and high size are less reliable and more fault prone. The analysis of distribution of metrics among the sub-characteristics leads to the conclusion that recoverability is less covered. This is first due to the complexity of web applications architectures with their layered architectures and the variety of underlying technologies. However, recovery of websites could be even more critical than for traditional software as many companies' commercial activities rely on them.

Maintainability aims to reduce time and effort devoted to maintenance. We notice that the selected maintainability metrics are compliant with the principles generally adopted in software engineering. Indeed, they are to some extent related to size (script size, number of web pages, etc.), complexity (design optimization, lack of cohesion, etc.), and coupling (data abstraction coupling, responding methods, etc.). Considering the cohesion principle, if a web page lacks cohesion this could be due to heterogeneity of i) presentation styles or ii) implementation choices for the objects within the page or iii) the content semantics. In all these situations, the web page will be difficult to analyze, difficult to change and also difficult to test.

A website must be correctly displayed using any web browser and any browser version. However, error messages and alerts, informing you that you are not using the right browser or the right version of the browser, are frequent. Portability quality metrics measure the effort needed to transfer an application from an environment (hardware and software) to another. It requires measuring: (1) the adaptation effort of the application code, (2) the installation effort on a given platform using a given operating system such as mobile devices, (3) replacing parts or modules of the application with taking into account that (4) several, heterogeneous and sometimes incompatible, implementation techniques must be managed. These four aspects are more complex in web development than in traditional software developments due to the variety of underlying technologies (HTML code, style files etc.). In addition to that, many web developers are not always programmers and this explains partly the extensive use of tools in web developments making difficult the prediction of change efforts since the development expertise is partly embedded in the tools they use.

4   General Analysis

The distribution of web metrics at the characteristics level is sketched by the pie chart of Figure 1 (a). It shows that two characteristics, namely Maintainability and Usability totalize nearly 60% of the metrics. Moreover, Reliability characteristic attracted less than 10% of the metrics analyzed as well as Efficacy.

A previous study [41] highlighted a different situation (see Figure 1b). Let us keep in mind that it was seven years ago. Thus it is interesting to analyze how the situation evolved. There is an overlap between the two sub sets of metrics studied, but our analysis incorporates also more recent work, subsequent to the research of Calero.

The first observation is that maintainability metrics seem to capture a growing interest with 34% of the total of metrics. Thanks to their attractiveness, websites become more popular for individuals and even for companies. In the same time, they tend to be more complex, thus generating high maintenance cost and time. This complexity is inherent to their underlying architectures and technologies. It is also a consequence of their rapid evolution due to their attractiveness and the pressure of market. Preventive approaches in software quality, based on evaluation metrics, allowed considering quality earlier in the development process. This led to a reduction of maintenance costs. We can deduce that the same phenomenon is observed in websites development.

Usability attracts 25% of metrics, which is lower than the value observed in [41]. However, this does not mean that it was more important seven years ago. It only means that some characteristics relatively gained in interest. On the one hand, websites are most of the time used by persons having no competencies in computer based technologies. On the other hand, the success of these applications depends on their acceptance by these non skilled persons. This illustrates the importance of usability, and more precisely understandability. Portability also evolved, due to the diversity and heterogeneity of used technologies. Efficacy and reliability still attract little interest.

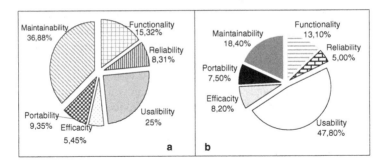

Fig. 1. Global analysis of web quality characteristics (a) vs. [41] (b)

This is probably due to new hardware solutions (relying on standby servers, setting up recovery procedures etc.). Preventive solutions, based on metrics, could however provide good complementary solutions by well targeting the problems. However, we would like to highlight the limitations of our study that has not considered all the work related to web quality metrics as it would require more substantial effort. Nevertheless, the main contributions of this paper are to illustrate i) how the various metrics largely cover the sub-characteristics of ISO 9126 quality model, ii) that these metrics are either general software quality metrics or specific web application metrics, iii) that most metrics can only be evaluated when the web application is online, iv) the very prolific activity in this field, leading us to conclude that current standards will still have to be updated.

5   Conclusion and Future Research

The importance of websites for companies convinces designers and developers to evaluate the quality of them. In this paper, we proposed a brief state-of-the-art of standards, models, methods, and tools for website quality assessment, with a particular emphasis on the metrics dedicated to the evaluation process. Even if quality models are often presented as hierarchical, we observe that some metrics are linked to several sub-characteristics and sometimes to different quality characteristics. Thus, the quality models, such as ISO/IEC 9126 are not composed of independent dimensions. This encourages us to propose a global evaluation of website quality, based on a compromise between the quality dimensions. The literature on this subject contains papers dedicated to quality criteria definition, and others on quality metrics without an explicit link with a quality factor. Our literature analysis also revealed that current approaches mainly evaluate external website quality, when the application is already online. For example, [42] describes a systematic mapping study of the usability evaluation methods for the web covering 206 papers selected among 2703 published over the last 14 years. Finally, some quality factors, such as security, have received very little attention. This analysis convinced us that there is a necessity to propose a website design method encompassing the evaluation and improvement of quality based on a complete quality model, covering most ISO proposals.

References

1. Huizingh, E.: The content and design of web sites: an empirical study. Information & Management 37, 123–134 (2000)
2. Luo, J., Ba, S., Zhang, H.: The effectiveness of online shopping characteristics and well-designed websites on satisfaction. MIS Quarterly 36(4) (2012)
3. ISO/IEC 9126-1:2001, Software engineering – Product quality – Part1: Quality model, http://www.iso.org
4. ISO/IEC 25010:2011, Systems and software engineering – Systems and software quality requirements and evaluation (SQuaRE) – System and software quality models, http://www.iso.org
5. McCall, J.A., Richards, P.K., Walters, G.F.: Factors in Software Quality. National Technology Information Service 1-3 (1977)
6. Boehm, B.: Characteristics of software quality. TRW series on software technology, vol. 1. North-Holland, Amsterdam (1978)
7. Kappel, G., Michlmayr, E., Pröll, B., Reich, S., Retschitzegger, W.: Web Engineering - Old Wine in New Bottles? In: Koch, N., Fraternali, P., Wirsing, M. (eds.) ICWE 2004. LNCS, vol. 3140, pp. 6–12. Springer, Heidelberg (2004)
8. Signore, O.: A Comprehensive Model for Web Sites Quality. In: Seventh IEEE International Symposium on Web Site Evolution (WSE 2005), pp. 30–36 (2005)
9. Ruiz, J., Calero, C., Piattini, M.: A Three Dimensional Web Quality Model. In: Cueva Lovelle, J.M., Rodríguez, B.M.G., Gayo, J.E.L., Ruiz, M.d.P.P., Aguilar, L.J. (eds.) ICWE 2003. LNCS, vol. 2722, pp. 384–385. Springer, Heidelberg (2003)
10. Mich, L., Franch, M., Gaio, L.: Evaluating and Designing the Quality of Web Sites. IEEE Multimedia, 34–43 (2003)

11. Olsina, L., Lafuente, G., Rossi, G.: Specifying Quality Characteristics and Attributes for Websites. In: Murugesan, S., Desphande, Y. (eds.) Web Engineering. LNCS, vol. 2016, pp. 266–277. Springer, Heidelberg (2001)
12. Olsina, L., Rossi, G.: Measuring Web Application Quality with WebQEM. IEEE Multimedia, 20–29 (2002)
13. Cimino, S., Micali, F.: Web Q-Model: a new approach to the quality. In: International Conference on Computer Human Interaction, CHI 2008. ACM (2008)
14. Mavromoustakos, S., Andreou, A.S.: WAQE: a Web Application Quality Evaluation model. International Journal of Web Engineering and Technology 3, 96–120 (2007)
15. Di Blas, N., Guermand Emilia Romagna M. P., Orsini C., Paolini P.: Evaluating The Features Of Museum Websites (The Bologna Report). Museums and the Web (2002)
16. Elling, S.K.: Evaluating website quality: Five studies on user-focused evaluation methods. LOT Dissertations Series, vol. 308 (2012)
17. Dominic, P.D.D., Jati, H.: A comparison of Asian airlines websites quality: using a nonparametric test. International Journal of Business Innovation and Research 5(5), 599–623 (2011)
18. Rekik, R., Kallel, I.: Fuzzy reduced method for evaluating the quality of institutional web sites. In: 7th International Conference on Next Generation Web Services Practices (NWeSP), pp. 296–301 (2011)
19. Malak, G., Sahraoui, H.A., Badri, L., Badri, M.: Modeling web quality using a probabilistic approach: An empirical validation. ACM Transactions on the Web (TWEB) 4(3), 1–31 (2010)
20. Fernandes, N., Costa, D., Duarte, C., Carriço, L.: Evaluating the accessibility of web applications. Procedia Computer Science (14), 28–35 (2012)
21. Ivory, M.Y.: An empirical foundation for automated web interface evaluation. PhD thesis, University of California at Berkeley (2001)
22. Saba, H., de Freitas Jorge, E.M., Franco Costa, V., Borges de Barros Pereira, H.: WEBTESTE: A Stress Test Tool, WEBIST 2006, Proceedings of the Second International Conference on Web Information Systems and Technologies: Internet Technology Web Interface and Applications, Setúbal, Portugal, pp. 246–249 (2006)
23. Guillemot, M., König, D.: Web Testing Made Easy. In: OOPSLA 2006, Portland, Oregon, USA, October 22-26, pp. 692–693 (2006)
24. http://www.tawdis.net/
25. http://webaim.org/
26. http://www.powermapper.com/
27. http://www.linkpopularity.com/
28. http://www.web.qualt.co.uk
29. Rio, A., Brito e Abreu, F.: Websites quality: Does it depend on the application domain? In: uality of Information and Communications Technology, 7th Int. Conf. on the Quality of Information and Communications Technology, QUATIC 2010, pp. 493–498 (2010)
30. Stefani, A., Xenos, M.: Meta-metric Evaluation of E-Commerce-related Metrics. Electronic Notes in Theoretical Computer Science 233, 59–72 (2009)
31. Chae, H.S., Kim, T.Y., Jung, W., Lee, J.: Using metrics for estimating maintainability of web applications: An empirical study. In: 6th Annual IEEE/ACIS International Conference on Computer and Information Science (ICIS 2007), Melbourne, Australia, July 11-13, pp. 1053–1059 (2007)
32. de Silva, A., Ponti de Mattos Fortes, R.: Web quality metrics: an analysis using machine learning systems. In: International Conference on Information Systems, Analysis and Synthesis, World Multiconference on Systemics, Cybernetics and Informatics, Information Systems Technology, SCI 2001/ISAS 2001, vol. XI (2001)

33. Bajaj, A., Krishnan, R.: CMU-WEB: a conceptual model for designing usable web applications. Journal of Database Management 10(4), 33–43 (1999)
34. Ghosheh, E., Black, S., Qaddour, J.: Design metrics for web application maintainability measurement. In: The 6th ACS/IEEE International Conference on Computer Systems and Applications, AICCSA 2008, Doha, Qatar, March 31- April 4, pp. 778–784 (2008)
35. Charland, F., Badri, L., Malak, G.: WEBQUALITY: Towards a Tool Supporting the Assessment of Web-Based Applications Quality. In: CAINE 2007, pp. 115–121 (2007)
36. Mendes, E., Mosley, N., Counsell, S.: Estimating design and authoring effort. IEEE MultiMedia, Special Issue, pp. 50-7 (January-March 2001)
37. Singh, Y., Malhotra, R., Gupta, P.: Empirical Validation of Web Metrics for Improving the Quality of Web Page. Int. Jal. Advanced Computer Science and Applications 2(5) (2011)
38. Di Lucca, G.A., Fasolino, A.R., Tramontata, P., Visaggio, C.A.: Towards the Definition of a Maintainability Model for Web Applications. In: 8th European Conference on Software Maintenance and Re-engineering, pp. 279–287 (2004)
39. Sommerville, I.: Software Engineering, 5th edn. Addison Wesley Longman Publishing Co., Inc., Redwood City (1995)
40. Rosenberg, L., Hammer, T., Shaw, J.: Software Metrics and Reliability. In: Proceedings of IEEE International Symposium on Software Reliability Engineering (1998)
41. Calero, C., Ruiz, J., Piattini, M.: Classifying web metrics using the web quality model. Online Information Review 29(3), 227–248 (2005)
42. Fernandez, A., Insfran, E., Abrahao, S.: Usability evaluation methods for the web: A systematic mapping study. Information and Software Technology 53, 789–817 (2011)

A Hybrid Approach to Web Information System Modularization

Jingang Zhou[1,2], Zuozhong Yang[2], Dazhe Zhao[2], and Jiren Liu[2]

[1] College of Information Science and Engineering,
Northeastern University, 110004, Shenyang, China
[2] State Key Laboratory of Software Architecture (Neusoft Corporation),
11017, Shenyang, China
{zhou-jg,yang-zz,zhaodz,liujr}@neusoft.com

Abstract. Web information systems (WISs) are the norm of current business systems, but the development and maintenance of such systems are still challenging because their size are becoming larger and larger. Modularity is the solution to this problem, however, the cost and risk to adopt the current modularization mechanisms are still high. In this paper, we provide a hybrid approach to implement modularization for WISs, which leverages OSGi technology as the foundation and provides a feasible way to componentization for WISs. Our approach is being tested and used in real industry environment.

1   Introduction

Web information system (WIS) is a long-lived domain which deliveries business services of a company or organization to its customers as well as other stakeholders through the Web [5], and a WIS typically covers many (technical/horizontal) domains like user interface, business process management, persistence, etc., and is related to a wide range of technologies like Java, JavaScript, XML, SQL, HTML, etc., and covers both software engineering and hypermedia engineering [22]. In addition, with IT development, more and more business services are incorporated in WISs and cause their size becoming larger and larger. Such characteristics of WISs make them complicated to develop and hard to maintain during their long service lifecycle.

To simplify WIS development, some technical frameworks and platforms are proposed, e.g., the mainstream Java EE technology platform as well as Spring, Struts, and Hibernate frameworks, which tackles many underlying technologies, like distributed computing, transactions processing, dependency injection (IoC), etc. [6], [7], [8]. Though they are helpful in alleviating some level of complexity of WIS development, it is still hard to develop and maintain a large WIS because there is not a standard modular mechanism beyond the class object level which is too fine-grained since a small business component will typically contain a number of classes [9]. Thus, a WIS can be easily to be monolithic and unmaintainable with system evolution. A good example provided by Accenture and Infosys shows that it cost nearly two years (2620 person-days) to refactor (modularize) only a half (7 million lines of code/MLOC) of a monolithic business system which was developed and evolved in ten years and the total code needs to be modularized is 12.5 MLOC [4].

J. Parsons and D. Chiu (Eds.): ER Workshops 2013, LNCS 8697, pp. 180–189, 2014.

Modularity and component-based software development (CBSD) are established principles of software engineering [1]. CBSD aims to compose systems from prebuilt software units or components rather than from scratch to improve software productivity and quality. In addition to reuse, another important purpose of CBSD with modern software engineering is to implement software decomposition and task assignment and serves as the foundation of "programming-in-the-large" [2]. However, due to the multi-technology domains involved, technical and execution environment constraints, the risks and challenges in WISs to enforce modularity are still high.

In a previous paper [15], we propose a lightweight CBSD approach for WISs development, which is based on OSGi technology and leverages many development facilities of Eclipse platform. In that approach, a WIS is decomposed by some business components which are mapped and implemented by OSGi bundles, and the final system is produced by a generation tool which transforms the business bundles to a standard Java EE web application, thus it can be deployed to any Java EE application servers. However, such approach only addresses the modularity of development time, which leads to system regeneration and restarting when a change must be made because there is no component concept in runtime.

In this paper, we propose a hybrid approach to OSGi based modularity mechanism for WISs to enable them to be manageable and evolvable in business component level, i.e., each business component has its own autonomy and lifecycle. Different to a pure OSGi based approach, the hybrid approach allows non OSGi bundles (e.g., ordinary Jars) coexist with bundles in a same WIS, thus lowering the adoption cost of a component-based approach since the transition from a non OSGi solution to a (pure) OSGi solution for large WISs may be unaffordable (our case). Our approach provides a pragmatic way to implementing modularity in WISs. We hope our experience can be beneficial to those who are looking for a modular approach in the WIS domains.

Outline. We elaborate the current modular approaches in WISs from an industrial perspective in Section 2 and propose the hybrid approach in Section 3. Related work is in Section 4. We conclude this paper with future directions in Section 5.

2   Modular WIS: State-of-the-Practice

Just as mentioned above, the prevailing components used in industry are still Java Beans, EJBs as well as POJOs, servlets and Spring Beans for the Java community [3]. All these component models are in the class level and no help for large application modularization. Java Package, as well as the default classloader mechanism, is the basic modularity mechanism in Java. But it only provides scoping and naming control for Java classes during compilation. No explicit interfaces (provided services, or API) declaration and no prevention its public classes from being accessed from other packages (components). The ordinary JAR file is just a packaging format without any further modularity enforcement.

Essentially, the modularization support of a Java application is determined by its underlying classloader model [23]. In terms of classloader scoping, we can divide the current modularization approaches into the following three categories [10]:

- Java Module System (JMS). This is a new language feature in Java to provide modularity mechanism introducing a new *module* construct which is a modular entity containing a number of types. A module declares explicitly what it depends on (other modules) and which parts of it are accessible from other modules. Other features like version, access control list, repository, etc. The modularity is assured in the standard JVM level. A reference implementation is the Jigsaw project[1]. However, since many issues are still in discussion, the introduction of such a feature in Java will be postponed to mid of 2015 in Java SE 9[2].

- OSGi. OSGi provides modularity support for *bundles* (OSGi term for modules) with a framework. A bundle is simply a JAR file with an OSGi manifest as its metadata used by the OSGi framework to resolve modularization processing among bundles. There are many OSGi-based solutions for WISs, such as OSGi HTTP service, ServletBridge [12], Virgo, PaxWeb as well as the OSGi-ed Spring and Struts frameworks and each addresses a part or facet of a WIS's modularization. Recently, OSGi alliance releases enterprise OSGi v5 [20] to address enterprise features (such as Web and persistence support) in a standard way, and some application servers are becoming to support it, e.g., IBM WebSphere. However, pure OSGi-based large WIS development is still costly and challengeable since it is in an early stage and lack of many necessary facilities [24].

- Other approaches use customized classloader or even a modified JVM to control the access among classes to achieve some kind of modularity, e.g. the Java module systems described in [9] and [11]. SAP provides another modular approach in its SC/DC component mode[3] for enterprise software. Components of this model allows APIs declaration, component aggregation (i.e., a hierarchical component model), and access control list. But these components are only supported by SAP application server in run time.

3   The Hybrid Modularity Approach

3.1   Why OSGi Matters

Developing a fully functional infrastructure to support modularity is a time-consuming task. Fortunately, OSGi provides some basic modularity support for WISs with the characteristics we need when considering its adoption in the industry [13]:

- OSGi provides modularity assurance and full lifecycle support for modules to allow them self evolution without "affecting" others parts of the system.
- OSGi is emerging in WIS domain with many open sourced implementation (e.g., Equinox, Felix) and plenty of documents for learn and reference.

---

[1] http://openjdk.java.net/projects/jigsaw/
[2] http://mreinhold.org/blog/on-the-next-train
[3] http://help.sap.com/saphelp_nw70ehp1/helpdata/en/1c/
bca99c220c0e45a1cae3c4cccf4346/content.htm

- OSGi provides version support and allows multi-versions of a component coexist (in different consistent class spaces), which alleviates the burden of component adaptation and is valuable for legacy applications.
- A module in OSGi is basically a JAR, which not only facilitates deployment and reuse, but also allows a proper granularity for business components.
- An OSGi framework can be deployed with WISs into a standard Java EE application server without any plugins or JVM modifications in the customer side for a production environment.

3.2   Hybrid Classloader Mechanism Support

Though OSGi provides modularity support, there are still some challenges when introducing it in WIS development due to its current immaturity in this field:

- No available bundles (sub-problem1). Most of today's large WISs are developed and executed with a business infrastructure platform. Many libs (JARs) in such a platform do not have their bundle counterpart and are probably developed by 3rd parties, it would be costly to bundlelize these libs. Furthermore, a strict and transmissible version check mechanism of OSGi for bundle compatibility worsens this situation in bundles integration.
- Not efficient support for UI layer (sub-problem2). OSGi has less support in UI layer, e.g., JSP, taglib support in OSGi is not convenient. Though some other libs (e.g., PaxWeb) provide such functionality, their introduction not only makes the platform hard to maintain, but also raises the problem of bundles compatibility (sub-problem1).
- The OSGi development paradigm put much burden on application developers to learn and transform to the new development approach (sub-problem3).

To address these problems, we map a WIS to a *component-based system* [14] with the business modules to the components and the underlying platform to the component platform (or framework). Thus, we adopt a hybrid strategy that uses two kinds of classloaders for a WIS: one kind of bundle classloaders for business modules, i.e., the business modules are OSGi bundles supported by an OSGi container; the other kind of classloader is the traditional web application classloader used for the component platform. The main purpose of this strategy is for addressing the sub-problem1 and avoiding the cost of bundlelize the component platform JARs.

Fig. 1 illustrates the technical architecture for the hybrid approach in runtime. We embed an OSGi container (actually the Equinox, denoted as OSGi core in Fig. 1) in a web application space of the application (or web) server. The reason that we use an embedded OSGi approach rather than, e.g., an embedded HTTP server approach[4] is that the current norm of application deployment paradigm is deploying an application in a standard application server and we can not restrict our customers to change it, as well as the commercial application servers are not suitable for the latter approach. So that the embedded OSGi approach can be used in any application (or web) servers. The OSGi container is manipulated by a standard filter which, for one hand, controls the life cycle (e.g., start, stop) of the OSGi container; for other hand, servers as a bridge for accessing actions, servlets, JSPs and other static resource in the business

---

[4] http://www.eclipse.org/equinox/server/http_in_equinox.php

components, forwards HTTP requests and delivers application context to the OSGi extension so that the latter can locate proper resources in the business components. OSGi extension is a fragment bundle of the OSGi container and serves proxy of the functionalities of IoC, ER mapping, action and servlet processing of the component platform to make such processing feasible in a bundle environment. To allow bundles to access the classes and services of the ordinary Jars of the component platform, we set the parent class loader of the OSGi container as the class loader of the web application when OSGi container is being initialized.

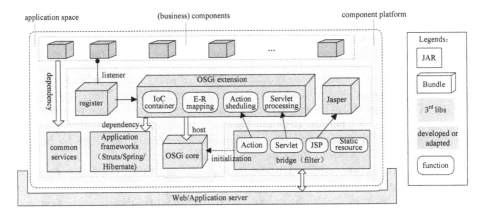

Fig. 1. The hybrid class loader architecture for our approach

To fully support JSP in bundles (sub-problem2), we adapt JSP Servlet of Jasper (an open source lib used to compile a JSP to a servlet) for its JSP request processing:

1) Get the component name (*name*) according to the JSP request.
2) Get bundle (component) object (*bundle*) according to *name*.
3) Get *bundle*'s class loader *parentCL*.
4) Create a child class loader of *parentCL* (*childCL*).
5) Load and compile JSP by *childCL* with TLD (Tag lib) location option.

This allows a JSP to process tags and access Java classes from other bundles. We also use component's class loader to initialize filters of the component and insert them into the application's filter chain to fully support the filter mechanism.

To make the traditional application frameworks, e.g., the Spring framework in the component platform handle classes in business components (sub-problem1) properly and allow developers to use these frameworks in a similar way to the traditional approach (sub-problem3), we adapt these frameworks with the OSGi extension. Fig. 2 illustrates this adaptation for Spring framework. The main process is to prepare correct environment (e.g., bean class path) and class loaders for Spring to initialize these beans. We use the extender pattern[5] to launch the process when bundles change.

---

[5] http://blog.osgi.org/2007/02/osgi-extender-model.html

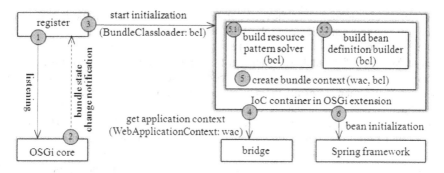

Fig. 2. Bundle-oriented processing mechanism for Spring extension

A particular process mechanism is the Hibernate adaption. Hibernate only supports static entity processing, i.e., it will handle all Java entities in given paths and set them in a sessionFactory (*sf*) object in one time. However, the ideal componentization is to handle entities as dynamically as their hosting components. Furthermore, the "private" and "final" constraints in the Hibernate source code prevent us adapting it in an elegant way. To overcome this problem, we add the entities definitions into the search path via Java reflection and rebuild *sf* each time a business component containing entities changes, which leads to all entities reconstruction and brings a little performance loss. To avoid *sf* being directly depended in this circumstance otherwise a wrong state may occur, we use a stable wrapper of *sf* for proxy.

3.3   Evaluation and Lessons Learned

In our approach, each component declares the entities, actions, Spring beans, servlets, etc. it hosts in its own configuration files to realize maximized component autonomy. However, since the component platform are still ordinary JARs, they do not have dynamicity. But it is acceptable in current practices since it always needs restarting the system when its the platform changes. Also, the ordinary JARs in the platform can be transformed to bundles gradually when the resources available. Thus, our approach provides a staged way to full componentization for WISs.

Note, one purpose of our approach is to minimize the impact on develop habit change for developers, hence, we do not make any enhancement in functionality except the modular support of the component platform in the current implementation, e.g., the usage of beans wiring and transaction management supported by Spring framework is the same as before.

Our approach is being tested in Apache Tomcat v6/7 and Oracle WebLogic v9. We adopt this approach in two (sub)products of a cloud application management software suite [16], both of which are WISs. One of the products has 26 bundles with an average 20 Java classes in each bundle, the other has 10 bundles with a range of 10 to 50 Java classes and JSP files in each bundle. Currently, two customized systems derived from the two (sub)projects are being constructed.

We conducted a runtime performance evaluation for our approach in the Tomcat server v7 and found it is comparable with the traditional approach and without explicit performance lost though there are some custom objects creation, resource location, and different classloaders switchover operations. Another related issue is the performance lost due to sessionFactory rebuild of Hibernate. To peer this issue, we create 7 bundles each containing seven entity classes with a one-to-one mapping to total 91 tables of MySQL v5.5 database. Each entity contains eight fields in average. Such a table space size corresponds to a typical middle sized WIS. We install these bundles in sequence and then uninstall them to record the time spent on reconstruction the sessionFactory each time a bundle changes. We repeated this process 6 times on the Eclipse environment running in a PC with Intel Core2 Duo CPU, 2.93 GHz, and 2G memory and found that the average times spent for resolving these entity classes in one to seven bundles are 46, 78, 116, 163, 187, 217, 257ms, respectively. From these results, we can see that the reconstruction time is almost linear to the entities size and the order of a few hundred milliseconds can be tolerated.

With the component practices in WISs, we gain the following lessons:

- **The Version Mechanism of OSGi Bundles Is a Two-Edged Sword.** A strict version mechanism eases compatibility checking, but makes it hard to find a compatible bundle especially in complex integrations. Thus the balance should be taking into account in bundles design and a mechanism allowing flexible version checking would be appealing.
- **Balance Should Be Considered between Reuse and Autonomy of Components.** In components environment, reuse between components causes dependency among them, which may impair components autonomy and lead to other problems like, e.g., "resource can not be found" due to a wrong classloader being used. Though such problem can be solved by using the right classloader, it is favorable to allow some "clones" and cut the dependency some times because of the cost (effort spent and architecture degradation).
- **Customized Classloader Mechanism Is Sophisticated and Error-Prone,** which demands developers to have a good understanding on not only the classloader itself, but also the frameworks to be adapted. Sometimes, it is hard to determine and set the correct thread context classloader for modules hence have to resort to other approaches like, embed libs in a bundle's local class path. In addition, different servers may have different processing policy, e.g., WebLogic uses a different JSP processing policy from Tomcat, which needs different adaptation.

3.4   Ongoing Work

When the hybrid mechanism for runtime modularity support is established, we face immediately another problem, i.e., how to make the two kinds of components (bundles/business modules and ordinary JARs) live in harmony in the development phase since they have different dependency resolution mechanisms.

Apache Maven is the mainstream configuration management tool for JARs dependency and automated project build, also, Apache Felix provides Maven plugin[6] for bundle projects build. However, either one of them alone cannot handle the situation that both JARs and bundles in one system due to the following reasons:

---

[6] http://felix.apache.org/site/apache-felix-maven-bundle-plugin-bnd.html

- If Maven (alone) is being used for bundles, the JAR dependency would shadow the package dependency for bundles, which would cause package dependency errors in runtime;
- If the package dependency information detected from source code being inserted automatically into the MANIFEST.MF for bundles, it may lead to non-modular design and hard to differentiate whether the to be imported packages come from true bundles or just ordinary JARs.

Currently, we take an lightweight approach without taking much effort on a dedicated tool implementation (the future work). We use Maven for dependency management for both bundles and ordinary JARs (i.e., bundles are treated as ordinary JARs), and leave the task of declaring package dependency for bundles to developers. To easy this manual process and assure the correct package dependency declaration, we develop a consistency validation tool to check this information and avoid such errors occur in runtime in the scope of the current system.

4   Related Work

Enterprise OSGi [20] provides a layered solution for WISs, which covers Web (Web application specification), business logic (blueprint container specification), and data access (JDBC and JPA service specification). The implementations of these specifications can be found, e.g., in IBM WebSphere 6.1+ and the open source Gemini project. Such a layered approach set the whole Web layer of a WIS in one bundle (called Web bundle). While, our approach divides the whole Web layer into their hosting business components to allow them dynamically change and easy integration, which is more maintainable and the is best practices mentioned in [25].

Spring DM [21] (currently, the Gemini Blueprint project) provides a pure OSGi-based approach for Spring framework with an enhancement for bean services declaration and allows a service-oriented computing paradigm among beans. While our approach does not extend the programming capacities of the traditional Spring framework has though we can do it later when it is necessary.

Voluble [19] provides a similar approach to ours in concept for Hibernate's sessionFactory rebuild to implement the dynamisty according to the idea proposed by Peter Kriens[7], which allows Hibernate to be used with Spring DM in both Equinox and Felix environment. Ding and Klein [18] provide a modular approach to allow bundle specific sessionFactory and extend Spring's transaction management with sessionFactory wrapping and transaction synchronization to implement distributed transactions among bundles.

Granat [17] develops a bundle management server called Trinity, which supports the life cycle of dynamic applications from creation to deployment allowing developers to predict the behavior of OSGi applications in different configurations, to assure applications depending on specific bundles will work with other version or other implementation and reduce the compatibility and consistency problems in complex integration and configurations.

---

[7] http://blog.osgi.org/2007/06/osgi-and-hibernate.html

Kaegi et al. [12] develop a servlet bridge to allow an OSGi to be embedded in an application (or Web) server to provide an OSGi space in an application space. This approach also inspires our approach on filter implementation for the bridge. And more recently, the OSGi Enterprise Tools project was proposed as an open source project to aid enterprise application development align with this approach.

5   Conclusion

Modularity and componentization are established principles we should obey and pursue in software development. However, such a goal is not easy to achieve in the industrial environment with complex settings and constraints. In this paper, we provide a hybrid classloader approach for WISs, which allows business modules of a WIS to be modularized in a more easier way than a pure OSGi-based approach and provides an intermediate path to a full bundlelized solution. Our approach is being tested and used in real industry environment.

For future work, we focus two aspects, one is component management and deployment tool improvement to enhance the developers experience in components (including bundles) dependency and compatibility assurance, and the other is automated distributed modules scheduling according to performance probe on component level of the virtual machines in a cloud computing environment.

Acknowledgments. The authors are grateful to the anonymous reviewers for valuable comments on this paper. This work was partially supported by the National Basic Research Program of China under Grant No. 2012CB724107 and National Electronic Information Industry Development Fund under Grant No. [2012]407.

References

1. Crnković, I., Sentilles, S., Vulgarakis, A., Chaudron, M.: A Classification Framework for Software Component Models. IEEE Trans. Softw. Eng. 37(5), 593–615 (2011)
2. Shaw, M.: Three Patterns that help explain the development of Software Engineering. In: Dagstuhl Seminar 9635 on History of Software Engineering, pp. 52–56 (1996)
3. Szyperski, C.: Component Software: Beyond Object-Oriented Programming, 2nd edn. Addison-Wesley Professional (2002)
4. Sarkar, S., Ramachandran, S., Kumar, G., Iyengar, M., Rangarajan, K., Sivagnanam, S.: Modularization of a Large-Scale Business Application: A Case Study. IEEE Software 26(2), 28–35 (2009)
5. Offutt, J., Wu, Y.: Modeling presentation layers of web applications for testing. Software and Systems Modeling 9(2), 257–280 (2010)
6. Zhang, J., Chung, J.Y., Chang, C.K.: Towards Increasing Web Application Productivity. In: 2004 ACM Symposium on Applied Computing, pp. 1677–1681. ACM Press (2004)
7. Zhou, J., Zhang, X.: Architecture Platform based Systematic Software Reuse. In: Software Component Technology: The Practices Road of China, pp. 93–114. Publishing House of Electronics Industry, Beijing (2012) (in Chinese)
8. Zhou, J., Ji, Y., Zhao, D., Zhang, X.: Product Line Engineering in Enterprise Applications. In: Bosch, J., Lee, J. (eds.) SPLC 2010. LNCS, vol. 6287, p. 494. Springer, Heidelberg (2010)

9. Corwin, J., Bacon, D.F., Grove, D., Murthy, C. M.: A Rational Module System for Java and its Applications. In: ACM International Conference on Object-Oriented Programming Systems, Languages, and Applications, pp. 241–254. ACM Press (2003)
10. Zhou, J., Ji, Y., Zhao, D., Liu, J.: Using AOP to Ensure Component Interactions in Component-Based Software. In: International Conference on Computer and Automation Engineering, vol. 3, pp. 518–523. IEEE Press (2010)
11. Bauer, L., Appel, A.W., Felten, E.W.: Mechanisms for secure modular programming in Java. Software Practice and Experience 33(5), 461–480 (2003)
12. Kaegi, S.R., Deugo, D.: Modular Java Web Applications. In: 2008 ACM Symposium on Applied Computing, pp. 588–693. ACM Press (2008)
13. Zhou, J., Zhao, D., Ji, Y., Liu, J.: Examining OSGi from an Ideal Enterprise Software Component Model. In: IEEE International Conference on Software Engineering and Service Sciences, pp. 119–123. IEEE Press (2010)
14. Bachmann, F., Bass, L., Buhman, C., Comella-Dorda, S., Long, F., Robert, J., Seacord, R., Wallnau, K.: Volume II: Technical Concepts of Component-Based Software Engineering, 2nd edn. CMU/SEI-2000-TR-008 (2000)
15. Zhou, J., Zhao, D., Liu, J.: A Lightweight Component-based Development Approach for Enterprise Applications. In: 35th IEEE Annual Computer Software and Applications Conference Workshops, pp. 335–340. IEEE CS Press (2011)
16. Xu, L., Tan, G., Zhang, X., Zhou, J.: Aclome: Agile Cloud Environment Management Platform. In: 2013 International Conference on Computer Distributed Control System and Environment Monitoring. IEEE CS Press (2013) (to appear)
17. Granat, J.: Trinity: The OSGi module development server. Master's Thesis, Department of Computer Science, ETH Zurich (2008)
18. Ding, Y., Klein, K.: Modularizing the Hibernate SessionFactory with the Spring framework, http://www.theserverside.com/feature/Modularizing-the-Hibernate-SessionFactory-with-the-Spring-framework
19. voluble, http://code.google.com/p/voluble/wiki/OsgiHibernateSpringSpringDMSample
20. The OSGi Alliance.: OSGi Enterprise Release 5 (2012)
21. Spring Dynamic Modules, http://www.springsource.org/osgi
22. Ginige, A., Murugesan, S.: Web Engineering: An Introduction. IEEE MultiMedia 8(1), 14–18 (2001)
23. Liang, S., Bracha, G.: Dynamic class loading in the Java virtual machine. In: OOPSLA, pp. 36–44. ACM Press (1998)
24. Cummins, H., Ward, T.: Enterprise OSGi in Action. Manning Publications Co. (2013)
25. Package by feature, not layer, http://www.javapractices.com/topic/TopicAction.do?Id=205

Using Fixed-Price Auctions for Selection in Communities of Web Services

Erbin Lim* and Zakaria Maamar

[1] PReCISE Research Center
University of Namur, Namur, Belgium
[2] College of Information Technology
Zayed University, Dubai, U.A.E.
lerbin@fundp.ac.be,
zakaria.maamar@zu.ac.ae

Abstract. This paper introduces an approach that allows Web services to handle user requests where the price that the users are willing to pay is fixed. In such cases, a user search for the highest quality of service based on the submitted fixed price. Instead of searching for individual Web services, the user finds it more convenient to send requests to middlemen (or brokers) who act on behalf of a group of Web services. These middlemen then select a Web service within the group to handle the request. In this paper we demonstrate how fixed price requests can be included into the operation of a community of Web services. Our approach introduces auction theory into the selection process. Experiments using real world values are conducted to demonstrate the effectiveness of the approach.

1 Introduction

In recent years, Web services (WS) have emerged as one of the promising technologies that help implement Internet applications. A Web service is *"a software application identified by a URI, whose interfaces and binding are capable of being defined, described, and discovered by XML artifacts and supports direct interactions with other software applications using XML-based messages via Internet-based applications"* (3WC).

Users search the Internet looking for WS to handle their requests, often with the help of brokers. Brokers act as a middleman between Web services and users by matching the requests from the users to the Web services that handle the requests. This matching considers functional and non-functional properties (Quality of Service (QoS)) of Web services so that the "best" Web services is selected (focus of this paper).

One common approach is to select the Web service that maximizes the level of QoS provided to the client. This can be achieved with the use of a utility function as proposed in [3, 4]. By maximizing the utility function, the user receives

---

* Erbin Lim's research is supported by La Wallonie and the European Regional Development Fund (ERDF).

J. Parsons and D. Chiu (Eds.): ER Workshops 2013, LNCS 8697, pp. 190–201, 2014.
© Springer International Publishing Switzerland 2014

the highest possible utility from the Web services. One limitation with utility functions is the user inability to fix a value. For example, if the client would like the price (A QoS property) fixed at a certain value, utility functions alone are not able to solve the problem. Ardagna and Pernici in [2] go a step further by proposing possible constraints to the optimization problem. For example, the Web service can be selected only if its price or execution duration is lower than a certain threshold.

What is lacking are a proper framework with which the selection can be done in the situation where the client would like to fix the value of certain QoS properties. Such cases already occur frequently when it comes to budget constraints [6, 8]. The difficulty of selection in such a case is that the broker does not necessarily know the QoS levels that its Web services can provide at a certain price.

Our main contribution in this paper is to introduce an approach that allows Web services to use the platform of a community to handle requests where the user submits a fixed value of certain QoS properties. The framework of a community was chosen because of its feature of having multiple Web services that are able to handle the request. In our paper, we use the example of using price (a QoS property) as a fixed value that is submitted by the client. Within the community, our unique approach uses an auction type selection process in order to select the Web services to handle the request. There are two additional benefits to our approach, firstly, it allows the possibility of continuous service levels, and secondly, it allows the broker to monitor the possible QoS levels that the WSs can provide.

The rest of the paper is organised as follows. Section 2 discusses the related literature concerning our proposed auction system. Section 3 describes the preliminary details required for the paper, including the architecture of a community as well as how auction theory can be implemented into communities. Section 4 defines the auction system protocol proposed in this paper. Section 5 presents the results of our experiments using real-world values. Finally Section 6 concludes this paper and discuss possible future work.

2   Related Work

Section 2.1 discusses specific auction concepts that help explain our approach. The related work where auctions are used in the selection process is first described in the field of Multi-Agent Systems (MAS) in Section 2.2 and in the field of network resource sharing in Section 2.3. Next in Section 2.4 we discuss the related work on fixed-revenue auctions.

2.1   Auction Basics

Concepts related to auctions include *English auction, Dutch auction, first price sealed auction, second price sealed auction* and basic auction theory terms such as *private value, common value, correlated value, risk averse, risk seeking,* and *risk neutral.* More details on auction theory are given in [14].

In this paper, we do use 3 auction properties that require elaboration:

– Truthful Dominant Strategy (TDS) indicates whether each bidder will have the dominant strategy where he bids its own true value. This cuts down on any possible counterspeculation and forces the bidder to always tell the truth.
– Final Bid Value (FBV) compares the final bid value according to a determined currency.
– Time-requirement defines the amount of time required to conduct the bid. For example, sealed bid auctions would end earlier than an English auction.

The time-requirements imposed on Web services can be critical depending on the nature of the request. Examples of these can include estimating the prices of stocks in a stock exchange. This implies that the time taken to execute the auction can significantly impact the QoS provided.

2.2   Auctions in Multi-Agent Systems

Vulkan and Jennings in [20] describe how an auction is conducted for providing a quote to design a network for a customer. They introduce a mechanism that allows multi-dimensional auctions to take place. This involves a utility function that compares multi-dimensional bids. The utility function approach, also used in [9] is adapted in this paper. Thiel in [9] argue that having a time-limited English auction is preferable to the Vickrey auction system because the former is more robust in order to sustain its truth-telling dominant strategy property. The same author argues that the amount of time to wait for the auction to end has to be set long enough for an interested agent to be able to carry out its calculations and submit an offer.

The Vickrey auction is commonly used in the context of Multi-Agent Systems due to its truthtelling and counterspeculation avoidance properties [5,11,17,21].

2.3   Auctions in Network Resource Sharing

In network resource sharing, a single bandwidth is divided into multiple pieces to be auctioned off to interested bidders. Each bidder bids on one piece of the bandwidth.

In terms of time requirements, the bidders bid for the usage of the bandwidth at some point in the future. The time-requirements of conducting the auction itself is thus not relevant to Network Resource Sharing auctions. An English auction was used in [19] by the American government for a bid of airwaves bandwidth for some time in the future. Another distinction in the same paper is that several licenses were up for bid at the same time.

The Vickrey-Clarke-Groves (VCG) auction is used in [10,12,13,15] in order to maximize total utility [18]. The truthtelling nature of the Vickrey has a high appeal to network resource sharing auction systems. The maximization of total utility or efficiency (throughput) of the network is generally the main consideration for network resource sharing models. This differs in our model since the item auctioned is not divisible.

Table 1. Truthful and Revenues for Different Fixed Revenue Auction Systems

	English	Dutch	First-Price Sealed	Second-Price Sealed
TDS	Yes	No	No	Yes
FBV	3	3	1	1

2.4 Fixed-Revenue Auctions

Extensive work on the properties of auctions with a fixed price has been done in [7] (known as Fixed-Revenue Reverse Auction). A seller wishing to raise a fixed revenue sells a quantity of a certain good. This fixed revenue is known and bidders bid on the amount which the bidders are willing to buy. The bidder who bids on the lowest quantity of good wins the bid. The results indicate that in such a system of fixed-revenue, the characteristics are similar to standard auction theory (i.e. English and Second-Price sealed auction have the TDS property). However, they did stress that sealed bid auction systems lead to lower quantities (similar to higher prices in a fixed quantity auction, a more favourable situation for the seller). Quantity equivalence also does not hold across the different auction systems when having a fixed-revenue. We summarize the findings in Table 1.

An important finding in [7] indicates that the outcomes are not affected by the dimension (number of properties) of the auction. This means that a model with 3 QoS properties will have the same outcome as a model with 9 QoS properties. A similar conclusion was reached in multi-dimensional auctions [9]. This finding is important in our paper because the number of QoS properties in different models can vary greatly.

3 Preliminaries

In this section we describe the preliminary information required to present our approach of selecting Web services in a community. Section 3.1 gives a brief overview of communities. Section 3.2 describes in detail the Contract Net Protocol (CNP) that is used in a community. Section 3.3 describes how auction theory can be used in a community of Web services. Finally, Section 3.4 describes the utility function and its role in a community.

3.1 Community of Web Services

A community of Web services consists of 2 main components: a Master Web Service (MWS)and Slave Web Service (SWS). The MWS acts as a broker for the community, receiving requests from the user and replying with the help of SWSs. The MWS is also responsible for the management of the community, this includes deciding which Web services to enter or leave the community as well as the selection and substitution processes. A more detailed description of communities of Web services can be found in [16].

3.2   Contract Net Protocol in a Community

A community of Web service uses the CNP as described in [16] in order to select appropriate SWS in response to specific requests. We highlight steps 2, 3 and 4 in the CNP protocol.

– Step 2: The MWS asks the SWSs for bids;
– Step 3: The SWSs make their bid to the MWS;
– Step 4: The MWS selects which SWS will handle the request;

Using the CNP ensures that all requests and answers go through the MWS. It also allows the MWS to have control over who handles the request. Finally, it gives the MWS the responsibility of solving failures. If a SWS fails, the MWS will be responsible for finding a SWS to substitute the original SWS.

We mentioned in Section 1 that we are concerned with the selection process. This is represented by steps 2, 3 and 4 in the CNP. We define the time-requirement as the maximum time to start and complete successfully each selection process.

3.3   Auction in Communities

In this section we go into detail on how auction theory can be implemented into a community in order to handle fixed-price requests. To this we replace steps 2 and 3 of the CNP. For a fixed-price request, when the MWS receives the request, the MWS forwards it to the SWSs in the community. The SWSs then make a bid consisting of the level of QoS that they are willing to provide based on the price of the request. This is known as a fixed revenue reverse auction [7] (Figure 1).

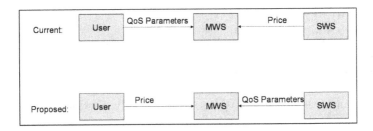

Fig. 1. Fixed Quantity Auction versus Fixed Revenue Auction

The fixed revenue reverse auction does not change the fact that multiple SWSs are competing against each other to provide a certain service to the user. There are three properties associated with this type of auction:

- The fixed revenue reverse auction handles the situation where users have a fixed budget and are looking for the best service that they can get.
- SWSs are allowed to submit bids according to their strengths. The proposal allows the SWS to make its own assessment on how good its service is and submit this bid to the MWS.
- One challenge which the community faces when it comes to managing SWSs is the estimation of the QoS of each SWS. This QoS can change over time due to equipment failure, power shortages, software errors, etc. This proposal allows the community to assess the level of QoS that each SWS can provide. The community will still have to monitor the eventual level of QoS that the selected SWS provides and compares that with the bid of the same SWS. With more bids, the community is able to get a better idea of the level of QoS the SWS can provide, based on the prices that users provide.

In this paper, since our focus is on handling requests with a fixed-price, we decide to call the auction *fixed price second-QoS sealed auction*. The way this auction works is by having the client submit a fixed-price to the community, the SWSs within the community submit their respective bids consisting of the level of QoS that each SWS can handle for the request. The MWS makes a selection among SWSs in the community and the selected SWS handles the request at the second-highest submitted QoS if it is able to. A more detailed explanation of the protocol is given in Section 4.2.

We choose to use the second-QoS sealed auction for three reasons. The first is that it returns a higher amount of QoS to the user, as shown in Table 1. The second is due to the time requirement of the second-QoS sealed auction. There is no need for multiple exchange of bids (for example in the Dutch and English auctions) between the auctioneer and the bidders. The third is due to its TDS property, each SWS will make a bid truthfully, thus avoiding any wasted resources counter-speculating.

3.4   Utility Function and Other Properties

The use of a utility function [9, 18] gives the flexibility to the user to provide its preference with regard to the specific properties. The utility function is a weighted function of the QoS properties. The values of the weights are provided by the user. The utility function allows the MWS to calculate the potential score that each SWS can provide upon receiving each bid. We define the score derived from the calculation of the utility function as the *utility function score*.

In order to model the selection process, we need to define the *other property score*. This latter is dependent on the MWS's value of the SWS to handle the request that is not derived from the utility function. This could be the MWS's own internal biasness of certain SWSs over others. This property is important because it gives the MWS the flexibility to select SWSs not purely on the utility it can provide to the user. The MWS may want to select a SWS on the utility the SWS can provide to the community.

4 Protocol

In this section we describe the protocol for the fixed price second-QoS sealed auction proposed for use in a community of Web services. The protocol can be applied to both the selection and substitution processes. Section 4.1 introduces the protocol. Section 4.2 defines the fixed price second-QoS sealed auction.

4.1 Introduction to Protocol

We describe the request, r, sent by the user to the community as a pair of price p_r, and the utility function f_r. This utility function is based on QoS properties $q_{r-0} \cdots q_{r-n}$, where n is the number of QoS properties used in the model. The maximization of the utility function implies that the use receives the highest possible utility from the community.

When each SWS submits a bid to the MWS, this bid comprises a list of values corresponding to $q_0 \ldots q_n$. This allows the MWS to calculate the utility function score of each SWS based on the utility function that was provided by the user. A score of 0 indicates that the SWS is not able to handle the request and is considered the lowest possible score.

We use a weighted sum of the utility function score and the other property score to determine the total score of a SWS to handle a request. The value of the weights are determined by the MWS. This allows the MWS to determine on its own how much importance to give to the utility function against other properties.

4.2 Fixed Price Second-QoS Sealed Auction Protocol

When the MWS receives from the user request, r, with price p_r and utility function, f_r, the MWS proceeds as follows:

1. MWS sends p_r and f_r to the SWSs.
2. Each SWS calculates the bid depending on the level of QoS it can provide based on the price.
3. Each SWS then submits this bid (a list of values corresponding to $q_0 \ldots q_n$) to the MWS
4. To terminate the auction, the MWS calculates the total score of all SWSs. The SWS with the highest total score is then selected to handle the request at the level of QoS that the second highest SWS made a bid for, in return for p_r. In the event that the level of QoS of the SWS with the highest total score is less than the level of QoS of the SWS with the second highest total score, then the selected SWS is expected to handle the request at the level of QoS that it submitted. The MWS will subsequently broadcast to all other SWSs that the auction for request r has ended.

5   Experiments

In order to illustrate the benefits of our approach to select Web services, we simulate experiments where the number of handled requests as well as the client satisfaction is compared across different approaches. Client satisfaction is determined by considering the QoS of the handled requests against the requested QoS of the client. In our experiments, although the approach allows the client to only submit the price, to illustrate the client satisfaction, we have to also consider other QoS property requirements from the client. The different approaches are defined by the different frameworks. The frameworks that we compare against each other are:

1. Basic method of selecting the SWS to handle the request based on the CNP (Framework 1)
2. Auction based selection where the MWS sends the SWSs all QoS requirements except the price (Framework 2)
3. Fixed price auction where the MWS only sends the price to the SWSs (Framework 3)

We first define the client satisfaction in Section 5.1. Next we proceed to define more experimental properties in Section 5.2. We then present our first experiments showing the number of handled requests across the different frameworks in Section 5.3. Finally we look at the client satisfaction in Section 5.4.

5.1   Client Satisfaction

We first define the QoS properties that define a request, as well as the notations used. The QoS properties used in this paper are:

– Availability - probability that the SWS is up and ready for consumption
– Reliability - probability that the SWS returns a reply that the client expects
– Capacity - number of requests which the SWS can handle at any point in time
– Execution Duration - amount of time which the SWS takes to handle the request
– Price - amount of currency which the SWS charges for handling a request

It is the responsibility of the client to determine the value of the QoS properties. The properties, their definitions, and notations are listed in Table 2 for request r that is sent by client c at time t. The notation C^t represents the set of all clients that sent requests to the community at time t. We also define the QoS properties of the handled request in Table 3.

We introduce the experiment client satisfaction for availability, reliability, and execution duration in Equation 1, Equation 2, and Equation 3, respectively.

$$clientSatisAv_{c-r}^t = \begin{cases} 1 & \text{if } reqAv_{c-r}^t \le hanAv_{c-r}^t \\ \frac{hanAv_{c-r}^t}{reqAv_{c-r}^t} & \text{if } reqAv_{c-r}^t > hanAv_{c-r}^t \end{cases} \tag{1}$$

Table 2. List of Request Properties

Property	Notation
Requested Availability	$reqAv_{c-r}^t$
Requested Reliability	$reqRl_{c-r}^t$
Requested Execution Duration	$reqEx_{c-r}^t$
Requested Price	$reqPr_{c-r}^t$

Table 3. List of Handled Properties

Property	Notation
Handled Availability	$hanAv_{c-r}^t$
Handled Reliability	$hanRl_{c-r}^t$
Handled Execution Duration	$hanEd_{c-r}^t$
Handled Price	$hanPr_{c-r}^t$

$$clientSatisRl_{c-r}^t = \begin{cases} 1 & \text{if } reqRl_{c-r}^t \leq hanRl_{c-r}^t \\ \frac{hanRl_{c-r}^t}{reqRl_{c-r}^t} & \text{if } reqRl_{c-r}^t > hanRl_{c-r}^t \end{cases} \quad (2)$$

$$clientSatisEd_{c-r}^t = \begin{cases} \frac{reqEd_{c-r}^t}{hanEd_{c-r}^t} & \text{if } reqEd_{c-r}^t < hanEd_{c-r}^t \\ 1 & \text{if } reqEd_{c-r}^t \geq hanEd_{c-r}^t \end{cases} \quad (3)$$

Finally we can define the overall client satisfaction in Equation 4.

$$\begin{aligned} clientSatis_{c-r}^t = & \; w_{clientSatisAv} \cdot clientSatisAv_{c-r}^t \\ & + w_{clientSatisRl} \cdot clientSatisRl_{c-r}^t \\ & + w_{clientSatisEd} \cdot clientSatisEd_{c-r}^t \end{aligned} \quad (4)$$

Where $w_{clientSatisAv}$, $w_{clientSatisRl}$, $w_{clientSatisEd}$ are the weights for the experiment client satisfaction for availability, reliability, execution duration and price respectively.

For the purposes of the simulations, we have set these 3 weights to be of the same value. In practice, a system administrator is free to set them differently according to its own priorities.

The price satisfaction is calculated separately in Equation 5. This is because the satisfaction is only applicable in the framework where the MWS sends all QoS except to the price to the SWSs. In the other two frameworks, the handled price is always the same as the requested price.

$$clientSatisPr_{c-r}^t = 1 - \frac{hanPr_{c-r}^t}{reqPr_{c-r}^t} \quad (5)$$

5.2   Experiments – Properties

Most of the values of the experimental properties had to be simulated. Although we were able to get most of the values of the SWS properties from a real dataset [1], some experimental values still had to be simulated. Simulated values were chosen in order to best simulate the real world situation.

Each experiment was simulated 100 times and the average was taken. In these experiments we simulate 50 SWSs over 10 time units. At the end of each time unit, the QoS requirements for the requested availability, requested reliability was increased by 10% while the requested execution duration was decreased by

10%. In order to illustrate the benefits of the frameworks, the community was sent more requests that it can handle (according to its capacity determined by the SWSs). In the experiment we set this number to 400 requests per unit time.

Other property values in our experiment are, SWS price with a minimum of 10 and a maximum of 14, SWS failure probability with a minimum of 0% and a maximum of 20%, requested budget with a minimum of 10 and a maximum of 20, requested availability with a minimum of 30% and a maximum of 35%, requested reliability with a minimum of 20% and a maximum of 25%, and the requested execution duration with a minimum of 3500 and a maximum of 5000.

5.3   Number of Handled Requests

For the first 2 frameworks, individual SWSs do not bid if they cannot match the QoS requirements.

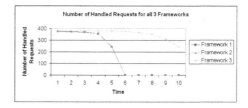

Fig. 2. Number of Handled Requests for all 3 Frameworks

In Figure 2, we display the number of handled requests for all 3 approaches. We see that when the client increases the QoS requirements to a certain point, the first two approaches fail to handle any requests. This happens when the community does not receive a single bid from the SWSs. In the third approach, SWSs are allowed to return a QoS bid which allows the SWS to handle the request at a lower QoS. In the third approach, the limit of the number of requests that are handled depends on the capacities of the SWSs in the community.

5.4   Client Satisfaction

Although all the requests are handled in the third approach, the lower QoS provided by the SWSs lead to a lower client satisfaction (Figure 3). Another important observation in the client satisfaction is that in the initial period when the first 2 frameworks are able to handle the requests, there is not much difference between the client satisfaction. This means that during the period which the first 2 mechanisms can handle all requests, the third framework can perform equally as the first 2 frameworks. Since client satisfaction for each request is 0 when the request is not handled, we observe that the client satisfaction for the first 2 frameworks drop to 0 when the number of handled requests for both approaches drop to 0.

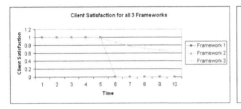

Fig. 3. Client Satisfaction   **Fig. 4.** Price Satisfaction

Finally, we look at the benefit of framework 2 over framework 1. In framework 2, since the SWSs are allowed to make a lower price bid than the requested price, the client may have a higher price satisfaction than 0 since it saves money. We notice the price satisfaction in Figure 4 that drops over time, this is because of the higher QoS requirements from the client means a higher price it has to pay. The price satisfaction drops to 0 when the requests are not being handled.

6   Conclusion and Future Work

In this paper we proposed a new approach that allows clients to submit only the price that they are willing to pay to a community of Web services. Such a need can be handy in this increasing world where financial constraints play a major role in deciding which service to use. In return, the community selects the Web service that is able to provide the highest level of QoS based on the price. This selection is done via the proposed fixed price second-QoS sealed auction protocol. The approach also allows the client to propose its preferences via a utility function. Finally we demonstrated this framework and compared its results with other frameworks in the experiments section. Some of the QoS values used in the experiments were taken from real world Web services.

We consider another property - the amount of bandwidth required to conduct the auction, however we decided not to include it in our approach. The main reason is because in today's context of Web services, the amount of bandwidth required to conduct the auction is negligible.

Further analysis on this framework could be carried out in a real world situation where the framework is applied. The level of QoS could then be more accurately measured based on real world scenarios. Further application into specific areas such as Web Information Systems or specific other areas could be looked into.

References

1. Al-Masri, E., Mahmoud, Q.H.: Discovering the best web service. In: Proceedings of the 16th International Conference on World Wide Web, pp. 1257–1258 (2007)
2. Ardagna, D., Pernici, B.: Global and local QoS guarantee in web service selection. In: Bussler, C.J., Haller, A. (eds.) BPM 2005. LNCS, vol. 3812, pp. 32–46. Springer, Heidelberg (2006)

3. Benatallah, B., Sheng, Q.Z., Duman, M.: The Self-Serv Environment for Web Services Composition. IEEE Internet Computing 7(1), 40–48 (2003)
4. Berbner, R., Spahn, M., Repp, N., Heckmann, O., Steinmetz, R.: Heuristics for qos-aware web service composition. In: Proceedings of the IEEE International Conference on Web Services, pp. 72–82 (2006), http://dx.doi.org/10.1109/ICWS.2006.69
5. Collins, J., Tsvetovat, M., Mobasher, B., Gini, M.: Magnet: A multi-agent contracting system for plan execution. In: Proceedings of SIGMAN, pp. 63–68 (1998)
6. Dastidar, K.G.: On procurement auctions with fixed budgets. Research in Economics 62(2), 72–91 (2008)
7. Deck, C., Wilson, B.J.: Fixed revenue auctions: Theory and behavior. Economic Inquiry 46(3), 342–354 (2008)
8. Ding, M., Eliashberg, J., Huber, J., Saini, R.: Emotional bidders: An analytical and experimental examination of consumers behavior in priceline-like reverse auctions. Management Science 51(3), 352–364 (2005)
9. Thiel, S.E.: Multidimensional auctions. Economics Letters 28(1), 37–40 (1988)
10. Huang, J., Han, Z., Chiang, M., Poor, H.V.: Auction-based resource allocation for cooperative communications. IEEE Journal on Selected Areas in Communications 26, 1226–1237 (2008)
11. Huberman, B.A., Clearwater, S.H.: A Multi-Agent system for controlling building environments. In: ICMAS, pp. 171–176 (1995)
12. Sun, J., Modiano, E., Zheng, L.: Wireless channel allocation using an auction algorithm. IEEE Journal on Selected Areas in Communications 24, 1085–1096 (2006)
13. Johari, R., Tsitsiklis, J.N.: Efficiency loss in a network resource allocation game. Mathematics of Operations Research 29(3), 407–435 (2004)
14. Krishna, V.: Auction Theory, 2nd edn. Academic Press (2009)
15. Lazar, A.A., Semret, N.: The progressive second price auction mechanism for network resource sharing. In: 8th International Symposium on Dynamic Games, pp. 359–365 (1998)
16. Maamar, Z., Subramanian, S., Thiran, P., Benslimane, D., Bentahar, J.: An Approach to Engineer Communities of Web Services - Concepts, Architecture, Operation, and Deployment. International Journal of E-Business Research 5(4), 1–21 (2009)
17. MacKie-Mason, J.K., Varian, H.R.: Pricing the Internet, pp. 269–314. MIT Press, Cambridge (1995), http://dl.acm.org/citation.cfm?id=212764.212778
18. Mas-Collel, A., Whinston, M.D., Green, J.: Microeconomic Theory. Oxford University Press (1995)
19. Mcafee, R.P., Mcmillan, J.: Analyzing the airwaves auction. Journal of Economic Perspectives 10, 159–175 (1998)
20. Vulkan, N., Jennings, N.R.: Efficient mechanisms for the supply of services in multi-agent environments. Decision Support Systems 28(1), 5–19 (2000)
21. Waldspurger, C.A., Hogg, T., Huberman, B.A., Kephart, J.O., Stornetta, W.S.: Spawn: A distributed computational economy. IEEE Transactions on Software Engineering 18(2), 103–117 (1992), http://dl.acm.org/citation.cfm?id=129792.129794

Preface to DaSEM 2013

As the development of World Wide Web, social networking sites, wikis and folksonomies are becoming more and more popular, the above resources gives a new ground for mining useful information for object modeling, where semantics can play an important role. Along with the interactions between users and computers, more and more information can potentially be mined from the Web by using semantic computing technology, such as ontology engineering for social network and personalization, mining user reviews, user profiling in social network, sentiment analysis for user opinion mining, and so on. Connecting semantic computing and data mining can enhance object modeling. It combines data mining with semantic computing as a promising direction and offers opportunities for developing novel algorithms, methods and tools ranging from text to multimedia.

The International Workshop on Data mining and semantic computing for object modeling (DaSeM) in conjunction with ER 2013 is held in Nov. 13, 2013. The goal of the workshop is to bring together the academia, researchers and industrial practitioners from computer science, information systems, psychology, behavior science and organization science discipline, and provide a forum for recent advances in the field of data mining, semantic computing and object modeling, from the perspectives of information mining and management.

For this first workshop, the Program Committee selects three papers for inclusion in the workshop proceedings. We would like to thank the valuable contribution of all the Program Committee members and reviewers. Also, we would like to acknowledge the ER 2013 Conference General Co-Chairs and Workshop Co-chairs for their great support in ensuring the success of DaSeM 2013 workshop.

November 2013   Yi Cai

Products Competitive Relationships Mining

Jun Li[1], Tao Wang[2,*], Shuyue Hu[2], Qingchuan Zhao[2], and Huaqing Min[2,]

[1] Information Science and Technology School, Zhanjiang Normal University, Zhanjiang, China
[2] School of Software Engineering, South China University of Technology, Guangzhou, China
wtgmme@gmail.com

Abstract. Mining companies' relationship network from the internet is one of the objectives of business intelligence (BI). In previous works of companies' relationship mining, researchers usually applied linguistic analysis tools and methods like natural language processing (NLP) to extract such relationship from online financial articles. In this paper, we propose a new bottom-up algorithm for the mining of companies' competitive relationship network. The algorithm generate a products' competitive relationship network.

We use Tablets and Video Cards data from e-stores to examine the effectiveness of our method, the results are relatively satisfactory. They could present dynamic and asymmetry competitive relationships among companies and could provide useful information for manages to make decisions.

1 Introduction

Accompanied with the development of the internet, some new business and social styles have changed people's lives. Amazon, EBay and the like could let people buy things online, etc. Those recent inventions not only provide people convenience life style but also fuel an explosive growth of data. Such data are valuable and could be used to exploit business intelligence (BI) and develop deep insights about their customers, business partners and competitors [1] [2]. However, manual analysis of such sheer of data is unpractical due to the problem of information overload [10] [11]. As a result, using artificial intelligent (AI) techniques, instead of the people themselves, to automatically analyze those sheer of data and then to provide useful information for managers has attracted some scientists and researchers.

In this paper, we focused on the product competitive relationship mining.The contributions of our work are follows:

- Proposing a three-dimension model combining SWOT method and KANO Model to calculate the intensity of competition between any two products.
- Asymmetrical and dynamic relationship could be showed in products' competitive networks.
- Adopting data from e-stores instead of online financial articles to mine products' competitive networks.

---

* Corresponding author.

J. Parsons and D. Chiu (Eds.): ER Workshops 2013, LNCS 8697, pp. 205–215, 2014.

This paper is structured as follows. Section 2 introduces the related works. In section 3, we propose a three-dimension model for products' competitive network generating and our bottom-up algorithm to generate business entities competitive network. In section 4, we present our experiments. Section 5 concludes the paper and introduces potential future work.

2   Related Works

Competitors identification is a major component of any approach to formulating marketing strategy and there are two approaches to competitor identification, a supply-based and demand-based approach [3]. In this paper, we only focus on the competitive relationship between companies. Chen [4] proposed a competitor identification model, a three-dimension classification of competitors, which concerns attack and response, product market commonality and resource similarity. Feng et al. [13] mentioned a way to combine KANO'S model with SWOT to analyze competition. Zhong [12] used cluster analysis to identify dynamic competitors. But previous works did not pay enough attention to the data flooded in the internet. In this paper, we borrow the idea from these previous analysis and make them adaptable to the new source of data from e-store.

Recently, researchers have realized the utility of the internet and some methods have been proposed to facilitate analysis in business based on the data from internet. Linguistic rules or heuristic are often applied to identify specific types of entities such as people, organizations, places, etc. [5]. And the CoMiner system made use of Natural Language Processing (NLP) techniques and several pre-defined lexical-syntactic patterns (e.g., company-A"against" company-B) to identify competitive company relations based on a Web corpus [6]. Ma et al. [7] developed a network-based approach to extract business competition relations from online financial news articles. However, the main weakness of their approaches are that they extract objective business competitive relations, ironically, from subjective materials such as news articles. In this paper, our computational method generate objective business competitive relationships only from objective data sources, e.g. data from e-stores.

Liu Bing and Minqing Hu [8] proposed a method to extract the specific features of a product that customers have opinions on from customer reviews on e-commerce. Wenping Zhang [9] developed a semi-supervised text mining method to generate dynamic business network based on online articles and customers reviews. Although they realize the value of the information from e-commerce or e-store, they did not pay attention to the new form of information e-commerce and e-store could provide. Their approaches are still using subjective sources, new objective form of information like customers' rating star and sales ranking of a product are ignored. Our proposed method will only use objective information crawl from e-store, such as sales ranking of a product, customers' rating star, the hardware features of a product, etc.

3   Computational Methods

In our algorithm, the input is a pair of companies (comparing companies), such as "Apple" and "Samsung". The output is a dynamic product competitive relationship network of the two comparing companies.

The algorithm performs in three steps:

- First step, gathering all products of the target company and then identifying all competitive products for each product of the target company.
- Second step, generating products competitive network.

3.1 Competitive Products Identification and Competitive Products Set Generation

To analyze the competitive relationship among products, the first thing is to identify what properties should a product has if this product is a competitive product of another product. We begin to solve this issue with some observations:

Observation 1: For two products p_a and p_b, they are competitive if they satisfy the following conditions: (1) the category of p_a is the same with that of p_b; (2) p_a and p_b could be purchased in the same period of time; (3) the price difference between p_a and p_b must be acceptable.

Based on Observation 1, we formalize the product competitive relationship conditions of p_a and p_b as follows:

$$\left\{ \begin{array}{c} \dfrac{|p_{a,price} - p_{b,price}|}{MAX(p_{a,price}, p_{b,price})} \leq \Omega \\ p_{a,cate} = p_{b,cate} \\ p_{a,date} \leq year \| p_{b,date} \leq year \end{array} \right\} \Leftrightarrow p_b \in CPS_{p_a} \qquad (1)$$

where $p_{a,price}$ means the price of product p_a; $MAX(p_{a,price}, p_{b,price})$ is max one of $p_{a,price}$ and $p_{b,price}$; Ω is a variable, which indicates how much difference in money of two competitive products could customers accept; $p_{a,cate}$ means the category that product p_a falls in; $p_{a,date}$ means the latest date in year that product p_a could be purchased; $year$ is the date that could purchase;

All its competitive products for a particular product p_a form a competitive product set of p_a, which is defined as follows:

Definition 1: A competitive products set of product p_a, denoted by CPS_{p_a}, is a set contains all competitive products of product p_a.

$$CPS_{p_a} = (p_{a,1}, p_{a,2}, p_{a,3}, \cdots, p_{a,n})$$

where $p_{a,i}$ is the ith competitive product of p_a; n is the number of products in CPS_{p_a}

Furthermore, such competitive relationship is invertible:

$$p_b \in CPS_{p_a} \Leftrightarrow p_a \in CPS_{p_b}$$

Based on Observation 1 and definition 1, three steps were designed to generate competitive products set for products of the target company:

- Step 1: cluster all products belong to the target company and store them in a set P^C, where C is the name of the target company:

$$P^C = (p_1^C, p_2^C, p_3^C, \cdots, p_n^C)$$

where p_i^C is the ith product of target company C

- Step 2: for each p_i^C in set P^C, cluster all products belong to other companies, those products are in the same category with that of p_i^C, and then store them in set $CPS_{p_i^C}$
- Step 3: for each product in every set $CPS_{p_i^C}$, remain those whose price is similar to the price of p_i^C and those products must could be purchased in the same period time with that of p_i^C.

3.2   Product Competitive Network Generation

Product competitive network (PCN) of asymmetry and dynamics is one of our contributions in this paper. We proposed a three dimensional model for calculating the intensity of products competition and applied a method that combined SWOT method and KANO Model in one of those three dimensions analysis.

The PCN is defined as follows:

Definition 2: Product competitive network(PCN) is a binary tuple PCN = (G, tp) where $G = (V, E)$ is a weighted directed graph and tp is the time point when the graph G is valid. The set V represents the set of nodes (products) and the set E denotes the set of edges (competitive relationship) of G. Each edge $e_{x,y} \in E$ is an ordered pair of nodes (x, y) which indicates that the competitive relationship is from $x \in V$ to $y \in V$, in regard of $x \in V$. The weight of an edge (intensity of competitive relationship) is denoted as $w(e_{x,y})$.

From Definition 2, the dynamic feature could be indicated by tp for the reason that some products may be withdraw from the market and will not exist in that G; the asymmetrical feature can be indicated by the direct edge and its weight, the weight of edge from $x \in V$ to $y \in V$ is not the same with that of edge from $y \in V$ to $x \in V$.

Chen [4] classifies his competition analysis concept into three factors which are *attack and response*, *market commonality* and *resource similarity*. However, his analysis focuses competitions in the level of company, it is required to make some adjustments to make a new model that is suitable to measure competition between products.

We find that in products' competition, attack and response factor is not exist due to it belongs to company strategies. Market commonality factor is to measure the influence of companies in the market, and this factor should be considered when analyzing products' competition and need to be adjusted. Resource similarity is to measure the similarity of the usage of resources, and the measurement of the similarity in the products' competition is also important, so some adjustments had to be made.

In our model, we also have three factors and we let them be three dimensions, in each dimension, the value of it could be positive and negative, positive means better than and negative means worse. The first dimension is products' hardware specifications (PHS), which is to measure the similarity between products; the second one is products' brand effect (PBE), which is to measure products' market influence; and the third one is the new one we create, we name it products' attraction (PA), which is to measure the ability to attract customers.

Product's Brand Effect Dimension. This dimension measures the difference of product's brand effect between two competitive products. The product's brand effect (PBE) of a product indicates this product's influence in the market. The higher a PBE of a product is, the more powerful influence this product plays in the market. The more powerful influence of a product means this product could influence the trend in its category.

As our observations, the PBE of a product could be measured by two factors, products' recognition degree(PRD) and products' added value(PAV). These two factors will be discussed in follows. Based on these observations, in this dimension, the difference of PBE between product p_a and product p_b in regard of p_a, denoted as $F_{PBE}(p_a, p_b)$, could be calculated as follows:

$$F_{PBE}(p_a, p_b) = \alpha_1 \times F_{PAV}(p_a, p_b) + \alpha_2 \times F_{PRD}(p_a, p_b) \qquad (2)$$

where α_1 is the weight of $F_{PAV}(p_a, p_b)$, α_2 is the weight of $F_{PRD}(p_a, p_b)$ and $\alpha_1 + \alpha_2 = 1$(in our experiments, we set $\alpha_1 = 0.6$ and $\alpha_2 = 0.4$); the value of $F_{PAV}(p_a, p_b)$ is the difference of PAV between product p_a and product p_b in regard of p_a and the value $F_{PRD}(p_a, p_b)$ is the difference of PRD between product p_a and product p_b in regard of p_a.

Commonly, a more powerful influence product is often more expensive than that of a product with similar functions and quality but whose influence is not so powerful. Added value could be used to measure different level of this influence. The more powerful the influence of a product is, the more added value there in this product. So **Products' added value(PAV)** could be used to describe the power of influence of a product.

And then how to calculate PAV of a product? Our observations of this issue is follows:

Observation 2: The higher the a product's PAV, the lower its performance price ratio(PPR)

With the observation 2 above, we define the value of a product p_a's PAV:

$$PAV_{p_a} = \frac{1}{PPR_{p_a}} \qquad (3)$$

where PPR_{p_a} is the performance price ratio of product p_a, and the value of it defined as:

$$PPR_{p_a} = \frac{\sum_{i=1}^{n} \delta_i \times p_{a,f_i}}{p_{a,price}} \qquad (4)$$

where n is the number of features of product p_a; $p_{a,price}$ is the price of product p_a; p_{a,f_i} is the ith feature of product p_a and δ_i is the weight of it, $\sum_{i=1}^{n} \delta_i = 1, n$ is the number of features of product p_a.

And the difference of PAV between product p_a and product p_b in regard of product p_a, denoted as $F_{PAV}(p_a, p_b)$, could be calculated by following function:
$F_{PAV}(p_a, p_b) =$

$$\begin{cases} -e^{\frac{PAV_{p_a} - PAV_{p_b}}{PAV_{p_a}}}, & \text{if } PAV_{p_a} > PAV_{p_b} \\ 0, & \text{if } PAV_{p_a} = PAV_{p_b} \\ e^{\frac{PAV_{p_a} - PAV_{p_b}}{PAV_{p_a}}}, & \text{if } PAV_{p_a} < PAV_{p_b} \end{cases} \qquad (5)$$

Intuitively, a more powerful influence product could attract more customers and the market shares it accounted for is larger. With larger market shares, the higher recognition degree of this product, which means that people acknowledge the performance of this product. So **Products' recognition degree (PRD)** could be used to measure the power of influence of a product. Before introducing how to calculate it, we first present our observation to this issue as follows:

Observation 3: In e-stores, customers will be required to rate products they have bought, people would be denied to rate if they have not bought, so the higher a product's PRD, the more customers rated.

With the observation above, we define the value of p_a's PRD, PRD_{p_a} is the total number of customers who rate product p_a.

Products' Attraction Dimension. This dimension measures the difference of product's attraction(PA) between two competitive products. Product's attraction (PA) of a product indicates the ability of this product to let customers buy it when customers comparing this product with its competitive products.

As our observations of customers purchasing online, besides specifications of hardware, there are four factors could change customers choice, we name them performance price ratio (PPR), user rating (UR), sales ranking (SR) and price effect(PE). Each of these factors will be discussed in follows. Based on these observations, in this dimension, the difference of PA between product p_a and product p_b in regard of p_a, denoted as $F_{PA}(p_a, p_b)$, could be calculated as following:

$$F_{PA}(p_a, p_b) = (\beta_1 \times F_{PPR}(p_a, p_b) + \beta_2 \times F_{UR}(p_a, p_b)) \times \\ \beta_3 \times F_{SR}(p_a, p_b) \times \beta_4 \times F_{PE}(p_a, p_b) \qquad (6)$$

where β_1 is the weight of $F_{PPR}(p_a, p_b)$, β_2 is the weight of $F_{UR}(p_a, p_b)$, β_3 is the weight of $F_{SR}(p_a, p_b)$ and β_4 is the weight of $F_{PE}(p_a, p_b)$; (in our experiments, we set $\beta_1 = 0.35, \beta_2 = 0.65, \beta_3 = 5, \beta_4 = 1$)
the value of $F_{PR}(p_a, p_b)$ is the difference of PPR between product p_a and product p_b in regard of p_a; the value of $F_{UR}(p_a, p_b)$ is the difference of UR of product p_a and product p_b in regard of p_a; the value of $F_{SR}(p_a, p_b)$ is the difference of SR of product p_a and product p_b in regard of p_a; the value of $F_{PE}(p_a, p_b)$ is the difference of PE of product p_a and product p_b in regard of p_a.

Among many factors that could effect customers choices, the **Performance price ratio (PPR)** is a very important factor. It is all known that higher PPR will attract more customers. So PPR could be used to measure the PA of a product.

The score rated by customers is a unique feature that e-stores could provide, and this feature could express the customers' satisfactory. The higher the score, the more satisfactory customers would have. As our observation, the average score of a product is another consideration of customers when they buying online, customers tend to purchase products with higher scores. So the average score, **User rating(UR)**, could be used to measure the PA of a product.

The difference of UR between product p_a and product p_b in regard of p_a, denoted as $F_{UR}(p_a, p_b)$, could be calculated by following function:

$$F_{UR}(p_a, p_b) = \begin{cases} -e^{\frac{UR_{p_a} - UR_{p_b}}{UR_{p_a}}}, & \text{if } UR_{p_a} > UR_{p_b} \\ 0, & \text{if } UR_{p_a} = UR_{p_b} \\ e^{\frac{UR_{p_a} - UR_{p_b}}{UR_{p_a}}}, & \text{if } UR_{p_a} < UR_{p_b} \end{cases} \tag{7}$$

The sales ranking of a product is also a unique feature of e-stores. This feature could express the degree of popularity of a product among customers. The higher the sales ranking of a product, the more popular this product would be among customers. As our observations, customers tend to purchase products with higher sales ranking. And customers often connect sales ranking of a product with its quality and performance. For customers, a product with higher sales ranking, its quality and performance will also be great. So **Sales ranking(SR)** could be used to measure the PA of a product.

The difference of SR between between product p_a and product p_b in regard of p_a, denoted as $F_{SR}(p_a, p_b)$, could be calculated by following function:

$$F_{SR}(p_a, p_b) = \tan(\frac{\pi \times |SR_{p_a} - SR_{p_b}|}{2 \times \varepsilon}) \tag{8}$$

where ε is a variable to let $\frac{\pi \times |SR_{p_a} - SR_{p_b}|}{2 \times \varepsilon} \in [0, \frac{\pi}{2})$

The most attractable and important factor is the price of a product. This feature can change customer's choice, because people tend to like cheaper ones. As our observations, customers tend to purchase a cheaper one if two competitive products are similar in other aspects. So the price of products, **Price effect(PE)**, could be used to measure the PA of a product.

Products' Hardware Specification Dimension. This dimension measures the difference between products' hardware specifications(PHS). Comparing products' hardware specifications is to compare their hardware similarities and then to find their advantages and disadvantages. Different from products market influence and its marketing performance in attracting customers, analysis in products' hardware specifications could focus only on products themselves. In this dimension, we adopt a method that combining KANO Model and SWOT method [13]to analyze advantages and disadvantages of a product when competing with its competitive products and then calculate the intensity of competitive relationships between products.

The difference of PHS of product p_a and product p_b in regard of p_a, denoted as $F_{PHS}(p_a, p_b)$, could be calculated as following:

$$F_{PHS}(p_a, p_b) = \gamma_1 \times F_s(p_a, p_b) + \gamma_2 \times F_w(p_a, p_b) \tag{9}$$

where γ_1 is the weight of $F_s(p_a, p_b)$, γ_2 is the weight of $F_w(p_a, p_b)$(in our experiments, we set $\gamma_1 = 0.8, \gamma_2 = -0.2$); the value of $S(p_a, p_b)$ is the strength or opportunity of product p_a in competing with product p_b; and the value of $W(p_a, p_b)$ is the weak or threaten of productp_a in competing with product p_b.

4 Experiments and Results

In our experiments, the data we get from Amazon.com is not complete. For tablet data set, we scrawled 436 tablets' information until September 1, 2012. While for some reasons, some the information of products' is missed. One reason is because Amazon.com does not provide such information for some products, like some kinds of hardware specifications and ranking. Another reason is our technique limitation that it is hard to scrawl those information.

Table 1. Part of product iPad MC705LL/A competitive product result

name	iPad MC705LL/A	TF300BL	TF300WH	P5100
price	514.00	391.72	382.00	475.99
company	Apple	ASUS	ASUS	Samsung
rank	8	36	45	73
star	4.3	3.9	3.9	5.0
total	313	435	435	2
fiveStar	211	211	211	2
screenSize	9.7	10.1	10.1	10.1
processor	1	1.2	1.2	1
core	2	4	4	2
RAM	1	1	1	0.5
hard driver	16	32	32	64
wireless	1	1	1	1
compScore		0.4548	0.4604	0.6334
RICPS		5	3	10

To resolve such missing information, we do following steps:

– Firstly, we eliminate those products who miss most its information, and only remain those who only miss 1 or 2 of its information.
– Secondly, some of information which could be inferred from other information, we fill them after processing, and some of information we give it a random number.(For different data set, such information will be different, this will be indicated in every data set.)

In tables 1 and 2, we can see that it is part of the result of product iPad MC705LL/A's competitive products. In the form, 'star' means the average stars that customers rated, 'total' means the total number of customers who have rated this product, 'fiveStar' means how many customers rated five stars for this product, 'processor' means the frequency of the CPU, 'core' means the number of cores in CPU, 'hard driver' means the capacity of storage of the hard driver, 'wireless' means whether such device is able to connect to the wireless network, 1 means could, 0 means could not; 'RICPS' means ranking in set CPS, 'compScore' means their weight of the direct path. In these three tables, we only present part of the whole result in order to show representative features of our method, asymmetry competitive relationship.

Table 2. Part of product iPad2 MC916LL/A competitive product result

name	iPad2 MC916LL/A	TF201	XOOM	Xoom Quad
company	Apple	ASUS	Motorola	Motorola
price	544.98	462.57	404.99	398.99
rank	29	67	59	98
star	4.3	3.7	4.1	3.8
total	1013	606	678	24
fiveStar	683	307	396	12
screenSize	9.7	10.1	10.1	10.1
processor	1	1.66	1.0	1.0
core	2	2	2	2
RAM	0.5	1	1	1
hard driver	64	32	32	32
wireless	1	1	1	1
compScore		0.0989	0.0971	0.1651
RICPS		2	4	14

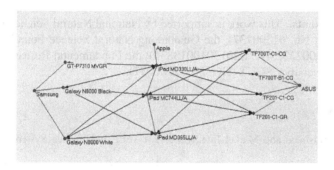

Fig. 1. Parts of competitive products of Apple in Tablets, 2012

In table 1, for the two products TF300BL and TF300WH, they are the same product shares the same hardware specifications expect their colors. We can see that TF300BL is 10 dollars higher than TF300WH, while TF300BL ranks in the 36th place and TF300WH ranks in the 45th place in their category. From their compScore, we could see that, and we could say in this price level, 10 dollars play less important than ranking in analyzing the intensity of competitive relationship, which is an empirical realization that for the same price difference, the higher the price level, the less important it is to effect customers choices.

But in table 2, the target product is iPad MC705LL/A. For the product TF201 and XOOM, TF201 is almost 60 dollars closer to iPad MC705LL/A in price than that of XOOM, even if TF201's ranking difference is 8 larger than that of XOOM to the target product, as well as in other factors XOOM is much closer to the target product, TF201 is much more competitive than XOOM, because 60 dollars in this price level is a big deal.

Fig 1 shows parts of competitive products of Apple in 2012 in Tablets market. In Fig 2, we present 3 products of "Apple", "iPad MD330LL/A", "iPad MC744LL/A" and "iPad MD365LL/A"; 3 competitive products belong to "Samsung", "GT-P7310 MVGR", "Galaxy N8000 White" and "Galaxy N8000 Black"; 4 competitive products belong to "ASUS", "TF700T-C1-CG", "TF700T-B1-CG", "TF201-C1-CG" and "TF201-C1-CR". The arrowed line in this Fig means that there is a competitive relationship between the two products, e.g. "Apple"'s "iPad MD330LL/A" has competitive relationship with "ASUS"'s "TF700T-C1-CG".

5   Conclusion

Although some research works realized the value of information from e-stores, their works still limit on linguistic analysis and few of companies relationship mining could show the asymmetry of competition. The main contribution of this paper is the usage of the new features of the date crawl from e-stores, proposed an algorithm to transfer products competition to companies competition and show the asymmetry of competitive relationship. Experiments results of our proposed method are relatively satisfactory.

Acknowledgements. This work is supported by National Natural Science Foundation of China (Grant No. 61300137); the Guangdong Natural Science Foundation, China (NO. S2011040002222, NO.S2013010013836); the Fundamental Research Funds for the Central Universities,SCUT (NO. 2012ZM0077).

References

1. Chen, H.: Business and Market Intelligence 2.0. IEEE Intelligence System 25(1), 68–71 (2010)
2. Chen, H., Zimbra, D.: AI and Opinion Mining. IEEE Intelligent Systems 25(3), 74–80 (2010)
3. Clark, B.H., Montgomery, D.B.: Managerial Identification of Competitors. Journal of Marketing 63, 67–83 (1999)
4. Chen, M.-J., Hambrick, D.: Speed. Stealth and selective attack: How small firms differ from large firms in competitive behavior. Academy of Management Journal 38(2), 453–482 (1995)
5. Budi, I., Bressan, S.: Application of association rules mining to named entity recognition and co-reference resolution for the Indonesian language. International Journal of BI and DM 2, 426–446 (2007)
6. Bao, S., Li, R., Yu, Y., Cao, Y.: Competitor Mining with the Web. IEEE Transactions on Knowledge and Data Engineering 20(10), 1297–1310 (2008)
7. Ma, Z., Pant, G., Sheng, O.R.L.: A Network-based Approach to Mining Competitor Relationships from Online News. In: Proceedings of the, International Conference on Information Systems. Completed Research Paper 59 (2009b)
8. Liu, B., Minqing, H.: Mining Opinion Features in Customers Reviews. In: American Association for Artificial Intelligence(2004)
9. Zhang, W., Cai, Y., Lau, R.Y.K., Liao, S.S.Y., Kwok, R.C.-W.: Semi-Supervised Text Mining For Dynamic Business Network Discovery. In: PACIS 2012, vol. 138 (2012)
10. Lau, R.Y.K., Bruza, P.D., Song, D.: Towards a Belief Revision Based Adaptive and Context Sensitive Informaiton Retrieval System.ACM Transactions on Information System 26(2) (2008)

11. Yan, X., Lau, R.Y., Song, D., Li, X., Ma, J.: Towards a Semantic Granularity Model for Domain-specific Information Retrieval. ACM Transactions on Information Systems 29(3), Article 15 (2011)
12. Zheng, Z.: The identification of enterprise dynamic competitor based on cluster analysis. In: International Conference on Information Management, Innovation Management and Industrial Engineering (2011), doi: 10.1109/ICIII.2011.80
13. Feng, W.J., Hou, Z., Li, Z., Zhou, K.Q.: Research on Product Competition Strategy. Construction Machinery and Equipment 39(5), 50–52 (2008)

Exploring Set Recommendation
from a Financial Perspective

Yu Liu, Yi Cai, Shuyue Hu, Yifeng Shao, Tao Wang*, and Huaqing Min

School of Software Engineering, South China University of Technology,
Guangzhou, China
wtgmme@gmail.com

Abstract. All current recommendation algorithms try to handle the
problem of recommending single item to a user. However, there are many
cases that we need to consume a set of items at one time in our real life,
e.g., many restaurants may provide some food set for users to choose and
a travel agent may provide many travel routes or itineraries which can
contain different interest places. In this paper, inspired by the modern
portfolio theory, we propose three set recommendation algorithms which
return a list of item-set for users. We conduct experiments on a real-life
dataset by comparing the performance of our proposed approaches. The
experimental results fit our expectation and show the effectiveness of
proposed methods.

1 Introduction

As the development of World Wide Web and E-Commerce, people need to spend
more time on browsing web pages so as to get information in their need, and such
a task is time-consuming. Thus, effective recommendation systems is needed to
assist users to find out what they need. The task of recommendation system is
to estimate preference or ratings of a user on the items.

All current works try to handle the problem of recommending single item to
a user. However, there are many cases that we need to consume a set of items
at one time in our real life. For example, many restaurants may provide some
food set, and we can choose different salad, main course, dessert, soup and so
on. Especially in Chinese restaurant, there may be many dishes for customers
to choose to combine their favorite dinning food set. For another example, for a
travel agent, it may provide many travel routes or itineraries which can contain
different interest places, a user can choose different interest places to form his
personalized favorite travel routes for his holidays. One common distinct feature
of these cases is that what we want to recommend to a user is a set of items
(e.g., dishes and interest places). In other words, there are many cases in which
users consume a set of goods instead of only a single good at a time. For these
prevalent cases, these is little work on handle them. Current recommendation
systems only try to recommend a single item to a user and can not recommend
a set of items to a user well at a time. We consider that recommending a set of

---

* Corresponding author.

J. Parsons and D. Chiu (Eds.): ER Workshops 2013, LNCS 8697, pp. 216–225, 2014.

items at a time to a user is a new problem which is different from traditional single item recommendation and we name it as *Set Recommendation.*

For the new problem of set recommendation, its task is to recommend a set items (instead of only one item) to a user for one consumption and expect that the user will be satisfied with such a consumption of a set of items with a highest satisfaction degree. If we look into the field of finance, we find that such a set recommendation task have an analogy with the investment problem in financial markets. As one of the most influential economic theories dealing with finance and investment, the Modern Portfolio Theory (MPT) was motivated on the basis of the following two observations. 1) The future return of a stock is unknown and cannot be calculated with absolute certainty. Investors have different preferences of the risk associated with uncertainty. Therefore, it is highly desirable to have a method of quantifying this uncertainty or risk, and reflect them and incorporate users' risk preferences when selecting stocks. 2) Since in practice the future returns of stocks are correlated, assuming independence between the returns and selecting them independently to construct a portfolio is not preferable. Realizing the two fundamental issues, the MPT emphasizes that risk (uncertainty) is an inherent part of future return, and quantifies it by using the variance (or the standard deviation) of the return. The theory suggests that, for a risk-averse decision, an investor should both maximize the return as a desirable thing and minimize the variance of the return as an undesirable thing.

Considering set recommendation problem, we also have two similar critical issues: 1) In set recommendation, the return (satisfaction degree) of a set of items is unknown and cannot be estimated with absolute certainty from current recommendation methods. There are many sources of uncertainty such as specific user preferences, the deviation of prediction from actual users' rating and so on. 2) The estimation of satisfaction degree of individual items are also correlated. Thus, we consider that it may be great helpful to borrow the idea of portfolio theory from finance to handle the set recommendation problem. The contributions of this paper are listed below.

- We formulate the problem of set recommendation and have a deep discussion on it.
- As a new research field, we propose a naive and a preference-based methods as the basic implementations of set recommendation.
- For further development, we propose a risk-optimized approach based on the MPT for set recommendation.
- We conduct experiments on the real-life dataset by comparing the performance of our proposed approaches. The experimental results fit our expectations.

2   Background and Related Work

In this section we briefly introduce the background of the modern recommender systems as well as some basic concepts in this field. Due to the hard work of the scholar around the world, modern recommender systems is becoming more and more mature. Current recommendation methods are usually classified into collaborative filtering (e.g., [7]), content-based (e.g., [6][5]) and hybrid methods (e.g., [4][1] [3]). CB methods estimate the preference degree of a user u_a on an item i_x based on the preference degree of u_a on the other items that are similar with i_x, while the key idea of CF methods is that similar users have similar taste(user-based) and similar items will attract the same user(item-based). The main difference between CB and item-based CF is the similarity measurement strategy. CB measures the similarity between two items based on their content, while item-based CF is based on the common users that rate both the two items. Due to its' scalability, CF is more popular and widely used than CB in recent recommender systems. There are many work on CF and most of them can achieve a better performance in specific occasion. Recently, matrix factorization(MF) has been one of the most popular CF algorithm, which was firstly proposed by Koren et al[11] in the netflix prize. MF is proved to outperform most existing state-of-the art algorithms in most cases.

3   Problem Formulation

In this section, we formulate the problem of set recommendation. As mentioned above, set recommendation is to recommend a set of items to a specific user and the user will satisfy the item set with a highest degree. Given a set S of items and a user i denoted by u_i, the set recommendation method(SRM) can return a *top-k recommended item-set list* denoted by L as following:

$$L = SRM(S, u_i)$$

The top-k list consists of k item sets which are ranked by an evaluated value in a decreasing order as following:

$$L = \{P_1, P_2, \cdots, P_k\}$$

where P_x is an item set with at least two items inside and the size of each item set is various. In order to evaluate each item set for user i, there needs to be a function f to measure the satisfaction degree of the user:

$$D_{i,x} = f(u_i, P_x)$$

where $D_{i,x}$ is the satisfaction degree of user i on the item set P_x. Obviously, searching all of the items to generate candidate sets is a tough process since it will produce a large amount of item sets. For example, when there are n items in total, the number of candidate sets will be $(C_n^2 + C_n^3 + \cdots + C_n^n)$. Therefore, in this paper, we do set recommendation after the user has already chosen an item which we named as *major item* here. The candidate item set denoted by C can be defined as following:

$$C = \{o_m, o_1, o_2, \cdots, o_n\}$$

where o_m is the *major item* and o_x is the item recommended to the user.

4   Method

4.1   A Naive Set Recommendation Method

From the last section we can know that each candidate set contains a *major item*, so the simple method to do set recommendation for someone is to recommend the item set which not only contains the *major item* but is also often chosen by users to him. The method we used here is called association-rule recommendation method. First we extract the association rules from the buying record, then we

Table 1. A binary 0/1 representation of purchase records

RID	mouse	keyboard	mouse pad	card reader	SD card
1	1	1	0	0	0
2	1	0	1	0	0
3	1	0	0	1	1
4	1	1	1	0	0

can use the rules to do some prediction. In Table 1, there are four purchase records. *1* represents that the item is in the purchase record and *0* represents that it is not. A record R_i is said to contain an item set X if X is a subset of R_i. For example, the first record in Table I contains the item set $\{mouse, keyboard\}$ but not $\{mouse, mousepad\}$. An important property of an item set is *support count*, which refers to the number of records that contains a particular item set[2]. Mathematically, the support count, $\sigma(X)$, for an item set X can be stated as follows:

$$\sigma(X) = |\{R_i | X \subseteq R_i, R_i \in U\}|$$

where the symbol $|\cdot|$ denote the number of elements in a set and U denote the set of all purchase records. In the data set shown in Table 1, the *support count* for $\{mouse, keyboard\}$ equals to two because there are two records that contains these two items. The association rule is an implication expression of the form $X \rightarrow Y$, where X and Y are disjoint item sets. Considered that the scenario of the set recommendation is to recommend the item set after the user has chosen the *major item* o_m, the rule is generally in the form of $o_i \rightarrow Y$. The strength of an association rule can be measured in terms of its *support* and *confidence*[2]. *Support* determines how often a rule is applicable to a given data set, while *confidence* determines how frequently items in Y appear in records that contains o_i. The formal definitions of these metrics are:

$$support(o_i \rightarrow Y) = \frac{\sigma(\{o_i\} \cup Y)}{\sigma(\{o_i\}) + \sigma(Y) - \sigma(\{o_i\} \cup Y)}$$

$$confidence(o_i \rightarrow Y) = \frac{\sigma(\{o_i\} \cup Y)}{\sigma(\{o_i\})}$$

When we want to do set recommendation with the association rules, first we find all the rules whose *support* and *confidence* are respectively larger than a threshold and in the form of $o_m \rightarrow Y$ to generate the candidate item sets. Then we evaluate each candidate item set according to their *support* and *confidence* to attain the top-k recommended list. Given the set of rules denoted by *RS*, *major item* denoted by o_m, the threshold of support denoted by *TS*, the threshold of confidence *TC* and the evaluation function *f*, we can attain the recommended list of item sets with the algorithm *Association-Rule*.

Input : RS, o_m, TS, TC, δ
Output: L

1 $L \leftarrow \emptyset$;

2 **for** $ru \in RS$ **do**
3 $\quad$ **if** $support(o_m \rightarrow Y) \geq TS$ and $confidence(o_m \rightarrow Y) \geq TC$ **then if** ru
   $\quad$ *is in the form of* $o_m \rightarrow Y$ **then** $L.insert(\{o_m\} \cup Y)$;
4 **end**
5 $MS = \max(support(o_m \rightarrow Y_i))((o_m \rightarrow Y_i) \in RS)$;

6 $MC = \max(confidence(o_m \rightarrow Y_i))((o_m \rightarrow Y_i) \in RS)$;

7 Sort $L = \{\{o_m\} \cup Y_1, \{o_m\} \cup Y_2, \cdots, \{o_m\} \cup Y_n\}$ by value
   $f(o_m \rightarrow Y_i, MS, MC, \delta)$;

8 RETURN L;

Algorithm 1. Association-Rule(RS, o_m, TS, TC, δ)

In this algorithm, the evaluation function f is used to evaluate the satisfaction degree of the candidate item set for user i as following:

$$f(o_m \rightarrow Y_i, MS, MC, \delta) = \delta * \frac{support(o_m \rightarrow Y_i)}{MS} + (1-\delta) * \frac{confidence(o_m \rightarrow Y_i)}{MC}$$

where variable δ is a number between *0* and *1*. For different *TS* and *TC*, we often have different δ to produce a better recommended list. The evaluated value of each item set have an analogy with the return of an investment in the financial market. We always want the investment has the best return. Also in this method for set recommendation, the more strongly the *major item* is associated with the other items in the item set, the higher satisfaction degree we think the user will have on the item set. With this algorithm, for any user who has chosen the same *major item* o_m will be recommended the same list of item sets.

4.2   Preference-Based Set Recommendation Approach

The naive recommendation method consider that the item set liked by a large amount of users will also be liked by any one, which is often not true since everyone has its own preference. So we proposed a preference-based approach to do set recommendation. Here *preference* of a user on a certain item can be represented as predicted rating drawn from the user's buying history. Any traditional recommendation methods can be used here, like collaborative filtering, etc. Given a single-item recommendation method(RM), the rating of an item set P with n items for a specific user u is the average rating of items in the set:

$$Rating(u, P) = \frac{\sum_{i=1}^{n} RM(u, o_i)}{n}$$

We can optimize the algorithm *Association-Rule* by predicted ratings replacing the evaluating function f with function *f-rating* defined as following:

$$f - rating(o_m \rightarrow Y_i, MS, MC, MR, u, \delta, \alpha) =$$
$$\alpha * f(o_m \rightarrow Y_i, MS, MC, \delta) + (1 - \alpha) * \frac{Rating(u, \{o_m\} \cup Y_i)}{MR}$$

where variable α is between *0* and *1* and MR denoted the maximal predicted rating of the item sets in the recommended list. In the definition of function f, we know that there is another variable named δ. For different TS, TC and RM, we can often has different pairs of (δ, α) to do better set recommendation. For this evaluation method, the return or satisfaction degree of an item set of a user is not only the association strength between the *major item* and the other items in the item set but also the ratings of the items. Here we gives the definition of the algorithm *Rating-ARule*.

4.3   Risk-Optimized Set Recommendation Approach

In Modern Portfolio Theory, we balance the return and risk or uncertainty to maximize some kind of utility. Follow this school of thinking, for set recommendation problem, we also has two similar critical issues: The return(the satisfaction degree we evaluated for a user on the item set) and the risk(the uncertainty or deviation of the satisfaction degree produced by our evaluation method). In Subsection A and B, we only consider the return of an item set ignoring the risk or uncertainty. In this subsection, we take the risk into consideration in order to optimize our method. For the preference-based set recommendation approach mentioned in Subsection B, there are two kinds of sources of risk: association rules and predicted ratings. 1) We can find that association rules are drawn from different amount of buying records in Subsection A. For example, in Table 1, we can get the rule $\{mouse\} \rightarrow \{keyboard\}$ with *support* of 0.5 and *confidence* of 0.5. The *support* and *confidence* is large but we still can't declare that the user who has chosen *mouse* will possibly choose *keyboard* since this rule is derived from only four buying records. However, if the same rule is extracted from one million buying records with the same *support* and *confidence*, the situation will be different. Thus, the risk of association rules denoted by *ARuleRisk* can be defined as following:

$$ARuleRisk(o_m \rightarrow Y_i) = 1 - \frac{\sigma(\{o_m\}) + \sigma(Y_i) - \sigma(\{o_m\} \cup Y_i)}{\sigma(\{o_m\}) + \sum_{t=1}^{n} \sigma(Y_t) - \sum_{t=1}^{n} \sigma(\{o_m\} \cup Y_t)}$$

where n denoted that there are n rules in the form of $o_m \to Y$. 2) There are many recommendation methods we can use to get the predicted ratings but it's uncertain whether ratings can really represent users' preferences. To evaluate the efficiency of the methods, we often use *mean absolute error*(MAE) defined as the average absolute difference between predicted ratings and actual ratings. Here we calculate MAE for each item o_i:

$$MAE(o_i) = \frac{\sum_{t=1}^{n}(a_{t,i} - p_{t,i})}{n}$$

where n is the number of users we have predicted for on o_i, $a_{t,i}$ is the actual rating of user t on item o_i while $p_{t,i}$ is the predicted rating. With the same recommendation method, the MAE of each item may be different. MAE is a good way to see the average deviation between the actual ratings and predicted ratings. In the real world, actual ratings reflect users' preferences, so we can say that the lower the MAE is, the more possible predicted ratings can stand for users' preferences. Here gives the definition of the risk of predicted ratings:

$$RatingRisk(o_i) = MAE(o_i)$$

To optimize the preference-based set recommendation method with *ARuleRisk*, we can change the evaluating function f into:

$$f(o_m \to Y_i, MS, MC, \delta, \theta) = \delta * \frac{support(o_m \to Y_i)}{MS} + (1-\delta) * \frac{confidence(o_m \to Y_i)}{MC}$$
$$- \theta * ARuleRisk(o_m \to Y_i)$$

where θ is a factor which can be changed to make a better recommending result. With *RatingRisk*, the predicted rating of an item set p for a specific user u can be redefined as following:

$$Rating(u, P, \beta) = \frac{\sum_{i=1}^{n} RM(u, o_i) - \beta * RatingRisk(o_i)}{n}$$

where β is a factor like θ. Therefore, for different TS, TC and RM, we can generally have different four tuples $(\delta, \alpha, \theta, \beta)$ to produce a better recommended list of item sets.

5   Experiments

5.1   Experimental Setup and Data Description

In this paper, we exploit purchase data from an e-commerce web site. There are totally 3,924,559 buying records in our data set. We synthesize 291,718 useful item sets with 226,033 customers and 2,534 items from it. On average, each user owns no more than two item sets. It is not hard to tell that the data set is sparse. Each row of the data set is like this:

$$\{u_i, o_1 : r_{i,1}, o_2 : r_{i,2}, \cdots, o_n : r_{i,n}\}$$

where $r_{i,x}$ is the real rating between *1* to *5* of user u_i on item o_x. *1* represents the worst satisfaction degree and *5* represent the best. $o_1, o_2, \cdots, o_n$ are items the user bought at the same time. In our experiment, the data set are divided into test set with 55,612 item sets and training set with 236,106 item sets.

5.2 Evaluation Metrics for Recommendation

In a real world, ratings for item sets are usually not conveniently available. So in our data set, there are no explicit ratings of item sets for validation. Therefore, we refer to the ranking accuracies. In the experiment, we adopt *Degree of Agreement*(DOA)as the evaluation metric for recommendation. DOA is used for ranking accuracies and describes the average rank accuracy for the item sets [8].DOA used in this paper is similar to [8].

5.3 Recommendation Performances

In this subsection, we present the performance comparison on recommendation accuracies among the three recommendation methods. The major difference of the three methods are the evaluation functions we used to sort the recommended list L of candidate item sets. So no matter what methods we use, L will stay no change unless we alter the thresholds of support(*TS*) or confidence(*TC*). With the increase of *TS* or *TC*, the number of the association rules will become smaller and smaller. It means that the recommended list will be getting shorter and shorter as we can see in Table 2. The ordinate is the average number of item sets in a list. To set the *TS* or *TC* too small or too big are both inappropriate. If they are too big, there will be not enough association rules for us to do predictions and too many candidate lists with only one item set. If they are too small, we will get too many meaningless rules. Therefore, in the experiment, we set four pairs of (*TS*, *TC*): (0.2,0.1), (0.1,0.15), (0.1,0.1) and (0.05,0.05). When we use the method *Rating-ARule*, we choose the user-based collaborative filtering(CF)[10] to predict ratings for single items. For *Risk-Optimized-Rating-ARule*, we have to calculate the value of MAE for CF. So we use the whole training set we divided from the data set before to train for CF. This training set is also used as a test set. The value of MAE we have attained is about 0.3 which is very low as a result of that real ratings in our data set are mainly 4 or 5.

Table 2. The average length of the list of candidate item sets

(TS,TC)	(0.2,0.1)	(0.1,0.15)	(0.1,0.1)	(0.05,0.05)
Length	1.13	1.38	1.53	1.68

In Figure 1, we can see that there are four groups of experiment and each group has different *TS* or *TC*. All methods perform better and better with the increase of *TS* or *TC*. As mentioned above, the smaller are the *TS* or *TC*, the more meaningless association rules will be used to do prediction which will weaken the accuracies of the methods. For example, for item set

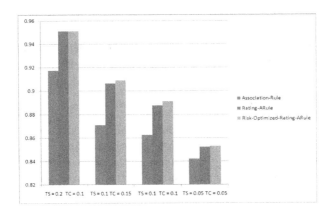

Fig. 1. A performance comparison based on DOA results

$\{mouse, radio\}$ and $\{mouse, fan\}$ of which the $(support, confidence)$ are respectively (0.053,0.053) and (0.050,0.050). We can't judge that between these two item sets, $\{mouse, radio\}$ is more possible for users to choose according to the size of their *support* and *confidence* since their *support* and *confidence* are both too low to be meaningful. *Rating-ARule* outperforms the *Association-Rule* in all groups and the improvement is between 1.1% to 4.1%. *Risk-Optimized-Rating-ARule* perform better than *Rating-ARule* except in the first group on the left which group has the smallest average number of item sets in a list. The optimizing from *Rating-ARule* to *Risk-Optimized-Rating-ARule* is not so remarkable as it from *Association-Rule* to *Rating-ARule*, only between 0.10% to 0.42% in our experiment based on DOA results. It is more easy to tell the optimizing of the performance among these methods in the second and the third group from left to right where the recommended lists are not too short and quality of the association rules are more acceptable.

6   Conclusion

In this paper, we focus on how to address the set recommendation problem. We first propose a naive method and a preference-based method as two basic methods for set recommendation. Then we propose the risk-optimized method based on the portfolio theory to improve the basic methods. The experimental results show that the proposed approaches are sensitive to the support and the confidence threshold. In most occasions the Rating-ARule outperforms the Association-Rule, and the Risk-Optimized-Rating-ARule performs better than Rating-ARule in some occasions.

Acknowledgements. This work is supported by National Natural Science Foundation of China (Grant No. 61300137); the Guangdong Natural Science Foundation, China (NO. S2011040002222, NO.S2013010013836); the Fundamental Research Funds for the Central Universities,SCUT (NO. 2012ZM0077).

References

1. Balabanović, M., Shoham, Y.: Fab: content-based, collaborative recommendation. Commun. ACM 40(3), 66–72 (1997)
2. Tan, P.-N., Steinbach, M., Kumar, V.: Introduction to Data Mining. China Machine Press 6(1), 328–330 (2010)
3. Ma, H., King, I., Lyu, M.R.: Effective missing data prediction for collaborative filtering. In: SIGIR 2007, pp. 39–46 (2007)
4. Melville, P., Mooney, R.J., Nagarajan, R.: Content-boosted collaborative filtering for improved recommendations. In: AAAI 2002, Menlo Park, CA, USA, pp. 187–192 (2002)
5. Mooney, R.J., Roy, L.: Content-based book recommending using learning for text categorization. In: DL 2000: Proceedings of the fifth ACM Conference on Digital Libraries, New York, NY, USA, pp. 195–204 (2000)
6. Pazzani, M., Billsus, D.: Learning and revising user profiles: The identification ofinteresting web sites. Mach. Learn. 27(3), 313–331 (1997)
7. Sarwar, B., Karypis, G., Konstan, J., Reidl, J.: Item-based collaborative filtering recommendation algorithms. In: WWW 2001, NY, USA, pp. 285–295 (2001)
8. Fouss, F., Pirotte, A., Renders, J.-M., et al.: Random-walk computation of similarities between nodes of a graph, with application to collaborative recommendation. IEEE TKDE 19(3), 355–369 (2007)
9. Thom, J.A., Scholar, F.: A comparison of evaluation measures given how users perform on search tasks. In: Twelfth Australasian Document Computing Symposium (2007)
10. Breese, J.S., Heckerman, D., Kadie, C.: Empirical analysis of predictive algorithms for collaborative filtering. In: Proc. of UAI (1998)
11. Koren, Y., Bell, R., Volinsky, C.: Matrix factorization techniques for recommender systems. Computer 42(8), 30–37 (2009)

Exploring Users' Preference
on Mobile Based on Customer Features

Gang Yu, Zhiyan Wang, and Jiang Xue

School of Computer Science and Engineering
South China University of Technology
Guangzhou, China

Abstract. Users' mobile model chosen can indicate their telecommunication network demand and consumption habit. The study of users' preference on mobile model has count for much meaning for mobile operators' business strategy and mobile model product sale. This paper looks for customer features as the basis for users' preference judgment from the basic features such as customer attributes, consumption and service usage, that most related to mobile model characteristics, using a genetic algorithm iteration method and k-means clustering algorithm. Our method performs well on how to judge user's preference on mobile model.

Keywords: telecommunication customer feature, feature selection, mobile model characteristic, k-means clustering algorithm, Adaptive genetic algorithm.

1 Introduction

In recent years, the development of mobile is very fast, its function is more and more fruitful, while its appearance is more and more fashionable and thin. What is more, a mobile can meet a large majority of people's daily need, such as communication and entertainment. Customers will choose a mobile model whose function, price and appearance can satisfy their requirements. The communication and data traffic consumption are largely based on the functions of a mobile model they have chosen, due to both are limited by its function. Based on the above analysis, it is important for telecommunications operator to explore users' preference on mobile model through the analysis of user behavior data. An effective users' preference on mobile model judgment strategy is useful for mobile operators to make their mobile model sale strategy, data flow amount marketing management and regular customer consolidation.

Extracting the appropriate features to classify mobile models into its associated preference class is the main difficulty in the study of the association between user attributes and users' preference on mobile model. Feature extraction is one of the key technologies in pattern recognition field. In general, only when the customer feature vector has enough classification information, the classifier can achieve the correct classification and identify the appropriate kinds of mobile models the user preferring precisely. However, it is hard to determine that whether we have got enough classification information. To improve the recognition rate of a classification model, the ordinary algorithms often extract features as many as possible. It results in that there are too many feature

J. Parsons and D. Chiu (Eds.): ER Workshops 2013, LNCS 8697, pp. 226–233, 2014.

dimensions, and the correlation and redundancy among the dimensions can be too high. Therefore, it is important to pick up the right customer features to define users' preference on mobile mode. It has great impact on many aspects of mobile selection, such as the recognition rate of the classification model, training time of the classification model and the amount of training samples of user data set. What is more, customer feature selection for classification is also very important on constructing the classifier.

According to the raw sampled data have pattern classes' information, the procedure of feature selection can be divided into supervised feature selection and unsupervised feature selection. Supervised feature selection works under pre-defined classes, it makes use the relationship between features and pre-defined classes and the relationship among features to select features. Unsupervised feature selection makes use of the relationship among the features of raw sampled data set to select features. We adopt unsupervised feature selection method in this paper. It is used to select an appropriate subset of user features that can best coverage the whole data, based on certain regulation about experience. The methods which are commonly used include feature selection using genetic algorithms, feature selection based on pattern similarity and feature selection based on information gain. The whole of them have no consideration about the correlation among features and the influence of the feature to classification. In this paper, we introduce a new method based on the influence of the customer features for exploring users' preference on mobile model classification and the correlation among customer features. It is a unsupervised feature selection method which using genetic algorithm and k-means clustering. The basic idea is to use genetic algorithm to select the feature subsets, and then use k-means clustering algorithm to determine how many classes we should have for each feature subsets, after that, we use database index regulation to set a formula to select features. Finally we delete those features which are high correlation to reduce redundancy.

The rest of this paper is organized as follows. In section 2, we review some related work. In section 3, we introduce Preliminary knowledge in details, including feature clustering and genetic algorithm. We introduce feature selection process in section 4. In section 5, we conduct experiment on a real data set to evaluate our proposed method. We summarize our work and discuss some potential extension in section 5.

2   Related Work

In this section we introduce the background in this field. Feature selection is the key of exploring users' preference on mobile model. Lei Yu and Huan Liu [6] explore an efficient feature selection method via analysis of relevance and redundancy. Lei Yu and Huan Liu [7] show that feature relevance alone is insufficient for efficient feature selection of high-dimensional data. They define feature redundancy and propose to perform explicit redundancy analysis in feature selection, and also develop a correlation-based method for relevance and redundancy analysis. Yuan et al. [1] explore application of HOOK technology in network covert communication. Jin et al. [2] give an introduction on copressive sampling and its applications. Shi et al. [3] propose an echo signal detection with ultro-low rate sampling based on compressed sensing. Johnson et al. [4] propose an interior point methodology for 3-D PET reconstruction. Galand and

Kabatiansky [5] try to explore information hiding by coverings. User preference modeling is also a related work for our work. Cai and Li [8] propose a new method to model user profiles and resource profiles in a collaborative tagging environment.

3   Preliminary

In this section we introduce the two important techniques in our proposed method, which are feature clustering and genetic algorithm.

3.1   Feature Clustering

We use two indexes in our method. One is for measuring the correlation between the features and clustering evaluation, while another is for distribution information inside a class and distances between clusters. The DB Index regulation we used in this paper measures these two indexes meanwhile.

Firstly, The formula definition of average distribution information inside a class is as follows.

$$P_i = \frac{1}{|L_i|} \sum_{A \in L_i} ||A - C_i|| \tag{1}$$

where C_i is the clustering center of L_i, $|L_i|$ is the count of samples in L_i.
Besides, the formula definition of distances between clusters is as follows.

$$D_{ij} = ||C_i - C_j|| \tag{2}$$

D_{ij} is the distances between the two clustering centers i and j.
Then, we describe DB Index regulation as follows:

$$DB_m = \frac{1}{m} \sum_{i=1}^{m} R_i , \ R_i = \max_{j=1,\cdots,m,j\neq i} \frac{p_i + p_j}{D_{ij}} \tag{3}$$

where m represents the count of clustering.

Finally, we need to measure the correlation between the two features, we use the below formula to calculate it in this paper.

$$\alpha_{ij} = \frac{\sum\limits_{k=1}^{n} (x_{ik} - C_i)(x_{jk} - C_j)}{\sqrt{\sum\limits_{k=1}^{n} (x_{ik} - C_i)^2 \sum\limits_{k=1}^{n} (x_{jk} - C_j)^2}} \tag{4}$$

The absolute value of α_{ij} shows the correlation between feature i and j. The bigger absolute value of α_{ij} represents the higher correlation between feature i and j.

3.2 Genetic Algorithm

Genetic algorithm is a global convergent algorithm which generates solutions to optimization problems by simulating the nature evolution process. When dealing with complex optimization and multi-extreme value function optimization, traditional genetic algorithm always cannot achieve global convergent and it only gets local optimal solution finally. The main parameters that determine the performance of genetic algorithm include population size n, crossover rate P_c and mutation rate P_m. P_c and P_m are the most critical factors that impact the algorithm performance when genetic algorithm try to find generally good global solutions. P_c mainly affects the algorithm's ability of finding new spaces of solution during global solutions generating. P_m mainly affects the algorithm's ability to converge towards a global solutions and the solution search spaces. Therefore, many experiments need to be conducted to determine the value of P_c and P_m for each different global optimization problems. The whole procedure is very tedious, and it is very hard to find a best choice with strong robustness. Thus, for the application in this paper, we choose the adaptive genetic algorithm to optimize feature selection. The advantage of this algorithm is that it can adjust the value of crossover rate P_c and mutation rate P_m timely based on the results of every step during the operation of genetic algorithm.

4 Feature Selection Process

In this section, we present a composite and innovative feature selection algorithm, which can obtain the directly correlation between customer characteristics and consume information and users' preference on mobile model. The main idea of algorithm is as following: based on a wide variety and greater redundancy customer information feature group, we try to find suitable feature sets capable of showing user properties, while this feature sets in the classification of customer preference should also have higher correlation than a certain threshold.

Therefore, the feature selection algorithm designed in this paper can be divided into two steps:

- Firstly, using adaptive genetic algorithm to select several types of high correlation feature aggregation sets from a large number sample set of customer features, and remove redundant features, as a candidate feature subset.
- Secondly, using feature clustering sorting algorithm, to find out the feature subset which have the maximum correlation between users' preference on mobile model decisions, as the final standard of judgment.

The details of algorithm process is described below: First of all, for large number of sample sets of each customer feature, we use the adaptive genetic algorithm to determine the sample set's correlation between features. Based on these correlations, we can preliminarily aggregate a series of related feature sets. In the application of adaptive genetic algorithm, we not only need to make sure that the genetic process does not fall into local optimal solution, but also need to ensure not reduce the search efficiency.

Therefore, in order to meet the actual needs of research and preserve the better performance feature clustering solution in sample groups, we design the adaptive probability adjustment criteria as follows:

- When the correlations of each individual in sample group tends to coincide or may fall into local optimal solution, the values of P_c and P_m increase;
- When the correlations of individual in sample group is dispersed, the values of P_c and P_m decrease.

Meanwhile, the feature which has a higher correlation than the average of sample group is given corresponding lower values of P_c and P_m, so that the proposed method can be guaranteed to enter the next iteration. While the feature which has a lower correlation than the average is given corresponding higher values of P_c and P_m, and the proposed method can be eliminated. P_c and P_m are defined as follows:

$$P_c = \begin{cases} (d_{max} - d)/(d_{max} - d_{avg}) & d \geq d_{avg} \\ 1 & d < d_{avg} \end{cases} \tag{5}$$

$$P_c = \begin{cases} (d_{max} - d)/2(d_{max} - d_{avg}) & d \geq d_{avg} \\ 0.5 & d < d_{avg} \end{cases} \tag{6}$$

where d_{max} represents the maximum correlation value of the feature group; d_{avg} represents the average correlation value of the correlation of each iteration; d represents the current calculated correlation value between two crossover features. Through multiple iterations of adaptive genetic algorithm, we can get several suitable customer feature subsets which can be used to characterize the properties of the customer.

In our method, we take advantage of feature clustering for selection. We select suitable feature subsets with higher correlations of the users' preference on mobile model from the candidate feature subset as the final feature set. Then, we use them to predicate customer mobile model preference.

For each candidate feature subset T_i, we use K-means clustering algorithm clustering feature subset and determine the final number k_i of clusters generated. Meanwhile, we use the DB Index regulation as the cluster validity judgments. For feature subsets T_i and T_j ($i = 1 \cdots m$, $j = 1 \cdots m$, $i \neq j$, m is the number of feature subsets), their corresponding features are not exactly the same. Therefore, for different feature subsets T_i and T_j, the obtained values DB_{k_j} and DB_{k_j} do not have direct comparison values. We normalize the obtained values DB_{k_j} and DB_{k_j} firstly, and then compare with each other and select the smaller value. We describe the whole feature clustering selection process as follows.

Let T_i be the original candidate feature subset, and its number is m, and the number of loop iterations is p. T_{best} is used to save the best feature subset selection.

The following figure shows a simplified flow of the algorithm:

1. For a subset T_i, using the formula Eq.1 Eq.2 Eq.3 yields the best classification number and DB value;
2. Compare the DB values, find the clustering method which make the DB value smallest.

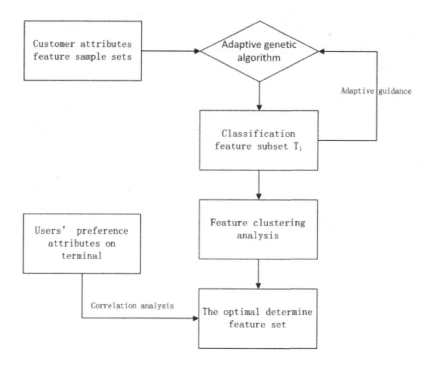

Fig. 1. Customer feature selection algorithm flow

3. Compare the correlation values of T_i and T_{best} with mobile model preference attribute. If T_i has a higher correlation value, then update T_{best}
4. Searching until it meets loop stop condition.

Figure 1 shows the simplified flow of the algorithm. In this algorithm, we adopt genetic algorithm first to obtain the classification subset, and then we use clustering on features and take user preference attributes on mobile model into consideration to obtain optimal determined feature subset.

5   User Preference Prediction

After we obtain the subset of features according to the method we proposed above, we apply the subset of features to help to predict user preferences on mobile models by adopting some existing classification methods, such as decision tree classification, to classify a user with a mobile model lable.

6   Experiment

In this section, we conduct experiments to evaluate the proposed method on predicting user preference on mobile model. We use a extracted data set from a communication operator company, which contains 660,000 users and their historical data. We apply decision tree as a classifier. We adopt three metrics, which are *precision, recall* and *improvement*. We select top-k results for evaluation, and we pick k from 5 to 50.

According to our method, we use k-means clustering method first to obtain similar features, and then use adaptive genetic algorithm to select several types of high correlation feature aggregation sets from a cluster and remove redundant features. Then we use feature clustering sorting algorithm, to find out the feature subset which have the maximum correlation between users' preference on mobile model decisions. We find out 7 major features for user preference prediction, which are WLAN, smart phone, operating system, networking, price, screen and brand.

According to Figure 2, we can find that as the increase of k, the precision decrease smoothly, and the recall increase rapidly. While k is equal to 25, then we can obtain a relative balance of precision and recall. The change of recall is bigger than that of precision. It means that it is easier to obtain an improvement on recall than precision. We also can observe that the improvement is not so significant as the increase of k.

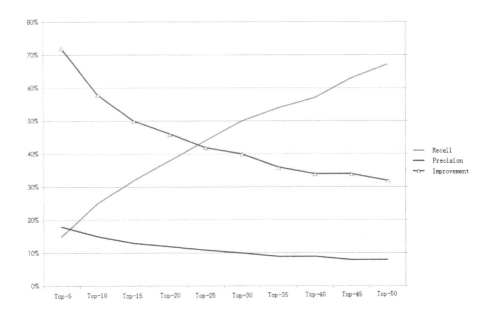

Fig. 2. Precision, Recall and Improvement

7   Conclusion and Future Work

Extracting the appropriate features to classify mobile models into its associated preference class is the main difficulty in the study of the association between user attributes and users preference on mobile model. Feature extraction is one of the key technologies in pattern recognition field. This paper looks for customer features as the basis for users' preference judgment from the basic features such as customer attributes, consumption and service usage. The basic idea is to use genetic algorithm to select the feature subsets, and then use k-means clustering algorithm to determine how many classes we should have for each feature subsets, after that, we use database index regulation to set a formula to select features. Finally we delete those features which are high correlation to reduce redundancy.

In our future work, we plan to try more clustering methods instead of k-means only. Also, we plan to apply another optimization methods such as Particle Swarm Optimization.

References

1. Jian, Y., Xue-Si, Z., Yong-feng, H.: Application of HOOK technology in network covert communication. In: Proceedings of 9th China Information Hiding Workshop, Chengdu, pp. 489–496 (2010)
2. Jin, J., Gu, Y.-T., Mei, S.-L.: An introduction to copressive sampling and its applications. Jounal of Electronics & Information Technology 32(2), 470–475 (2010)
3. Shi, G.-M., Lin, J., Chen, X.-Y.: UWB echo signal detection with ultro-low rate sampling based on compressed sensing. IEEE Transactions on Circuits and System Express Brifs 55(4), 379–383 (2008)
4. Johnson, C., Seidel, J., Sofer, A.: Interior point methodology for 3-D PET reconstruction. IEEE Transactions on Medical Imaging 19(4), 271–285 (2000)
5. Galand, F., Kabatiansky, G.: Information hiding by Coverings. In: Preceedings of the IEEE Information Theory WorkShop, Paris, pp. 151–154 (2003)
6. Yu, L., Liu, H.: Efficient Feature Selection via Analysis of Relevance and Redundancy. Journal Mach. Learn. Res. 20(5), 1205–1224 (2004)
7. Yu, L., Liu, H.: Toward integrating feature selection algorithms for classification and clustering. IEEE Transactions on Knowledge and Data Engineering 17(4), 491–502 (2005)
8. Cai, Y., Li, Q.: Personalized Search by Tag-based User Profile and Resource Profile in Collaborative Tagging Systems. In: Proceedings of The 19th ACM International Conference on Information and Knowledge Management, pp. 969–978 (2009)

Preface to SCME 2013

The 1st Symposium on Conceptual Modeling Education (SCME 2013) provides a forum for discussing the education and teaching of theoretical or practical concepts related to conceptual modeling, methods and tools for developing and communicating conceptual models, techniques for transforming conceptual models into effective implementations, case studies of interesting projects, and pedagogies of modeling education for our next generation.

We received 5 papers in response to the call for papers, each of which was reviewed by at least two PC members with a focus on selecting submissions that describe methods of teaching and educating conceptual modeling. In the end, we selected 2 submissions for presentation at the Symposium and for inclusion in the ER 2013 Workshop proceedings. In addition, the symposium also included an invited keynote "Teaching Undergraduates Conceptual Modelling: Why, What and How?", presented by John Mylopoulos (University of Trento), a leading expert in conceptual modeling and the winner of 2010 Peter Chen Award for his outstanding contributions to conceptual modeling.

We would like to express our sincere appreciation to all the authors, who submitted their papers to SCME 2013, for their efforts in promoting Conceptual Modeling education. We would also like to thank all the PC members for their hard work in evaluating the papers. We specially thank John Mylopoulos for giving the keynote at SCME 2013. Finally, we thank the ER Steering Committee Chair Antoni Olive, the ER 2013 General Chairs Qing Li and Ho-fung Leung for their help in organizing the Symposium, and the ER 2013 Workshop Chairs Jeffrey Parsons and Dickson Chiu who helped us with the proceedings.

July 17, 2013

James Cheng
Il-Yeol Song
SCME 2013 Chairs

Former Students' Views on the Usefulness of Conceptual Modeling Education

Albert Tort, Antoni Olivé, and Joan Antoni Pastor

Department of Service and Information System Engineering
Universitat Politècnica de Catalunya – BarcelonaTech
{atort,olive,pastor}@essi.upc.edu

Abstract. A big challenge for education and research in Requirements Engineering and Conceptual Modeling (RE/CM) is the need for much more empirical research about the use in practice of RE/CM, including the practical impact of CM education. Former students of RE/CM are potential prescriptors of the RE/CM concepts, methodologies and tools that they have learnt, but they are also conditioned by the current use of those same issues in practice. In this paper we focus on the views that former students of a RE/CM course have, now as young professionals, on the usefulness of the received CM education. We have surveyed over 70 former students to know their opinions on the usefulness of the education on a representative set of CM artifacts. Our results show that our former students find quite useful in general their received CM education, with different usefulness degrees for the various learned artifacts.

Keywords: Conceptual modeling, Education, Practice, Survey.

1 Introduction

It is widely recognized that there is a need for much more empirical investigation about the use of Requirements Engineering/Conceptual Modeling (RE/CM) in practice and the practical impact of its education [1,2,3]. In this paper, we focus on CM education and we try to provide some empirical data on its usefulness.

In the context of the well-known Kirpatrick's pedagogical framework for evaluating educational programs [4], the work reported here corresponds to the third evaluation level, which deals with evaluating student behavior. This aims at understanding what happens when students leave the classroom and enter jobs where they could apply what they learnt. In this paper we focus on the views that former students have, now as young practitioners, on the usefulness of the CM education that they received. To this end, we have surveyed over 70 former students in order to know their opinions and recommendations on the received education on a representative set of CM artifacts.

We have found in the literature some reports of surveys on former students' perceptions of the impact of the education they received on their professional activities [5,6], but they are set up at a general and wide educational range, dealing with the education they received during their whole studies. As far as we

J. Parsons and D. Chiu (Eds.): ER Workshops 2013, LNCS 8697, pp. 237–246, 2014.

know, there has been no prior attempt to evaluate the perceptions and behavior of former students of RE/CM, and this is the first time in which students of an informatics engineering university program are surveyed on their views of CM education and practice.

The structure of the paper is as follows. Section 2 briefly describes the RE/CM course taken by the students that later participated in the survey. Section 3 describes how we designed and conducted the survey. Section 4 presents the general results of the survey, with an emphasis on the former students' opinions of the CM education usefulness as well as their recommendations of learning. Section 5 presents the detailed results for each of the four artifacts surveyed. Finally, section 6 summarizes the conclusions.

2   The RE/CM Course

In this section we briefly describe the RE/CM course taken by the former students that participated in the survey.

The course started in 2005 as an elective course of the speciality in Software and Information Systems of the five-year program of *Informatics Engineering* taught at the *Barcelona School of Informatics* of the *Universitat Politècnica de Catalunya (UPC) – BarcelonaTech*. Typically, students take the course during their fourth year in the program, after (among others) an introductory course to software engineering.

The course is taught using a variant of the PBL (*Project-Based Learning*) approach. The main activity of the course is the requirements specification of a software system, including its conceptual schema. The structure of the requirements specification is an adaptation of the *Volere* template [7], which includes the definition of use cases and the glossary. The structure of the conceptual schema (specified in UML/OCL [8,9]) is the classical one: structural schema (including integrity constraints) and behavioral schema [10]. At the beginning of the course, the teachers establish a vision [11], which varies each course. The students -working in groups of 5-7 people- study the relevant methods, languages and techniques and apply them to the determination and specification of the requirements of a system that realizes the vision.

Students have available deliverables from previous editions of the course, which can be used as (good) examples. The conceptual schema must be defined using the USE tool [12], and be validated by means of example instantiations.

3   Survey Design and Conduct

We created a web-based survey [13] in order to collect the perceptions of the respondents about the current use of well-known conceptual modeling artifacts, and the usefulness for practice of the education received on these artifacts. The survey included two initial questions aiming at characterizing the number of years of professional experience, and the number of projects with a significant RE/CM activity in which the participant has been involved. The other parts of the survey focused on specific RE/CM artifacts. In this paper we focus only on the four artifacts more closely related to conceptual modeling, which are: (1) Use cases (scenarios); (2) Glossary; (3) Structural schema (UML class diagram, ER schema); and (4) Integrity constraints (UML invariants).

The names of the artifacts in the survey were as indicated above, but it was made clear that in practice they may be called with different names (examples are shown above within parentheses). It was also made clear that the questions referred to explicit artifacts written in any language and at any level of formality, not necessarily the same as those learnt in the RE/CM course.

We targeted the survey to past students of the indicated RE/CM course. The potential number of survey participants was 369, but we were able to know the current email address of 182 people (49.3%). We sent them an email invitation (and reminders) to visit the survey website. We collected survey responses during October-December 2012. The survey was implemented using the web-based SurveyMonkey tool. The survey was initially tested through personal interviews with two former students with wide experience as practitioners.

In this study, we focus, for each artifact $\mathcal{A}$, on the following three questions:

- The *Education usefulness* question ($\mathcal{E}$), aimed at collecting the current perception on the usefulness for practice of the received education:
  $\mathcal{E}$: *"In general, do you think the education received on the definition of the artifact $\mathcal{A}$ has been helpful in your professional practice?"*
- The *Learning recommendation* question ($\mathcal{L}$), aimed at collecting the recommendation of in-depth learning for each artifact:
  $\mathcal{L}$: *"In general, do you agree that conceptual modeling students should learn in depth the importance of defining the artifact $\mathcal{A}$ and how to do it?"*
- The *Usage* question ($\mathcal{U}$), aimed at collecting the current use of each artifact in professional practice.
  $\mathcal{U}$: *"In general, in the projects in which you have participated, the artifact $\mathcal{A}$ was created ... ?"*

If the answer of the participant to $\mathcal{U}$ indicates low usage, then the participant was also asked to answer the *Recommendation of use* question ($\mathcal{R}$):
$\mathcal{R}$: *"In the projects in which the artifact was not created, would you have recommended its creation, taking into account the situation and the resources available at that time?"*

The respondents were asked to answer questions $\mathcal{E}$ and $\mathcal{L}$ using a five-point Likert scale with the values: 1 (*strongly disagree*), 2 (*disagree*), 3 (*neither agree nor disagree*), 4 (*agree*) and 5 (*strongly agree*). Similarly, questions $\mathcal{U}$ and $\mathcal{R}$ were asked to be answered using a frequency Likert scale, with the values: 1 (*never*), 2 (*rarely*), 3 (*sometimes*), 4 (*often*) and 5 (*always*).

The survey participants were asked whether they were willing to participate in a post-survey meeting. A few of the most-experienced respondents were invited to a 90-minutes meeting aimed at validating the survey results.

Table 1. Participants by number of years and projects (%)

Years	Projects					
	0	1	2	3	>3	
≤ 2	1.39	2.78	5.56	0.00	1.39	**11.11**
3	0.00	4.17	6.94	5.56	2.78	**19.44**
4	1.39	0.00	0.00	4.17	8.33	**13.89**
5	2.78	4.17	2.78	1.39	16.67	**27.78**
≥ 6	1.39	2.78	2.78	2.78	18.06	**27.78**
	6.94	**13.89**	**18.06**	**13.89**	**47.22**	

4 Survey Results and Discussion

In this section, we describe the general results of the survey. Our aim is to provide an analysis about the relevance of the received education for practice, from the point of view of our former students with professional experience. In subsection 4.1 we summarize the number of participants in the survey by the number of years since they took the course, and the number of projects with a significant CM activity in which the participants have been involved. Subsections 4.2-4.5 define the analysis indicators and present the main general assessments.

4.1 Participant Characteristics

We received 72 complete responses to our survey, which represents a response rate of 39.6%. Table 1 shows the percentage of participants by the number of years since the course was taken, and the number of projects with a significant RE/CM activity in which the participant has been involved. It can be seen that 55% of the participants took the course five or more years ago, and that 61% have participated in three or more relevant projects.

These results indicate that a large fraction of the respondents have a considerable experience in RE/CM. The table also shows that 6,94% of the respondents have not participated in any project with a significant RE/CM activity. These responses have been ignored in the results reported in this paper.

4.2 Education Usefulness ($\mathcal{EU}$)

The first objective of our work was to obtain an assessment of the perceived *Education Usefulness* ($\mathcal{EU}$) for the professional practice, regarding each CM artifact. A first assessment can be obtained from the answers to the $\mathcal{E}$ question.

Table 2 gives the mean (M) and the standard deviation (SD) of $\mathcal{EU}$ for each artifact. It can be observed that there are differences depending on the artifact. Some general trends (in average) can be observed: the structural schema and the use cases are the artifacts with the highest $\mathcal{EU}$ mean (4.31 and 4.02), and also with the lowest SD. (2) The $\mathcal{EU}$ mean for integrity constraints (3.47) shows that

Table 2. $\mathcal{EU}$, $\mathcal{LR}$ and $\mathcal{CP}$ for each artifact (*Likert scale*)

	$\mathcal{EU}$		$\mathcal{LR}$		$\mathcal{CP}$	
	M	SD	M	SD	M	SD
Use Cases	**4.02**	0.83	**4.42**	0.80	**3.10**	1.13
Glossary	**2.94**	0.96	**3.68**	0.91	**2.62**	1.24
Structural Schema	**4.31**	0.74	**4.58**	0.69	**3.56**	1.20
Integrity Constraints	**3.47**	1.07	**4.07**	0.91	**2.64**	1.30

education on this artifact is quite useful. (3) The glossary has the lowest mean (2.94), which is below the answer *neither agree nor disagree* in the *Likert scale*.

Table 2 also shows M and SD for the answers to question $\mathcal{U}$, which indicate the perception on the current practice of each artifact, denoted by *Current Practice* ($\mathcal{CP}$). These values suggest that the higher $\mathcal{CP}$ is observed for an artifact, the higher $\mathcal{EU}$ is perceived. It is also important to note that, for all artifacts, the mean of $\mathcal{EU}$ is higher than the mean of $\mathcal{CP}$, so that other factors than the current direct application of the artifacts contribute to positive perceptions on the education usefulness.

4.3   Learning Recommendation ($\mathcal{LR}$)

The second objective of our work was to obtain an assessment of the *Learning Recommendation* ($\mathcal{LR}$) for each CM artifact, from the perspective of the former students that participated in the study. A first assessment is provided by the answers to the question $\mathcal{L}$.

Table 2 shows the mean (M) and the standard deviation (SD) of $\mathcal{LR}$ for each artifact. We can observe that $\mathcal{LR}$ and $\mathcal{EU}$ follow similar trends, although there is more emphasis on the learning recommendation for each artifact. These results suggest that the learning recommendation is mainly influenced by the perception on the usefulness for practice of the received education. It is also important to note that for all artifacts the mean of $\mathcal{LR}$ is greater than the neutral value (3) in the Likert scale. However, learning about the structural schema and the use cases clearly have a higher recommendation, in comparison with integrity constraints and glossaries.

4.4   High/Low Education Usefulness and Learning Recommendation

In order to go in depth in the relationship between the perception on the education usefulness for practice ($\mathcal{EU}$) and the learning recommendation ($\mathcal{LR}$), we classified the answers to questions $\mathcal{E}$ and $\mathcal{L}$ into two groups:

- *High agreement* answers: Those that correspond to the values *agree* (4) or *strongly agree* (5) in the Likert scale.
- *Low agreement* answers: Those that correspond to the values *neither agree nor disagree* (3) or *disagree* (2) or *strongly disagree* (1).

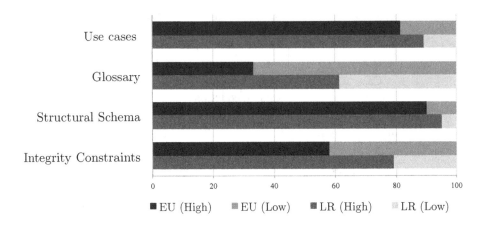

Fig. 1. High and Low indicators for $\mathcal{EU}$ and $\mathcal{LR}$

This classification allows to formally define the *high* ($\mathcal{H}$) and *low* ($\mathcal{L}$) indicators for $\mathcal{EU}$ and $\mathcal{LR}$ as follows for each $\mathcal{A}$ artifact:

$$\mathcal{EU}_{\mathcal{H}}(\mathcal{A}) = \frac{\mathcal{E}_4(\mathcal{A}) + \mathcal{E}_5(\mathcal{A})}{\mathcal{E}(\mathcal{A})} * 100 \qquad \mathcal{EU}_{\mathcal{L}}(\mathcal{A}) = \frac{\mathcal{E}_1(\mathcal{A}) + \mathcal{E}_2(\mathcal{A}) + \mathcal{E}_3(\mathcal{A})}{\mathcal{E}(\mathcal{A})} * 100$$

$$\mathcal{LR}_{\mathcal{H}}(\mathcal{A}) = \frac{\mathcal{L}_4(\mathcal{A}) + \mathcal{L}_5(\mathcal{A})}{\mathcal{L}(\mathcal{A})} * 100 \qquad \mathcal{LR}_{\mathcal{L}}(\mathcal{A}) = \frac{\mathcal{L}_1(\mathcal{A}) + \mathcal{L}_2(\mathcal{A}) + \mathcal{L}_3(\mathcal{A})}{\mathcal{L}(\mathcal{A})} * 100$$

where $\mathcal{E}_i(\mathcal{A})$, $i = 1..5$, is the number of respondents that answered i in the Likert scale of the $\mathcal{E}$ question of artifact $\mathcal{A}$. Similarly, $\mathcal{L}_i(\mathcal{A})$, $i = 1..5$, is the number of respondents that answered i in the Likert scale of the $\mathcal{L}$ question of artifact $\mathcal{A}$. $\mathcal{E}(\mathcal{A})$ and $\mathcal{L}(\mathcal{A})$ are the total number of respondents to each question. Note that $\mathcal{EU}_{\mathcal{H}}(\mathcal{A}) + \mathcal{EU}_{\mathcal{L}}(\mathcal{A}) = 100$ and $\mathcal{LR}_{\mathcal{H}}(\mathcal{A}) + \mathcal{LR}_{\mathcal{L}}(\mathcal{A}) = 100$.

Fig. 1 shows the relationship between $\mathcal{EU}$ and $\mathcal{LR}$ by means of two bars for each artifact. The first bar classifies the percentage of responses between those that are in the *High Education Usefulness* ($\mathcal{EU}_{\mathcal{H}}$) situation, and those that are in the *Low Education Usefulness* ($\mathcal{EU}_{\mathcal{L}}$) situation. Similarly, the second bar classifies the percentage of respondents in two groups: those that are in the *High Learning Recommendation* ($\mathcal{LR}_{\mathcal{H}}$) situation, and those that are in the *Low Learning Recommendation* ($\mathcal{LR}_{\mathcal{L}}$) situation.

The bar chart in Fig. 1 reinforces the idea that the usefulness of the received education for practice is an important influence factor on the positive learning recommendation, since first and second bars for each artifact follow a similar trend.

4.5   Current Practice Influence on Education

In this section we analyze in depth the influence of the current practice on the *Education Usefulness* ($\mathcal{EU}$) perception and the *Learning Recommendation* ($\mathcal{LR}$) according to the view of the participants in the survey.

Table 3. $\mathcal{EU_H}$ and $\mathcal{EU_L}$ responses (%) classified into $\mathcal{CP}$ situations

| | $\mathcal{EU_H}$ | | | | $\mathcal{EU_L}$ | | | |
	$\mathcal{CHP}$	$\mathcal{IP}$	$\mathcal{ALP}$	Total	$\mathcal{CHP}$	$\mathcal{IP}$	$\mathcal{ALP}$	Total
Use Cases	81.5	0.0	0.0	**81.5**	0.0	10.8	7.7	**18.5**
Glossary	33.3	0.0	0.0	**33.3**	0.0	34.9	31.7	**66.7**
Structural Schema	90.2	0.0	0.0	**90.2**	0.0	6.6	3.3	**9.8**
Integrity Constraints	58.1	0.0	0.0	**58.1**	0.0	22.6	19.4	**41.9**

Tables 3 and 4 classify the answers of $\mathcal{EU_H}/\mathcal{EU_L}$ and $\mathcal{LR_H}/\mathcal{LR_L}$ in three *Current Practice* ($\mathcal{CP}$) situations, according to the analysis in conjunction of questions $\mathcal{U}$ and $\mathcal{R}$ [14]:

- *Current High Practice* ($\mathcal{CHP}$). These are the situations in which, according to the answer to question $\mathcal{U}$, the artifact is *often* (4) or *always* (5) used.
- For *Current Low Practice* ($\mathcal{CLP}$) situations (in which the artifact is *never* (1) or *rarely* (2) or *sometimes* (3) used according to the answer to question $\mathcal{U}$), the answer to the *recommendation of use* $\mathcal{R}$ question, allows us to distinguish the following situations:
  - *Improvement Potential* ($\mathcal{IP}$) if the answer was *often* (4) or *always* (5).
  - *Accepted Low Practice* ($\mathcal{ALP}$) if the answer was *never* (1), *rarely* (2) or *sometimes* (3).

Our rationale for the definition of $\mathcal{IP}(\mathcal{A})$ is that we consider that situations have potential for improvement if they are in $\mathcal{CLP}$ but the respondents would have recommended *often* or *always* the creation of the corresponding artifact. That is, if the recommendation had been followed in the given situation, then it would have been in the $\mathcal{CHP}$ situation.

Similarly, $\mathcal{ALP}$ situations are defined as those that are in $\mathcal{CLP}$ and the respondents would have not recommended *often* or *always* the creation of the artifact.

Table 3 points out that there is a strong relationship between high education usefulness perception ($\mathcal{EU_H}$) and current high practice ($\mathcal{CHP}$), since all respondents that perceive an artifact as highly applied in practice also consider the received education useful. In contrast, those that perceive a low current use also perceive a low usefulness of the education for current practice ($\mathcal{EU_L}$), regardless they expect an improvement potential on the use ($\mathcal{IP}$ situation) or not ($\mathcal{ALP}$).

In Table 4, it can be observed that most of the respondents in the low recommendation of learning ($\mathcal{LR_L}$) situation are those that accept a low current practice of the artifact ($\mathcal{ALP}$). There are also very few respondents for each artifact who, although they consider that the education on the artifact may be useful, they would not recommend to learn it in depth. On the other hand, respondents who highly recommend to learn an artifact ($\mathcal{LR_H}$) are those that consider either that (1) the artifact has a current high practice ($\mathcal{CHP}$), or (2) there is an improvement potential ($\mathcal{IP}$) situation, in which they would recommend the use of the artifact if they would lead the project.

Table 4. $\mathcal{LR}_\mathcal{H}$ and $\mathcal{LR}_\mathcal{L}$ responses (%) classified into $\mathcal{CP}$ situations

	$\mathcal{LR}_\mathcal{H}$				$\mathcal{LR}_\mathcal{L}$			
	$\mathcal{CHP}$	$\mathcal{IP}$	$\mathcal{ALP}$	Total	$\mathcal{CHP}$	$\mathcal{IP}$	$\mathcal{ALP}$	Total
Use Cases	78.5	10.8	0.0	**89.2**	3.1	0.0	7.7	**10.8**
Glossary	25.8	35.5	0.0	**61.3**	6.5	0.0	32.3	**38.7**
Structural Schema	88.5	6.6	0.0	**95.1**	1.6	0.0	3.3	**4.9**
Integrity Constraints	56.5	22.6	0.0	**79.0**	1.6	0.0	19.4	**21.0**

5   Results per Artifact

In this section we focus on each of the four artifacts and we briefly describe the analysis about its education relevance for practice, based on the indicators presented in Section 4.

5.1   Use Cases

Table 2 shows that, for the use cases artifact, $\mathcal{EU}$ (4.02) and $\mathcal{LR}$ (4.42) have a value in the Likert scale greater than 4. In Fig. 1, it is also clear that $\mathcal{EU}_\mathcal{H}$ and $\mathcal{LR}_\mathcal{H}$ are significantly greater than $\mathcal{EU}_\mathcal{L}$ and $\mathcal{LR}_\mathcal{L}$. These results indicate that use cases are relevant artifacts for the professional practice and that learning them in-depth may be useful for practitioners.

According to Table 3, 81.5% of the respondents consider that use cases have a current high usage in practice ($\mathcal{CHP}$), and that the education on this artifact is useful ($\mathcal{EU}_\mathcal{H}$). Table 4 also shows that the 89.2% of respondents recommend to learn the artifact ($\mathcal{LR}_\mathcal{H}$). These respondents correspond to those that either perceive use cases as currently highly used ($\mathcal{CHP}$) in practice (78.5%) or would recommend ($\mathcal{IP}$) its use (10.8%).

5.2   Glossary

As illustrated in Table 2, $\mathcal{EU}(glossary)$ is lower than the neutral value in the Likert Scale (2.94) and, consequently, its relevance for practice is quite low. However, its $\mathcal{LR}$ mean is 3.68, so that several respondents recommend to learn about the glossary. Fig. 1 shows that this is the only artifact for which $\mathcal{EU}_\mathcal{L}$ is greater than $\mathcal{EU}_\mathcal{H}$. The analysis suggests that the education on the specification of glossaries has the lowest relevance perception for practice.

In Table 3, it can be observed that 66.7% of the respondents consider that glossaries have a current low usage in practice and that the education on this artifact has a low usefulness perception. Only 33.3% of the respondents consider that the glossary is highly used and that the education is useful for current practice. Nevertheless, according to Table 4, an important percentage of the respondents (35.5%) are in the $\mathcal{IP}$ situation and recommend to learn about the glossary, together with those that perceived them as already highly used (25.8%).

5.3 Structural Schema

Table 2 shows that, for this artifact, the mean of $\mathcal{EU}$ is 4.31 and the mean of $\mathcal{LR}$ is 4.42. These are the highest values in comparison with the rest of artifacts considered in the study. This results are also confirmed in Fig. 1, where it is clear that $\mathcal{EU_H}$ and $\mathcal{LR_H}$ are greater than 90%, while $\mathcal{EU_L}$ and $\mathcal{LR_L}$ are very low. These results indicate that the education on the elicitation and specification of the structural schema of an information system is considered very relevant for practice and its learning is highly recommended.

Tables 3 and 4 clearly show that the dominant situation is that of respondents in the $\mathcal{CHP}$ situation (those that perceive a high usage of conceptual schemas in practice) who also consider the education on structural schemas very useful (90.2%) while they recommend its learning (95.1%).

5.4 Integrity Constraints

As illustrated in Table 2, $\mathcal{EU}(integrity\ constraints)$ is 3.47 and $\mathcal{LR}(integrity\ constraints)$ is 4.07. Fig. 1 also shows that, although $\mathcal{EU_H}$ is lower than the same value for the structural schema and the use cases, near 60% of the respondents recommend that students learn about integrity constraints.

Table 3 confirms that the highest education usefulness on integrity constraints $(\mathcal{EU_H})$ is perceived for those that are in the $\mathcal{CHP}$ situation (58.1%). However, Table 4 shows that there is an important percentage of respondents (22.6%) in the $\mathcal{IP}$ situation that highly recommend to learn about the integrity constraints, together with those (56.6%) that already consider that their use is high ($\mathcal{CHP}$). Only 19.4% of the respondents accept the low practice ($\mathcal{ALP}$) of integrity constraints and do not recommend their learning ($\mathcal{LR_L}$).

6   Conclusions

In this paper, we have analyzed the perceptions on the usefulness for the professional practice of CM education, based on a survey answered by over 70 former students of a RE/CM course within an informatics engineering university program. The survey was aimed at knowing their opinions and recommendations, as practitioners, on the received education on a representative set of CM artifacts. As far as we know, this is the first attempt to evaluate the perceptions of RE/CM former students about the received education for their current practice.

In general, the survey results indicate that our former students consider their received CM education as useful for their professional work. The analysis of the results also points out that there are differences on theses perceptions depending on the artifact. In particular, they consider very useful the structural schema and the use cases, both with very high levels of perceived usefulness. Consistently, they highly recommend in-depth education on these artifacts. For integrity constraints, the perceptions on their education usefulness are lower, although many participants recommend to learn them in-depth. In contrast, the education received on the specification of glossaries has the lowest perception of usefulness for practice.

The results reported in this paper are subject to some threats to their validity beyond our local context. The main threat is the geographic and domain bias of the survey, created by drawing the respondents from the former students of an RE/CM course offered by a particular university.

We consider that the analysis reported in this paper can be useful for improving the effectiveness of our RE/CM course, taking into account the views and recommendations of our former students with professional experience in software development. Hopefully, these results could be of interest to other similar courses on conceptual modeling.

References

1. Bubenko, J.A.: Challenges in requirements engineering. In: 2nd IEEE International Symposium on Requirements Engineering, pp. 160–162. IEEE (1995)
2. Davies, I., Green, P., Rosemann, M., Indulska, M., Gallo, S.: How do practitioners use conceptual modeling in practice? Data and Knowledge Engineering 58, 358–380 (2006)
3. Milton, S.K., Rajapakse, J., Weber, R.: Conceptual modeling in practice: An evidence-based process-oriented theory. In: ICIAFs 2010, pp. 533–536. IEEE (2010)
4. Kirkpatrick, D.L.: Evaluating Training Programs: The Four Levels, 2nd edn. Berrett-Koehler Publishers, San Francisco (2008)
5. Wever, A., Maiden, N.: What are the day-to-day factors that are preventing business analysts from effective business analysis? In: RE 2011, pp. 293–298. IEEE (2011)
6. University of Idaho: 2006 survey of graduates classes of 1998, 1999, 2000 and 2001. Technical report (2007), http://www.webs.uidaho.edu/ira/assess/grad_alum_survey/GAS%20UI%20Summary%202011-2012%20.pdf
7. Robertson, S.: Mastering the Requirements Process. Addison-Wesley (2006)
8. OMG. UML Superstructure v.2.4.1 (2011) http://www.omg.org/spec/UML
9. OMG. Object Constraint Language v.2.3.1 (2012), http://www.omg.org/spec/OCL
10. Olivé, A.: Conceptual Modeling of Information Systems. Springer, Berlin (2007)
11. Jarke, M., Pohl, K.: Establishing visions in context: Towards a model of requirements processes. In: ICIS 1993, pp. 23–24 (1993)
12. Gogolla, M., Büttner, F., Richters, M.: Use: A UML-based specification environment for validating UML and OCL. Science of Computer Programming 69(1-3), 27–34 (2007)
13. Tort, A., Olivé, A., Pastor, J.A.: Survey on requirements engineering and conceptual modeling in practice. Technical report, Universitat Politécnica de Catalunya (2013), http://hdl.handle.net/2117/19768
14. Tort, A., Olivé, A., Pastor, J.A.: Former students' perception of improvement potential of conceptual modeling in practice. In: Ng, W., Storey, V.C., Trujillo, J.C. (eds.) ER 2013. LNCS, vol. 8217, pp. 395–402. Springer, Heidelberg (2013)

Teaching Conceptual Design Capture

Karen C. Davis

University of Cincinnati, Cincinnati, Ohio, USA
`karen.davis@uc.edu`

Abstract. In this paper, a framework for scholarly teaching is discussed and applied to teaching conceptual modeling in a database design course. The learning objectives are identified and used to select appropriate learning experiences and evaluation mechanisms. Student learning is evaluated via exam questions and a design capture project. A novel contribution of the assignment is that it includes both individual and team work, and the students revise their initial designs with instructor feedback as well as peer interaction. Results of assessment of student learning are given; the performance improvement of students on the assignment after feedback and with a partner is statistically significant. The framework is demonstrated to be useful for faculty to focus on guiding students to achieve competency and develop conceptual modeling knowledge and skills.

Keywords: conceptual modeling, database design, entity-relationship model.

1 Introduction

Richlin condenses decades of best practices taken from the literature on the scholarship of teaching and learning in her handbook for course design [R06]. This paper describes an application of her process and selected techniques in order to create and evaluate learning experiences to support achievement of learning objectives and course goals for an introductory database design course. The stages in the process are as follows:

1. identify big questions in the course,
2. select teaching goals,
3. design learning objectives,
4. consult the literature,
5. choose and use learning experiences,
6. conduct systematic observation and assessment,
7. document observations,
8. analyze results, and
9. obtain peer evaluation.

The big questions are "intriguing problems that your course will help students confront, answer, and solve" [R06]. In the introductory database course, answering these

J. Parsons and D. Chiu (Eds.): ER Workshops 2013, LNCS 8697, pp. 247–256, 2014.
© Springer International Publishing Switzerland 2014

questions leads to course learning objectives. For the course described here, the learning objectives are that students will:

1. use a fundamental conceptual modeling technique to capture database requirements in a graphical representation,
2. learn relational database terminology and concepts and derive an implementation schema from their conceptual design,
3. apply relational normalization theory to evaluate good design practices,
4. learn query processing techniques by writing queries using a standard language and studying the impact of physical storage options such as indexing, and
5. learn fundamental practices in database systems to ensure transaction concurrency and recovery from failure.

The teaching goals are what the instructor hopes to achieve in the course, but the goals do not have to be tied to measurable or observable outcomes. Certainly the teaching goals include student competency with the subject material, but they can also include the professor's philosophy of classroom management, for example. The primary teaching goal addressed in this course (that is not related directly to subject knowledge) is how the class is conducted. The instructional delivery emphasizes student ownership of learning through a variety of mechanisms, including interactive, collaborative experiences in the classroom as well as outside of the classroom. Public domain software programs such as Dia [Dia13] and free educational software such as WinRDBI [W13] are also utilized to practice and reinforce concepts.

The remainder of this paper focuses on the learning outcomes, learning experiences, evaluation, and observations related to conceptual modeling in an introductory database design course. A review of related literature and topics for future work conclude the paper.

2   Learning Objectives

The learning objectives related to conceptual modeling can be summarized as (1) given an Entity-Relationship (ER) schema, interpret the meaning of constructs used in it, and (2) given a description of requirements, design an ER schema (design capture). The in-class activities are geared toward understanding, applying, and analyzing small examples, while the outside of class activities are geared toward evaluation and creation of knowledge, as described in Bloom's taxonomy [K02].

In Richlin's framework, *learning objectives* are the abilities students are expected to have upon completing the course. *Learning experiences* are activities for meeting those objectives. The *evaluation plan* devises assessments that directly reflect achievement of learning goals. The course planning framework includes these three aspects and four cognitive dimensions as well. The *factual* dimension refers to learning and understanding terminology, the *conceptual* dimension refers to understanding context and ideas, the *procedural* dimension refers to actions performed by the student, and the *meta-cognition* dimension refers to reflections on learning and knowledge gained. Course learning aspects (objectives, experiences, evaluation) and cognitive dimensions are summarized in Table 1. By refining and classifying the objectives according to Richlin's conceptual taxonomy, balance between learning levels can be observed.

Table 1. Student Perspective of Learning Aspects and Cognitive Dimensions

	factual	conceptual	procedural	meta-cognition
learning objective	Become familiar with ER model terminology and graphical conventions	Use a design process to analyze requirements and create an ERD	Create an individual ER schema from a requirements specification	Discuss and modify solutions with a partner
learning experience	Use symbol chart and example schemas to answer questions in class and as homework	Observe step-by-step examples and practice in class and as homework	(1) Analyze requirements (analyze) (2) Create schema (3) Render ERD in Dia (4) Document design decisions	(1) Revise ERDs with partner and merge schemas (2) Render mutual ERD in Dia
evaluation plan	Discuss solutions in class; solve a problem on the midterm exam	Discuss solutions in class	Revew graded feedback on design capture flaws	Review graded feedback on design prior to relational implementation

3   Learning Experiences

The first section below describes experiences in the factual dimension, while the second describes design capture in the conceptual, procedural, and meta-cognition dimensions.

3.1   Terminology and Interpretation

In order for students to become aware of ER concepts and graphical modeling conventions, students use a handout with the notation to answer questions about different applications represented using the ER model. The instructor interacts with the class to do this for an example in class, followed by the students working together in pairs to interpret additional sample ERDs. Student solutions are presented and reviewed in class. Students are asked to interpret a new ERD in the same way as an exam question. A healthcare ERD from the Fall 2012 midterm exam appears in Figure 1. Students are asked questions about the ERD and asked to briefly justify their answers. Some sample questions include:

1. Can a medication have 0, 1, or many active ingredients? (circle all that apply)
2. Can a condition have 0, 1, or many icd9codes? (circle all that apply)

3. Can a patient have 0, 1, or many dates of diagnosis associated with their primary condition? (circle all that apply)
4. Can a patient have no condition?
5. Can a condition have no patients?

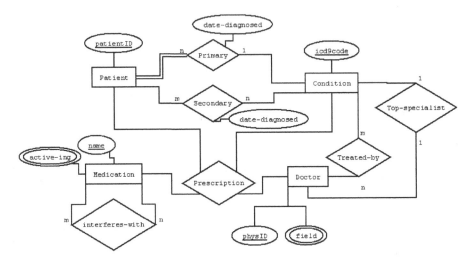

Fig. 1. A Healthcare ERD

The use of Dia for drawing ERDs has numerous advantages. The drawing tool is free and it can be installed on both Windows and Linux platforms. The ER package in Dia is completely self-contained for the purposes of creating ERDs using the basic conventions covered in introductory database design; the learning curve is very small since students need only focus on a few relevant concepts. Everything the students need to know is demonstrated in a 5 minute screen capture video created by the instructor [D13]. Dia allows students to create and submit professional quality conceptual schema designs that can be electronically revised after receiving feedback and collaborating with teammates. In addition, Dia is a tremendous time-saver for the instructor for creating example exercises and evaluation questions.

3.2   Design Capture

To experience design capture, students complete an ER modeling assignment in two phases. Each time the course is offered, a new requirement specification is created by the instructor. In the Fall 2012 offering of the course, the web-based software case study was selected from a thesis containing ten case studies [Z12]. The requirements were altered so that students could not directly use the solutions presented in the thesis. The application description given to students appears in Figure 2. An outline of project responsibilities and documentation is given below.

Project Responsibilities

1. Each student should read the requirements document and prepare an ERD as well as a list of questions that arise while attempting to create the ERD (Phase 1 submission).
2. The graded Phase 1 submission with extensive feedback is returned and teams (pairs of students) are assigned. In a team meeting, each student should review his or her design and questions with the other (the beginning of Phase 2).
3. The team should arrive at a mutually acceptable second draft (ERD and assumptions) by merging and refining their individual ideas.
4. One team member should prepare the merged version for submission (format) and the other should review it against the requirements.
5. If further revisions are required, the team members should swap roles (formatting vs. reviewing).

Project Documentation

1. graded Phase 1 ERDs and question/assumption lists,
2. meeting logs including: date, time, duration, location of meetings, and brief description of activities during the meeting,
3. results of design reviews and who performed what roles with what responsibilities, and
4. final version of ERD and assumptions.

Our website manages software projects for downloads to users. Some projects may depend on other projects and we keep track of the dependency. Each project is developed by a group of developers, who are subscribers, and uploaded to our website in one or more transactions. Anyone in the group is considered an owner of the project, but only one person is designated as the primary developer.

A software project has a unique ID, a name, a description, a testing stage (A=alpha, B=beta, R=released, U=unavailable), and a category number. Categories have descriptions.

A user can be a guest user or a subscriber. A user has a name, an email address, and a unique user ID. Subscribers have passwords they set themselves and we track the beginning date of the subscription.

Subscribers use their passwords to file bug reports, upload software projects, or update patches. A user can download any project, and the number of downloads per user per project is recorded.

Every bug has a unique ID and a description. A bug report refers to a single project and reports a single bug. Each bug report is made by a single subscriber. A bug has a status (R=resolved, O=open), and a severity level (1, 2, or 3).

Some subscribers are developers. They can post software projects and updates (patches) for their own projects.

Each project post or update is created by a single developer. Each update patch is uploaded to the site in a transaction. A transaction has a unique ID per project and the date it took place. An update patch may refer to specific bug reports.

Fig. 2. The WebForge Application Requirements

Team assignments were made after the individual ERDs were created (Phase 1) to promote individual responsibility for learning ER concepts prior to teaming. Students were confidentially surveyed about their preferences and non-preferences for team-mates, and teams were assigned that considered this information for the completion of Phase 2 (the team work phase) of the project. Grades on Phase 1 were also consi-dered in the assignment of teammates. Students were paired with other sudents who scored similarly on the first assignment when possible. In 2012, all pairs were within 5 points of each other and most were within 2 points.

A second project (not detailed here) has the students revise (if necessary) and im-plement their relational schema on a database platform of their choice; they then po-pulate it and query it.

4   Evaluation Results

Evaluation of student learning for ERD interpretation and design capture are dis-cussed below. The 53 students in the introductory course in Fall 2012 were from three different populations: (1) 16 undergraduate computer science students (3rd year) required to take the course, (2) 15 senior (5th year) electrical and computer engineer-ing students taking the course as an elective, and (3) 23 first year graduate students[1] in computer science and engineering. During the teaming phase, undergraduates were paired together and graduate students were paired togther. Achievement results for each group are reported below.

4.1   Test Question and Student Achievement

On the midterm exam, all students had the same ERD interpretation problem (using the diagram in Figure 1 and 8 questions) for a total of 20 points. The average and standard deviation for each group are reported in Table 2. The graduate student per-formance was lower than expected.

Table 2. Exam Question Scores

	CS (3rd year)	ECE (5th year)	CSE grad
number of students	16	15	23
average	16.50	17.19	15.78
standard deviation	2.24	2.01	1.76

To address the low performance, an optional bonus question on this material was offered to the students after completing their final exam (which is only over the ma-terial from the second half of the course). Earned points would be added to the mid-term exam (up to 4 points), but there was no penalty for attempting the question. It was hoped that students would demonstrate better mastery of the concepts after

---

[1] The lecture notes and activities are the same, however, the graduate students have additional test questions and an additional homework assignment using WinRDBI to answer tuple rela-tional calculus queries.

completing the project and having more experience with the topic. Some students attempted it without any additional preparation because they felt they had "nothing to lose." For comparison purposes, the question was scored a second time (not for credit) on the same point scale as the midterm question. Of the 18 graduate students who submitted the bonus, 5 outperformed their midterm question grade. Of the 11 CS undergrads who attempted the problem, only 3 improved their performance; of the 14 ECE undergrads attempting the problem, 4 improved their performance. Even though this is a convenience sample only, not a well-formed experiment, overall 28% of the students who attempted the second problem achieved a higher score than they did on the first.

4.2   Project Performance

Paired difference t-tests (Phase 1 score minus Phase 2 score) were performed on each of the three project performance data sets to determine if the difference in performance is meaningful; the resulting t-values are statistically significant in each case. Thus the differences between the students' performance on Phases 1 and 2 of the assignment are too large to be explained by random chance. In fact, only one student in the course in Fall 2012 did not improve his/her grade in the second phase. Average improvement in the scores for the two phases of the design capture project along with t statistics and p values are given in Table 3.

Table 3. Project Scores

	CS (3rd year)	ECE (5th year)	CSE grad
number of students	15	16	23
average Phase 1 score (%)	69.6	73.5	76.3
average Phase 2 score (%)	89.2	91.3	95.1
paired difference average (%)	19.6	17.8	18.8
standard deviation	12.58	11.67	12.56
t statistic	6.05	6.08	7.17
p value	1.50^{-5}	1.05^{-5}	1.72^{-7}

4.3   Student Perception of Learning

Students were asked an open response question in an anonymous survey: "Why did you do better on the second part of the project?" Selected responses are given here:

- *just got a better understanding of the requirements after talking with partner*
- *talking with my partner about when I can use relationships and multivalued attributes*
- *having 2 heads working on the project, you pick up new details that one person doesn't see; also, more assumptions are made and recorded.*
- *better understanding of ERDs and how they relate to RDBs*

- *not so much concrete things, but I have a better feel for interpreting the requirements into an ERD*
- *learned how cardinality works*
- *ER designs don't have to be complicated to convey a lot of information*

The responses were coded into 7 categories and the frequencies are shown in Figure 3. Working with a partner and fixing mistakes based on feedback were the most frequent reasons students attributed to their improved scores on Phase 2.

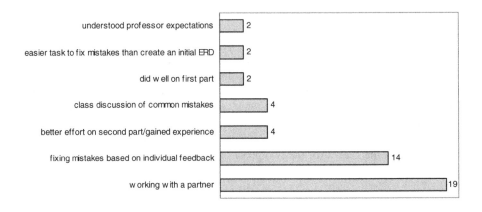

Fig. 3. Frequency of Responses about Improved Performance on Phase 2

In conclusion, some students demonstrated higher mastery of ER concepts at the end of the course, and students significantly improved performance on a second phase of the ER design capture assignment. Reflection on the reasons for their improvement via a survey also substantiate the importance of being able to revise their designs.

5   Related Work

Several research efforts focus on practitioners and examine causes for the difficulty novice users encounter when creating a database [BS94, STR95, TR02, MS03, B07, T07]. Storey et al. propose a framework based on skill/knowledge dimensions from the literature to evaluate database design expert systems at novice, intermediate, and expert levels. Our work focuses training human users at the novice level, defined as a familiar application domain, a known data model, a known methodology, and straightforward complexity (a small case study) [STR95]. A topic for future research would be to create a teaching methodology to take novice users to the intermediate level and validate the results with a study. Moody and Shanks [MS03] describe the importance of detecting and correcting mistakes early in the application development process with a particular focus on the quality of schema design. A topic for future work would be to couple the ideas from their Data Model Quality Advisor tool with Dia diagrams as input to provide feedback to students on their schema designs.

Dietrich and Urban [DU96] describe experiences with cooperative learning in a group project that is similar to ours; both have a conceptual modeling phase, a relational design phase, and a relational implementation phase. One major difference is that their project has 4-5 students per team and they identify and develop requirements for different applications in their initial phase, whereas we have individual and then paired conceptual design activities starting with the same case study. Connolly and Begg [CB06] propose a constructivist approach to teaching database analysis and design that includes a *cognitive apprenticeship* and *project-based learning*; students learning by exploring the problem independently and with their peers, guided by the faculty as facilitators who coach and model problem-solving processes, geared toward an end-product rather than a completely open-ended inquiry (as in problem-based learning.) Both projects have larger scope than ours (they include requirements gathering, for example), but are similar in teaching philosophy. Theirs do not, however, include the explicit second revision phase we introduce here. Their projects offer more real-world authentic experience, while ours controls application scope and offers greater individual accountability for learning the concepts as well as the ability to offer targeted feedback related to a common application in the classroom.

6   Conclusions and Future Work

Following Richlin's course design framework is a useful instructional design methodology and a step toward scholarly teaching that leverages pedagogical research and best practices from the literature. It is an effective way to ensure coverage of topics while varying the emphasis and depth appropriately, planning learning experiences, and assessing learning.

Many instructors teach conceptual modeling and likely already have an assignment similar to ours. Some of the potentially helpful ideas for instructors offered here include:

1. recommendation of case studies [Z12] to adapt for new requirements for projects,
2. demonstration of the impact on student learning achieved with a two-phase assignment; the first phase allows for an initial individual experience with modeling, and the second phase allows for a deeper engagement with the concepts and practice of modeling, and
3. use of Dia to create ERDs easily and quickly that are useful for teaching ERD interpretation, making up new exam and quiz questions, and later for teaching ERD to relational model translation.

One improvement that could be made to the course in the future is better delineation of the big questions addressed by the course content; the instructor currently includes examples of MS and PhD thesis topics illustrating how the course content provides a foundation for research, but relevant problems from the professor's consulting experience could be better incorporated to build intuition about practical challenges that can be solved using database modeling and systems principles. Other areas for improvement to the learning experience would be to:

1. incorporate a rubric for student use and grading developed from the practitioner studies for schema quality [STR95, TR02, MS03, S07],
2. address identified areas of difficulty with additional practice [STR95, B07, P07], and
3. consider use of automated tools for evaluation [BS94, MS03] and animations for teaching concepts [MS+04, MG09].

References

[BS94] Batra, D., Sein, M.K.: Improving conceptual database design through feedback. International Journal of Human-Computer Studies 40(4), 653–676 (1994)

[B07]   Batra, D.: Cognitive complexity in data modeling: causes and recommendations. Requirements Engineering 12(4), 231–244 (2007)

[CB06] Connolly, T.M., Begg, C.E.: A constructivist-based approach to teaching database analysis and design. Journal of Information Systems Education 17(1), 43 (2006)

[D13]   Davis, K.C.: Using Dia to Create Entity Relationship Diagrams. demonstration video, http://tinyurl.com/ER-Dia-video (date accessed: May 29, 2013)

[Dia13] Dia, https://live.gnome.org/Dia (date accessed: May 29, 2013)

[DU96] Dietrich, S.W., Urban, S.D.: Database theory in practice: learning from cooperative group projects. ACM SIGCSE Bulletin 28(1) (1996)

[K02]   Krathwohl, D.R.: A revision of Bloom's taxonomy: An overview. Theory into Practice 41(4), 212–218 (2002)

[MS+04] Mitrovic, A., Suraweera, P., Martin, B., Weerasinghe, A.: DB-suite: Experiences with three intelligent, web-based database tutors. Journal of Interactive Learning Research 15(4), 409–432 (2004)

[MS03] Moody, D.L., Shanks, G.G.: Improving the quality of data models: empirical validation of a quality management framework. Information Systems 28(6), 619–650 (2003)

[MG09] Murray, M., Guimaraes, M.: Animated Courseware Support for Teaching Database Design. Issues in Informing Science and Information Technology 6, 201–211 (2009)

[P07]   Philip, G.C.: Teaching database modeling and design: areas of confusion and helpful hints. Journal of Information Technology Education 6, 481–497 (2007)

[R06]   Richlin, L.: Blueprint for Learning: Constructing College Courses to Facilitate, Access, and Document Learning. Stylus Publishing, VA (2006)

[S07]   Shanks, G.: Conceptual data modelling: an empirical study of expert and novice data modellers. Australasian Journal of Information Systems 4(2) (2007)

[STR95] Storey, V.C., Thompson, C.B., Ram, S.: Understanding data-base design expertise. Data & Knowledge Engineering 16(2), 97–124 (1995)

[W13]   WinRDBI Educational Tool, http://winrdbi.asu.edu/ (date accessed: May 29, 2013)

[TR02] Topi, H., Ramesh, V.: Human factors research on data modeling: a review of prior research, an extended framework and future research directions. Journal of Database Management (JDM) 13(2), 3–19 (2002)

[Z12]   Zhang, W.: A Suite of Case Studies in Relational Database Design. M.S. thesis, McMaster University, Ontario, Canada (2012)

A Semantic DBMS Prototype*

Liu Chen and Ting Yu

State Key Lab of Software Engineering
School of Computer
Wuhan University, China

Abstract. The dominant database management systems such as Oracle
and DB2 are based on the object-relational model, which grew out of the
research in 1990s by extending the relational model with object-oriented
features. They provide extended modeling power to users to build complex applications as it has shortened the distance from the conceptual
model to the logical model. However there are three main problems with
this approach. Firstly, it does not allow object migration so that the application development is unnecessarily complicated, time consuming and
difficult to evolve. Secondly, it don't support inverse relationship so that
the user has to manually define them and maintain their consistency.
Thirdly, as the current implementations simply convert object-oriented
features into various flat relations, the object manipulation and query
processing are quite inefficient. Information Network Model is a novel
conceptual model that can directly represent real-world organizational
structures and different kinds of relationships and their inverse relationships between real-world entities and corresponding context-dependent
properties so that the design and development of complex data applications is greatly simplified. Over the past three years, we have systematically designed and implemented this semantic database management
system based on INM. In this paper, we describe the system.

1 Introduction

In early 1990s, various object-oriented models were proposed to support the
direct modeling of real-world entities by means of object identity, complex values,
typing, classification, property inheritance, etc. [1,2]. The object-relational model
extends the relational model with these key object-oriented features [3,4] and has
been adopted by the dominant database management systems such as Oracle and
DB2. They do so by adding an object-relational layer on top of the relational
engine so that it appears to be object-relational but the data is actually split
and stored in various underlying relations. This approach provides users with
extended modeling power to build complex applications. However, there are three
main problems with this approach. Firstly, it does not allow object migration
as an object must have a direct class and cannot change its membership during
its life time. This limitation makes the application development unnecessarily

---

* This work is supported by National Natural Science Funds of China under grant No.
61202100.

J. Parsons and D. Chiu (Eds.): ER Workshops 2013, LNCS 8697, pp. 257–266, 2014.

complicated, time consuming and difficult to evolve. Secondly, it don't support the representation of the inverse relationship as in ODMG 3.0 [5]. The user has to manually define them and maintain their consistency. Thirdly, as the current implementations simply convert object-oriented features into various flat relations, the object manipulation and query processing are quite inefficient as many underlying relations are involved.

To solve these problems, Information Network Model (INM) has been proposed [6]. It supports two kinds of classes: object classes and role classes, two kinds of attributes: simple and composite, six kinds of relationships: normal, contain, context, role, role-based and composite. With these constructs, we can directly represent real-world organizational structures, various relationships and their inverse relationships between real-world entities and corresponding context-dependent properties. Indeed, INM is a conceptual model that is more expressive than existing ones such as UML [7] and ER [8]. It is quite easy to create the conceptual model of an application with INM. INM has three languages: data definition language (IDL), data manipulation language (IML) and query language (IQL). Based on the object class and relationship definitions in IDL, various role classes for the roles that entities play in the relationships can be generated automatically and objects can evolve to different role classes when needed. In INM, all information regarding a real-world entity is represented as a single object with a unique object identifier and one or more names. The object can belong to several classes to reflect the dynamic, many-faceted and evolutional aspects of the entity and objects are networked through various relationships and their inverse relationships. The object contains attribute/relationship names together with their values so that data in the object is self-describing. Furthermore, we use not only oids but also object names as relationship values so that the user can see what objects this object has relationships with, without jumping to linked objects to find their names.

Over the past three years, we have designed and implemented a semantic database management system based on INM to solve the problems with dominant database management systems. In this paper, we describe our implementation of the system. First, we give a brief overview of the INM modeling languages and then the architecture of INM database management system, which employs a conventional thin client/fat server software architecture. Also, we elaborate the core processing module, schema manager, instance manager, storage manager and query manager in which we use the advantage of object-oriented programming language and techniques, and at last the conclusion.

2   Overview of INM Languages

To introduce INM modeling, let us take university information modeling as an example. A university has a number of departments and locates in a city. Within a department, there are a number of faculty members and students, and each faculty member supervises some students. A person has an attribute birthdate and resides in a city, a country contains some provinces which in turn contain some cities. The following examples show several ways to use Information Definition Language (IDL), Information Manipulation Language (IML) and Information Query Language (IQL) for this application.

Example 1. First, we can use a nested relation so that all properties of Univ are nested as composite attributes, such as address, departments, faculty, students, etc. The following is the corresponding IDL statement, where * indicate the attribute is multi-valued.

```
create class Univ [
    @yearfounded: int,
    @category: {public,private},
    @address: [no:int,street:string,city:string,postcode:string],
    @departments*: [
        name:string,
        faculty*: [
            name:string,
            address: [no:int,street:string,city:string,postcode:string],
            birthdate: [day:int,month:int,year:int],
            students*: [name:string,
                address: [no:int,street:string,city:string,postcode:string],
                birthdate: [day:int,month:int,year:int]]]]];
```

Example 2. Different kinds of entities can be represented as INM objects of some classes, such as Univ, Country, Province, City and Person. In addition, faculty and student are the roles persons play in a department, so they are represented using role relationships. While playing the roles, these entities can have properties: a faculty member supervises students. Every relationship has a unique inverse, which can be a user-define one or a system generated default one if the inverse clause is not given. Also, we can represent cardinality constraints on the relationship and its inverse. For example, we can use (1:N) or * express one to many. The following IDL statements define classes and their various relationships.

```
create class Univ [normal address(N:1): City(inverse hasUniv),
    contain depts*: Department(inverse belongTo)];
create class Department [role Student*: Person(inverse studiesIn),
    role Faculty [role_based supervise*: Student(inverse supervisor)]*
        :Person(inverse worksIn)];
create class Person [@birthdate: [day:int,month:int,year:int],
    address(N:1): City(inverse hasPerson)];
create class Country [contain provinces*: Province(inverse belongTo) ];
create class Province [contain cities*: City(inverse belongTo)];
```

Example 3. The following IML statements show how to insert the facts that Department CS has a Student Jack and a Faculty Mike whose birthdate is 1960-1-1 and resides in Beijing, and supervises Student Jack.

```
insert Person Mike [@birthdate: [@day: 1,@month: 1,@year: 1960],address: Beijing];
insert Department CS [role Student: Jack, role Faculty: Mike [supervise: Jack]];
```

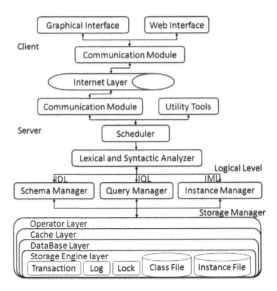

Fig. 1. Diagram of system architecture

Example 4. The following IQL statement finds and displays the birthyear of Mike and the student Mike supervises. Note that unlike SQL which mix querying and result constructing together, IQL strictly separates them so that queries are easier to write and understand.

query $x=Mike[birthdate/year:$y,//supervise:$s]
construct Professor $x[birthyear:$y,Student:$s];

In the query clause, logical variables $x matches the name Mike, $y and $s in the path expressions match the year 1960 and name Jack respectively. The construct clause specifies how to output the query result.

3   Overview of INM Database Management System

The INM database management system is a full-fledged database management system implemented in C++ on top of a PC running Linux. The lexical and syntactic analyzer is implemented using Flex 2.5.35 and Bison 2.4.1. The implementation employs a conventional thin client/fat server software architecture, as shown in Fig.1.

Client. The client of the database management system is organized into two layers: the *graphical/web interface* and the *communication module*. The graphical/web interface sends user requests to the server via the communication module and takes the query results from the server for proper display. The second layer is the communication module. It sends user requests from the first layer to the server for parsing and execution, and obtains query results from the server and then sends them back to the first layer.

Server. The server is organized into five layers. The first layer is the *communication module* which communicates with the communication modules of clients. It accepts user requests from clients, sends them to the scheduler, and ships the results back to these clients. Also, we provide on the server side a *Utility Tools* and available commands that for administrators to manage database, like batch file, statistics, clearing database, opening database listener, etc.

The second layer is the *scheduler*. It obtains multiple user requests from the communication module and the utility tools, schedules user requests, and ships them to the lexical and syntactical parser.

The third layer is the *lexical and syntactical analyzer* which performs lexical and syntactical analysis of user requests. It filters out invalid requests, transforms strings of valid requests into standard forms, and sends them to the schema manager, instance manager and query manager, which collectively referred to as the logical level.

The forth layer is the *logical level* which is in charge of class definition, object creation and modification and query processing. The *schema manager* validates operations and checks various integrity constrains. The *instance manager* matches objects with classes, and it is in charge of storing, modifying and deleting objects in the database. The *query manager* decides on what evaluation strategies to use according to the nature of the query, and it invokes the schema and the instance manager to handle queries of classes and objects respectively.

The last layer is the *storage manager*. It is responsible for the management of disk-based data structures and moves the data between disk and memory as needed. It is implemented in four layers, operator, cache, database and storage engine and each outer layer encapsulates the next inner layer respectively. It provides rapid access to classes, objects and other meta information about them on the disk.

3.1   Schema Manager

Schema manager is in charge of the logical processing of classes' definitions and updates and responsible for the interfaces to instance manager for objects' validation.

The structure of INM class consists of class identifier, class name, attributes and various relationships. The class identifier is generated automatically by the system as the key for each class. Attributes are prefixed with the symbol @ and there are two kinds of attributes in INM: simple and composite. In Example 1, attributes *yearfounded* and *category* are simple whereas the rest are composite. Also, attributes can either be single valued or multi-valued.

There are six kinds of relationships: role relationship, context relationship, role-based relationship, normal relationship, composite relationship and contain relationship. Schema manager insures that every relationship has a unique corresponding inverse relationship.

All classes are stored in the class primary file, in which the key of each record is the class identifier and the value is a byte array of the class's tree structure.Furthermore, there is a class name index whose key column stores the string

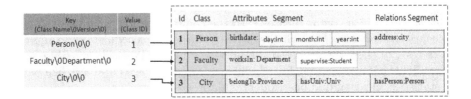

Fig. 2. A sample of the Class Name Index and the Class Primary File

which consists of the class name and the class version and value column stores the ID of the corresponding class.

Fig.2 displays several data records of the class primary file and a part of the class name index of the Example 2. Role class Department.Faculty induced from the corresponding role relationship in the class Department generates the context relationship worksIn and the role-based relationship supervise. In addition, there is no direct definition for the class City in Example 2, but for the inverse relationship mechanism, City has the relationship belongTo with Province and the relationship hasPerson with Person.

3.2 Instance Manager

Instance manager takes care of object generating, object modifying and object removing. It firstly executes validation check of the intermediary object structure and merges the objects confirmed to be the same entity. Three principles established to simplify object creation are partial instantiation, multi-inheritance and consistency maintaining.

The entire structure of an object contains object name, identifier, version, belonging classes, attributes and relationships. Only name, ID and a belonging class are necessary to construct basic objects. So objects can be partially instantiated in two ways: via instance creation command as (1) (3) in Fig.3, and via relationship target as (2) (4) in Fig.3. Segments of the same object are merged and stored as an entire object in the instance primary file.

Target of role relationship usually generates multi-inheritance for the target object already exists as an instance of an object class. The new generated role instance will be merged with the object instance referring to Example 3, as shown in Fig. 3(3).

Whenever a relationship is created with object generation, the inverse relationship with binding attributes and sub-relationships will be generated in the target object. The same thing happens during modifying and removing procedure to maintain the data consistency. Various indexes are created to raise efficiency of data access. The instance primary file is divided into the *object ID index*, the *object file* and the *large object file* to reduce memory fragments. In the object ID index, the key column stores the object ID and the value column keeps a marker bit marking in which file, the object file or the large object file, the object is stored. In both the object file and the large object file, the object ID is

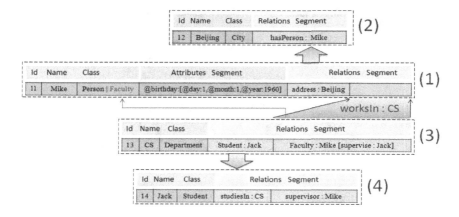

Fig. 3. Partial instantiation and multi-inheritance of object in the instance file

stored as the key and the byte array of the object's tree structure as the value. Objects with the size smaller than 1 KB are stored in the object file, while others stored in the large object file. The page size of the large object file is 32 KB, 8 times larger than the object file. There are four other indexes: the *instance name index*, the *class identifier index*, the *attribute/relationship name index* and the *attribute value index*, which will be introduced in the query processing example in Section 3.4.

3.3   Storage Manager

Storage manager is responsible for the interfaces for the logical level. We divide storage module into four layers, the *operator layer*, the *cache layer*, the *database layer* and the *storage engine layer*, as shown in Fig.1.

Operator Layer. According to the needs of the logical level, the operator layer consists of two parts: schema operator and instance operator. The operator layer schedules the cache layer and the database layer and provides interfaces of data access for the logical level. For example, the instance operator encapsulates methods that getting an object by object name or oid and methods that removing an object from database, etc. The logical level cannot directly access the other layers, but the operator layer.

Cache Layer. Corresponding to the two parts of the operator layer, the cache layer also contains two aspects, and each aspect packs a cache table. The cache table is used to buffer the deserialized data.

Database Layer. Like the cache layer, the database layer also has two parts in accordance with the operator layer. It creates indexes, serializes data, and fetches data by means provided by the storage engine layer.

Storage Engine Layer. The storage engine layer is the Berkeley DB [9]. It provides the fundamental database management service, including the access to

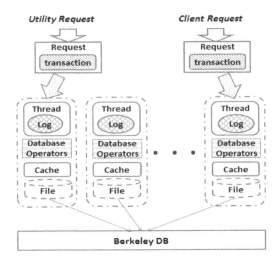

Fig. 4. Process diagram

the record in the class file and the instance file, transaction management, log, lock, buffer, etc.

As in Fig.4, when a process is created, firstly the database will be opened, in which the class file, the class index file, the instance file, and the instance index files are opened by calling methods of the storage engine level, and we call those data collectively *Global Data*. When the listener service is open, eight threads will be created and each thread possesses a pointer to the Global Data, a schema operator, a instance operator and a log file. When a thread receives any data from the client, a request and a transaction will be created, and the transaction is encapsulated in the request.

For example, when a new class is created and needs to be stored into the database, the logical level will invoke the class-inserting method in the schema operator, then the schema operator will pass the data to the schema cache level, and the data will be marked dirty. For the dirty records are not written to database instantly, the class name index is updated here to make sure this newly created class can be searched if following operations need. After the request finishes, the data marked dirty will be serialized and stored into the database through the storage engine level. In addition, the cache level will be cleared as the request's end, and if there occur any errors during the procedure, the transaction will roll back, otherwise, the transaction will be committed.

3.4   Query Manager

Query Manager includes query optimization, return pattern extraction, result construction and query output handler. Parser processing generates a query tree with variables/values bindings, which is used to store the variables, values as well as the hierarchy fetched from query expression.

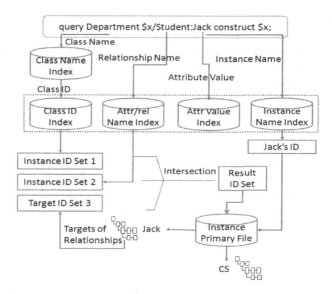

Fig. 5. Example of query processing

Result variables fetched from the construction expression of query command can scatter everywhere in the query tree. According to the position of result variables, appropriate querying strategy is chosen to make an effective querying.

After using querying strategy, values of each variable are binding as the sub-node of the variable in the query tree. The return pattern extraction extracts variables from construction expression in query tree to check if the result variables are in the query expression or not. If there is a result variable not in query expression, query output handler will commit the error information. Otherwise, the result construction will build a result graph to hold query result.

The Fig.5 shows a query processing that finding the department which has the student Jack. To optimize the query processing, we take advantage of indexes of class and instance as we have designed and maintained in schema manager and instance manager. From the left to the right in Fig.5, firstly we get the class identifier of the class Department via the class name index, then we get identifers of instances which belong to the class Department through the class identifier index, and we collects those instance identifiers in set 1. Secondly, we obtain identifiers of instances which have a relationship student via the at-tribute/relationship name index, and we put those instance identifiers in set 2. At last the value Jack, we firstly treat it as an attribute value for the attribute value index, the instances whose attributes have the value Jack will be returned, and here the result will be empty. We also treat Jack as a relationship target, that is an instance, via the instance name index and the instance primary file, easily we get the complete object Jack. For the inverse relationship mechanism, within the targets of relationships in object Jack, there must be one which is the result. So we get an instance identifer set 3. Finally, the intersection of the three sets will be the result object CS.

4 Conclusion

In this paper, we have described a prototype implementation of a novel semantic database management system based on Information Networking Model [6]. The complete implementation has been completed and the system is available from the svn address: mars.whu.edu.cn/inmproject.

The system has the following novel features. All information regarding a real-world entity is stored in a single object with a unique oid and one or more names. The object can belong to several classes to reflect the dynamic, many-faceted and evolutional aspects of the entity and objects are networked through various relationships and their inverse relationships. The object contains attribute/relationship names together with their values so that data in the object is self-describing, there is no limit on the number of attributes/relationships that objects can have, and space is not reserved for properties that are null. Furthermore, we use not only oids but also object names as relationship values so that the user can see what objects this object has relationships with, without jumping to linked objects to find their names.

Several applications based on the system have been developed such as the human resource management system for Wuhan University. We are also trying to improve the efficiency of object manipulation and query processing. We plan to extend the system to parallel distributed environment.

References

1. Kim, W.: Introduction to object-oriented databases. Computer Systems (1990)
2. Bancilhon, F., Delobel, C., Kanellakis, P.C.: Building an object-oriented database system, the story of o2 (1992)
3. Stonebraker, M., Moore, D.: Object Relational DBMSs: The Next Great Wave. Morgan Kaufmann Publishers Inc., San Francisco (1995)
4. Subramanian, M., Krishnamurthy, V.: Performance challenges in object-relational dbmss. IEEE Data Eng. Bull. 27–31 (1999)
5. Cattell, R., Barry, D., Berler, M., Eastman, J., Jordan, D., Russel, C., Schadow, O., Stanienda, T., Velez, F.: The Object Data Standard: ODMG 3.0. Morgan Kaufmann Publishers (2000)
6. Liu, M., Hu, J.: Information networking model. In: Laender, A.H.F., Castano, S., Dayal, U., Casati, F., de Oliveira, J.P.M. (eds.) ER 2009. LNCS, vol. 5829, pp. 131–144. Springer, Heidelberg (2009)
7. Hamilton, M.: Software Development: Building Reliable Systems, 1st edn. Prentice-Hall (April 1999)
8. Chen, P.P.: The entity-relationship model - toward a unified view of data. ACM Trans. Database Syst., 9–36 (1976)
9. Oracle (Berkeley DB),
   http://www.oracle.com/technology/products/berkeley-db/index.html

Towards a Domain Specific Modeling Language for Agent-Based Modeling of Land Use/Cover Change

Cédric Grueau[1,2]

[1] Departamento de Sistemas e Informática
Escola Superior de Tecnologia de Setúbal - Instituto Politécnico de Setúbal
Campus do IPS, Estefanilha, 2910-761 Setúbal, Portugal
[2] Centro de Informática e Tecnologias da Informação - CITI (DI/FCT/UNL)
Faculdade de Ciências e Tecnologia, Universidade Nova de Lisboa,
Quinta da Torre, 2829-516 Caparica, Portugal
cedric.grueau@estsetubal.ips.pt

Abstract. While agent-based models are widely used for the simulation of human-natural systems, it remains challenging for scientists to specify their models in a manner in which they can be understood and used by others. In this research project, we survey existing solutions that have emerged to cope with models specification issues. We then propose another approach: a domain specific modeling language for agent-based simulations of land use/cover change. This language is intended to constitute a means to promote models' validation and reuse. We also present the general methodology for the development of the modeling language which consists in extending existing conceptual modeling languages with domain-specific language profiles. We also present the first step towards its development comprising a domain model based on a domain ontology.

Keywords: Domain ontology, Multi-Agents Systems, Domain Specific Modeling Language, Land-Use Science.

1 Introduction

Computer-based simulations have become an important asset to understand the complex interactions between human societies and the land resources on which they depend. Many of these simulations rely on agent-based modeling (ABM) to represent social interactions. A spatial context (static or dynamic) is provided to represent the context where social interactions occur. In the particular domain of agent-based modeling of land use/cover change (ABM/LUCC), simulations are used to understand and test possible effects of alternative policy or management interventions in the socio-spatial system under study. Through simulation, modelers can understand and reproduce, with virtual experiments, the emergence of nearly any kind of macro-structure or macro-dynamics from the interactions of lower level computer processes, called agents. Building such simulations is

J. Parsons and D. Chiu (Eds.): ER Workshops 2013, LNCS 8697, pp. 267–276, 2014.

challenging but ABM have been enthusiastically adopted by ABM/LUCC scientists during the last decade. [24], [14] and [1] provide a broad range of examples of ABM/LUCC applications as diverse as innovation diffusion, city size distributions study, demographic and lot effects of agriculture in the Brazilian Amazon or forest management in Asia. However the fast development of this type of applications quickly raised concerns related to transparency issues [20]. Transparency pertains to how easy it is for an external person to understand a simulation model. ABM transparency issues are directly related to the manner in which models are described and specified by their authors. In practice, the representation of the model (and submodels) of the system in scientific papers will differ according to the background of the system's designer. These descriptions integrate pieces of natural language, mathematical formulas, pseudo code, UML diagrams and sometimes computer code. The diversity and lack of consistency between representations make it difficult to reuse and validate models. If design documents are unavailable, it is necessary to reverse-engineer the program back to the design to link with the high-level description of the model given in any source text [20] . Moreover, when, for example, reusing a model published in a scientific journal paper, one has no guaranty that the model was correctly implemented and that the results of the simulations conform to the model described. Such concerns represent a real challenge for the users and decision makers that rely on the simulations results.

2   Research Questions and Objectives

In order to respond to ABM/LUCC transparency issues, we propose to follow an approach that will address three questions. The first question is how to represent ABM/LUCC information structure in a manner in which it is decoupled from the simulation software and can be independently processed. The second question to address relates to the level of abstraction to achieve in order to represent the concepts of the domain. In fact, the abstraction should enable the representation of concepts and relationships for a multidisciplinary audience who is not necessarily expert in computer science, but, at the same time be precise enough to represent all concepts of the domain. A third question to answer is how can we ensure that an executable implementation conforms to a system's model?
To respond to these questions we propose to adopt a research approach consisting in the development of a Domain Specific Modeling Language (DSML). The objective of the DSML is to define an abstract representation of the ABM/LUCC domain, a domain model, and use it to instantiate executable systems (e.g. source code for simulation). By following such an approach, a particular system can be represented using the concepts defined in the domain model and its properties can be clearly specified using the modeling language. The objective of providing this DSML is moving towards a unified design that would facilitate the interpretation of the system by developers or practitioners that would want to reuse the system. It should answer the first two questions raised above. Our goal is to provide a modeling language that would meet users needs and that would

be straightforward enough to be adopted by the main users of the domain. By following a model-driven approach we also pretend to diminish the gap between system representation and system implementation. Providing the possibility of deriving executable code from the modeling language, using model transformations, would allow us to respond to the third question of our research.

3 State of the Art

3.1 Model-Driven Engineering and Ontology-Driven Conceptual Modeling

In MDE, models are described by modeling languages, where modeling languages themselves are described by so called metamodeling languages. A modeling language consists of an abstract syntax, at least one concrete syntax and semantics. Domain-Specific Modeling Languages (DSML) are specification languages that offer, through appropriate notations and abstractions, expressive power focused on, and usually restricted to, particular problem domains [4]. A DSML can be used to generate members of a family of systems in an application domain. The well-designed DSML is based on a thorough understanding of the underlying application domain, giving exactly the expressive power to generate required family members easily. Thus, a prerequisite for the design of a DSML is a detailed analysis and structuring of the application domain. Guidelines for acquiring such an understanding are provided by the research area of domain analysis, which investigates forms to model domains. Domain models are artefacts produced at the early stage of the software development process and illustrates specific conceptual knowledge in a problem domain, excluding irrelevant knowledge from this domain.

Relevant to our work is ontology-based domain analysis. The term Ontology originates in philosophy, where it was used to characterize a science about the nature of things: the types of things that exist and the relationships among them. In Computer Science environments, ontologies have been used, among others purposes, for building Domain Oriented Software Development Environments. Incorporating ontologies in the Software Engineering life cycle offers several advantages [23], ontologies seem to be well suited for an evolutionary approach to the specification of requirements and domain knowledge. Moreover, ontologies can be used to support requirements management and traceability. Formal specification may be a prerequisite in the design and implementation phases, in model driven approaches. In this context, ontologies can be incorporated into the DSML design phase, instead of other techniques [2], to produce a domain model. A domain ontology specifies the invariant conditions of the domain of interest which should be respected by any model built for that domain. The transition from an ontology to a domain modeling language might be obtained by a transformation between a language expressing the ontology and the DSML. It is also possible to apply domain ontologies to conceptual schema development by extending existing conceptual modeling languages, such as the Unified

Modeling Language (UML), with domain-specific language profiles that are defined through domain ontologies [6]. Since, ideally, domain ontologies should be grounded in foundational ontologies [10], we decided to develop our domain ontology taking as basis the Unified Foundational Ontology (UFO) [12], [11]. This choice is motivated by our concern in building a grounded domain ontology that could be expanded, compared or merged with other ontologies. Domain ontologies that use common foundation ontologies can be merged easily or compared. UFO is a foundational ontology that has been based on a number of theories from Formal Ontology, Philosophical Logics, Philosophy of Language, Linguistics and Cognitive Psychology. UFO has been used to evaluate, redesign and integrate (meta) models of conceptual modeling languages, as well as to evaluate, re-design and give real-world semantics to domain ontologies. It is composed by three main parts. UFO-A is an ontology of endurants, and it is the core of UFO. UFO-B is an ontology of perdurants (events) that is suitable to represent discrete events simulations. UFO-C is an ontology of social entities (both endurants and perdurants) built on the top of UFO-A and UFO-B. UFO-C distinguishes agents and objects. Agents are capable of performing actions with some intention, while objects only participate in events. UFO is appropriate to build our domain ontology as it provides support to represent ABM simulation through UFO-B and UFO-C.

3.2   Agent-Based Modeling and Simulation for Land Use/Cover Change

Some authors have recently addressed the problem of communicating about ABM. The ODD (Overview, Design concepts, Details) protocol, described in [7] has been defined for describing individual-based models and agent-based models. ODD is aimed at describing these types of models in scientific publications and is essentially focused on communication and reimplementation of ABM. But ODD is designed to describe only one definite model version [8] and can not be directly compiled to computer code. ODD can only represent the first step on the way to establish a general protocol for describing individual- and agent-based models [21]. Other authors have concentrated in ABM representation issues. In [13], a development environment for the definition of multi-agent systems (MAS), called Dsml4mas, is proposed. It is a model-driven framework that encompasses the platform independent specification of MAS, the model validation, the model transformation and code generation, as well as the execution of generated source code. However, Dsml4mas does not offer the possibility to represent important elements of the ABM/LUCC domain such as the agents' environment. Moreover, it is not based on a foundational ontology.

In [3], authors present an ontology defining an agent-based simulation framework and discuss the possibilities for using the Web Ontology Language's (OWL) automated reasoning capabilities. How to benefit from OWL and Semantic Web technologies for simulation is also the topic of other works. In [22] Polhill and colleagues illustrate how deploying an agent-based model on the Semantic Grid facilitates international collaboration on investigations using such a model, and contributes to establishing rigorous working practices with agent-based models as part of good science in social simulation. The experimental work-flow is described explicitly using an ontology, and a Semantic Grid service with a web interface implementing the work-flow. Users are able to compare their parameter settings and results, and relate their work with the model to wider the scientific debate. But this work mainly focuses on simulations parameters and the ontology used does not describe the models themselves.

MR POTATOHEAD [18] is another approach that tackles the design of agent-based models of land use change. This framework involves the creation of a standard design patterns at the conceptual level to enable the comparison of of agent-based models of land use/land-cover change. MR POTATOHEAD is tailored to a particular subset of models and enables a more detailed comparison to be made than the more generally applicable ODD. The MR POTATOHEAD framework is implemented using OWL.

Polhill and Gotts [20] presented another interesting approach to address ABM/ LUCC transparency issues. The authors propose to implement ABM simulations using ontologies, instead of object-oriented languages. Their work illustrates that using OWL to represent ABM as an ontology and executing an inference process, enables representing each step of a simulation as a particular ontology. This approach responds directly to transparency issues such as model validation because it is possible at any time to access the state of simulation and understand how a model behaves. However, the implementation in OWL limits the number of entities that can be represented in the model, as opposed to OO languages. Authors also point out that ontologies are not best suited to describe the algorithmic processes by which the state of the model is changed. Our ontology seems better suited for this task as it relies on the OO paradigm. All of these works represent a step forward to more transparent ABM but they individually only respond partially to the issues we want to address in our research.

4   Research Methodology

As the research project sought to produce and assess an artifact (a DSML), we based our research approach on other approaches that focus on the development and performance of (designed) artifacts in a context. Design science [15] and Action Research [5] are two research approaches that aim to increase the relevance of research by incorporating a social problem-solving activity in research without sacrificing rigour. Some authors ([5] and [17]) have combined both to offer guidelines and frameworks to conduct research projects. To achieve our research goals, we designed a research approach that carries out a series of tasks that are synthesized in figure 1. We included, in the methodology, some of the concepts advocated in Design Science, which include artefacts validation and design evaluation. The problem investigation phase is supported by a systematic literature review (SLR) [16], in order to rank the papers of main journals and conferences in our domain which tackle the issues related with ABM/LUCC specification. Based on this selection, we will systematically characterize the consequences of ABM/LUCC transparency issues and select main stakeholders.

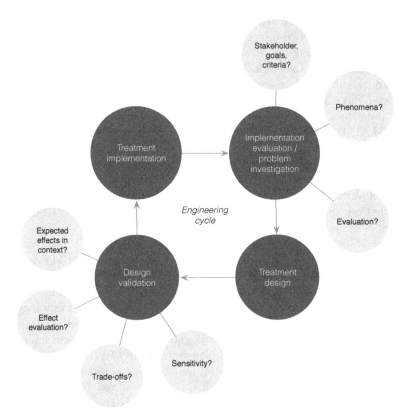

Fig. 1. Research methodology, adapted from [24]

Before starting to design the DSML, we will conduct a survey to evaluate how scientists and practitioners capture requirements for their systems and how they perform the analysis activity. The target population for answering the survey is composed by our stakeholders: the authors of the papers the have been ranked and selected during the SLR. The survey will also focus on the CASE tools that are used to model ABM/LUCC and on the properties that a DSML should provide for stakeholders. The treatment design phase focuses on the design of the DSML. The initial stage of this phase consists in the definition of a domain model supported by a domain ontology (see section 5). During the treatment design phase, we will need to build an editor that enables the construction of conceptual schemas of the phenomena belonging to the domain. It requires the creation of an UML profile based upon the domain ontology that specifies a domain axiomatization in terms of concepts, relationships between concepts and the rules that govern these relationships (i.e. the invariant conditions that define the domain). This operation will be implemented using the Object Constraints Language (OCL). We will target a specific Agent-based Modeling and Simulation

Platform (ABMSP)[1] to produce the code corresponding to the implementation of a conceptual schema of a domain subsystem. The outcome of these implementations are simulation runs which provide insight to model designers and decision makers. To properly test our DSML, we will perform, during the design validation phase, a usability and a quality analysis of our DSML. These analyses should provide insight on how users manage to learn and use the language and what is the outcome of the modeling of the same subsystem, by different groups of users. We will first evaluate the DSML usability with a population of graduate students, to provide feedback from preceding to the following tasks and carry out necessary adjustments and correction to the DSML. In the last phase, the Treatment Implementation, we will scale up the evaluation using domain experts. As advocated in [5], this operation can be performed using the Action Research approach and will allow to measure the acceptance of the artifact using a population of targeted stakeholders.

5   First Results

After a first attempt to characterize the ABM/LUCC domain [9], we decided on a more grounded approach to construct our domain model. As tackled in previous sections, we opted to build a domain ontology based on UFO where relevant MAS/LUCC concepts to be considered for the language are included. In the context of this paper, we will only illustrate a small part of the ontology including some of the concepts specific to the MAS/LUCC domain. Figure 2 shows a fragment of the UML classe diagram illustrating the type of agents that can be defined and the representation of the agents' environment. It illustrates that two types of agents exist in ABM/LUCC. Stereotypes represent the foundational ontology concepts and the class names, the domain concepts. For instance, to represent groups of agents with a social role, the UML class SocialAgent is created with the « InstitutionAgent » stereotypes which represents the equivalent concept in the eUFO-C3 ontology layer.

The classes describe our domain concepts and classes' stereotypes represents the corresponding UFO ontology concepts.

Working Example

The Ontology is currently under a validation process, which consists in adapting a published model and verifying if it supports the ontology. We have chosen to represent SLUDGE model (Simulated Land Use Dependent on eDGe Effect externalities), [21] for its representativeness of ABM/LUCC. SLUDGE is a simple combined cellular automaton and agent-based model designed to explore the effects of positive and negative distance-dependent spatial externalities on economic and landscape pattern outcomes. The first results of this validation process allowed to highlight some limitations of the ontology to represent spatial concepts. We are now working on incrementing the required spatial references.

---

[1] Such as RePast (repast.sourceforge.net)

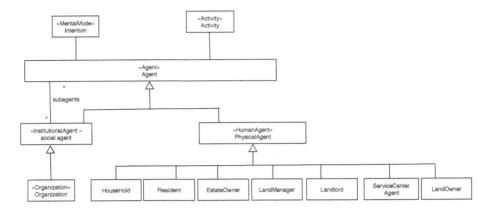

Fig. 2. Extract from the MAS/LUCC domain ontology - the agents' layer

6   Expected Contribution

By providing a DSML to the ABM/LUCC community we aim at providing its users with a common platform to represent and communicate the systems and sub-models they are working on. We also aim to contribute to the validation and reuse of the sub-models by reducing the gap between conceptualization and implementation. We also expect that the choice we made about using a foundational ontology as a basis for our domain ontology will facilitate the adoption and extension of our DSML to other related domains.

7   Conclusions and Further Work

In this paper, we have introduced transparency issues in ABM/LUCC domain. We have proposed the development of a Domain Specific Modeling Language for this domain and described the methodology we will follow to respond to the research questions we have raised. We also presented a domain model based on a domain ontology. The next step in our work will consist in validating the domain ontology by confronting its capacity to represent MAS/LUCC models existing in the literature. After this validation, we will pursue by designing a UML profile for the ontology domain axioms and formalize them as Object Constraint Language (OCL) constraints. We will also implement an editor in Eclipse that will enable the design of conceptual schemas in conformity with the UML profile.

References

1. Bousquet, F., Trébuil, G.: Introduction to companion modeling and multi-agent systems for integrated natural resource management in Asia, pp. 1–17. IRRI Publications, Los Banos (2005)

2. Ceh, I., Crepinsek, M., Kosar, T., Mernik, M.: Ontology driven development of domain-specific languages. Comput. Sci. Inf. Syst. 8(2), 317–342 (2011)
3. Christley, S., Xiang, X., Madey, G.: An ontology for agent-based modeling and simulation. In: Agent 2004 Conference on Social Dynamics: Interaction, Reflexivity and Emergence (2004)
4. van Deursen, A., Klint, P., Visser, J.: Domain-specific languages: An annotated bibliography. ACM SIGPLAN Notices 35(6), 26–36 (2000)
5. Fatemi, H., van Sinderen, M.J., Wieringa, R.J.: A trust ontology for business collaborations. In: Sandkuhl, K., Seigerroth, U., Stirna, J. (eds.) Short Paper Proceedings of the 5th IFIP WG 8.1 Working Conference on the Practice of Enterprise Modeling, Rostock, Germany, Aachen. CEUR Workshop Proceedings, vol. 933, p. 5. CEUR-WS.org (November 2012)
6. Gailly, F., Poels, G.: Conceptual modelling using domain ontologies: Improving the domain-specific quality of conceptual schemas. Working papers of faculty of economics and business administration, Ghent University, Faculty of Economics and Business Administration, Belgium (2009)
7. Grimm, V., Berger, U., Bastiansen, F., Eliassen, S., Ginot, V., Giske, J., Goss-Custard, J., Grand, T., Heinz, S.K., Huse, G., Huth, A., Jepsen, J.U., Jørgensen, C., Mooij, W.M., Müller, B., Pe'er, G., Piou, C., Railsback, S.F., Robbins, A.M., Robbins, M.M., Rossmanith, E., Rüger, N., Strand, E., Souissi, S., Stillman, R.A., Vabø, R., Visser, U., DeAngelis, D.L.: A standard protocol for describing individual-based and agent-based models. Ecological Modelling 198(1-2), 115–126 (2006)
8. Grimm, V., Berger, U., DeAngelis, D.L., Polhill, J.G., Giske, J., Railsback, S.F.: The odd protocol: A review and first update. Ecological Modelling 221(23), 2760–2768 (2010)
9. Grueau, C., Araujo, J.: Towards a domain specific modeling language for agent-based models in land use science. In: Proceedings of the 28th Symposium on Applied Computing, Coimbra, Portugal (2013)
10. Guarino, N.: Formal Ontology in Information Systems: Proceedings of the 1st International Conference, 1st edn., Trento, Italy, June 6-8. IOS Press, Amsterdam (1998)
11. Guizzardi, G.: Ontological foundations for structural conceptual models. PhD thesis, University of Twente, Enschede, The Netherlands (October 2005)
12. Guizzardi, G., Wagner, G.: Towards an ontological foundation of agent-based simulation. In: Winter Simulation Conference, pp. 284–295 (2011)
13. Hahn, C.: A domain specific modeling language for multiagent systems. In: Proceedings of 7th International Conference on Autonomous Agents and Multi-Agent Systems (AAMAS), pp. 233–240 (2008)
14. Heppenstall, A., Crooks, A., See, L., Batty, M. (eds.): Agent-based Models of Geographical Systems. Springer, Dordrecht (2012), http://www.springer.com/social+sciences/population+studies/book/978-90-481-8926-7
15. Hevner, A.R., March, S.T., Park, J., Ram, S.: Design science in information systems research. MIS Quarterly 28(1), 75–105 (2004)
16. Kitchenham, B., Pearl Brereton, O., Budgen, D., Turner, M., Bailey, J., Linkman, S.: Systematic literature reviews in software engineering - a systematic literature review. Inf. Softw. Technol. 51(1), 7–15 (2009)
17. Lee, A.: Action is an artifact. In: Kock, N. (ed.) Information Systems Action Research. Integrated Series in Information Systems, vol. 13, pp. 43–60. Springer US (2007)

18. Parker, D.C., Brown, D.G., Polhill, J.G., Deadman, P.J.M.: Illustrating a new conceptual design pattern for agent-based models of land use via five case studies: the MR POTATOHEAD framework. In: Agent-Based Modelling in Natural Resource Management, Valladolid, Spain, pp. 29–62 (2008)

19. Parker, D.C., Manson, S.M., Janssen, M.A., Hoffmann, M.J., Deadman, P.: Multi-agent systems for the simulation of land-use and land-cover change: A review. Annals of the Association of American Geographers 93(2), 314–337 (2003), http://dx.doi.org/10.1111/1467-8306.9302004

20. Polhill, J., Gotts, N.: Ontologies for transparent integrated human-natural system modelling. Landscape Ecology 24(9), 1255–1267 (2009)

21. Polhill, J.G., Parker, D., Brown, D., Grimm, V.: Using the odd protocol for describing three agent-based social simulation models of land-use change. Journal of Artificial Societies and Social Simulation 11(2), 3 (2008)

22. Polhill, J.G., Pignotti, E., Gotts, N.M., Edwards, P., Preece, A.: A semantic grid service for experimentation with an agent-based model of land-use change. Journal of Artificial Societies and Social Simulation 10(2), 2 (2007)

23. Seedorf, S., Informatik, F.F., Mannheim, U.: Applications of ontologies in software engineering. In: 2nd International Workshop on Semantic Web Enabled Software Engineering (SWESE), held at the 5th International Semantic Web Conference, ISWC (2006)

24. Wieringa, R., Moralı, A.: Technical action research as a validation method in information systems design science. In: Peffers, K., Rothenberger, M., Kuechler, B. (eds.) DESRIST 2012. LNCS, vol. 7286, pp. 220–238. Springer, Heidelberg (2012)

The Role Concept for Relational Database Management Systems

Tobias Jaekel

Department of Computer Science
Technische Universität Dresden
01062 Dresden, Germany
tobias.jaekel@tu-dresden.de

Abstract. More complex applications lead to worse maintainability and extensibility. Flexible and dynamic concepts can help to balance maintainability and complexity. The role concept is an approach that is used in software systems and programming languages to enable dynamic objects. Database systems with dynamic data objects are not available, which leads to complex mappers if the data have to be stored relationally. In this paper we outline research towards a role-concept-enabled relational database system. We describe a definition of this concept based on existing results and discuss open research questions related to our definition. Since today's RDBMSs cannot handle the role concept inherently, we also detail architecture and query language extensions.

Keywords: relational database system, role concept definition, modeling language, query language, relational architecture extension.

1 Introduction

Modern software applications are becoming increasingly complex, and growth in complexity worsens maintainability and extensibility. To keep applications maintainable, more flexibility is desired, and not only in programming contexts. Database systems also have to keep pace with this development. Nowadays, software is usually written in an object-oriented (OO) style with special persistence layers that map objects onto relational tables. The problem of mapping entities onto tables gets more complex if the software uses concepts, like the *role concept*, that enable dynamic objects. This concept was initially proposed as extension of the network model for databases [1] and has since been adapted to OO programming languages to get dynamic objects.

The idea of the role concept is based on the observation that real-world entities are role-oriented [1]. In the role model, an entity need not represent all aspects at the same time, as entities are constrained to do in the relational model. Figure 1 illustrates an example schema and its changes over time. It shows two data object types, each of which consists of a core object type and two role types. *Person* and *public facility* represent core objects that can be extended by roles. These roles are *student* and *employee* for *person* and *university* and *employer*

J. Parsons and D. Chiu (Eds.): ER Workshops 2013, LNCS 8697, pp. 277–286, 2014.
© Springer International Publishing Switzerland 2014

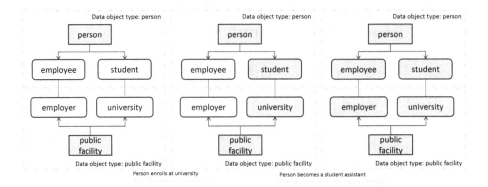

Fig. 1. Schema flexible data objects

for *public facility*. Both, core objects and roles come with their own attributes. E.g. a person has a first name and a last as well as a date of birth and the role student a student ID. The left part of this figure represents the state when no role is active and only the core object instances exist (active types are shaded gray). At a particular time, an instance of the *person* core object enrolls at a university and thus, becomes a *student*. Because of the *student* role, the *person* gets in a relationship to a *public facility* that plays a *university* role as shown in the middle of Figure 1. At some future date the same person becomes a student assistant at the same university. For this reason, the *person* acquires the role *employee* and the *public facility* the role *employer*. The schema of this *person* data object instance has changed a second time now and compasses all attributes of *person*, *student*, and *employee*. The example's final state is shown on the right in the figure, but at runtime this state could change again, e.g. the *person* stops being an *employee* at the *university*.

The example shows the main advantage of this approach. Objects can be retyped at runtime by acquiring or abandoning roles dynamically without losing their identity. Where it started being typed as a *person*, the data object is retyped to *person–student* and later to *person–student–employee*. In most object-oriented systems, an object must be an instance of a specific type for its whole lifetime. If the object evolves, it would not be an instance of this type anymore and must be transformed into a new instance. Furthermore, the role concept reduces the number of entity types. To type instances precisely, an entity type for each entity–role combination must be defined. Taking into consideration that roles can be played several times without limitation, the definition would never end. With the role concept, entities and roles are defined only once and by combining them, the type is defined implicitly. Imagine a person who is a student and simultaneously has a student-assistant job at the university. An entity type that holds all these attributes simultaneously must be instantiated and each time the person acquires or abandons a role, a new instance is required.

In the software technology community, the role concept is more accepted than in the relational database community. The role concept is accepted in modeling software and modeling data; and there exist programming language extensions that enable this concept at runtime. Furthermore, systems exist that perform object-relational mapping for dynamic objects, but on the application level and not in the DBMS. The DBMS still cannot handle these flexible objects, because role concept semantics are in the application or mapping layer. Our goal is to develop a relational database system that is able to deal with dynamic data objects where these objects are represented by the role concept. In consequence, both applications and the DBMS can benefit of this approach. First, if application and database system communicate by using the same language, the object-relational mapper would significantly be simplified. Second, the database system can distinguish between entities and roles by having a richer semantics than traditional relational systems. Finally, the role concept gets transactional support by the DBMS.

Numerous approaches have been developed and each of these approaches has its own notion of the concept, but no universally accepted definition of the term "role" exists. One study [2] analyzed most approaches and found 15 characteristics of roles that are generally related to the term "role" in modeling. Based on these results, the authors created a more general definition [2]. Relational database systems are not capable of handling roles inherently and for this reason we have to solve several problems. Defining our notion of the role concept is the first task. To visualize the definition, we need a lightweight modeling language, and to communicate with applications we need an extended query language. Finally, the database architecture, including logical and physical representation, must be aligned to the role concept.

The rest of the paper is structured as follows: The next section describes our definition of the role concept together with the open research question related to that definition. Section 3 comprises all research questions related to the relational database management system extension, to be able to handle roles. The related work in Section 4 and Section 5 finishes the paper by summarizing the main contributions and the paper generally.

2   Our Role Concept Notion

In four decades of research related to the role concept, many somewhat conflicting approaches have been developed. To clearly specify our notion of the concept, in Section 2.1 we put the concept into a set-theoretical model to describe general relations. Next we define the elements *natural type* and *role type* in detail. In a DBMS, there exists not only entities of certain types, but there also exist constraints between those entities or attribute-related constraints (e.g. "not NULL" or "only numeric" for a ZIP-code). The role concept contains different kinds of constraints that we present in Section 2.2. In Section 2.3, we discuss related open research questions.

2.1   Role Concept Definition

The role concept we want to specify here is based on Guarino's [3] ontological distinction between *role types* and *natural types* and is also related to the definition of Lodwick presented in [2]. To distinguish the natural types from role types, we have to take in consideration two properties of the concepts: *foundation* and *rigidity*. The *foundation* property denotes the element's dependency on another element, or rather it depends on a relationship to this element. For example, a student cannot be a student without being enrolled at a university. Here, existence of the student role clearly depends on the relationship of a student to a university. *Founded types* are always part of a relation and they cannot exist without this relationship. *Rigidity* denotes the fact that an individual cannot drop its type without losing its identity. A human person will always be a human person. If the person stops being a person, it would not be the same object. With these properties we can distinguish natural types and role types. Natural types, like "person," are semantically rigid but not founded. On the other hand, role types are founded but lack semantic rigidity. In consequence of our definition, only role types can be part of a relationship.

Set-Theoretical Definition. Our system consists of a set of natural types and role types, generally. Role types (R) can be played by certain natural types (N), hence, the role types have a relation $(\leq_{NR})$ to natural types. Set-theoretically this relation is defined as:

$$\leq_{NR} \subseteq N \times R$$

To associate a certain role type (r) with a certain natural type (n) we write:

$$n \leq_{NR} r$$

Further, it is required that each role be associated to at least one natural type, i.e. an isolated role is prohibited.

$$\forall r \, \exists n \, (n \leq_{NR} r); n \in N, r \in R$$

Roles always have to be part of a relationship to other roles. This relation $(\leq_{RR})$ is defined by:

$$\leq_{RR} \subseteq R \times R$$

To specify that a role (r_1) is in a relationship with another role (r_2) we write:

$$r_1 \leq_{RR} r_2$$

It is also required that each role be part of a relationship, since roles cannot be played without a relation.

$$\forall r_1 \, \exists r_2 \, (r_1 \leq_{RR} r_2); \, r_1, r_2 \in R$$

The $\leq_{RR}$ relation is left-total and unidirectional. This means that each role must be in at least one relationship with a role r_2 (left-total) and $r_1 \leq_{RR} r_2$

does not imply $r_2 \leq_{RR} r_1$ (unidirectional). The left part of $\leq_{RR}$ describes the role that must be in a relationship with the role on the right side. All these relationships are mandatory to r_1, the role on the left. Furthermore, a role can only participate in relationships that are part of its role definition, there are no optional relationships. In fact, we can find many examples where the natural language indicates relationships of a role that are not mandatory by definition. Consider the student example that we discussed previously. A student visits a movie theater with a special discount and thus, he is involved into a relationship with this movie theater. Actually, s/he does not visit the movie theater as a student, but rather as a person that plays the role of movie-goer, which is defined by a relationship to a cinema role. The student role is only the requirement to get the student discount. Thus we can see that a relationship of role r_1 to a role r_n that is not mandatory to r_1 can be modeled by a special auxiliary role r_s, which the natural type has to acquire instead. The special role r_s is defined by a relation to the role r_n.

Element Definition. Up to now, we have handled natural types and role types as elements of sets without any information about them. Now, we want to define the two types in detail.

A *natural type*, the core element, is defined by:

$$n : (A)$$

Its schema contains a name (n) and a set of attributes (A). The natural type can be compared with a standard schema of a table in a database system.

A role is defined by the following tuple:

$$r : (A, N, R)$$

A role has a name (r) and a set of attributes (A) like the natural types have. In addition, a role references the natural types (N) that can play this role and the mandatory relations to other roles (R).

Defining the running student example in detail could lead to the following natural type definitions:

1. *public_facility* : ({*name, address, number_students*})
2. *person* : ({*first_name, last_name, birthdate, place_of_birth, address*})

The corresponding roles could be defined as follows:

1. *university* : ({*number_of_professors*}, {*public_facility*}, {*other_role*})
2. *student* : ({*student_id, semester*}, {*person*}, {*university*})

2.2   Constraints

Another important use case of roles is constraints between them. In the real world there exist many limitations, such as the constraint that a member of the scientific staff in a research group has to be an alumnus of the corresponding university. Here, the role "alumnus" is a requirement to play the role "member of scientific staff." Likewise, being a student, retiree, or disabled person is a pre-condition to receiving discounts at museums or movie theaters. Furthermore, there are limitations that are related to time. For instance, a member of the supervisory board of a company must not be in the management board for at least three years. Another example is an employment contract that is limited to one year. The associated role should be valid only for the given year. As we can see, limitations and constraints can be very complex. We found five different types of constraints that are not yet formalized:

1. Concurrency of roles (e.g. the roles "retiree" and "employee" must not be played by the same person)
2. Changeover of roles (e.g. if a student finishes his or her studies, s/he has to abandon the role "student" and acquire the role "alumnus")
3. Transfer of roles (e.g. if natural type n_1 abandons a role, n_2 has to take over this role)
4. Cardinality of roles (e.g. there can only be a single prime minister in relationship to a particular country)
5. Temporal aspects of roles (e.g. the "prime minister" role is only valid for the corresponding legislative period)

In many scenarios we must connect several constraints logically. In the discount scenario we described above, it is sufficient to play one of the roles "student," "retiree," or "disabled person" to get a discount at the museum. Here, the roles are constrained and connected by disjunction. The implemented system has to support such logical operations on constraints.

2.3   Open Research Questions

In the field of concept formalization, at least three research tasks remain. First, constraints need a formal and comprehensive definition, since roles may depend on other roles or be limited in cardinality. Since roles come with temporal aspects, we also should investigate which techniques of temporal databases can be used to ensure temporal requirements. The second task comprises the definition of our concept on the level of instances. Roles are related to natural-type instances and can be played several times simultaneously. Each role has to be identifiable and referenceable to other roles and natural types. We have to investigate how value-based references can be used, especially if two roles are referencing each other mutually. A visualization of the concept, as a bridge between data modeling and database management systems, by a lightweight modeling language is the third task.

3   Database Architecture Extension

The role concept can enable dynamics not only for software systems, but also database systems can benefit by understanding the notion of roles. Unfortunately, traditional RDBMSs are not able to handle such dynamics inherently. For this reason, we have to adjust the DBMS architecture to our notion of the role concept.

3.1 Query Language

In consequence of the extended relational model, an extended query language has to be designed as well. Here, the first question is whether standard SQL is sufficient for our purpose. Over time, SQL has become increasingly powerful with many new language constructs. In the latest version of SQL, SQL:2011, the feature of temporal databases was essentially improved. Nevertheless, SQL does not support all aspects of the role concept semantics, like the differences between role types and natural types.

Of course, the new query language has to support our notion of the role concept. That includes defining, updating, and querying natural types and role types. With a role-concept-specific query language, novel query potentials arise. A natural-type instance that plays a certain role is logically a single element. Querying one of the role's attributes should return the role with the corresponding natural type. By querying only a natural type's attribute, all attributes related to roles should not be returned. Consider the student example again. We would certainly expect that a person will not play only the student role over his or her whole lifetime. At some point in future, a student becomes a student assistant at the university where he or she studies. Querying this person's student role should only return the attributes of person and student. But, querying for the student assistant role, the attributes of role student should be accessible as well, because to be a student assistant it is required that this individual is a student as well.

Temporal facets must be considered by the query language as well. For example, consider the situation where a role can only be acquired if a certain role has not been played for at least three years, and this constraint is known by the DBMS. The DBMS has to block role acquisition if this constraint is violated.

In the end, we have to create a new connectivity to the enhanced database model. This connectivity has to support the role concept notion and query language as well.

The research tasks related to the query language topic are:

1. Defining a query language whose semantics represent the roles concept.
2. How can the different types, including the temporal aspects of them, be queried by a query language?
3. Which attributes should be visible if natural types or role types are queried?

3.2 Internal Representation and Storage Layout

Internal representation manages access and how the data are handled inside of the DBMS. Traditionally, relational data objects are represented as tables with a fixed schema. In our case we have dynamic data objects with a flexible schema, since roles are acquired and abandoned dynamically. These flexible data objects must be stored relationally. By definition, each role can be played simultaneously several times. A table that holds all attributes of a natural-type instance and its corresponding roles is not sufficient, since there is no maximal number of simultaneously-played roles. A suitable solution could be to store roles in a nested model, like the non-first-normal-form [4], but there are other possibilities as well.

Regardless of the logical representation we have to investigate the physical representation. Because our system consists of more than a single meta type and in a relational DBMS only entity types exist, the storage-model decision affects two abstraction levels: (1) types and (2) instances.

On the level of types several options are conceivable, e.g. storing the whole data object in a block or separately. It can be seen as a type-level decision between a block-wise storage model, where the entity is stored with its currently played roles, or a columnar storage model, where entities and roles are stored separately, or a mix of both. A block-wise storage model implies that the storage is able to handle schema-flexible data objects. Each time a role is acquired or abandoned, the schema changes. Further, the space the objects occupy changes with each role change and thus, the page has to be reorganized continuously. This approach would be advantageous if natural-type instances are queried in conjunction with their corresponding roles, since all information is stored in clusters.

Accordingly, storing in a columnar fashion means storing natural-type instances and currently played roles separately. A flexible storage is nonessential compared to a block-wise storage. With decomposed data objects, the reconstruction and linkage of parts is more important. Each role type would be stored in particular pages and special pages would link the natural-type instances to roles. In this scenario, the logical data object would have to be reconstructed when roles are queried. Hence, we are enhancing the relational data model and both types consist of attributes, like in RDBMSs, and thus we can use the well-known techniques like NSM or DSM [5] on the level of instances.

Besides the logical and physical representations, we also have to investigate efficient access paths. In RDBMS there are usually three options to navigate: (1) scanning a table, (2) using a non-composite index such as B-Trees or hashing, or (3) using a composite index such as multi-key hashing. Depending on the internal representation, the access paths have to be aligned. For accessing only the natural type's attributes, a non-composite index would be sufficient if a primary key exists. In case roles are queried in conjunction with attributes of the natural-type instance, a composite index, which references both keys, would be efficient. In general, the number of currently played distinct roles defines the dimensionality of a composite index, if we want to access a natural-type instance and role combination within a single index access.

Since roles can be constrained with temporal aspects, abandoned roles have to be stored. The research questions here are both how and how long to store abandoned roles. In general, a natural-type instance can reacquire in the future the same role it played in the past, e.g. an employee returns to work for a company he or she previously left. It is the same natural type and the old employee role could be reactivated. Furthermore, for some legal reasons or other constraints archiving roles may be necessary.

To summarize the research tasks for database architecture alignment, we have to solve the following problems:

1. Defining a query language that is capable of representing the defined role concept.
2. Investigating different options for the internal representation including the logical, physical, and temporal design.
3. Analyzing options to access dynamic data objects efficiently.

4 Related Work

The term "role" is used in many varied domains and contexts such as linguistics or acting, and thus many definitions for this term exist. Here, we discussed a "role" term and its underlying concept, which goes back to [1] and [6] in the 1970s. Especially in modeling, this concept was adopted to solve certain problems. The application area ranges from conceptual modeling [7], data modeling [1], and knowledge representation [8] to specialized object-oriented programming languages [9] or a generalized approach [2].

This work aims to develop a role concept definition that can be implemented into an enhanced relational database system. Thus, the related work comprises conceptual and data modeling as well as programming and implementation approaches. On the level of conceptual and data modeling much research has been done. Steimann has given an overview of research up to the year 2000 [10]. This habilitation thesis analyzes most of the research in modeling with roles. The level of implementation, especially for database systems, did not get much attention. Only DOOR [11] can be seen as an approach that enables roles in a DBMS, particularly an object-oriented DBMS.

5 Contribution and Summary

In this work we aim to bring together flexible data structures based on the role concept and relational database management systems. There are three main contributions in this work. The first contribution comprises the definition of the role concept enabled relational data model and how the components (natural types and role types) can be assembled. The second contribution is the relational transformation of this data model. Here, we have to analyze which relational and object–relational techniques can be exploited and in case any of these techniques are sufficient to meet our goal, we have to develop new approaches. Within the second contribution, our goal is to ensure efficient storage of these flexible data structures. The third contribution encompasses the development of an extended query language. This query language bridges the gap between our storage layer and applications.

In this paper we outlined our research to bring the relational data model and role concept together to take advantage of both models. On the one hand, the relational model has been researched for more than 40 years and is well-known.

On the other hand, the role concept provides dynamics by handling several aspects of entities as roles.

There are many different and partly oppositional definitions of the role concept and for that reason we defined our notion of the role concept in a first step. Following Guarino's [3] ontological distinction between natural types and role types, we formalized these two types both set-theoretically and on the model level in Section 2. As open research questions of the data model, formalization of constraints and instance-level definition together with the modeling language as visualization remain as future work. To get the role concept into a RDBMS, we detailed feasible modifications in Section 3. Open research questions related to the relational database management system are defining a query language suitable for our role concept notion along with defining the internal representation. In Section 4 we gave a short overview of related work. We look forward to continuing our development of this important research area. A solid, generally accepted role mechanism as we envision it would make for a better information systems development and management infrastructure.

References

1. Bachman, C.W., Daya, M.: The role concept in data models. In: Proceedings of the Third International Conference on Very Large Data Bases, VLDB 1977, vol. 3, pp. 464–476. VLDB Endowment (1977)
2. Steimann, F.: On the representation of roles in object-oriented and conceptual modelling. Data & Knowledge Engineering 35(1), 83–106 (1999)
3. Guarino, N.: Concepts, attributes and arbitrary relations: Some linguistic and ontological criteria for structuring knowledge bases. Data & Knowledge Engineering 8(3), 249–261 (1992)
4. Jaeschke, G., Schek, H.J.: Remarks on the algebra of non first normal form relations. In: Proceedings of the 1st ACM SIGACT-SIGMOD Symposium on Principles of Database Systems, pp. 124–138 (1982)
5. Copeland, G.P., Khoshafian, S.N.: A decomposition storage model. In: Proceedings of the 1985 ACM SIGMOD, SIGMOD 1985, pp. 268–279 (1985)
6. Falkenberg, E.D.: Concepts for modelling information. In: IFIP Working Conference on Modelling in Data Base Management Systems, pp. 95–109 (1976)
7. Halpin, T.: Orm/niam object-role modeling. In: Bernus, P., Mertins, K., Schmidt, G. (eds.) Handbook on Architectures of Information Systems. International Handbooks on Information Systems, pp. 81–101. Springer, Heidelberg (1998)
8. Brachman, R.J., Schmolze, J.G.: An overview of the kl-one knowledge representation system. Cognitive Science 9(2), 171–216 (1985)
9. Monpratarnchai, S., Tetsuo, T.: The design and implementation of a role model based language, epsilonj. In: Electrical Engineering/Electronics, Computer, Telecommunications and Information Technology, vol. 1, pp. 37–40 (2008)
10. Steimann, F.: Formale Modellierung mit Rollen (2000)
11. Wong, R.K., Chau, H.L., Lochovsky, F.H.: A data model and semantics of objects with dynamic roles (1996)

Store Review Spammer Detection Based on Review Relationship

Qingxi Peng

State Key Laboratory of Software Engineering, Wuhan University,
Luojiashan Road, 430072 Wuhan, China
pengqingxi@google.com

Abstract. Reviews and comments play important role in online shopping. It can help people getting more information about stores and products. The potential customers tend to make decision according to it. However, driven by profit and fame, spammers post spurious reviews to mislead the customers by promoting or demoting target store. Previous studies mainly focused on the text features and ratings to identify fake reviews. However, these studies ignore the importance of relationship between store and reviewer. This paper first proposes sentiment analysis techniques to calculate the sentiment score of reviews. Then a relationship-based method has been proposed to identify the spammers. We also present an algorithm which can detect both single-mode spammers and multi-mode spammers. A subset of highly suspicious reviewers is selected for evaluation by human judges. Experimental results show that the proposed method can find out the review spammer efficiently.

Keywords: review spam, review relationship, sentiment analysis.

1 Introduction

With the development of Web 2.0, online shopping has become a popular activity of many peoples life. Previously, people usually transfer experience within small scope such as friends and relatives. Nowadays, customers prefer to share their experiences about store and product by posting reviews, while potential customers tend to gain indirect experience by watching user generating reviews before online shopping. The online comments have also been used by stores to identify their product and service problems to attract more customers. However, Spammers publish spurious reviews to promote or demote target online store, inducing users buy or not to buy something from particular store. More and more spam reviews emerge in major review websites such as Epinion.com, Resellerrating.com, and Shopzilla.com. Therefore, detecting such spurious reviews and spammers become a pressing issue.

Previous works have paid more emphasis on text features of reviews. Similarity of text has been regarded as main evidence to identify the spam reviews. While cunning spammers avoid writing near duplicated text, the text-based methods dont work now. Other works use rating score and feedback score as indicator to

J. Parsons and D. Chiu (Eds.): ER Workshops 2013, LNCS 8697, pp. 287–298, 2014.
© Springer International Publishing Switzerland 2014

detect the spam reviews. In this paper, we study the relationship between store, reviewer and review. We also incorporate the sentiment analysis techniques into spam review detection.

There are two typical spammers: single-mode spammers and multi-mode spammers. Single-mode spammer is spammer who only uses one userid to post reviews. In [15], time series analysis has been employed to detect the single-mode spammers. Multi-mode spammers usually post several reviews using one userid [4]. Previous works either capture single-mode spammers by time-series analysis of reviews, or capture multi-mode spammers by means of review graph. Due to the analysis of relationship between stores and reviewers, our method can capture both single-mode spammers and multi-mode spammers, which is different from previous works.

In this paper, our researches mainly focus on the relationship between store and reviewer. Firstly we incorporate the sentiment analysis techniques to calculate the sentiment score. Then deviation of sentiment and rating has been analyzed by a relationship-based method. We also propose an algorithm to capture the spammers mentioned above. It is important to note that our idea is different from [9] even if we all use relationships. We map the reviewers and stores into a heterogeneous graph, and consider the entities and the relationship between them. To our knowledge, this is first study detecting both single-mode and multi-mode spammers.

Our contributions in this paper are then as follows:

1. We incorporate the sentiment analysis techniques into spam review detection, and propose a method to calculate the sentiment score of reviews.

2. We map the reviews and stores into a heterogeneous graph, and propose a relationship-based approach to calculate the deviation of sentiment and rating scores.

3. We propose an algorithm to detect both single-mode spammers and multi-mode spammers. Experimental results demonstrate the effectiveness of the proposed method.

The remainder of the paper is organized as follows. Section 2 discusses related work in the area of spam detection and their limitations. In Section 3, we first propose sentiment analysis method to calculate sentiment score of reviews. Then the deviation of review has been calculated. Finally, an algorithm has been proposed to capture both single-mode and multi-mode spammers by means of store-reviewer relationship. In section 4 we present an evaluation of the spammer detecting on the real world dataset. Finally, conclusions and directions for future work are given in section5.

2 Related Work

In this section we summarize the previous approaches, and how our method differs from them.

2.1 Spam Review Detection

In [1], Web spam was defined as a phenomenon that web pages exist only to mislead search engine into leading user to certain web sites. Term-based methods and link-based methods were proposed in many studies [2, 3]. Email spam and Blog spam also have been studied in [4] and [5].

The problem of detecting review or opinion spam was first introduced in [6], which treated review spam detection as a classification problem. Supervised learning was employed while duplicated and near duplicated reviews were regarded as positive training data. In [14], three approaches were proposed to identify deceptive reviews. A classifier was developed for specific domain dataset. [12] characterize spam by a set of frequently occurring sequential patterns and enhancement it by using a min-closed sequence. [7] identify unusual review patterns which represent suspicious behaviors of reviewers, and formulate the problem as finding unexpected rules.

Due to the complexity of the problem, many complementary approaches were employed to solve the problem. [8] identify several characteristic behaviors of review spammers by using the rating score, and model this behaviors to detect the spammers. In [11], feedback of review and the returned customers were employed to explore the inconsistency problem between the evaluation scores and review contents. [10] propose several behavior features derived from collusion among spurious reviewers, and introduce a model named GSRank, which can be considered a relationships among groups, individual reviewers and products.

2.2 Sentiment Analysis

User-generated-content in the Web such as review, blog and microblog usually express the authors emotion. The extraction, analysis and summarization of sentiment become an important research field. In [16], the features of the product are extracted. A summarization system has been built to show the users sentiment to every feature of the product. In [17], Ding et al. present a holistic lexicon-based approach to analyze the sentiment of both explicit and implicit aspect of product, and realize an opinion mining system. In [18], sentiment analysis is classified at word and sentence level. A series of definition about sentiment, sentiment holder and sentiment polarity are presented in [19]. In [20], Senti-WordNet lexical resource has been applied in automatic sentiment classification. In [21], signals have been incorporated into unsupervised sentiment analysis to model two main categories: emotion indication and emotion correlation. In [22], Twitter as a corpus has been automatically collected, and sentiment classifier has been built to determine sentiment polarity. In [23], sentiment analysis has been combined with K-means clustering and support vector machine (SVM) to develop unsupervised text mining approach in the forum hotspot detection and forecast. In [24], classifying sentiment in microblogs has been found easier than in blogs and reviews. In [25], a concept-level sentiment analysis has been seamlessly integrated into lexicon-based opinion mining.

In order to study the sentiment analysis, it is important to extract product features. Two approaches have been proposed to solve this problem. One method is based on dependency parser. According to previous studies, product features are almost noun phrase. Therefore, product features can be extracted by phrase dependency parsing [26-28]. The other method is based on probabilistic topic model such as LDA and PLSA. Through unsupervised learning, not only product features but also their corresponding sentiment can be extracted simultaneously [29-31].

It is important to note that our idea is different from [9] even if we all use relationships. We map the reviewers and stores into a heterogeneous graph, and consider the entities and the relationship between them. In [9], only multi-mode spammers have been taken into consideration. Single-mode spammers will be ignored in [9].

However, both single-mode spammers and multi-mode spammers have been studied in this paper. The proposed method can capture both of them.

3   The Proposed Method

In this section, we first compute sentiment score of review through sentiment analysis. Then several deviations between sentiment and rating score have been presented based on review relationship. Finally, an algorithm has been proposed to capture both single-mode spammers and multi-mode spammers.

3.1   Sentiment Analysis of Reviews

Our goal in this section is to incorporate sentiment analysis into the spam review detection. To achieve this aim, two tasks should be considered. The first task is to generate a sentiment lexicon. The second task is to compute the sentiment score. For ease of presentation, we give the notations listed in Table 1.

Table 1. Notations

Notation	Definition
w	The word in a review.
s	The sentence in a review.
V	Word vocabulary.
C_N	The number of negation word in in one feature.
d	A review
$\mid d \mid$	The number of sentence of review d
$o(*)$	The sentiment polarity of a word, sentence, or review. $o(*) \in [-1,1]$
$e(d)$	The rating of a review. $e(d) \in [-1,1]$

Sentiment Lexicon Generation. In the opinion mining and sentiment analysis research field, there are many sentiment lexicons such as SentiWordNet and MPQA [32, 33].

We choose it as general sentiment lexicon respectively. However, store reviews have their characteristics in natural language text. To improve the accuracy, sentiment lexicon special for store should be prepared in this task.

We extract the reviews from Resellerrating.com from October, 26, 2012 to November 20, 2012. 2000 reviews with four stars to five stars are regarded as positive samples while 500 reviews with one star to two stars as negative samples. We choose Information Gain for feature selection.

Equation (1) is the definition of information entropy. Equation (2) is the Information Gain.

$$entropy(D) = - \sum_{j=1}^{|c|} P(c_j) log_2 P(c_j), \sum_{j=1}^{|c|} P(c_j) = 1 \tag{1}$$

$$IG(t) = entropy(D) - entropy(c|t) \tag{2}$$

The Information Gain of the sentiment words in the product reviews are calculated after preprocessing. Then the sentiment words are listed in descending order respectively. We choose 260 positive words and 180 negative words special for store manually. The whole lexicon has been built by SentiWordNet plus MPQA plus sentiment word special for product respectively.

Computing Sentiment Score. In this section, the task is to determine the sentiment score of each review. Several definitions are presented as below.

Definition 1 (Sentiment Score). Sentiment score (denoted by) is a score of a review , which means the sentiment strength of review. For ease of understanding and computation, we limit the range of in [-1, 1].

The extraction methods are proposed in lots of previous works [26, 27]. We propose an equation computing sentiment score considering the negation words. All the word scores are summed up using the following equation (3):

$$o(s) = \sum_{w_j \in s \land w_j \in V} (-1)^{c_N} O(w_j) \tag{3}$$

In equation (3), means the sentiment polarity of the word . A positive word is assigned the sentiment polarity score of +1, and a negative word is assigned the sentiment polarity score of -1. means the number of negation word in sentence. If there is no negation word, equals 0. While there is one negation word, the polarity of the sentiment is reversed through multiply by -1. The sentence score of each review is listed in Equation (4).

$$o(d) = \sum_{s_i \in d} o(s)/|d| \tag{4}$$

3.2   Deviation Analysis of Reviews

An important observation in this paper is the inconsistency of sentiment score and rating score. Compared with rating score, the content of the reviews will represent more accurate sentiment of the reviewer. Therefore it will indeed influence the potential customer. Three main observations about the rating and content of the reviews are listed below.

(1) The inconsistency between rating and sentiment polarity exist in reviews. There is large number of reviews whose rating and the sentiment polarity is inconsistent. There are two reviews listed in Figure 1, which are collected from the whole lexicon dataset. It is obviously that the rating and the sentiment polarity of two reviews are contradicted. We choose 1000 reviews randomly from the dataset, and find that 132 reviews belong to this inconsistent case.

(2) The sentiment strength expressed in the review varies considerably. According to [34], the sentiment strength of review The picture quality is very good and the review I like the camera are different. Although all the sentiment polarity is positive, the former review has specific description of the product feature. The latter review just has rough evaluation. Therefore they have different sentiment strength.

(3) The sentiment strength differs when two reviews have different number of sentences. For instance, two reviews have the same rating scores. However, one review has lots of sentences, and has detail description about the shopping procedure, usage of the product and service quality as well. The other review has just one or two sentences with simple comment without trustful fact to support. It is obviously that the former will be convincing than the latter.

According to the analysis mentioned above, the content of reviews is more important than rating score. In addition, we can also take advantage of the contradiction of the rating score and the content of the review.

Review	Rating	Review Content
A	5	Great! Too bad shipping costs are so high since that essentially doubled the price
B	1	Very good. Very prompt sending when in stock. I really like the way they tell you when you order a book you already have. Keep up the good work.

Fig. 1. Rating and Content of the Reviews

We already get the sentiment score of review last section. If sentiment score of one review contradict with its rating score, spamming may occur. Therefore, we take the deviation of sentiment score with rating score as indicator to measure spamming.

For each review d, the interior deviation measure the sentiment and rating deviation. $o(d)$ and $e(d)$ represent sentiment score and rating score of one review respectively. If one reviewer posts review whose rating score contradict sentiment score, he is suspicious reviewer.

$$id(d) = |o(d) - e(d)| \tag{5}$$

In [8], a reasonable customer is expected to give rating similar to others of the same store. As spammers attempt to promote or demote the store or product, his rating score will different from others. We take deviation of rating score with others as indicator.

$$sd_G(d) = |o(d) - avg_{d' \epsilon G} o(d')| \tag{6}$$

Sentiment Deviation of Review measures the sentiment score of one review with mean score of review group G.

$$rd_G(d) = |e(d) - avg_{d' \epsilon G} e(d')| \tag{7}$$

3.3   Relationship-Based Detection Algorithm

The customer may post reviews to many stores. In Figure 2, r, d and s represent the reviewer, review and store respectively. To identify the spammer, two clues can be taken advantage of. One is the deviation of review connected with him. The other is the suspicious store connected with him. We use deviation as indicators to measure the spam degree. The deviation of a store is defined as:

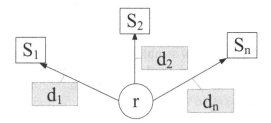

Fig. 2. Relationship between store-reviewer

We model the reviewer spam (rs for short) as a linear regression of id(d), sdG(d), and rdg(d). The algorithm is listed below.

Algorithm: Review Spammer Detection
Input: the set of review D, store S and reviewer R,$o(d_i), e(d_i)$
Begin
for each $d \in D$
compute id(d)
end
for each $s \in S$
compute $sd_s(d), rd_s(d)$
end

for each $r \in R$
compute rs(r)
sort rs(r) and corresponding v,r
end
return Descending sort list of r, List of v
end

4   Experimental Evaluation

4.1   Experiment Setup

We use the data set from Resellerrating.com for the experiment. Resellerrating.com is a large active store review website. The data of 5 categories out of 20 categories were crawled which include: Books & Magazines; Computer Hardware & Software; Consumer Electronics; DVD and VHS Videos; Music, Instruments, CDs. Our data set has 8737 stores, 628707 reviews and 561703 reviewers.

Table 2. Statistic information for datasets

Dataset	BeforePreprocessing	AfterPreprocessing
# of reviewers	561703	457463
# of stores	8737	7933.
# of reviews	628707	590605

In many previous works, a few samples are prepared for experiment. However, spam degree should be calculated iteratively. Therefore, we use the whole dataset for the experiment. The stop words are removed in the dataset. Then we use Porter Stemming tool to stem all the words.

4.2   Experiment Result

According to the previous researches [7-10], evaluating the detection of the spam mainly depends on manually work. We recruit three undergraduates to read the reviews after calculation and use their intuitions to make the judgments. There are several challenges in store review detection. Firstly, the number of suspicious reviewers that calculated from our methods is several hundred and it is impossible for our human evaluators to judge everyone. Evaluating a review is a very time consuming work. It needs the evaluators patience. Secondly, it is lack of ground truth for us to tell which review is a spam or which reviewer is suspicious in the review data set.

We solve the first issue by choosing a relative small subset of reviewers to be evaluated. These suspicious reviewers are calculated from our proposed method. Sampling in small subset is a frequently used method in information retrieval

(IR) task evaluation. Therefore, we can also examine the small subset of the suspicious reviewers. We choose 50 suspicious reviewers according to the spamicity descending. It is obvious that these 50 suspicious reviewers may be most harmful as we discussed on the above section. To solve the second issue, we mainly rely on the intuition of the evaluators and the method to check the consistency between different reviewers. A report named 30 Ways You Can Spot Fake Online Reviews introduced some useful techniques to identify the spammers.

Our evaluators work independently on spammer detection. In this evaluation, if more than one evaluator regards a reviewer as a spammer, we label it as a suspicious spammer. Our evaluators identified about 29 out of 50 suspicious reviewers. Then the precision is 58%. The table shows the agreement of different evaluators. Evaluator 1 finds 29 spammers out of 50 suspicious reviewers by our method. 20 out of which are identified by evaluator 2, and 19 out of which are confirmed by evaluator 3.

Table 3. Evaluation Result

	Evaluator1	Evaluator2	Evaluator3
Evaluator1	29	23	21
Evaluator2		27	24
Evaluator3			29

The agreement between three evaluators can be measured by [35]. It is an inter-evaluator agreement measure mainly for the observer. This method is usually used in medical clinical diagnosis. The Kappa between evaluator 1 and 2 is 59%, and the Kappa between evaluator 1 and 3 is 56%. According to the criterion, the kappa shows the substantial agreement among three evaluators. This result proved the trustiness of our experiment.

Our evaluation is better than previous work [8], since our solution mainly focus on the spammer-targeting stores.

4.3   Result Comparison

We use four types of baseline for comparison.

TP- This is a model used to detect the spam reviewers in different product. If a reviewer posts multiple similar reviews to one store, he might be a spammer [3].

GD- This is a model based on deviation from the average rating on the same store [3].

RG- This is a model based on the review graph. It takes advantage of rating deviation as measurement for detection [9].

TS- This is a model based on time series analysis of rating score burst phenomenon to detect the spammers [15].

With the labeled spammers, we train the linear regression model to predict the parameter α , β , γ . We minimize the mean square error, and get α=0.63, β=0.20, γ=0.17. This value is used as the default setting in our experiment. The result also show that the interior deviation play important role in reviewer spam detection.

We take NDCG(Normalized Discounted Cumulative Gain) to compare the results from the model and those from the evaluators. NDCG is a popular measure for spam reviewer detection. We examine the NDCG for different top k positions (k= 1 to 50) in the rank list produced by each method. As shown in Figure 2, the proposed model generates the best ranking list. It performs better than any of others.

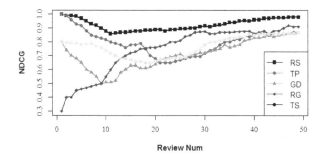

Fig. 3. Comparison with the baselines

5   Conclusion

We presented in this paper a method to detect the store review spammer based on review relationship. Our work is the first to consider the deviation of sentiment and the preference of the spammers. We first calculate the sentiment score of reviews. Then relationship between store and reviews has been studied, an algorithm has been proposed to detect the spammers. Experimental result show that proposed method can identify both single-mode and multi-mode spammers efficiently with good precision.

Acknowledgments. This work is supported by The Fundamental Research Funds for the Central Universities, No. 201121102020005, and also partially supported by National Science Foundation of China under grant No. 61272275.

References

1. Bachman, C.W., Daya, M.: The role concept in data models. In: Proceedings of the Third International Conference on Very Large Data Bases, VLDB 1977, vol. 3, pp. 464–476. VLDB Endowment (1977)

2. Gyongyi, Z., Garcia-Molina, H.: Web spam taxonomy. In: First International Workshop on Adversarial Information Retrieval on the Web, AIRWeb 2005 (2005)
3. Wu, B., Davison, B.D.: Identifying link farm spam pages. In: Special Interest Tracks and Posters of the 14th International Conference on World Wide Web. ACM (2005)
4. Fallows, D.: Spam: How it is hurting email and degrading life on the internet. Technical report, Pew Internet and American Life Project (October 2003)
5. Thomason, A.: Blog Spam: A Review. In: CEAS (2007)
6. Jindal, N., Chang, B.L.: Review Spam Detection. In: WWW 2007 (2007)
7. Jindal, N., Liu, B., Lim, E.P.: Finding Unusual Review Patterns using Unexpected Rules. In: CIKM 2010 (2010)
8. Lim, E.P., Nguyen, V.A., Jindal, N., Liu, B., Lauw, H.W.: Detecting product review spammers using rating behaviors. In: CIKM 2010 (2010)
9. Wang, G., Xie, S., Liu, B., Philip, S.Y.: Identify Online Store Review Spammers via Social Review Graph. ACM Transactions on Intelligent Systems and Technology 3(4), Article No. 61 (September 2012)
10. Mukherjee, A., Liu, B., Glance, N.: Spotting Fake Reviewer Groups in Consumer Reviews. In: WWW 2012 (2012)
11. Zhang, R., Sha, C., Zhou, M., Zhou, A.: Exploiting shopping and reviewing behavior to rescore online evaluations. In: WWW 2012 (2012)
12. Kant, R., Sengamedu, S.H., Kumar, K.S.: Comment spam detection by sequence mining. In: WWW 2012 (2012)
13. Li, F., Huang, M., Yang, Y., Zhu, X.: Learning to identify review spam. In: IJCAI 2011 (2011)
14. Ott, M., Choi, Y., Cardie, C., Hancock, J.T.: Finding deceptive opinion spam by any stretch of the imagination. In: HLT 2011 (2011)
15. Xie, S., et al.: Review spam detection via temporal pattern discovery. In: Proceedings of the 18th ACM SIGKDD International Conference on Knowledge Discovery and Data Mining. ACM (2012)
16. Hu, M., Liu, B.: Mining and summarizing customer reviews. In: Proceedings of the 10th ACM SIGKDD International Conference on Knowledge Discovery and Data Mining, pp. 168–177. ACM Press, New York (2004)
17. Ding, X., Liu, B., Yu, P.S., et al.: A holistic lexicon-based approach to opinion mining. In: Proceedings of the 2008 International Conference on Web Search and Data Mining, pp. 231–240. ACM Press, New York (2008)
18. Kim, S.-M., Hovy, E.: Determining the sentiment of opinions. In: Proceedings of the 20th International Conference on Computational Linguistics, p. 1367. Association for Computational Linguistics, Philadelphia (2004)
19. Indurkhya, N., Damerau, F.J.: Handbook of natural language processing. In: 2nd. Chapman and Hall/CRC (2010)
20. Ohana, B., Tierney, B.: Sentiment classification of reviews using SentiWordNet. In: 9th IT & T Conference, p. 13 (2009)
21. Hu, X., Tang, J., Gao, H., et al.: Unsupervised sentiment analysis with emotional signals. In: Proceedings of the 22nd International Conference on World Wide Web. International World Wide Web Conferences Steering Committee, pp. 607–618 (2013)
22. Pak, A., Paroubek, P.: Twitter as a Corpus for Sentiment Analysis and Opinion Mining. In: LREC (2010)
23. Li, N., Wu, D.D.: Using text mining and sentiment analysis for online forums hotspot detection and forecast. Decision Support Systems 48(2), 354–368 (1981, 2010)

24. Bermingham, A., Smeaton, A.F.: Classifying sentiment in microblogs: is brevity an advantage? In: Proceedings of the 19th ACM International Conference on Information and Knowledge Management, pp. 1833–1836. ACM (2010)

25. Mudinas, A., Zhang, D., Levene, M.: Combining lexicon and learning based approaches for concept-level sentiment analysis. In: Proceedings of the First International Workshop on Issues of Sentiment Discovery and Opinion Mining, p. 5. ACM (2012)

26. Zhang, Q., Wu, Y., Li, T., et al.: Mining product reviews based on shallow dependency parsing. In: Proceedings of the 32nd International ACM SIGIR Conference on Research and development in Information Retrieval, pp. 726–727. ACM (2009)

27. Wu, Y., Zhang, Q., Huang, X., et al.: Phrase dependency parsing for opinion mining. In: Proceedings of the 2009 Conference on Empirical Methods in Natural Language Processing, vol. 3, pp. 1533–1541. Association for Computational Linguistics (2009)

28. Joshi, M., Penstein-Ros, C.: Generalizing dependency features for opinion mining. In: Proceedings of the ACL-IJCNLP 2009 Conference Short Papers, pp. 313–316. Association for Computational Linguistics (2009)

29. Zhao, W.X., et al.: Jointly modeling aspects and opinions with a MaxEnt-LDA hybrid. In: Proceedings of the 2010 Conference on Empirical Methods in Natural Language Processing. Association for Computational Linguistics (2010)

30. Thet, T.T., Na, J.-C., Khoo, C.S.G.: Aspect-based sentiment analysis of movie reviews on discussion boards. Journal of Information Science 36(6), 823–848 (2010)

31. Mei, Q., et al.: Topic sentiment mixture: modeling facets and opinions in weblogs. In: Proceedings of the 16th International Conference on World Wide Web. ACM (2007)

32. Esuli, A., Sebastiani, F.: Sentiwordnet: A publicly available lexical resource for opinion mining. In: Proceedings of LREC, vol. 6 (2006)

33. Wilson, T., et al.: OpinionFinder: A system for subjectivity analysis. In: Proceedings of HLT/EMNLP on Interactive Demonstrations. Association for Computational Linguistics (2005)

34. Jindal, N., Liu, B.: Mining comparative sentences and relations. In: AAAI, vol. 22 (2006)

35. Fleiss, J.L., Cohen, J.: The equivalence of weighted kappa and the intraclass correlation coefficient as measures of reliability. Educational and Psychological Measurement

Author Index

Arenas, Helbert 117

Bakillah, Mohamed 107
Bhardwaj, Hanu 39
Bizid, Imen 77
Blanco, Carlos 21
Boursier, Patrice 77

Cai, Yi 203, 216
Cámara, José 29
Capelle, Michel 160
Chen, Liu 257
Cheng, James 235
Cherfi, Samira Si-saïd 170
Chiu, Dickson 7
Comyn-Wattiau, Isabelle 170
Cruz, Christophe 117

Davis, Karen C. 247
de Gregorio, Elisa 29
de Macedo, José Antonio Fernandes 127
de Oliveira, José Palazzo Moreira 139
Do Tuan, Anh 170

Faiz, Sami 77
Frasincar, Flavius 137

Gil, David 21
Gkantouna, Vassiliki 14
Gnaho, Christophe 59
Grueau, Cédric 267
Guilbert, Eric 87

Harbelot, Benjamin 117
Hogenboom, Frederik 160
Horkoff, Jennifer 49
Houben, Geert-Jan 137
Hu, Shuyue 205, 216

Ioannou, Zafeiria-Marina 14

Jaekel, Tobias 277

Kafeza, Eleanna 7
Kanavos, Andreas 7
Karam, Roula 97
Kusumah, Indra 51

Laleau, Regine 59
Li, Jun 205
Liang, Steve H.L. 107
Lim, Erbin 190
Lin, Jing 51
Liu, Jiren 180
Liu, Lin 49
Liu, Yu 216

Maamar, Zakaria 190
Machado, Alencar 139
Makris, Christos 7
Maté, Alejandro 29
Melchiori, Michele 97
Milea, Viorel 150
Min, Huaqing 205, 216
Moerland, Marnix 160
Mostafavi, Mir Abolfazl 75
Mouratidis, Theofilos 1

Olivé, Antoni 237
Özkan, Gülru 51

Papastefanatos, George 23
Pastor, Joan Antoni 237
Peng, Qingxi 287
Pernas, Ana Marilza 139
Prakash, Deepika 68
Prakash, Naveen 39, 68

Raffaetà, Alessandra 127
Renso, Chiara 127
Rohleder, Clotilde 51
Rolland, Collette 49
Roncato, Alessandro 127

Saux, Eric 87
Semmak, Farida 59
Shao, Yifeng 216
Sharma, Deepak Kumar 68
Singh, Dheerendra 68

Sioutas, Spyros   1
Song, Il-Yeol   21, 235
Spathis, Dimitris   1

Thiran, Philippe   137
Tort, Albert   237
Trasarti, Roberto   127
Trujillo, Juan   29
Tsakalidis, Athanasios   1, 14
Tsaknakis, John   14
Tzimas, Giannis   14

Vandic, Damir   150

Wagner, Ricardo   127
Wang, Tao   205, 216

Wang, Zhiyan   226
Wives, Leandro Krug   139

Xue, Jiang   226

Yan, Jingya   87
Yang, Zuozhong   180
Yu, Eric   49
Yu, Gang   226
Yu, Ting   257
Yusuf, Jawahir Che Mustapha   77

Zhao, Dazhe   180
Zhao, Qingchuan   205
Zhou, Jingang   180
Zimanyi, Esteban   75